WOMEN COAUTHORS

Women
Coauthors

HOLLY A. LAIRD

UNIVERSITY OF ILLINOIS PRESS

URBANA AND CHICAGO

Library of Congress Cataloging-in-Publication Data
Laird, Holly A., 1953–
Women coauthors / Holly A. Laird.
p.   cm.
ISBN 0-252-02547-4 (alk. paper)
1. English literature—Women authors—History and criticism.
2. American literature—Women authors—History and criticism.
3. English literature—19th century—History and criticism.
4. English literature—20th century—History and criticism.
5. Authorship—Sex differences—History.
6. Authorship—Collaboration—History.
7. Women—Authorship—History.
8. Ghostwriting—History.
9. Feminism and literature.
10. Women and literature. I. Title.
PR115.L33   2000
820.9'9287—dc21   99-006863
C   5   4   3   2   1

For Lars

Contents

Acknowledgments

ALTHOUGH THIS BOOK falls short even of "approximate collaboration" as described within these pages, I feel indebted to many people, occasions, and prior texts. In addition to the influences of important conference occasions and previous critical and theoretical works detailed in the notes to this study, I am especially grateful for and to the following individuals and groups: to Joyce Elbrecht and Lydia Fakundiny for their willingness to be written about and to read the first version of my treatment of *The Restorationist;* to the 22d annual Twentieth-Century Literature Conference directors (1994) and, in particular, Suzette Henke for inviting me to present the opening address, where I first aired my comparative analysis of Field and Juba; to Linda K. Hughes for the thoughtful reading she gave my essay on Field's contradictions in preparation for publication in her special issue of *Victorian Poetry* (1995); to Carolyn Dinshaw, Susan Belasco, and Joseph Kestner for their receptive responses to early pieces of this book; to Alice Gambrell, Melissa Zeiger, and Susan Fraiman for enthusiastically reading the completed manuscript; to Pamela Caughie, Ania Loomba, Susan Stanford Friedman, Sandra Gilbert, and Ellen Cronan Rose for warm support of this project; to my two anonymous readers for the University of Illinois Press, subsequently revealed as Dale M. Bauer and Susan J. Leonardi; to Seung-hee Roh, Rebecca Dyer, and Sarah Theobald Hall, who served as research assistants at different times in this project; to Johanna Dehler and Pauline Newton for undertaking a final check of the book's numerous citations; to the women in two undergraduate and graduate seminars on collaborative writing for their responsiveness as an audience and deep engagement in discussion;

to Ann Lowry, assistant director of the University of Illinois Press, for her efficient and business-like squiring of the book; to James Watson, chair of the English department, Thomas Horne, dean of the Henry Kendall College of Arts and Sciences, and the University of Tulsa for their support of this project; to Joli Jensen, Pat Newman, and Linda Frazier for their friendship, intelligence, and conversation, often about the struggles of writing a book while doing "everything else"; to Lars Engle for reading the penultimate draft and providing editorial help, but also for his amazing partnership and seemingly endless optimism—this book is dedicated to him; to my father, mother, brother, and sister for their steady kindness and belief in me; to my son, Carl, and my mother-in-law, Jay, for their generous understanding and interest and for Jay's proofreading of the first complete draft of the manuscript; and to my daughter, Sage, just for coming along. All the remaining shortcomings of this book are even more my own than usual.

An earlier version of chapter 3 and of the brief section on "A Girl" in the Introduction appeared as "Contradictory Legacies: Michael Field and Feminist Restoration," in *Victorian Poetry* 33.1 (1995), 111–28.

WOMEN COAUTHORS

Introduction:
Collaborative Desire

Women's Literary Coauthorship

THIS STUDY INVESTIGATES Victorian and twentieth-century literary coauthorships in English in which women have played central roles. Such collaborations,[1] coauthorships in which women's names or pseudonyms (sometimes male, sometimes female) appear on the title page, are of particular interest in a feminist literary history. Framed in time by the feminist and abolitionist movements of the mid-nineteenth century and the ongoing civil rights movements of our own, written in England, North America, and Europe, these texts are preoccupied with collaboration in relation to, at times as a path to, various kinds of equity, both socioliterary and erotic. Some of these writers are our contemporaries, but all of them treat issues that are alive for us; they breathe down our necks, their beliefs and anxieties impinging closely on our own. Thus I consider the turn-of-the-century British poet-dramatists Michael Field (the pseudonym for Katherine Bradley and Edith Cooper) and the Anglo-Irish novelists Edith Somerville and Martin Ross (the latter the adopted name of Violet Martin), the contemporary Native American writers Louise Erdrich and Michael Dorris (who early in their collaboration published works under the pseudonym Milou North), the British contemporary novelist-poets Penelope Shuttle and Peter Redgrove (coauthors of one of the first feminist studies of menstruation), the Canadian avant-garde lesbian poets Daphne Marlatt and Betsy Warland, and Jael

B. Juba (pseudonymous author-character of the contemporary American novelists Lydia Fakundiny and Joyce Elbrecht, whose names appear with Juba's on dustjackets). This book deals also with partial collaborations, in which full mutually acknowledged coauthorship does not occur, including the collaborations of John Stuart Mill and Harriet Taylor (her name never appeared with his on a book), Harriet Brent Jacobs and Lydia Child (the first composed the narrative; the second revised it), H.D., Freud, and Bryher (neither Freud nor Bryher lifted a pen to help H.D. write), . Gertrude Stein and Alice B. Toklas (the conventional wisdom is that Stein wrote the "autobiography" of Toklas, while Toklas acted as amanuensis), and the Delany sisters and Ossie Guffy (who narrated their stories orally to Amy Hill Hearth and Caryl Ledner, respectively). The subject of women's collaborations led me inexorably to such apparently asymmetric writing relationships; each brings to the fore specific issues or themes that are pivotal in recontextualizing more complete or mutual collaborations.

Despite contemporary demystification, a particular authorial life behind a work has long been an almost necessary adjunct both to a sympathetic reception and to the work's survival as an object of commentary. Not only has such an author been perceived as originator and authenticator, but she or he also has been perceived as validating a work, offering an individual human point of attachment for readers, enhancing even its aesthetic value. Coauthored works disrupt this scheme, and in their announcement of a preexisting relationship, they thwart such attachment. When two people come together to write and openly sign both their names, they are met with incredulity and dismay. Today's social systems of authorship are not designed to cope with variability in the number of authors involved, not just for autobiographies (where one would expect problems in the event of multiple authorship) but also for novels. Most reviewers become instantly skeptical, as they proved in reviews of Erdrich and Dorris's excellent cosigned novel, *The Crown of Columbus*, and book cataloguers become confused. Readers generally accept the fiction of single authorship; the self-representations of collaborators arouse suspicion.

Until quite recently, collaborative texts were barely noticed by critics and, when noticed, were generally dismissed or dismantled by scholars. Whatever the reason—whether it is the result of overinvestment in the concept of solitary genius, as recent scholars such as Lisa Ede and Andrea Lunsford (in the field of composition theory) and Jack Stillinger argue, or reflects a more obscure, underlying anxiety about homoeroticism, as Wayne Koestenbaum hints, or is fundamentally a manifestation of modern capitalism in which texts function as another form of private property—it is an unfortunate legacy under which to labor.[2] It would be difficult to find an author who has not written with someone else—under other writers' influence, with the aid of editors' revisions, in response to generative conversation, or literally together with someone else. Although modern literary texts are rarely cosigned, Stillinger and Koestenbaum show, contrary to popular perception, how widespread literary collaboration has been in men's writing in the nineteenth and twentieth centuries. Stillinger appends to his book a list of ninety-seven collaborators. As the interactive computer network shares the stage with print, collaborative writing will become not only less easily avoided, but more inviting and easier to attempt.[3] I doubt that the current study will be the last of its kind.

To date, however, critics have devoted attention almost entirely to famous male writers. Koestenbaum briefly discusses coauthorship between women in the final pages of his book, whereas women appear in Stillinger's book as subordinate figures to major male writers, and the most prolific women collaborators (Mary Howitt, Jane and Ann Taylor, Faye Huntington, Michael Field, Somerville and Ross, Penelope Shuttle, and Louise Erdrich) are not listed in his appendix.[4] Unless they worked in conjunction with a famous male writer, groundbreaking women coauthors remain noncanonical, despite their initial success in getting their work published. Whereas a woman such as Dorothy Wordsworth has always been assured a scholarly audience, if only for the light she throws on her renowned brother, women who have not supported a great male writer in collaboration face far greater obstacles to sustained recognition. Scholars are writing increasingly about female "powers behind the throne" but continue to neglect collaborations in which women played central roles.[5] Most of the women writers I have selected here do not labor under the shadow of more famous male coauthors; these women worked with each other or achieved reputations equal to or beyond those of their male partners. A major aim of this project thus is restorative:[6] to introduce important but lesser-known coauthors (Field, Somerville and Ross, Redgrove and Shuttle, Marlatt and Warland, Ossie Guffy, Elbrecht and Fakundiny, most of them not yet well known to critics, particularly outside the writers' national borders) in juxtaposition with better-known but less fully collaborative writers (Taylor, Jacobs, H.D., Stein, Erdrich and Dorris, and the Delany sisters), whose work acquires a new dimension when placed in the context of literary collaboration.

The few scholars and critics who have written about literary coauthors (including pioneers Wayne Koestenbaum and Jack Stillinger) have been intent on dissecting the relationship between the people behind the signature or signatures. Focusing on the authors' correspondence and manuscripts, critics have sought to sort out who contributed what and, moreover, who dominated whom in the relationship and in the writing. But as Somerville and Ross repeatedly point out, in a full collaboration even manuscript evidence cannot reliably tell us which is which. For Somerville and Ross, it does not matter "which of us held the pen"—what matters is the process behind and around it of conversation, revision, more conversation, and more revision.[7]

My concern in this book is instead with collaborators' self-representations. To redirect attention as far as possible from the "true" lives lived (as if lives themselves were not multiple, concocted in part by the people inside them and the social structures circumscribing them) to the stories they have written, I suggest that a reader think of collaboration as itself reproduced and thematized in writing.

One of the two books previously written on modern collaborative literature, Stillinger's *Multiple Authorship and the Myth of Solitary Genius*, retains the notion of at least potentially separable authorship, whereas the other, Koestenbaum's *Double Talk: The Erotics of Male Literary Collaboration*, espouses what can seem most subversive and transgressive in collaborative writing. Yet rather than opening up the idea of writing to a range of kinds of authorship, they take sides on the battleline between single authorship and collaborative writing. Despite Stillinger's argument that "solitary genius" is a myth—a conclusion he reaches through close study of textual evidence—he speaks of the alternative not as collaborative writing but as "multiple authorship" because he wants to retain a belief in genius and sees it as possible and valuable to establish hierarchies within multiple authorship (for example, John Stuart Mill remains the genius behind his autobiography, even as he is aided in his work by the lesser talents of his wife and other relatives and editors). Koestenbaum, meanwhile, begins his study of well-known male writers (mostly at the turn of the century) by unearthing an assumption of collaborative writers as "promiscuous" and their work as illegitimate; he sees the term *collaboration* as burdened in the nineteenth century with sexual associations and thus adopts eroticism as his central source of metaphors for collaborative writing (1, 3). Koestenbaum's emphasis on collaborative writing as covert "double talk" and its transgressions as erotic succeeds in portraying coauthorship as ambivalently poised between colluding with and undermining the myth of solitary male genius. But his suggestion that these pairs of male writers continually fall into dominant-submissive patterns results in a model of coauthorship as divided and divisive.

Collaborative women writers and scholars also interest themselves in "double talk," but for feminists the idea of writing as double talk is nothing new. Numerous feminist and women writers and critics (throughout the centuries) have seen women as compelled to write duplicitously, in imitation of men, while evading male-constructed norms.[8] For feminist collaborators, however, what is notable about collaborative writing is the room it creates for them to talk together. The numerous models and metaphors that appear in collaborative feminist scholars' discussions of their coauthorship[9] touch mostly on the playfulness rather than the labor involved (including, in comments by women and feminist collaborators, metaphors of dance, mosaic, quilt, jazz, and cookery), and the conversation model appears more pervasively than any other.[10] Literary collaborators blur the boundaries not only between each other in writing, but between text and speech, between a text and its contexts. For some women writers, collaboration makes it possible to write with other women; others write with men. In either case, collaboration allows women writers to turn their attention from how to write between the lines of an inherited tradition to how they may write together. Among the larger purposes of this project, I mean to reintroduce the "co-" (the togetherness) into authorship, to reinsert the factor of speech in text, to reemphasize the necessity of affinity and continuity in relational processes of this sort, and (as Jane Gallop argues in revising Jacques Lacan) to reinvoke the genitally female sense of contiguity against the lonely phallic "I."[11]

This study begins, then, not with the assumption that one can, should, or would want to divide coauthored texts back up into single originators, but rather with the assumption, the desire, and (to my mind) the obligation to analyze these texts as collaboratively written, as texts in which it is usually impossible to tell which was which. Instead of dissecting the relationships behind the writing, this study reads coauthored texts as the realization of relationships. These writers' relationships reach their audiences through stories, whether or not what is available to the public includes collaborative self-description in published correspondence or interviews.

Reading these texts as acts and representations of collaboration makes a decisive difference in the analyses I undertake here. Thus, for example, in striking contrast even to critics who see the authorship of *The Autobiography of Alice B. Toklas* as a rhetorical question raised by this text, my analysis of this autobiography indicates the difference it makes to describe the authors and narrators of this text as both Stein and Toklas rather than either Stein or Toklas. This shift in focus affects the largest conclusions I draw; it brings attention to the many borders approached, blurred, or dissolved in these texts, not only between one author and another, but also between one set of cultural differences and another, between one reality and another, and between difference and sameness themselves. Any one person's sense of reality is never more directly challenged than by the difficult recognition of another person's reality, so coauthors find themselves often speculating about modern ontological distinctions, reimagining the relations between one rational, civilized, sane, or ordinary world and another. Collaboration ultimately assumes a crossing between differences and samenesses; it issues in and through what are, by turns, troubled, rhapsodic, torn, pleasurable realizations of difference within sameness, of sameness amid difference.

With the revised assumption that we neither can nor ought to try to tell coauthors apart, I open this study by offering a speculative model of collaborative desire wherein one might reconsider the relationship between coauthors and (co)subjects in accordance not exclusively with a Freudian/Lacanian model of gaps and hierarchical power differentials between the desiring and the desired, but with a collaborative model of reciprocally operating power exchanges between two desiring subjects. Although I do not go out of my way to imagine tensions or struggles between authors in this study, I nonetheless investigate the problematics of these collaborations, probing their contradictions and their enmeshment in larger systems (such as the Western canon of solitary authors). It may be no accident that collaboration still is strongly associated with the meaning it acquired during the Nazi occupation of France, where to collaborate was to collude with the enemy. Collaboration has played the villain's role in modern liberation movements ("solidarity" gets to be the good guy), and the term *collaboration* has thus become sedimented in a highly political, unstable binary between free individualism and enslaving totalitarianism. It is necessary somehow to keep both faces of this term in play, collaboration as collaborationism and as cooperation, and to discern how we can move from emphasizing one to emphasizing the other.

This study explores the problematics of collaboration, beginning with approximate, mutually beneficial, but not thoroughgoing coauthorships between authors and their editors (chapters 1 and 2), moving on to the socially embedded contradictions and uncanny suppressions involved in full coauthorships between turn-of-the-century women couples (chapters 3 and 4), and culminating with several sets of modernist and contemporary approximate and cosigned collaborations, all of which partially revise old habits of thinking about writing (chapters 5–7). These various twentieth-century experimental and postmodern cowriters question assumptions about the isolated artist's creative mind or psyche, autonomous artifact or impersonal *écriture*, and democratically individual textual ownership or claim to retell American history. Although the problems touched on and the cultural differences confronted by these writers recur in varying forms from one couple to another, no one example can display them all equally or do justice to the complex interactions among them. The aim of this study is not to set forth one kind of collaboration as ideal or even as better in some sense than another, but to learn what can be gleaned from the juxtapositions of different kinds and degrees of collaboration.

Indeed, full collaborations—that is, writers who collaborate at every stage of composition, playing all these roles of verbal companion and author, writer and editor, with each other—are not necessarily more balanced, more equitable, or more mutually rewarding than partial or "approximate" (a term I adopt and develop in chapter 2, on Jacobs and Child) collaborations between authors and editors, speakers and writers. Because tensions and inequities are often more lively, more entrenched, or more deeply concealed in long-term intimate relationships than in more temporary, contractual, or casual arrangements, the latter in some cases may be politically more mutually beneficial than the former. Nonetheless, when the relationship between two people who talk together is extended into every stage of the process of writing, authorship becomes thoroughly collaborative and these collaborative accomplishments merit acknowledgment.

At certain points, this project becomes a study of collaborative autobiography. The distinctive multiply authored autobiographies analyzed suggest that the apparent guarantee of single authorship in the name of the genre may be deceptive. Mill and Taylor's autobiography of John Stuart Mill reminds us how deeply entrenched the assumption has been that an autobiography is merited only when its subject is a single great man and thus how difficult it is, in that context, to reimagine either a "life" or its "graph" as collaborative. The Delany sisters' autobiography would not be possible at all, however, if autobiography were determinedly singular. Autobiographies as different as those of Stein and Toklas and Ossie Guffy would gain in interest for critics if they were to worry less about authenticity and credibility and concern themselves more with the various ways in which these texts enact and resist collaborative relationships. Both these autobiographies and the many nonautobiographical texts in this study—the novels, poems, and prose poems[12]—demonstrate the fuzziness critics have increasingly noticed between autobiography and its fictive others. The current study contributes yet another reevaluation of the constructedness of autobiography, a reevaluation that focuses on what can be discerned from thinking of the "auto" as plural.

At other points, this study offers a reconsideration of the function of the literary uncanny, turning from Freud's rationalist model to a revised model of the uncanny as the place where the real and unreal, known and unknown, intersect. Although this theme emerges in the early chapters and then is treated centrally in chapters 4 and 5, especially in relation to Somerville and Ross and H.D., it is prevalent in most of these writers' texts. Erdrich and Dorris are as keen to map uncanny intersections as any of the writers discussed here, and Dorris and Erdrich's fictive characters who admit the unknown find mystery, as H.D. does, where others have found only horror. Then again, the Delany sisters joke in their autobiography, as do other coauthors, about their telepathic conversations, and claim that with Bessie in the house, they do not need a telephone to know what is going on in the world. This project thus contributes to recent reconsiderations by scholars of the problem of spiritualism in writers in a skeptical, rationalist age.

In addition, I often touch on the relations between oral and textual collaboration. As Stillinger shows, authors and their editors are much more tightly bound to each other, far less separable, than orthodox theorists of intention and of textual editing have assumed, but as I have already suggested, coauthorship depends as much on the conversations that precede and surround writing as on the writing itself. As Janice Doane and Devon Hodges put this in relation to their own collaboration, "Our method of working has not only been enriched, but has come to rely predominantly upon the oral—conversation, composing aloud—which recent theory emphasizing textuality has obscured. That is, notions of intertextuality seem to leave no place for the ways in which discourse is also shaped by human dialogue."[13] Of the writers considered in this study, Marlatt and Warland go furthest to retheorize the relations between orality and textuality in particular and the complex dynamics of collaboration in general. If authors and editors mark one end of a spectrum of full collaboration—usually producing the concluding stages of a written work— the relationship between conversation and writing is still more crucial, doing more than merely marking the place where collaboration starts. In conversation a creative work is contextualized and conceptually generated as well as inaugurated.

Throughout this study, I show not only how in collaborative representations numerous hierarchies come undone, their borders weakened or threatened with collapse, but also how a playful intercourse, loop, indeterminate multiplication, elusive excess, or mocking performance of differences is produced. Such polarities include the now-standard list of dichotomized pairs—binaries of gender, race, class, and sexuality—but also polarizations that are imposed on age, the mind's faculties, the real, and the relations between a text and its contexts. If I shift focus from one mode of elusion of these binaries to another from one chapter to the next, it is because escape routes are as various as the traps in which coauthors' protagonists find themselves.

In its choices of women coauthors, this study is not an egg hunt for the most obscure coauthors one could find nestled in archives. I look only at writers who have succeeded in the literary marketplace or have already received some attention (and should receive more). The pre–World War II writers in this study were considered significant in their own time and have received some critical attention; the contemporary writers represented vary in the degree to which they are known to the literate public, but they have published widely or received previous critical attention. *The Restorationist,* a 1993 first novel by Jael B. Juba (Elbrecht and Fakundiny), is the one exception—a remarkable text discussed later in this introduction that I hope to bring to the attention of a wider audience. Its authors themselves have published an intriguing essay-story on their collaboration.[14] Several prolific women collaborators are not treated here: the late-nineteenth-century writer "Pansy" (Isabella M. Alden), who coauthored work with C. M. Livingston, Faye Huntington (pseudonym of Theodosia M. Foster), and others; the late-nineteenth-century Scottish writers E. D. Gerard (pseudonym of the sisters Emily and Dorothea Gerard); and the mid-twentieth-century Australian writers M. Barnard Eldershaw (pseudonym of Marjorie Barnard and Flora Eldershaw).[15] It is clear to me, from excursions into libraries here and in England, that collaborative writing as an area of research would benefit from further archival digging. But when opening up a new area of study, it is useful to begin selectively and with what already can be glimpsed in corners of the existing landscape. Choosing authors who remain visible to readers today in reprinted texts and histories has enabled me to look more closely at specific examples of the reception of collaboration and to reconsider the vexed relationship of coauthors to the modern literary marketplace and to modern literary canons—in other words, to rethink the ways in which we have conceptualized and evaluated collaborative texts.

I have found full collaborations between African-American women writers to be even less visible than those between Caucasian women; my choice here of approximate collaborations between black and white women is partly a consequence of that invisibility, but primarily a result of my desire to draw attention to the problems of interaction between a black woman's narrative and a white female's editing, transcription, and reading. White feminists like me, encountering the challenging criticism of many women of color in the last two decades, have faced the hard lesson of their own myopia and are less prone in 1999 than in 1979 to describe the "woman" writer of the past as if she must be white and middle-class. Yet, as African-Americanists have shown, writing about an African-American woman's text can become another form of appropriation. When a white American woman engages a text by a woman of color, she involves herself in the history of American racism, a history she cannot escape entirely. To face these issues as directly as possible, I have selected texts by African-American women that participate overtly in this dilemma; Jacobs's text in particular dramatizes the politics by which a black woman writer's text is produced through the medium of a white editor or transcriber. Chapter 2 thus makes explicit the problematics of my treatment of differences throughout this study.

In the opinions of the authors here who collaborate most fully with each other, two are better than one. But are two better than three? And what happens when the number of collaborators is increased to four, or seven, or thirty-seven?[16] Like Koestenbaum, who hints at added excitements, tensions, or rivalries among writers when more than two conjoin but does not look closely at examples, I only occasionally guess at what differences it makes when the number of coauthors increases. (Stillinger's study includes multiple groupings because he is concerned with multiple editorships, but he does not investigate the interpersonal dynamics, group psychology, or social and ideological implications of several writers working together simultaneously.)[17] Important differences develop in intersubjective relations among groups of two, three, four, five, six, or more.

Marjorie Garber argues that couples are produced through triangles and that the triangle is a far more prevalent, indeed normal, phenomenon than the exclusive couple.[18] In literary cosignatories, there is rarely a third author, but collaborative relationships may pivot on a partially excluded third person (and writer), as is the case in many of the homosocial collaborations Koestenbaum writes about (for example, Vivien Eliot and Dorothy Wordsworth play third-party roles in the collaborations of Eliot and Pound, Wordsworth and Coleridge). With the exception of Amy Hill Hearth's role in interviewing the Delany sisters and Bryher's role in her psychic "writing" with H.D., however, I did not discover important third partners to the ongoing literary collaborations discussed in this book, and feminist collaborative scholars often comment on the inapplicability of Koestenbaum's model to their relationships, so this Girardian theme plays a minor role in this study. Meanwhile, the full group literary collaborations I have found, involving more than three writers, are collections of noncosigned stories.[19]

Perhaps more important, the intimacies of dual collaboration so fascinated me that I found myself continually adding new dual collaborations to the list of those I wanted to examine while reaching dead ends and losing interest in researching work by group collaborative teams. As a result, this book studies a phenomenon more private, possibly less socially representative or reconstructive than it might otherwise have been. The texts themselves often introduce triangulations, families, and groups, and these necessarily intertwine with my discussions of couples, but this study remains centrally a description of couples working together. Similarly, because of my emphasis on enduring literary collaborations (those that have succeeded, partly through persistence, in gaining critical attention), the couples I consider are not, in Koestenbaum's terms, "promiscuous"— they rarely, if ever, write with anyone other than their primary partners. Nonetheless, I have not neglected the failures, limits, and mystifications of coupled collaborative relations in favor of their successes, innovations, and courage. And I do not see collaborative writing as restricted to the kinds of relationships described here; rather, I see the couple as the most propitious site at present for collaborative writing to develop and receive recognition—to become visible in today's literary marketplace.

The experience of entering a bottomless closet, in the domestic as well as the socioerotic sense of the term, is a vivid aspect of my study of these couples, one that has remained an important but elusive strand in tracing their various relations. Naming and describing these collaborations has inevitably involved rehearsing gossip about the couple's life and some information about their collaboration. Implicated in the first way of construing the frequent questions I have received ("Who are they? Who were they?"), and deliberately implied in my metaphor of the closet, is a second sociopsychological question: Were the female couples lesbian? Are the female/male couples heterosexual or transgendered? Who they are, in this sense, can be both very easy to answer (if they have asserted an identity for themselves) and not easy to answer at all (for these identities are unstable and complex). The texts selected represent sexual relations between women and women and between women and men far more often than between men and men; nonetheless, they range widely from presenting highly conventional heterosexual relations (in Somerville and Ross's novels) to presenting queer ones (in Shuttle and Redgrove). Even the most normative plots are marked by curious breaking points where sexual identity is destabilized (for example, by hints of decadence in Somerville and Ross), and the most radically experimental coauthors also reproduce heterosexual norms (as in the equivocal treatment of transsexualism in Shuttle and Redgrove's nonfictional writing).

I would not argue that these various forms of the question "Who" should not be asked or that answers to it, provisional as they must be, serve no purpose. These are questions people ask about each other and will surely go on asking. My focus in this study is on the construction of collaborative authorial identities rather than on authors' "real lives" and on the ways coauthored texts themselves raise questions of identity rather than the ways authorial identity questions might be solved through biographical detection or dissection. In particular, chapter 3, which focuses on the contradictions in Field's construction of an authorial identity, indicates some of the problems involved in attempts to reach definitive— or singular—answers to such questions. Throughout this study, brief biographical descriptions demonstrate how different collaborators can be from each other. Yet I also question whether collaborators are really eccentric or anomalous and propose that we recontextualize the puzzle of these collaborations in the perhaps less puzzling circumstances of modern literary production, in order to look not at how they lived or what they thought exactly, but at what models of psychosocial interaction their texts provide.

Both their eccentricities and the extraordinary parallels that emerge among them (from their frequent inability to separate their contributions in the final work to their recurrent preoccupation with the uncanny and spiritualism) seem to point to patterns of authorship and thought that, though mostly unacknowledged in this century, are finally beginning to be exposed by critics such as Koestenbaum, Stillinger, Ede and Lunsford, and Carey Kaplan and Ellen Cronan Rose.[20] Juxtaposing the texts of women's collaborations yields a blueprint for practicable feminist collaboration. Three models emerge from this analysis:

— A model of coauthorship as distinct from both solitary genius and an authorless textuality. In this model a large range of different kinds of coauthorship includes, surrounds, and renders anomalous the idea of the autonomous, original author.
— A model of fertile coupling as distinct from both Harold Bloom's Freudian agon with the father and oceanic merging. Here again a broad, varied field of relationships would render anomalous the idea of influence as fatal struggle for dominance between a single author and his precursors.
— A model of local social coalition as distinct from both heroic individualism and complete class or group solidarity. Here multiple socially constructed differences and samenesses are at play with each other.

In addition, examination specifically of dual coauthorship enables a general reevaluation of the ways in which concepts of authorship rest on very different perceptions of a reader's relation to a writer and to a text. For those who privilege the notion of the solitary author, literature characteristically provides vicarious pleasure even while distancing the writer from the reader; literature provides voyeuristic seeing, possessive knowing, or teasing seduction. For those who interest themselves in collaborative writing, literature is reimagined as a place where people meet, where they must negotiate their differences, where they may contest each other's powers, and where, while retaining their bodily borders, they may momentarily, ecstatically merge. Drawing on Lacan's discussion of *jouissance* as "ex-istence," one may define such "ecstasy" not as homogenizing "fusion" and not merely as multiplicitous "*jouissance*," but as the excitement implied by the roots of "ec-stasy," or (in Lacan's phrasing) "that which puts us on the path of ex-istence":[21] sliding out of a staid or stuck singular subject position. When "I" crosses over to "I," "we" produce not an immobile singularity but ec-static *jouissance*.

I may sound utopian here, intoxicated by a French-influenced feminism in its celebratory mode, but a celebratory redescription of coauthorship and of relational and group dynamics need not fail to get at the ways these also remain implicated in limiting or oppressive ideologies or structures. The dual valences of "collaboration" mark the work of all these writers. Yet the coauthors in this study also experiment, obviously, with alternative forms of authorship, they explore varied interpersonal relations, and they produce critical representations of hierarchical social institutions. As Field once protested to Robert Browning when he expressed discomfort with their unorthodox relationship, "We must be free as dramatists to work out in the open air of nature—exposed to her vicissitudes, witnessing her terrors: we cannot be stifled in drawing-room conventionalities."[22]

If a theory underlies this book, then, it is a revisionary theory of the relation between power and desire in writing. I devote the rest of this introduction to what I have found most desirable in collaborative writing, what I would argue its collaborators have desired—and gotten from— their writing together, and how reconsideration of collaboration entails a theory of desire.

Desire and Power: Michael Field and Jael B. Juba

R: The work we produce separately is different in content and tone from the work we do together. Our work together has a different voice. To demand to know which mind produced what seems beside the point; it's a refusal to see the work as the product of a re-

lationship, an alliance. So, given our project's status as a collaboration, to say nothing of its feminist and queer politics, we do
this work knowing we probably won't be rewarded for it. You
might say that we do it for love.
S: Or sex.
R: Are we on to that so soon?
S: I'm afraid so.[23]

The writings of the two couples I take as examples in this section
derive from widely separated historical moments and are markedly different. The ways they represent their collaborations, however, join in suggesting a model of desire that differs in interesting ways from the Freud-
ian/Lacanian paradigm that has dominated much contemporary feminist
theory of desire. The short essay on which I focus initially, Barbara Johnson's "Lesbian Spectacles," was not intended to rehearse all the complexities of the Freudian/Lacanian model, but it nonetheless provides a useful point of departure because Johnson seeks to describe the shape of
desire specifically between women—"lesbian desire," she calls it—and
she does so in contemporary novels and films that are far more familiar
to readers than are the collaborations I discuss here.[24] Moreover, she an-
alyzes four different relationships between women whose "identity" as
lesbians is *not* predicated in the texts she chooses; it is feminist readers
and viewers who have discerned lesbian identity here. Similarly, whether Field should be called "lesbian" has been a matter of debate among
their[25] twentieth-century critics, and the word *lesbian* never appears on
or between the covers of *The Restorationist*. What interests me throughout this study is the desire of two likenesses (not identicalities) for each
other—whether of two women, of two writers, or of a woman (writer) for
herself (a text of her own)—even in the midst of their differences. Enacted in shared projects, "collaborative desire," I argue, is a process of reciprocally operating power exchanges between two desiring subjects who
are attracted as much (or more) by their affinities and contiguity as by
what they may have to gain from each other. Thus it is not my aim to
decide whether these writers' intercourse occurs in a genitally sexual way
as well as a textual one. As critics such as Bonnie Zimmerman, Carey
Kaplan, and Ellen Cronan Rose argue, a same-sex metaphor is useful *as*
a metaphor, not only as an identity label,[26] but I have not adopted the term
lesbian as a central trope for this study as a whole for the same reasons
that I have not chosen to look only at same-sex couples: To do so would
be to embrace a single identity and to suggest that an equitable collaborative relation is possible only between two people identified as women.
Johnson gets personal in her analysis, so that her argument is based

as much on one viewer/reader's response—her own—as on theorization of desire; not presuming to decide whether the texts or their authors are lesbian, Johnson undertakes an intimate analysis of the act of reading "as a lesbian" (160). Johnson thus departs from previous critics not only in not seeking to establish identity—whether singular or multiple—for the texts themselves or for the characters in them, but also in analyzing the structure of her own desire for women in response to the women in the texts. Johnson's bold choice to speak of herself as a reader enables her to develop conclusions that combine the kind of deconstructive analysis she has long produced with personal feminist anecdote. She offers analysis that admits its own interests—both personal and political—in its subject and treats her responses as facts just as worthy of consideration as any theory that might undergird them. Indeed, it is only in her conclusion that Johnson incorporates a psychoanalytic explanation of desire, but in doing so her essay reveals how deeply influential this model has been on theorists of all types despite any arguments that have been developed to refine or refute it. Yet this model is reductive. Both Johnson's analysis and her concluding interpretation of desire are informed by sociopsychoanalytic theories of feminist film criticism, and so turn out to be examples of a particular model of psychodynamic relationship that, I argue, circumscribes possibilities for more various personal and political responses.

Comparing her reactions first to the novels *Sula* and *Passing* (which have been analyzed by Barbara Smith and Deborah McDowell, respectively, as lesbian novels)[27] and then to the films *Thelma and Louise* and *The Accused* (the former received as lesbian by many viewers, the second not), Johnson felt that *Sula* did not "work as a lesbian novel," but *Passing* did, and that *Thelma and Louise* did not work for her as a lesbian film, but *The Accused* did (161, 163). *Sula* and *Thelma and Louise* show women achieving "genuine intimacy and recogniz[ing] each other's value," and they criticize contemporary patriarchal society—thus enacting both sides of what Adrienne Rich first argued in her classic essay "Compulsory Heterosexuality" is integral to lesbian resistance (161–62)[28]—yet they do not match Johnson's sense of the "lesbian plot" or persuade her as representations of erotic desire between two women, whereas the other two works do. Why? Johnson answers this question by focusing on an explanation of why *Passing* and *The Accused* intrigue her.

In *Passing* and *The Accused* (but not in *Sula* or *Thelma and Louise*), long, tantalizing gazes are exchanged between the women, and the relationships in *Passing* and *The Accused* are "overinvested," with the women experiencing a protracted series of "involuntary re-encounters ungrounded in conscious positive feelings" (162). As Johnson says in speaking of *The Accused*, the actresses "fill each other's screen as objects of fascination" (163). Unexplainable as friendship, excessive in intensity, and focused on and through the gaze, the attraction between the women in the two latter texts enacts desire in a classic, cinematic form—in the form, indeed, that has been of greatest interest to feminist film critics. Yet, as Johnson goes on to point out, the relationship in *Passing* is a murderous one, and the relationship in *The Accused* occurs from "*within* the patriarchal institution" and without challenging it (162, 165). Indeed, Murphy in *The Accused* is attractive to Johnson "because she is a powerful woman turning her full attention toward another woman" (165). Johnson concludes from this that her response is a simple case of transference onto "the phallic mother, the woman whose appeal arises from her position in a power structure" (165). Johnson does not advocate this kind of appeal and, after acknowledging it, she attributes her response to a more general sociopsychic condition: "I have to acknowledge the role of the patriarchal institution not in impeding [my] fantasies but in enabling them" (165).

Johnson begins this essay by explaining it as a project to "catch" herself in the "act of reading as a lesbian" in moments unprocessed "through media-induced images of what a lesbian is or through my own idealizations of what a lesbian *should* be" (160). But, she concludes, her fantasies themselves are mediated through the "patriarchal institution," through the unconscious, and—I would add—through "media-induced images," not of what a lesbian is or should be, but of how desire works and should work. Johnson deftly hints at a deconstructive way out of these repetitively constraining structures by arguing, in the final lines of her essay, that the disparity between her feminist political views and her fantasies need not end in an impasse: "Any attempt to go on from this reading to theorize (my) lesbian desire would therefore have to confront the possibility of a real disjunction between my political ideals and my libidinal investments. But if the unconscious is structured by repetition and the political by the desire for change, there is nothing surprising about this. The question, still, would remain one of knowing what the unconscious changes, and what politics repeats" (166). Noting the false binary between changeable social institutions and unchanging unconscious structures, she upends the suggestion in her previous analysis of a monolithic, unchanging patriarchal institution mirroring itself in repetitive unconscious fantasy.

Nonetheless, the ease with which she had previously discovered a one-to-one correspondence between the data of her "experience" and a psychoanalytic explanation remains a potent residue of this essay—in some ways all the more potent for being unfiltered before the sudden deconstructive move she makes at the end. As she says, her response is unequivocally simple: "It is . . . [Murphy's] position in a power structure, that infuses my reading of the film, simple as that" (165). But does Johnson always respond in the same way to the same kinds of representations of women or even to the same text? How solid a fact is this description of her response? This observation about herself lacks consideration of any circumstantial, developmental, and differential contingencies. The ease with which she accepts her discovery of erotic nonfeeling or feeling in response to these four texts has the effect of making the psychoanalytic explanation seem natural, inevitable, possibly even universal, and the deconstructive twist at the end cannot entirely undo this.

What Johnson's response also shows us, however, is that different self-declared "lesbian" readers (Johnson and Smith, for example) respond differently to the same texts. Her reading reminds us to be wary of treating the relations between likenesses (whether women, women's novels, or coauthors) as undifferentiated, or—in Teresa de Lauretis's terms—as a matter of "sexual (in)difference."[29] "Same-sex" readers are no more like each other than are "same-sex" texts. I myself respond differently from Johnson to these texts, two of which (*Passing* and *Thelma and Louise*) I encountered before reading any criticism about them or hearing them discussed. My primary response is better described by Eve Sedgwick's more colloquial understanding of "indifference": Sedgwick reminds us of "the plain fact . . . that most people in the world, whatever their gender or sexuality, don't form or maintain libidinal cathexes toward most other people in the world."[30] On first impression, I found none of these texts erotically tantalizing or akin to my sense of a "lesbian plot."

After reading Smith, McDowell, and eventually Johnson, and then rereading or reseeing these texts, I found one moment (but only one) in one of the texts erotically charged—namely, the passage Smith cites in *Sula,* a moment early in the relationship between Sula and Nel: "It was in dreams that the two girls had first met. . . . Always, watching the dream along with her, were some smiling sympathetic eyes. Someone as interested as she herself in the flow of her imagined hair, the thickness of the mattress of flowers, the voile sleeves that closed below her elbows in gold-threaded cuffs."[31] What occurs here (that seems to be missing from the relationships in the rest of this novel as well as in the other novel and films) is mutual enjoyment of an autoerotic fantasy that is as tactile as it is visual and whose sensual pleasure is unmixed: Both self and other are enjoyed, both girls enjoy this with each other, and there are no mitigating elements of displeasure with each other (whether of hostility, resentment, regret, intimidation, or even anxiety). My response is not uncommon and it is not inexplicable, although it is better described by a nonpatriarchal (nonphallic) model than by a patriarchal model of power. Yet my response is also not a universal one, and it is partly contextualized by the pleasurable escape it affords from the more standard power hierarchy of heterosexual relations to which I became profoundly accustomed as a girl.

I would not deny that desire operates in part in the fashion many feminist film critics describe: The central Freudian/Lacanian insight that desire is constituted by the gap between subject and (m)other is a compelling one, not so much (in my view) for its elegant logic as for its descriptive power. As Mary Ann Doane paraphrases this theory, "Distance from the 'origin' (the maternal) is the prerequisite to desire; and insofar as desire is defined as the excess of demand over a need aligned with the maternal figure, the woman is left behind. Voyeurism, according to Christian Metz, is a perfect type of desire insofar as it presupposes and activates as its fundamental condition a spatial distance between subject and object."[32] But the possibility of closeness, proximity, contiguity is already embedded in this sense of distance, so that desire, as I would argue—and as I have experienced it—is elicited by the play between the gap and its closure, not by the gap alone.[33] "Power" itself operates in such situations more as a tantalizing oscillation between subject and object than as a property or force belonging either to the viewing subject or to the viewed object.[34] In this introduction my concern is to discern the ways in which an alternative (antipatriarchal) desire operates through combinatory, transformative, and mutual power play—a process enabled by collaboration.

Desire reproduces itself and combines with other affects in complex ways at different stages of a relationship. We get to see a long-term friendship develop in *Sula*, and we join Thelma and Louise in the midst of one, whereas the relationship in *Passing* comes and goes with great gaps in between, and in *The Accused* it is an ephemeral byproduct of the legal system. In other words, despite modernity's preoccupation with the earliest stages of sexual attraction—with the earliest moments of a child's cognition, with romantic first love, or with sudden, anonymous attraction between strangers—desire actually occurs in varied contexts and at variable depths. It often transpires and may be most likely to last between people who (for all kinds of reasons) appear to each other comparably yet differentially powerful. If we are each other's "phallic mothers," we may

actually move each other through and away from asymmetric power relations to relations of complex yet mutual empowerment. This eventu-
ality is one of the things that many of us most desire.

This last possibility is not realized in any of the texts Johnson describes, however, and although I enjoy reading Smith's, McDowell's, and
Johnson's readings of them (finding moments in each of these readings
exciting), the women in these novels and films, with the partial exception of Sula, do not strike me as desirable, and their relations with each
other seem unexciting. The women in these texts never recognize that
they want each other except as mysteries to be solved, friends to hold
onto, problems to be resolved, or allies to secure. Smith, McDowell, and
Johnson record thrilling opportunities for recognition that are lost on the
characters. What is missing for me in these texts rises to the surface in
Field and Juba.

To most readers, Michael Field and Jael B. Juba are unknown writers, so something first should be said about who they are. Considerably
more about Field appears in chapters 3 and 4. The brief profiles here introduce the contexts in which Field and Juba are currently being read by
setting forth the facts about their identities as coauthors made available,
in the case of Field, through memoirs, a 1922 biography, and a "short and
personal" 1998 biography[35] and, in the case of Juba, through bookjacket
blurbs and a self-analyzing published essay. Not much more is available.

Michael Field was the pen and pet name of two turn-of-the-century
women writers: they often called each other (and their friends called
them) "Michael" and "Field" or "Michael and Henry Field." Their legal
names were Katherine Bradley (1846–1914) and Edith Cooper (1862–1913).
Michael and Henry lived together throughout their lives. Janet Todd's
reference guide to British women writers relates the outlines of their story
in this way:

> Katherine Bradley and Edith Cooper were constant companions from
> 1865, when Bradley joined the household of [Bradley's] invalid older sis-
> ter, [who was] Cooper's mother, and [Bradley] assumed the care and tu-
> telage of her niece. . . . In 1878 the family moved to Bristol, where Brad-
> ley and Cooper attended University College together, participating in
> debating societies, women's suffrage organizations, and anti-vivisection-
> ist activities. By the time Cooper was 20, the two women had sworn
> "Against the world, to be / Poets and lovers evermore." . . . When [Coo-
> per] subsequently developed cancer, [Bradley] nursed her until her death
> then she herself died of the same illness within six months.[36]

As their 1998 biographer, Emma Donoghue, notes, "The most common misconceptions about them are factual" (8). According to Donoghue and other sources, Bradley was raised by her mother and her mother's sister, Emma ("Lissie"), and when Emma married James Cooper in 1860, Bradley's mother and she became nearly constant inmates of the Cooper household, where Edith was born in 1862.[37] Together Michael and Henry studied classics and philosophy—both at the university and on their own—and eventually they published more than twenty-five coauthored plays and eight cosigned books of poems.

Jael B. Juba is the pseudonym of the two authors of *The Restorationist: Text One* (1993).[38] Its cover calls it a "collaborative fiction" and its real-life collaborators are listed on the cover: Joyce Elbrecht and Lydia Fakundiny. A note on the back cover adds that "their fields are philosophy and literature" and locates them in Ithaca, New York.[39] *The Restorationist: Text One* is their first novel, although their title and the novel itself make it clear that they intend this to be the first volume of a series. In a memoir—which is part essay, part conversation, part science fiction story—about their collaboration, they say little about themselves, but they do include a convenient abstract of their novel:

> In [*The Restorationist*], Elizabeth Harding Dumot, known as Harding—a Southerner and a teacher of literature resettled in the Northeast—tells about restoring a rundown antebellum house on the Florida Gulf Coast one summer in the late 1970s. The story develops as a conflict between this woman who works herself to the bone restoring the old house, in which she envisions a life good in all senses, and a community corrupted in all senses by a struggle for survival and status going back to the landing of Spanish conquistadors in the New World. It moves inescapably toward violence and murder. Nearly a decade later, Harding's friend and former student, Jael B. Juba, faithfully writes out this half-gothic, half-naturalistic narrative, as compelled in her own way by the project of authorship as her narrator is by the feat of restoration. Hers is a speculative, blackly humorous self-presentation in an invented form she calls the "psycheme"; thrown among Harding's tales of restoration, Juba's psychemes are equally fraught with mystery and peril as she finds herself without a home, with no community to speak of, running—as she puts it to herself—culturally wild in the process. ("Scenes from a Collaboration" 241)

The Restorationist thus formally resembles the collaborative relation between its authors by bringing together a narrator-protagonist with an author-character. Their essay informs us further that the ethnic differences between these two characters—one a Southerner, the other of eastern European descent—mirror those of the authors (256). But Elbrecht and Fakundiny's essay also tells us that both authors were responsible for creating both characters.

I bring these two couples together here to foreground the pleasures of coauthorship because in the rest of this book I focus more extensively on its problems. I wish to disclose in this Introduction not a set of attributes possessed by one set of writings rather than another but a way of reading desire: Revising Barbara Johnson's phrase, one might call this "collaborative desire." At the same time, there is a material as well as a textual basis to this reading that would be missing in cases of single authors or, if one judges by Stillinger and Koestenbaum's descriptions, from dual male collaborations. Collaborative women writers write about and enact with each other the relations I explore in this Introduction. Both Field and Juba conceive of collaboration as often thoroughly integrated; both willingly join their names under one—but also two—signature(s) in their texts. Moreover, they overtly explore in their writing alternative kinds of relations—for and between women—to those offered by the predominantly heterosexual courtship tradition (which Field encountered) or the heterosexist sexual marketplace (which Juba describes).

Widely divided by time, space, and style, they share parallel constructions of authorial identity. Most obviously, they present their dual authorship under a single, fictionalized name and often insist on the indivisibility of their coauthorship. Yet they also play with their pseudonym and with alternative pseudonyms. In this playfulness, they permit differences to reemerge (Field dividing into Michael and Field or Michael and Henry, Juba becoming a character in her novel and ultimately a coauthor with Harding of their novel). They describe this playful interaction in similar ways as well, as dancing and weaving, for example. Field writes, "the work is perfect mosaic: we cross and interlace like a company of dancing summer flies";[40] Juba writes, "We turn around each to the other," "to and fro, [we] . . . live in the world being spun out" ("Scenes from a Collaboration" 247–49)—a mutual, mobile reflexivity of samenesses and differences. They are fascinated by the act of authorship, self-consciously writing (in Field's case) about poetry and poets or (in Juba's case) about narratology and authorship. In fact, this metatextual fascination takes precedence over other representations of their relationship with each other. Field extols the status of "the poet"; Juba broods on their activity as "author." Thus they write of desire as if it both is and isn't their own: Desire and song are equated to each other by Field, and desire and narrative hinge on each other for Juba. Their texts are places where they meet, and the radical transformation that occurs when two people write together makes both the gaps and the transferences between texts and selves even more obvious than they are to the solo author seeking "self-expression."

Are their relationships also sexual? This question has been hotly debated by one critic in relation to Field[41] (the "Fields" called themselves "closer married" than the Brownings),[42] and it is likely to emerge quickly for Juba ("Why do we [collaborate]?" asks "Lydia" in their essay. "You've already said it, I think, the operative word being *want*. Desire," answers "Joyce" ["Scenes from a Collaboration" 251]). But the permeable relations and potentially treacherous crossovers between public and private are a key theme for Juba and were a sore point for Bradley and Cooper as they endeavored to construct a successful single author between the two of them. Both pairs evade inquiry into their personal situations, yet do not shut it off; they create works formally distinct from biography without excluding autobiographical elements. But rather than writing semiautobiographical narratives like *Jane Eyre* or *The Autobiography of Alice B. Toklas,* they position themselves as archivalists and latecomers in their work, collaboratively rewriting previous texts, restoring historical periods and personalities, citing their authorities even as they revise them (Field often cites scholars and histories they have consulted, and while Harding is at work restoring her antebellum house, Juba recreates the traditional narrative, splicing in allusions to other literature and contemporary theorists). Thus they possess hermeneutic similarities as well. The fictions they choose to restore often focus on representations of strong, intellectual, and passionate women, and also on men's subjugation of women and children.

Even their aesthetic strategies bear comparison: They both ground their works in traditional lyric and narrative conventions, yet image and event become indeterminate in meaning, multiple in effect in their works. Their range of textures moves from the lush thematics of pagan or ordinary pleasures or toils to the complex psychodynamics of affect—of desire, fear, hatred, triumph, abjection, and bodily pain. They are thoroughly engaged, in other words, both in the confining structures of the text and in its pleasures. If Elizabeth Barrett Browning was, as Ellen Moers judged her, "the literary woman's writer,"[43] Field and Juba are a contemporary feminist critic's dream, almost too perfect for a critic interested in feminist literary collaboration.

They are both ripe for commentary: Field's century of neglect by scholars has barely ended, and Juba's first novel is yet to be substantially discussed. I will ask not how they lived, but how they represent authorial and psychosocial relations in their texts. What I present here may at times seem an idealized redescription of authorship and psychosocial relations. If so, the idealization is a result of my approach rather than theirs. Neither Field nor Juba has created utopian fictions; in fact, Field's narratives are mostly tragedies and *The Restorationist* is chameleonic, at times anarchistic, and often satiric. These two sets of writers nonetheless deploy an alternative form of authorship, and through it they imagine alternative interpersonal relations.

In the poem most often cited for its assertion of the collaborative relationship between Michael and Henry, we are invited to share one person's gaze upon another:

> A girl,
>   Her soul a deep-wave pearl
> Dim, lucent of all lovely mysteries;
>   A face flowered for heart's ease,
>   A brow's grace soft as seas
>   Seen through faint forest-trees:
>   A mouth, the lips apart,
> Like aspen-leaflets trembling in the breeze
>   From her tempestuous heart.
>   Such: and our souls so knit,
>   I leave a page half-writ—
>   The work begun
> Will be to heaven's conception done,
>   If she come to it.[44]

As in the cinematic representations that concern feminist film critics, we vicariously look in this poem at "a girl," and our gaze is seductively drawn to a translucent veil wavering before her face and body; we cannot quite see her, but peer as if through forest leaves at a seascape, "a deep-wave pearl." And we peer at lips parted for our further intrusion.

At this moment, however, the lips seem to be respond, "trembling" before us "in the breeze / From her tempestuous heart." Her breath breaks forth toward us, and the picture that seemed to await our plunge into it now appears to possess its own subjectivity and turbulent motion. The gaze stops abruptly here, with "such," a pregnant word indicating the immediate texture of the moment (its "suchness") and the poet's grasp of the picture in a final word ("such") and implying an embrace of the girl, for in the next phrase "our souls" are "so knit." In this context, the "knitting" suggests an embrace as physical as it is "soulful." "We" mean-

while becomes quietly ambiguous: "We" may be the speaker and onlook-
er seizing the girl, but perhaps the girl has met the speaker's embrace
halfway.

The poem itself shifts at this juncture, opening itself to a counter-
move from the girl, one in which the previous description may merely
act as an allegory ("such" and "so") of a relationship that is incomplete
and unsatisfactory in its one-sidedness until the "other" tells her version:
"I leave a page half-writ / The work begun," only to be completed "if she
come to it." In this last line, the work is done and the relationship consummated only if a reciprocal, quite possibly different response is made,
which the first speaker does not attempt to predict. The monodirection-
al cinematic image with which the poem began is set aside as its narrator awaits the other's voice and writing. The speaker acknowledges not
only the existence of life and subjectivity in a seen object but also their
insubstantiality as long as they go unuttered or unexpressed; some kind
of differential movement is necessary for completion of the poem and the
relationship.

Although this poem may come closer than any other to describing
Field's process of collaborative composition, it retains the shape of a traditional love lyric, addressed from one speaker to a silent listener. Like
most of their work, it was published under a joint male name (Michael
Field), so the reader is led to see the poem as yet another love lyric by a
male poet to a female object. Angela Leighton, in *Victorian Women Poets: Writing against the Heart,* complicates such a reading somewhat
when she recalls the Sapphic fragment ("To a Girl" or "To Brochea"),
which this poem possibly rewrites (231); the Sapphic echoes would render the genders of the participants ambiguous. The poem might also be
seen less as a representation of an actual relationship than as a restoration of previous lyric moments. But Leighton herself, following Field's
1922 biographer, Mary Sturgeon, instead claims, "The poem, 'A Girl,'
. . . was almost certainly written by Katherine for Edith" (231). Whatever Leighton's reasons for this attribution, the result is that the reader is redirected from regarding the poem as a collaborative text to reading it as a lyric written by one person about and for another.[45] The poem
itself describes only the opening gesture of love, the erotic moment in
which a lover first sees a beloved (love at first sight), and gazing is usually crucial in the onset of a relationship between two people. Analog-
ically, the poem can be read as the moment in which one of two coauthors begins to write—thus a moment in which poetic as well as erotic
conception begins.

In my view, however, a reading of this poem should not end there. As Wayne Koestenbaum argues, the question of who wrote the poem is open: "Michael or Henry? Michael Field frees the love lyric, long a genre of possession, into an ownerless, borderless 'field' without master or serf" (174). Many of Field's contemporaries knew by 1893 who Field was, so in a book that appeared under their collaborative signature, its audience could have been expected to read it, in part, as a joint production. However "A Girl" was originally composed, the circumstances of publication are these: Bradley and Cooper produced, published, and cosigned their plays and poetry at a fast and steady rate between 1884 (after they began to publish their plays under the name Michael Field) and 1893, when they published "A Girl"; in 1893 Cooper was thirty-one years old, certainly mature enough to write, revise, or advise a poem of this sort herself.[46]

If we take into account all the frames into which this poem invites us, two important conclusions can be drawn about it. The first is that in grounding their poem in the prior textual conventions of both male lyricists *and* Sappho's woman-centered lyricism, and in then rewriting the love lyric under their own now-notorious name (signifying usurpation of the male position by two female writers), Field produced a doubly indeterminate utterance in which the gender *and* number of the speaker(s) and thus also the kind of relationship enacted become tantalizingly uncertain, or multiple, permitting a simultaneity of different relationships. The second is that the structure of desire is reshaped not only by the assumption of multiple authorship, but also by the turn within the poem's narrative. It is no longer produced in a unidirectional movement between the power-seeking (male) gaze and voice and the passively recipient, silent female object, but is instead structured as an invitation to gaze together at each other or to gaze at a mirroring image that reflects each of them back to the other. The poem invites us to be each other's objects, to explore each other's silences, to expect each other's speech, to receive each other's movements—in Juba's words, to "turn to and fro," "dwelling" together ("Scenes from a Collaboration" 248–49).

I see this poem as a typical but particularly intriguing example of Field's socioerotic poetics. In their book of Sapphics, emotional and relational variations often (but not always) having to do with lesbian community are woven through seventy poems. A perhaps more revealing and more convenient second example may be found in a passage in which they imagine the relationship of a woman with herself. The poem, "The Sleeping Venus," offers ekphrastic commentary on Giorgione's painting of the same title; the poem appeared in an 1892 volume titled *Sight and Song*.

After gazing awhile at Venus and exploring a detailed analogy to the open landscape in which she rests "shameless[ly]" naked, Field describes the pleasure Venus seems to take in herself:[47]

> Her hand the thigh's tense surface leaves,
>   Falling inward. Not even sleep
>   Dare invalidate the deep,
>   Universal pleasure sex
>   Must unto itself annex—
>   Even the stillest sleep; at peace,
>   More profound with rest's increase,
>   She enjoys the good
>   Of delicious womanhood. (101–2)

At the outset we join the speaker in a voyeuristic gaze at an unconscious woman, watching Venus's seductive hand "falling" not outward to the lush Italian countryside that surrounds her, but inward toward a paradise regained. Then the gaze stops, penetrating no further, and we are transferred to the more abstract but sensually palpable interior of the pleasure zone, shifted from gazing at an object to resting within a sphere— or multiple spheres, multiple conditions—of sleep, pleasure, and sex. Sex appears to be at once an inviolate space and an actively pleasure-seeking force. "Not even sleep / Dare" block the threshold as Venus enters it, or dare undo Venus's pleasure once she is there.

At the heart of the passage is the false opposition between pleasure or sex and sleep, between conscious experience and blank unconsciousness, between sensation and oblivion. Unlike senseless sleep, sex sensibly annexes pleasure "unto itself." Even when confined (as we might think it) to a single body, sex acts unto itself, as two bodies interact. We tend these days to associate annexation with colonialism, but in this context it seems to suggest rather the self-reflexive actions of self-ownership and self-possession.

Self-reflexive interaction becomes the primary action of this passage, so that even the opposition I have just noted between sleep and sex is eventually undone and replaced by the intertwining of sleep with sex and with pleasure. Venus and sleep seem to join each other both in body and in rhyme, in the triple "deeps" of sleep, sex, and pleasure. The paradoxical conjoining of sleep and sex suggests obviously that sex consummates itself *through* submergence in sleep and pursues its pleasures even as it sinks into a bottomless unconsciousness; more interestingly, for our purposes, it also suggests that sleep must collaborate with, not oppose, sex. Similarly, in the fourth line, the conjunction "pleasure sex" makes it difficult to separate pleasure from sex or, grammatically, to separate subject from object. The rest of the passage becomes increasingly deconstructive as it plays on the paradoxes that pleasure and sex increase even as they become more still and that increase may be found in rest as well as in sex. This play enacts the kind of pleasure the poem as a whole describes: an activity in which no one term dominates the other, but in which all terms become implicated in each other: "She is of the things that are" (105).

The last lines of the verse passage I have cited add a further set of suggestions. Sex in this passage has moved from within the voyeuristic frame of Giorgione's painting (in which "I" gaze at "her") to develop her sex's autoerotic pleasures (between "it" and "itself") and here, finally, to permit a lesbian relation between two samenesses ("her" and "her"): If the "she" who enjoys sex enjoys herself, then the "she" who enjoys sex also enjoys womanhood. This is a poem in which Venus is thoroughly comfortable with herself (as indeed she seems in the painting); hers is clearly a long-term relationship, so her desires play among themselves as well as in communion with the landscape and "would continue" as long as "the sun strikes on the grass" (104, 105).

Self and other become, more entirely here than in "A Girl," buoyantly self-reflexive. I contrast this relation with the position of one who sees him or herself as entirely outside another body, either gazing at or being gazed at by a powerful other (as in *The Accused*) or who experiences him or herself as annihilating or being annihilated by the other (as in *Passing*). Field's collaborative poems open up an erotic relational zone that would possess the chaste strength of a marriage bond ("For the sex that forms them each [Earth and Venus] / Is a bond, a holiness" [99]), and, though traditionally associated with Britomart-like armed virginity, chastity is associated in Field's Sapphic poems with female erotic pleasure and shared sensuality, framed aesthetically and protected from external harm. That inviolate sphere of interactive pleasure offers an alternative model of desire, one that preempts and supplants standard hierarchical models of desire focused on a pathologically conceived female object: a passive, recipient object, an all-powerful possessor of the gaze, or, schizophrenically, both.

In an essay on collaboration, Joyce Elbrecht and Lydia Fakundiny converse together about collaboration as a form of conversation. Like their novel, this essay defies easy summary. But the concept of movement to and fro becomes a primary trope in their descriptions of collaboration as conversation, which they etymologize: "The route of borrowing, by way of early French, goes back not really to *convertere* but to the deponent form, *conversari*, literally 'to turn oneself about,' with the frequentative sense 'to move to and fro'" ("Scenes from a Collaboration" 249). Thus Lydia says, "When I collaborate with you, I turn to and fro, occupy, live in the world being spun out, the world on and in which we both labor by the turns we singly and reciprocally make." She continues, "People are always asking: 'How do you do it? How do you collaborate, don't your egos get in the way?' It's that tension they're curious about. But they're thinking of it as friction, as crises of appropriation." Here Joyce takes over: Their "tension" is "a sort of stretching . . . as in 'tensile.'" Lydia agrees: "Something more, then, like *ex*tension, the 'I' stretching—extending—to the place of the other, the place where the other is also 'I,' as though 'you' were somehow bypassed in the process—or, overpassed, like a gap across which 'I' always extend myself to 'I'" (249). And "without erasing our differences, leveling our histories, because the whole productive richness of collaboration owes its possibility to those differences," Joyce adds (250). The next question Lydia asks, "Why would anybody want to do that?" has an obvious answer; Joyce responds, "You've already said it, I think, the operative word being *want*. Desire. You have to desire the collaborative world under formation more than the unextended 'yours' and 'mine' of the old power structures." Lydia agrees: "That has a lot to do with the pleasure of this kind of work—of calling forth and using all your own resources for something other than your own power and survival" (251).

Like Michael Field in "A Girl," Elbrecht and Fakundiny reenact their collaboration as a form of reciprocal movement wherein the "I" encounters another "I" rather than an oppositional "her." Desire is conceived not as yearning for the withdrawn, all-powerful other, but as reciprocal motion where the "collaborative world under formation"—their collaborative creation—becomes the ultimate object of their joint desires. This pseudo-object (which becomes a fixed object only when it is finished) excites them as long as they are together producing it, as long as it remains in motion. In collaboration, one calls forth one's own powers for "something other than" the increase of one's own power or property—for the increase instead of an ongoing collaborative process and relationship wherein power continually oscillates between two "I's."

This language—and the entire conversation between Lydia and Joyce—is more optimistic than the novel, in which the author-character Jael B. Juba often reminds us of the "domination of signs" (233), the authority of prior sign systems framing Juba's text (much as earlier love lyrics and Giorgione's painting frame Field's poems). The term *collaboration* occurs in *The Restorationist* in almost exclusively negative contexts—in describing various forms of destructive collaborationism, usually between men (225, 239, 289). At one point in the essay itself, Juba writes that "there's no choice as to our cosmic working conditions . . . all falls into place in the collaborative chain." Nonetheless, she goes on to say with hedged optimism (which is as close as she gets to utopianism in the novel) that "perhaps there is some chance option as to whom and . . . what we collaborate with, some possibility of a fleeting escape from the cosmic collaborative web" (252). Juba speaks similarly in the novel both of this "cosmogonic web" in which each of us "lives her double existence as collaborative creator and collaboratively created" (383) and of the possibility of "escape" from the domination of discourse—the possibility that we may "collaborate to escape, not the activity of signing but the domination of signs. Almost." How do we do this? By "a turning of our bodies. Away from each other" (233). We may not escape entirely the domination of signs, but from within the activity of signing, Juba sees it as possible to make a psychic and bodily "turn away." As in the essay, this "movement away" is an act of "self-divestment," the giving up of power and privilege for the sake of something other.

These, then, are the conditions of freely chosen collaboration for Juba: acknowledgment of the chain of signs in which we are caught and partial escape through "turning away" from its domination and through self-divestiture. As Juba, Elbrecht, and Fakundiny describe it (and as the novel discloses it), self-divestiture is not an act of altruism, masochistic self-immolation, or self-emancipation; it is a relational gesture that acts to shift not only the balance, but also the direction of power. Power is reconceived and performed not as a fixed and binarized hierarchy (power/powerlessness) but as a mobile and plural splitting (of powers). This complex formula in the novel permits Juba (as author) and Harding (as restorationist) to evade appropriation and in the essay lets Lydia and Joyce choose each other. As Judith Butler argues, "construction is not opposed to agency; it is the necessary scene of agency, the very terms in which agency is articulated and becomes culturally intelligible."[48] Choice for these coauthors and their character-narrators thus occurs, paradoxically, in and through a preexistent "collaborative chain." That Juba also uses the term *web* for this chain further suggests that with all its "constitutive constraints" (in Butler's terminology),[49] the chain is itself multiplicitous, branching to provide choices.

In the novel, Juba and Harding continually remind the reader that further determinants, further signs, lurk to govern their movements. But as the novel unfolds its revisions of the realistic portrait of Harding restoring a house and of the murder plot that enmeshes her, it also demonstrates some of the ways in which choices come about. The novel emphasizes differences between the evasions Harding exercises and the attempts by various predatory male characters to dominate or appropriate. Harding simultaneously struggles to avoid becoming a victim of violence among the increasingly rivalrous workmen on the house she is restoring and to work *with* both the workmen and the obstructive community in which the house is located. She does these things not out of a desire to master either group, but because she has invested herself in restoring an old house, approaching and cultivating its beauties as if it were a beloved, doing violence only to the decay it has accrued through neglect. Moreover, only this combination of evasiveness, hard work, and a shifting of desire away from absolute possession of power or property can allow her to succeed. By the end of the novel, ownership of the house has passed to others; as a finished marketable product, it ceases to interest Harding, who sees it primarily as the sign of a completed hard-won collaboration between the workmen, the community, the house, and herself.

I am less concerned with the details of this narrative (one plotline—the simplest to follow—among several in this novel) than with the "psychemes" of its pseudonymous author, Juba, however. Free-associating in front of the reader, this author-character repeatedly interjects digressions about Harding's developing narrative and Juba's own authorship. Juba meditates with particular intensity on ways of eluding domination by sexual discourse, a discourse constantly on the tongues of the male characters. Sexual discourse is a major component of Harding's narrative; sex and violence are intertwined as thoroughly in this murder mystery as in any popular novel or film. Harding assiduously avoids sexual contact with the male workers, and sexual fantasies seem absent from her mind as she toils at her work. But, as it turns out, she cultivates this absence because she is perpetually pursued by the exploitive fantasies of her ex-husband, Paul. Juba eventually agrees to include his twenty-page story about Harding late in the novel. Paul tries to implicate Juba in (what he calls) a "collaborative" fantasy with him, inviting Juba to see her novel as a predatory fantasy about Harding (300). But Juba resists integrating Paul's piece into her narrative, carefully setting it off as a distinctly framed inset tale; it turns out to be a narcissistic recollection not of Harding, but of Paul's psychological abuse of her.

This tale raises a question, not unfamiliar in feminist readings of women's fiction: Where is the good love? Aside from Harding's relation to the house, is there a positive portrayal of erotic desire in the novel? Where does it transpire for its pseudonymous author, Juba? Juba turns "to and fro" in connection to her character Harding, and Harding, as narrator, reciprocates, so that Juba's and Harding's sections alternate with each other and occasionally intertwine. Specifically sexual desire seems either repressed or sublimated into Harding's house restoration and Juba's novel writing. Yet as the novel develops, an interesting countersuggestion emerges: Sublimation in its narrative is an avenue for the "movement away" from domination by others and inward into the silent body or house, and both Harding and Juba also undo the outward/inward, articulated/silent, public/private binaries by entertaining what could be called (borrowing a term from Juba) an "intransitive" condition (225) comparable to Field's inviolate, self-reflexive, erotic play.

Juba thinks a lot about sex, but finishes her meditations with gestures of self-repression. She often worries about the difficulty of any escape from the discourse of sexuality. At one point when Juba is thinking about pornography, she pessimistically analogizes the world to a marketplace of sadomasochistic sex exchange, where practically anything can be reduced to a sexual commodity. In concluding this passage, she offers it as the record of a kind of holocaust, vowing "never to forget again . . . the worldly transformations of sado-masochism" (97–98). Meanwhile, Juba seeks a collaborative relationship with the reader in which the reader and she could call forth their powers for the sake of something beyond their immediate personal interests—for the sake of a collaborative *reading* of the novel. But there is nothing easy or obvious about this, and Juba often frets under the imagined gaze of a reader she can't see (206). In the section about the sexual marketplace, her last sentence is directed to the reader: "I record myself standing under your gaze in order never to forget" (98). This gaze is figured, further, as what she would call a sadomasochistic transaction between giver and receiver. Juba worries too about her role in "seducing" the reader by offering the "feeling-of-meaning" in Harding's narrative and then withholding it in her own more postmodern sections, but then she senses the "pull" of the reader's "desires [on] her [for more meaning], suggesting all manner of commerce between us" (125–26).

The escape Juba finds from this dilemma emerges when she decides it is "easier" "to give up the power of seduction" than "to resist falling into [the reader's] hands, coming under your spell," and so she proclaims "unilateral disarmament" (126). Here it appears that Juba divests herself of power *in order to* avoid the exchange of gazes. But what else is there in that case, except to repress herself—which she does, by returning immediately to Harding's narrative? In the section I first quoted on "turning away" from signs, she speaks of this as a moment "free of eroticism, free of desire . . . satisfying in its Resistants" (232). Similarly, another passage answers Freud's question about what woman wants by asserting that "continuing satisfaction" can occur only "in being who we are wanting nothing," that "for me, my desire is intransitive: I want nothing more than I want. . . . To be left alone in my wanting, my desire, now *that's* life well-lived" (225). On the face of it, this sounds like a life of sexual death and a death of reciprocal desire.

Yet to read these passages exclusively in this way is to miss an alternative she suggests, an alternative that involves the possibility not only of choice but of an intransitive verbal condition not unlike that in Field's poem on Venus, where sleep and sex turn out to be linked and interchangeable rather than opposed and mutually exclusive conditions. Just before Juba includes Paul's piece, she presents an important theoretical context for her descriptions of sexual discourse and exchange. Inviting readers to skip Paul's narrative if they wish, she says,

> I share with [readers who dislike Paul's narrative] at the very least a resistance to contemporary pressure to be always and interminably talking about our sexual escapades, which presupposes not only that we must always be engaging in them but that nothing else matches them in interest or importance, whether in life or in art. I hold to the Foucaultian position that exposing oneself in sexual discourses has become a primary mode of mass pacification, the principal instrument of unreflective political subjection in Western societies. We all now have ample opportunity for abjection in the guise of consent; I can extol my captivation [by Harding and Paul's narratives] in the irony of naming none other than myself as captor/captive. (284)

This passage expresses Juba's concern not merely with dominance, but with monopolization by the discourse of sexuality, which Foucault tried to demystify in *The History of Sexuality*, showing it to be a "principal instrument" of social control. Her threefold strategy in this passage is, first, to acknowledge her position in this discourse; second, not to impose it on others (to "name" herself but "none other than" herself as "subjected"); and, third, to deconstruct the binarized structure of this discourse by recognizing (and internalizing) it as that of "captor/captive."[50] When subject (captor) and object (captive) become thus linked, the resulting grammar is "intransitive."

In an often overlooked passage in *The History of Sexuality*, Foucault himself offers an alternative to sexual discourse, proposing a *material* field of sexual desire, which the discourses of sexuality cannot entirely regulate—the "claims" of bodies, pleasures, and knowledges:

> We must not think that by saying yes to sex, one says no to power; on the contrary, one tracks along the course laid out by the general deployment of sexuality. It is the agency of sex that we must break away from, if we aim—through a tactical reversal of the various mechanisms of sexuality—to counter the grips of power with the claims of bodies, pleasures, and knowledges, in their multiplicity and their possibility of resistance. The rallying point for the counterattack against the deployment of sexuality ought not to be sex-desire, but bodies and pleasures.[51]

Butler has usefully critiqued other passages in Foucault that suggest a contradiction in his thinking between the constructedness of sexual discourse and a prior biologically based sexuality.[52] But it is not entirely clear how he might eventually have developed the "claims" described in the passage just cited, and this particular argument need not have been at odds with his central theory of language if he had proceeded to rethink the polarity between textuality and materiality.

Juba never offers a passage like this one in Foucault, remaining consistently concerned with the encompassing constitutive constraints of language; however, "bodies and pleasures" do seem available not only to Harding but to Juba, for they become a "matter" of textuality itself flowing elusively through Juba's discursive explanations and narratives. In the middle of the novel, Juba defines women's "sex acts" as all of women's daily routine activities, and the routines themselves are reperformed in the diversified descriptive terms of the text (195). Her narrative of Harding alludes to the richly various pleasures of a woman at work in her house. Indeed, even while Juba is struggling with theorizing the gaze and the commerce of sexuality, her own language is a punning maze of suggestive words and variant idioms. "Pleasure" is thus coterminous with both the bespoken body and the articulated text but is subdued or annihilated by neither. Instead of offering only sexual commerce, Juba invites us into the sensual sphere of language's myriad "material" impressions. (This never becomes *l'écriture féminine* because the novel's language rarely thematizes women's bodies.) Harding makes the complex relation between materiality and language as explicit as it ever becomes in the Prologue to the novel:

> Slats of sunlight snuggled over my arms and legs, breezes whiffled, and here I sat serenely tackling the problematic character of private life ex-

isting under the force of public intercourse, the place that remains private because it cannot be shared in language or otherwise, the place that is, quite simply, your body. No matter what the strategies of possession, including identification, I can't be your body and you can't be mine— well, "tackling" gets in altogether the wrong picture and, as much as I like the idea, so does "dallying." Dawdling is more like what I was doing up in that oversized window seat a little past eight A.M. my last morning in Old Tarragona. (6)

Bodies mark the inviolate private places that elude the fixtures of language, but around which language also is always snuggling and whiffling. In other words, bodies and words reciprocally constrain each other, conjoin each other, and toy with each other.

Without ignoring the sexual violence in sociolinguistic structures and insisting on the difficulty of escaping them, Juba thus seeks what I called in Field an "inviolate" sexuality—a sexuality that keeps itself unviolated by evading others and is nonviolent toward others. Juba and Field seek to "turn to and fro" in relation to others rather than to turn into others or to turn others into themselves. Bodies and words too may come together without violating each other in noncollaborationism; if they do, the process could be described as Juba describes it in Elbrecht and Fakundiny's essay: "There is, to be sure, a history leading to their choice of each other as fellow-workers, but no reason for it. It doubly happened, a haphazard happiness. I [Juba] never fight for my existence, never seek to perpetuate it, knowing no force . . . moves these two to the unity of their work. But if those who play together stay together, my coming and going is assured. I am the plaything of their collaboration, pleased to come and go in the knowledge that their separateness is necessary for my integrity" (252). Instead of possessing the asymmetric structure of hierarchical power relations, desire in these women's writings is enacted in the movements of subjects toward, around, and away from each other and in an exercise of power invested in something not exclusively focused even on each other—in the process of restoring a house for Harding, in the operations of narrative for Juba, and in coauthorship for Joyce and Lydia and for Field. Field's evasion of conventionalities and Juba's evasion of sign systems thus facilitate rather than obstruct as they pour their desires into activity: the making of a play or poem, the taking of a pleasure, the construction of a new house of fiction. It is the activity of collaborative writing, above all, in which Juba and Field, Juba and Harding, Joyce and Lydia are engaged in these texts. Collaboration, as they practice it, leads them to prefer over the discourse of sexuality, the pleasures and perils of conversational textuality.

Does collaboration, as Field and Juba conceive it, actually work? Echoing Johnson in her frank appreciation of *Passing* and *The Accused,* I could simply say that their textual enactments work for me. But beyond that, what are we to think about their presentation of collaborative desire? Both sets of authors become nearly silent on the question of whether collaboration such as theirs could provide the basis for social interactions more generally, although if Johnson and others are right in seeing desire as foundational (though not exclusively so) in the libidinal *and* the political, literary collaboration might suggest points of departure for rethinking social coalitions.

In modern history—the history of single authorship, compulsory heterosexuality, and models of desire premised on "absence"—there has seemed little possibility for Foucault's "bodies and pleasures," for Elbrecht and Fakundiny's "conversari," or (to cite yet another set of collaborators who conceive of desire differently, this time two collaborative male theorists) Deleuze and Guattari's "body without organs."[53] I have begun this book by offering a (possibly utopian) alternative, based on what collaborative writers and revisionists of the discourses of authorship and sexuality have to say about escape.[54] In what follows, I shift my emphasis to focus more closely on the problematics and challenges of various collaborations. The chapters that follow this Introduction relate, first, the contradictions (particularly in Parts 1 and 2) in which coauthorships are caught and, second, the ways coauthorships (particularly in Part 3) revise monolithic norms of thought, writing, and social interaction. In examining these contradictory legacies, one continues to discover transformative, collaborative desires.

PART I

Political Literary
Alliances of Two

1   Originality and Collaboration: John Stuart Mill and Harriet Taylor *in the* Autobiography

THE EPISODE THAT PROMPTED my interest in collaboration lasted less than an hour. That interest has widened over the years, as can be seen elsewhere in this book, but the following anecdote describes my start and explains why my first writing on this topic concerned John Stuart Mill's collaboration with Harriet Taylor. It has become common to begin feminist analyses with autobiographical anecdotes that reveal the political and personal intertwined, but things held in common—our commonplaces—are part of what this study is intended to emphasize, especially the commonalities we construct out of desire.

Mill caught my attention in the fall of 1982, my first year of teaching, when I was putting together the syllabus for a graduate seminar on Victorian literature. I had already decided to include Mill's *Autobiography* on the syllabus when the English department at the large university where I taught met to discuss the prospect of bringing a major theorist into its fold. Feminist theorists were not considered serious theorists by most of the faculty, and feminist criticism met with disdain, so feminist theorists were not considered in this discussion. Following the official meeting, several junior members of the department called for a grassroots meeting (as we called it in what was doubtless a political fantasy of our own) to discuss hiring a feminist scholar. Two senior faculty members with administrative positions attended. The discussion that followed had no immediate impact on hiring, but it had an impact on me. One of us proposed Sandra Gilbert and Susan Gubar as good prospects, but the objection was raised that, because Gilbert and Gubar had coauthored *The Madwoman in the Attic,* we could not determine the value or originality of either scholar's work. The tenured faculty wanted only the best in its ranks, and to write collaboratively evidently canceled one's individual claim to great or original scholarship.

This was my first personal contact with this particular take on scholarly originality. So when I reencountered it the same week in the critical reception of Mill's *Autobiography,* I jumped at the chance to discuss the problem with students. Dismissing Gilbert and Gubar's work in this way seemed especially ironic because *The Madwoman in the Attic* had put the question of originality at the center of its argument when it reworked Harold Bloom's revisionary theory of "intra-poetic relationships" and "anxiety of influence."[1] Although much has been written about anxiety, influence, and feminist revisions of these concepts since Bloom and Gilbert and Gubar's inaugural texts appeared, the relationship between Bloom's arguments and those of his early feminist revisers exemplifies, even now, the way issues of originality and collaboration have been polarized in twentieth-century scholarship, yet ultimately fail to exclude each other.

The "anxiety of influence" Bloom identifies in an almost entirely male canon and the "anxiety of authorship" Gilbert and Gubar locate in a female "tradition" offer a study in contrasts, but the contrast between them is not one of simple opposition.[2] Of course, Bloom argues that there is no such thing as originality in a poetic landscape dominated by powerful fathers, that the best an anxious poet-son can do is to pit himself against the father; he exhibits "strength" rather than "originality." Sons have no choice but to cooperate (a term Bloom studiously avoids) with their elders. Bloom's own argument exhibits some of the features of this theory, suppressing footnotes where scholars commonly acknowledge each other's work while attempting major revisions of, or "swerves" away from, the theories of previous critics.[3] But Bloom thus transvalues the fantasy, even while denying the reality, of originality and, above all, privileges the virile individualist. In contrast, Bloom's feminist revisers overtly defer to Bloom's theory and offer their arguments as collaborative complements to his. Gilbert and Gubar might describe their revisionary swerve away from Bloom in far more violent, Bloomian language than they do because they see women authors as facing a more fundamental challenge than that met by Bloom's strong men. Women writers confronted erasure and silence, the virtual non-existence of female authorship. To claim authorship was for the woman writer not only to produce history, but to stake out an origin. But Gilbert and Gubar describe this originality of women writers in opposite terms. They focus on an imagery of weakness—on "dis-ease"—rather than on Bloomian strength, and they see women as repeating their own self-effacement and imitating precursor male authors, expressing rebellious desires only in indirect or unconscious ways while seeking support from, collaborating with, the few other women writers discoverable (51). Gilbert and Gubar thus suppress the fantasy of originality even while acting out a Bloomian swerve under the guise of a counter-discourse of imitation and collaboration.

But while Gilbert and Gubar emphasize an imagery of weakness in their study of women writers, they also claim a kind of ecstasy for them that more than matches Bloom's portrait of male writers' passionate struggle. Gilbert and Gubar's language of cooperative writers first appears in their prefatory words about each other, in which women writers and critics are "exhilarated," made hilariously happy, enlivened by "working together":

> The process of writing this book has been as transformative for us as the process of "attempting the pen" was for so many of the women we discuss. And much of the exhilaration of writing has come from working together. Like most collaborators, we have divided our responsibilities. . . . We have continually exchanged and discussed our drafts, however, so that we feel our book represents not just a dialogue but a consensus. Redefining what has so far been male-defined literary history in the same way that women writers have revised "patriarchal poetics," we have found that the process of collaboration has given us the essential support we needed to complete such an ambitious project. (xiii)

This exhilaration emerges through release from bonds with men as well as through the formation of new bonds with women, but the emphasis of the passage falls on the delight of new collaboration. To restate this in erotic terms comparable to those Wayne Koestenbaum offers in his study of male collaborators, one might say that where Koestenbaum's male author "penetrates" the mind of his collaborator, Gilbert and Gubar's collaboration offers the satisfaction of what Jane Gallop (punning as always) calls "contiguity."[4] Rather than "submit to another's fertilizing will," as Koestenbaum puts it, these women collaborators are "exhilarated" by immediate contact and "consensus" with each other. At the same time, Gilbert and Gubar's preface reflects some of the ambiguity of "collaboration." "To collaborate" remains close to its original Latin roots—to work with someone else—but it also obviously means to work in solidarity against others (although the *Oxford English Dictionary* doesn't mention this, other dictionaries do). Not divided, but together, Gilbert and Gubar stand against the patriarchy surrounding them.

This spectacle of united womanhood was subsequently criticized by other feminists. The ideas of communities of women, common purposes, and supportive networks have been decried as the privilege of a monopolistic group of white, middle-class, educated women. Feminist critics have thus turned away from the communal "we" to a language of multiple, frictional differences. This counterevocation of difference does not return us to Bloom's model, which entails, if only in fantasy, eradication of the social landscape surrounding strong individuals. The notion of "differences" takes for granted a situation in which we rub against preexisting bodies, preexisting structures. I have returned here, nonetheless, to the textual relationships between Gilbert and Gubar and Bloom to show how contradictory styles of literary scholarship—that of revisionary intervention versus mutual collaboration—are compelled to cross each other. The rebel ephebe is undergirded not only by his family romance, but by professional communities he may be slow to acknowledge; collaborators, no matter how "connubial," are buoyed up by the extremity of their differences from others.

Mill's connubial *Autobiography* has emerged as a site of explicit contention in debates about originality and collaboration. Nearly all critics have found it necessary to account for Mill's tributes to Harriet Taylor Mill (whom I will simply call Taylor). Mill collaborated with Taylor (with whom he consorted for twenty years before the death of Taylor's husband allowed them to marry) in developing many of his works, including the *Autobiography* itself. Although the *Autobiography* has traditionally been approached as the authentic life story of a great, original thinker who preached an ethic of individual liberty and whose tributes to Taylor were exaggerated, several critics have taken an interest in the *Autobiography* as the documentary record of a collaborative team, a man and a woman, who preached an ethic of gender equity.[5] A few critics see it as neither of these things and describe the text as filled with gaps where it subverts itself or represses major influences other than that of Taylor. Although these general approaches are superficially incompatible with each other, there are good reasons why the *Autobiography* has spawned such different responses. I first discuss the still-unfolding debate on joint authorship between "originalists" and "collaborativists," showing the debate as rooted in the *Autobiography* itself and in the gaps the text leaves open. I then present a rereading of the *Autobiography* as a collaborative narrative—a narrative produced by and through the conflicts and excitements of collaborations with others.

The *Autobiography* offers support for both sides of the arguments about Mill's originality: It is torn between its protagonist's desire to narrate his life as the growth of an original thinker who achieved great things and his inclination to humble himself in the face of other people's achievements and influences. These contradictions have been noted by critics, but usually they are seen as a potentially resolvable problem of influence rather than as a necessary product of the tensions of collaboration, and as a problem in the representational design of the *Autobiography* rather than as an intrinsic feature of Mill's logic. I would argue that the *Autobiography* claims our interest—and has provoked numerous rereadings— in large part because it allows contradictions to tell against each other, however. One of Mill's primary purposes in writing the *Autobiography*, as he explained in its opening paragraph, was to acknowledge his debts to others, above all to Taylor, and the *Autobiography* persistently situates Mill's agency in and through clashes between contradictory influences: between father and wife, Benthamism and Romanticism, abstract theory and concrete practice, mind and emotion. In repeatedly positioning himself between rival oppositional terms, Mill becomes defined by and as the intersection of contradictory positions, not least those between the common and the uncommon, the collaborative and the uncollaborative. This contrariety in positioning is intimately linked to Mill's habits of collaboration.

There have been numerous rereadings of Mill's *Autobiography* in the last twenty years; I want to look closely at three of these in particular, focusing on the dispute about coauthorship. Jonathan Loesberg appears alone among critics in arguing that the *Autobiography* is enmeshed in a central paradox: the philosophic paradox of "free association," or "a place for free will within associationism."[6] Like his father, Mill believed that selves develop in response to external causes, but he found a place within that development for self-consciousness and hence for self-determination. These latter capacities arose in part through the availability of alternative influences among which he might choose—above all, for Mill, the influence of Taylor as an alternative to his upbringing. Loesberg argues further, however, that even biographical events recounted in the *Autobiography*—especially the story of Taylor's influence on Mill—are examples, not causes, of Mill's theory. Loesberg's conclusions about Taylor are predicated on arguments for Mill's originality. In Mill's relationship with Taylor, Loesberg argues, Mill paradoxically "freely chooses not to be free" and "makes his maker," thus turning Taylor into a figure for Mill's own creativity (47, 83). Loesberg casually dismisses "the whole overworked problem of joint authorship,"[7] reframing Taylor's help as "inspiration" (48–49). As female muse, Taylor not only ceases in this argument to possess a separate intelligence or creativity, but ceases to have been real.

In the twentieth century critics have increasingly insisted on reading the *Autobiography* as a fictionalized design and have recurrently accounted for Taylor as a "trope" produced by Mill; Loesberg simply accentuates this approach. It is all the more striking, then, to see him give so much attention to explaining the issue of Mill's "excessive" tribute to Taylor, an issue rooted in extratextual, sociocultural questions. Although I do not disagree entirely with accounts that begin by seeing the figure of Taylor in the *Autobiography* as an excessive one, I will later offer a reading that reevaluates the sources and effects of this excess. Critics have been so distracted by their concern with Mill and Taylor's comparative intellectual gifts, so anxious to rule on the exact nature of Taylor's influence on Mill, that—contrary to Loesberg's view of the problem of "joint authorship" as "overworked"—critics have failed almost completely to attend to the knotty processes and effects of authorial collaboration.

One of the few critics who has looked closely at Mill and Taylor's coauthorship—Jack Stillinger—interestingly illustrates both sides of the debate about Mill's originality, but without reconciling them. In 1961 Stillinger edited the early draft of the *Autobiography* and then in 1969 a Riverside paperback; these two editions deny Taylor a substantial role. But in 1991 he reversed his position on this matter in his book on multiple authorship. Stillinger's earlier views have shaped much subsequent criticism, so it is useful to consider them in detail.[8]

In the 1960s Stillinger made no secret of his distaste for Mill's tribute to Taylor in the *Autobiography*. The tribute undercut the factuality and stylistic integrity of the text as an autobiography; it tarnished claims for Mill's originality and honesty as a thinker. In his 1969 introduction to the Riverside edition, Stillinger writes that the tribute to Taylor is "a blemish on the work—not because we squirm at the notion that Mill owed so much to another, but simply because the claims do not carry conviction."[9] Stillinger apparently did squirm,[10] for one reason or another, at Mill's textual tribute: If only Mill had "simply thank[ed] his wife for encouragement, perhaps also for transcribing a manuscript or making an index, and let it go at that. But he was remarkably clear-sighted in most other things" (Introduction xix). Other passages in this introduction and in the introduction to the 1961 *Early Draft* of the *Autobiography* suggest that Stillinger was as concerned with Mill's intellectual dependency as with the truth claims of the *Autobiography*, however: If it turned out that Mill owed a lot to Taylor, his originality would be diminished.[11] So unhappy is Stillinger with Mill's tribute to his wife that, despite every effort to preserve Mill's stature, he comes close to devaluing Mill's intellectual acumen in this matter; he not only emphasizes Mill's professed helplessness in "practical affairs" but presents the tribute as support for Mill's claim, "Having grown up under a strong will, . . . he lacked initiative and responsibility" (Introduction xviii).

Nonetheless, the autobiography itself derives its claims to our interest, so Stillinger assumes, from Mill's reputation as an original thinker. For an editor, this raises the further problem of attribution: Whose authorship and whose intentions should one aim to preserve? Preserving the authority of his author, Stillinger assures us that "Harriet was no originator of ideas, however much she may have aided Mill by ordinary wifely discussion and debate" (Introduction xvii). Not leaving his critique of the tribute at the biographical and bibliographical, Stillinger raises also the issues of generic and narrative texture: "We should object to such extravagances in fiction, and similarly must object to them in autobiography" (Introduction xvii). Such "extravagances" produce a blot not only on Mill's reputation, but on the generic claims of autobiography as objective self-representation.

Stillinger does find one positive explanation for the "blemish" Taylor represents. "What must be grasped," he argues, "is the symbolic role she plays" as father-substitute; if James Mill is a "priest-figure" before Mill's conversion, Taylor replaces him as "a saint to be worshipped," "an imagined embodiment of the union of poetry and logic" (Introduction xvii–xviii). The reason thus offered for Mill's figuration of Taylor is psycholiterary. As a mere trope—both surrogate father and union of opposites—she need not cloud our appreciation for Mill's originality as a thinker, autonomy as an individual, credibility as an author, or consistency as a narrator. Conceding this, Stillinger easily dismisses Taylor's influence and so perceives Mill's tributes to her as minor aberrations in a great man's thinking. Stillinger writes in the 1960s with evident confidence in the agreement of both Mill's peers and his own, citing George Grote, a friend and collaborator of Mill: "Only John Mill's reputation could have survived such an exhibition" (Introduction xvii).

Stillinger eventually grew troubled by this evaluation of Mill's "extravagance." He now argues quite the opposite, that the *Autobiography* was produced through genuine collaboration, and he uses Mill's life story in his 1991 book, *Multiple Authorship and the Myth of Solitary Genius,* as a central example of multiple authorship. Stillinger first published his revised theory of the *Autobiography* in a 1983 article, where he argued that the *Autobiography* must be seen as having two authors and as part of a larger phenomenon "that literary scholars have just recently begun to be aware of—the joint or multiple authorship of works presented (and generally thought of) as having been written by a single author. . . . [This includes those of] Emily Dickinson, Ralph W. Emerson, Mark Twain, Thomas Hardy, Thomas Wolfe, Nathaniel Hawthorne."[12] "Mill and his wife revised jointly," says Stillinger, "interactively and interdependently—and, while we can say in general terms that Mill's contribution to the final text was considerably greater than his wife's, still the two are inseparably involved in the development of that text" ("Who Wrote" 10). This conclusion—with the *Autobiography* the product of direct collaboration, yet with Mill the "considerably greater" contributor to the text (following, one might note, Koestenbaum's "male" model of dominant-submissive collaboration rather than Gilbert and Gubar's "female" model of coequal partnership)—apparently resolves Stillinger's previous concerns about originality, authenticity, and narrative integrity along with those about the authorship of the *Autobiography.* The other issues simply evaporate, and Stillinger's affirmative treatment of multiple authorship is less value-laden than his attempt to purge it away.

Stronger defenses than this have been made for Mill's intellectual collaboration with his wife by Gertrude Himmelfarb, Michael St. John Packe, Alice Rossi, and Jo Ellen Jacobs. But I cite Stillinger's argument here not only because it focuses specifically on the problem of joint authorship in the *Autobiography* rather than on a more general survey of their relationship, but also because its limitations are illuminating. Despite his insistence on multiple authorship of this work, Stillinger's analysis of Taylor's contributions portrays her as an editor rather than author. This is not altogether surprising, given that he means to blur the distinction between editor and author in the single notion of multiple authorship. Although he blurs this distinction effectively in his general theory about textual editing, he reconstitutes the difference in his analysis of Taylor's actual contributions to the *Autobiography.* After a seemingly exhaustive description of the kinds of emendations she made, he concludes, "The question remains whether she did in fact contribute to, or alter, Mill's *ideas.* The short answer is: not much" ("Who Wrote" 19; *Multiple Authorship* 61). Mill provides great ideas; Taylor provides editorial emendation.

Moreover, Stillinger envisages her participation as a set of stereotypical female roles, sorting out her editorial work into four neat categories of "Copyeditor," "Mother-Protector," "Victorian Prude," and "Wicked Sister- and Daughter-in-Law" ("Who Wrote" 12, 14, 16, 18). In Stillinger's account, Taylor and Mill together do not make a convincing example of collaborative multiple authorship. Instead, Taylor becomes a straw woman with several aspects—a figure of the irritating, interfering female. This derogatory picture echoes a long history of gender-marked dismissals of Taylor as domineering spouse.[13] Unfortunately, the *Autobiography* is Stillinger's only example of literary collaboration between a man and a woman (and he discusses no work authored by women in collaboration with each other or with male editors).

The *Autobiography* itself is divided on the question of how we should regard its author. It moves from Bloom's model of authorship toward Gilbert and Gubar's and is true to neither. It begins by presenting John Stuart Mill as the dominated son who must swerve, against great odds, from his parent and finally does so with aid from that most Bloomian of father-substitutes, William Wordsworth. It then turns from this model to present us with John Stuart Taylor-Mill, joined in exhilarated collaboration with Taylor, who, as a woman, had been as subjugated as he. Yet, as Stillinger points out, Mill does not turn as far from the image of his father as he might have because he presents Taylor also as a father-substitute, directly superseding his father's influence in his life. Mill paints a portrait of Taylor that makes her "considerably greater" than himself (it is this estimate that most critics, including Stillinger in his revised 1983 account, have sought to reverse). Taylor thus emerges in the *Autobiography* paradoxically as both teamworker and awesome influence, both support and source for Mill's work.

In her 1991 book on Mill's *Autobiography*, Janice Carlisle impressively further complicates Mill's influences by exploring Mill's ambivalent relationship to a professional vocation. Carlisle shows us that although Mill focused on the drama of father and son in the *Autobiography*, his career was shaped by other major influences, especially his role in the East India Company and his compelling desire for a public vocation. In Bloomian fashion, Mill continually represses this unfulfilled desire for a vocation and swerves violently from it to focus on his career as thinker and writer, son and husband. For Carlisle, Mill's story ends ironically, not with a breakthrough in thought or lifestyle (or new mode of authorship) and not with a belief in himself as a great public figure, but with a vision of himself as a cog in a wheel, holding down a regular job where he joined with co-workers in a professional company.

While unearthing the traumatic episodes in Mill's struggle to make a career for himself, Carlisle condemns Taylor's role in Mill's career. Taylor remains a critical figure but not much support in Mill's development of a vocation because she cut Mill off from polite society and from other avenues of public involvement while depending on him to support her through a paid job. Gone in Carlisle's study is the exhilaration they claimed to feel in each other's company. Instead, Taylor looms threateningly over Mill's shoulder, "her pencil ready to scratch out whatever she, for one reason or another, might dislike" (95). Although he called her his "'precious guide philosopher & friend,'" she acted as his "censor," habitually treating him to "tongue-lashing" and "tirade[s] of criticism," a thoroughly "unpleasant wife" who left Mill "crippled by [her] influence" (95, 99, 97). Taylor may indeed have possessed a sharper tongue than Mill, whereas Mill retained control of a sharper pen, thus producing a parodically Ruskinian balance of powers rather than a meeting of matched minds such as Mill and Taylor had envisioned. But curt dismissals of what they said about their relationship and persistent attempts to bump Taylor from the pedestal into the bearpit do not produce credibly balanced analyses of this collaboration.

Stillinger and others show that what Taylor consistently disliked in the *Autobiography* were disparaging references to others or to Mill himself. And what the married Mills' letters to each other demonstrate is a mutual desire to justify their relationship to a critical world; their collaboration in the *Autobiography* was governed, above all, by their collaboration against others. To produce an attractive portrait of their relationship, they moderated distracting and offensive negative comments about others and presented their collaboration in unequivocally positive terms. In the *Autobiography* one sees the entire dynamic between Bloom and Gilbert and Gubar enacted: one writer barely escaping domination by another, two writers finding mutual support in one another, one writer failing to acknowledge indebtedness to fellow writers (and workers), and two writers joined in struggle against others.

At the same time, Taylor obviously was not a full collaborator in the text of the *Autobiography* in the sense that Gilbert and Gubar are, with both authors planning, composing, revising, and editing their work. Mill wrote most of the *Autobiography* when Taylor was not around. He invited her to help him compose the parts about their relationship, but she avoided doing that (not a surprising request for her to evade), responding by reiterating her general concern about preserving their reputations. I deliberately refer to this text as Mill's *Autobiography* not merely to follow scholarly convention or because it is written under his signature and as his voice, but because Mill and Taylor both saw Taylor as contributing to an *Autobiography* not her own; in a sense, Taylor thereby became coauthor of herself as a nonauthor. More importantly, if we misattribute coauthorship to Taylor, we obscure the ways in which she could not appropriately take part more actively than she did in writing this work. Unless the subject of the *Autobiography* had been stretched to include Taylor's life, it would have been odd for her to be a full participant in its composition. To reframe the narrative in that way would have been nearly inconceivable; precisely because of the prevailing doctrines about great and original male authorship, Mill thought of his *Autobiography*—as did Taylor—as documenting *his* life.

Taylor did become an important collaborator, however, and participated fully in the editorial stage in suggesting deletions and shifting emphases in Mill's self-portrait to protect them both. Thus far I have quoted criticism directed primarily at Taylor because although there have been occasional efforts to find redeeming evidence of Taylor's wit and affection or to condemn in Mill a masochistic collusion with his own domination, commentators on their relationship have occupied themselves primarily with "correcting" Mill in his perception of his wife. But critics from Mill's day to our own have also found this last fact—Taylor and Mill's collaboration against others—difficult to stomach, and this has affected evaluations of their work together. Taylor and Mill saw the *Autobiography* as their ultimate opportunity to make a collaborative statement against invidious critics: Mill wrote, "We have to consider, which we can only do together, how much of our story it is advisable to tell, in order to make head against the representations of enemies when we shall not be alive to add anything to it."[14]

Mill and Taylor's quasiadulterous relationship could never have been fully sanctioned by their peers; nonetheless, Mill's peers and later critics are unhappy with the exclusivity with which Mill and Taylor clung to each for support and cut themselves off from others. Mill and Taylor did not merely turn to each other for private support, but presented a common front against the world, including their friends and family. Critics point often to letters that show the Mills' sensitivity to slights from former friends and from Mill's family; they chafed against all signs of disapproval (signs produced mostly through a careful silence about their relationship) and rejected any half-gestures of reconciliation (like that of Mill's brother, who expressed his surprise at learning of their marriage). They thus divorced themselves from the good will of almost everyone in their society. Timid as they may seem to us and to their most progressive peers in their decision not to elope or, after the death of Taylor's

husband, not to cohabitate outside of marriage, they aggressively repudiated polite forms of disapproval, insisting on full, heartfelt acceptance
of their relationship as it was. Most critics chalk this stance up to over-
sensitivity to the opinions of others; critics miss any elements of thoughtful doctrine, and they attribute the bad blood to a mean-spirited Taylor.[15]
Yet it is hard to imagine an unconventional collaboration that would not
be accompanied by fierce passions and excessive expectations, particularly on the part of an ambitious wife. Odder than the Mills' sensitivity
is the fact that Mill and Taylor should still draw barbs for the way they
handled their social relations. That they do so is less the result of any
extraordinary character flaws or peculiarities in Taylor or Mill than of two
factors in contemporary scholarship: the intense vicarious interest in
psychobiographical portraits of the "eccentric" Victorians and the widespread lack of awareness (let alone analysis) not only of this particular
collaborative relationship, but of such relationships in general.

Far from being a blemish on this text, Taylor played a crucial role in
and behind the *Autobiography*; she resists dismissal by readers for whatever reason. My concern up to this point has been with the relation of
readers' assumptions about authorship to evaluations of Mill's collaboration with Taylor; I turn now to the figuration of Taylor within this text
and its complex function in the production of Mill's reputation. Stillinger's perhaps repented desire to suppress Mill's evocation of Taylor's
mind under the mark of an unsightly physical flaw is a familiar one and
easily exposed, thanks to the last three decades of feminist critique. It is
no accident that the feminist Alice Rossi was the first contemporary
scholar to put up an argument for Taylor as a thinker in her own right.
(As Rossi and Jacobs also point out, Taylor's own ideas and writing deserve closer scrutiny than they have received.[16] My focus is on the reconstruction of Mill and Taylor's collaboration in and by the *Autobiography*,
however, not the "true story" behind it, the facts of which previous scholars have sorted through many times.) Stillinger's suppression of Taylor
should have special resonance for us because it entails erasure of Taylor
in Mill's new Body Politic.

The ideal marriage is figured in *The Subjection of Women* as the
organic working-out of a relationship in which each partner would contribute equally to their joint intellectual and emotional life;[17] Mill's tributes to Taylor in the *Autobiography* establish her as the ideal partner for
him. What makes Mill's tributes in the *Autobiography* seem outlandish

is the fact that Mill went beyond figuration of their marriage as a full collaboration to an intensely adulatory portrait of Taylor. Although others have not put it this way, he embodied in the *single* figure of Taylor the doctrine of equality between the sexes.

Like Virginia Woolf's androgynous poet, Mill's Taylor has all the qualities traditionally attributed to both male and female and thus possesses in herself a fully collaborative mentality. In the terms advanced by the *Autobiography*, Taylor embodies right relations between logic and poetry, the abstract and the practical, thought and feeling.[18] And to combine gifts of feeling with powers of intellect was to reach beyond what either faculty could achieve by itself. In short, Taylor was what Mill yearned to be. No one, certainly not Mill, could compete with such perfection. As other critics point out, Taylor's portrait was inspired by romanticism,[19] a vision of the two warring poles of the mind finally made whole.

But Mill made of Taylor this consummate figure in order, paradoxically, to fulfill their doctrine of equality: She must be not merely Mill's complement (according to the standard view of woman held by Mill's contemporaries) but his equal,[20] as capable of intellect as of emotion.

> In general spiritual characteristics, as well as in temperament and organisation, I have often compared her, as she was at this time, to Shelley: but in thought and intellect, Shelley, so far as his powers were developed in his short life, was but a child compared with what she ultimately became. Alike in the highest regions of speculation and in the smallest practical concerns of daily life, her mind was the same perfect instrument, piercing to the very heart and marrow of the matter; always seizing the essential idea or principle. (195)

Deservedly controversial as this passage is, it is useful to remember that Mill associated Shelley (one of her favorite poets) strongly with Taylor and that Shelley did not then have the full weight of canonicity to render the comparison incongruous. As Jerome Buckley says, this encomium, "though to Harriet's advantage, must be taken as a high tribute to both."[21]

An important purpose of Mill's tributes, then, was to depict Taylor as the embodiment of a coequal intellect. Still, Mill was probably also compelled by less altruistic desires in writing passages like this. He needed to show that despite his dedication as a youth by his father to a life entirely of the mind, he had finally acquired powers of poetic feeling, which Taylor obviously already possessed. Mill effectively demonstrates his powers of feeling and imagination by envisaging his ambitions for himself, seeing his desires for himself, in the image of another, and by doing so in the most impassioned style he could muster. When Mill produces the vision of Taylor in this passage as the proper literary and historical climax to the *Autobiography*, he is himself writing a poem. He did this not to "make his maker," but to make himself.[22] Taylor comes to compensate for, to stand for, and to produce Mill's previously missing body of feeling. She is his poetic complement, the poetic figure of mediated opposites to which he aspires, and the poem with which he expresses his newly acquired imaginative powers, balancing his intellectual gifts. The extravagances of this text are by no means only those of a uxorious husband, but also those of a partisan (a political enthusiast) for another (a comrade) and those of a sonneteer for the beloved.

One suspects that, beyond the critics' strictly observed admiration for Mill's intellect and their careful separation of his intellect from his practical know-how, what worried them was the spectacle of Mill's feminization. In his uxorious devotion to his wife, in his dependent relationship to his father (a relationship in which he acted as his father's blank page), in his urgent desire to acknowledge the feelings that his father suppressed, Mill himself suffered the subjection of women and became a victim to retrospective stigmatization for it.[23]

At the same time, we should not necessarily expect such reactions from readers to evaporate through simple exposure of their antifeminism (in a kind of therapeutic cure). In fact, there are so many reasons for Taylor's place in the *Autobiography* that her purpose is overdetermined, and this ensures the effect of excess.[24] I argue that even in its repellent effects the *Autobiography* may be said to achieve one of its possible aims, however. In transgressing the rules of propriety, in opening itself up to scandal, the *Autobiography* insists not merely on the greater propriety of excellence in women, but on the unconventionality of the Mills' relationship. Moreover, the book promotes this scandal on its own terms, diverting attention from the moral controversy over their twenty-year extramarital relationship to Mill's impassioned description of their *intellectual* cohabitation.

—————

The passage of tribute to Taylor marks a culminating moment in the *Autobiography*, but it is not the only climactic moment or the only moment of excess. And although her textual intrusion should be taken more seriously than it has been, I also consider the references to Taylor a small part—small in extent—of an unsystematic series of intensified moments. Many critics point out that Mill's most intense relationship in the *Auto-*

biography is with his father, and the amazing education Mill describes is an extensive eulogy to that overwhelming influence. But there are numerous centers of excitement in the *Autobiography*. In addition to James Mill, Bentham, Marmontel, Wordsworth, and Taylor (all of whom critics often discuss), Mill's early reading of heroic histories, his own first efforts at writing and then again at speaking publicly, his burgeoning leadership among his contemporaries, his acquaintance with Thomas Carlyle, his relationship to Taylor's daughter Helen, and, as Carlisle argues, his elusive, always-beckoning vocation all serve as abrupt moments of intensification in feeling and as spurs, or incitements, to further mental activity. The tribute to Taylor appears excessive, yet again, because Mill brings his earlier excitements together in her person; she bears the burden of embodying his joy in writing, speaking, leading, socializing, developing his philosophy, and reforming the world. That she fails to act coherently as the vessel for all this should come as no surprise.

From the extratextual issues of authorship and collaboration and the textual issues of Taylor's excessive figuration as coequal partner, I wish to turn finally to the collaborative texture of the *Autobiography* as a narrative. The criticism is divided on the issue of narrative integrity as on everything else: between seeing the *Autobiography*, as Stillinger has done, as an integrated statement of Mill's life and seeing it, as Carlisle does, as a disintegrated statement that works harder to suppress than it does to express major events and figures in his life. A description I prefer is that of the body of this text as split—and squeezed—by pressures from without and pressures from within, by pressures to yield to others and urges to move them. Moreover, it is characterized as much by the contiguities of diverse purposes as by the alternate suppressions and penetrations of strong influences. The composition of this text was the product of divided minds, standing together for the time being; it was the product of different periods of composition, standing together in the written text.[25] Likewise, the narrative of the *Autobiography*, the body of this work is (to invoke another feminist commonplace, though in a somewhat less celebratory mood) an Irigarayan body; it is "not one."[26]

Many instigations to excessive energy or emotion were indeed suppressed, sometimes deliberately by the Mills. As is well known, what Taylor and Mill both considered excessive writing—as evidenced by their editorial decisions in the *Early Draft*—often marks spots where emotional spectacles other than Taylor intrude, especially those of his mother, his father, and Mill himself. Taylor and Mill colluded in obscuring and canceling all references to his mother, personal expressions of anguish at his father, expressions of self-adulation by Mill, and so forth. Possibly the most notorious of these suppressions was that of Mill's mother, Harriet Mill. Christine Di Stefano and (overtly following Di Stefano) Linda M.-G. Zerilli acutely argue that deleted references to Mill's mother mark sites where Mill's "feminism collapses on the terrain of *difference*" (Di Stefano, 167), and Di Stefano shows in other works by Mill a continual repulsion at pregnant women and mothers (203).[27] The *Autobiography* enthusiastically admits one set of important differences, the gender difference, even as it resists the pressure of others. Taylor also cut (with Mill's acquiescence) self-derogatory comments by Mill, attempting to prune Mill's excessive self-suppression—to little avail, of course. The signs of Mill's physical "inaptness" (as Mill put it), Mill's humiliation, are all too palpable from the start. Mill portrays himself as shaped by his father to have no physical needs, shaped to possess only intellectual needs, which were met by debate and study at his father's table.

But the classic, dialectical relationship between a suppression of physical demands and their return at the site of their suppression is thematized by Mill as the relationship between his father's oppression and the son's uncanny reemergence. One sees this even in the early pages of the *Autobiography*, when Mill is most thoroughly entombed in and by his father's educational plan. Four pages into the text, Mill writes of an "excite[ment]" at histories that goes beyond their educational purpose: "Robertson's histories, Hume, Gibbon . . . the heroic defence of the Knights of Malta against the Turks, and of the revolted provinces of the Netherlands against Spain." He "never wearied" of "Anson's *Voyage*, so delightful to most young persons, and a Collection . . . of Voyages round the World" (11); and *Robinson Crusoe* "continued to delight me through all my boyhood" (13). In these histories, Mill found the vicarious pleasures of physical heroism. The *Autobiography* may be read, similarly, as a history of heroic suffering in which Mill breaks sporadically from the father's dominion through collaboration with one alternative influence after another. These in turn contradict each other as Mill seeks to negotiate between, for example, Bentham and Wordsworth, Carlyle and Taylor, Taylor and a career of public action.

Thus, rather than standing apart, Taylor is inevitably caught up in Mill's cycles of self-reprisal. And the energy that is momentarily invested or overinvested in explicit tribute to her quickly dissipates (as excesses do) when the story presses on to other contrasting centers of excitement. Mill treats the ending of his text as if it were one more uncertain moment, poised between repudiation of the recent past and an urge to get on, an urge that is itself divided between possible action and possible defeat. "Since that time" (that is, the time of his activities in Parliament), little has occurred which there is need to commemorate in this place. . . . I have written various articles in periodicals . . . , have made a small number of speeches on public occasions, especially at the meetings of the Women's Suffrage Society, have published *The Subjection of Women*, written some years before, with some additions by my daughter and myself, and have commenced the preparation of matter for future books, of which it will be time to speak more particularly if I live to finish them. Here, therefore, for the present, this Memoir may close. (290)

Earlier in the *Autobiography*, Mill speaks of collaboration with Helen Taylor ("my daughter")[28] on important works originally conceived with his wife as in itself an exhilarating experience—a meet successor to his previous relationship with Harriet Taylor—but both collaborations are mere ripples in the wake of Mill's final gesture in this passage. This diminishment of Taylor and her memory occurs not only because Mill's attention has been diverted to the exciting question of his vocation and his time in Parliament (since which time "little has occurred"), but also because, as opposed to any self-contained closure or "proper" consummation for the *Autobiography* that an autobiographer might offer, Mill looks forward to a further excitement, that of living to finish future books, and to a more severe limit, that of his death.

Unlike his imaginative figuring of Taylor in this text, then, Mill does not produce a romantic vision of himself as a harmonious synthesis of diverse purposes. Equivocal to the end, squeezed by contradictory pressures, he rigidly contains his incitement toward future books by a further negation, marking this with a highly doubtful "if I live to finish them." Death may have seemed too excessive, possibly too physical, too finished, or too imposing a figure for him to call by its own name. Nonetheless, he manages to allude both to a future death and a future life in the same breath, and in the last sentence locates himself, as if parenthetically, between these possibilities: "Here, therefore, for the present, this Memoir may close." If this is a position Mill holds in common with many other autobiographers, we should not overlook its special resonance in this instance. The *Autobiography* of Mill offers a charged example of the ways in which a concatenation of divergent purposes and people produce the contradictory, coauthored text of a life.

2 Black/White, Author/Editor Friction: Incidents in the Life of a Slave Girl, Written by Herself

THERE COULD BE NO SUCH THING as solitary authorship for the southern slave; the slave's body, self, sexuality, and writing all were the property of whites. Thus Harriet Brent Jacobs's autobiography, *Incidents in the Life of a Slave Girl, Written by Herself,* is a particularly powerful story of the Millian triumph of reason and self against the "patriarchal institution" (a phrase she herself uses)[1] and oppressive power of slavery. Against enormous odds—including seven years in which Jacobs's autobiography claims she "escaped" slavery by voluntarily imprisoning herself in the leaky attic of an outhouse in her grandmother's yard—Jacobs gradually acquires knowledge, experience, and literacy sufficient to outwit her subjugators, ultimately publishing a work that goes beyond representing her own life to representing that of her people's quest for equality and freedom. Moreover, none of the features that have vexed readers of Mill's autobiography—especially the denigration of his own originality and his acknowledgment of dependency on relatives—appear improper when they show up in Jacobs's text. On the contrary, a former slave was expected to be modest about her intellectual powers and to express dependence on her friends and family. On the face of it, Jacobs's text exemplifies and legitimates, as Mill's never could, both the enlightenment and liberation narratives with which Mill has been so closely associated. But although Jacobs's text partakes of the power of these master narratives, it is not without contradiction. The contradictions that emerge around the sexual scandal of the Mills—covered over, renegotiated, and reperformed in the excesses of his text—are more than matched by the mixed messages surrounding the revelation of Jacobs's sexuality. Indeed, Jacobs's version demonstrates the importance of thinking of the subject not only as inscribed in preexistent social structures but as less determinately intersubjective, of sexuality not only as a product of discourse but as transformatively elusive, and of writing not only as laboring under influence but as collaborative.

As Jacobs's persona, Linda Brent, repeatedly asserts, she had not gained freedom from the oppressive legal and economic systems that included slavery, nor had her people, by the end of her narrative. Neither had Jacobs gained exclusive authorship of her text. Despite the bold assertion of her autobiography's subtitle, "Written by Herself," Jacobs reminds us—where Mill makes us forget—of the close relation of published writing with property ownership and of both these things with the public self. When freed, a former slave was still compelled to collaborate with editors and publishers, to permit his or her narrative to be molded to a standard formula. Although the literate Jacobs had more control than many over her text, her autobiography appeared, as it had to appear, as a joint production with white agents—in particular with Lydia Maria Child, a well-known abolitionist—and the copyright was taken out under Child's name. (Jacobs's name did not even appear on the title page; in the preface, as in the narrative, she adopted for her signature the pseudonym Linda Brent.)

But Child further arranged for Jacobs to sign an agreement guaranteeing proof that "in case of my death . . . the book is [Jacobs's] property."[2] One could thus argue that, much as Mill's collaborations enabled him to move forward, to pit one difficult influence against another, and to practice as well as preach an ethic of cooperation, collaboration enabled African-American writers to achieve solidarity with abolitionist whites in the larger antislavery movement in the United States. Many black Americans signed their works along with their editors and could thereby make a partial claim to the dream of authorship as well as of free selfhood. In contrast to the occasionally approving attention that has been given to Mill and Taylor as collaborators, however, no prior account has offered a detailed analysis of this text that is contextualized in an argument valuing Jacobs's and Child's literary relationship as a collaboration. Yet the partial benefits of these antislavery "approximate" collaborations are nowhere better demonstrated than in the case of Jacobs's text.

The politics of solidarity were themselves structured by racist, classist, and sexist hierarchies. Extolling the achievement of this particular collaboration risks displacing and reinscribing Jacobs's text in (given my own cultural context) a white middle-class academic woman's fantasy of harmonious sisterhood; Jacobs's narrative sharply critiques and disrupts such a notion. Problematic as it has been shown to be for an academic feminist like me to offer a reading of a black woman's text, however, it has been a greater mistake for white feminists not to do so. By focusing, in this study of feminist literary collaboration, on texts that are themselves engaged in the problem of a black woman's narrative being read and edited or interpreted by a white woman, it becomes possible to address this problem directly.

Thanks in large part to the groundbreaking work of African-American feminist scholars in the 1980s who attacked white feminists' racist focus on white writers, African-American women's texts have become much sought-after objects by white feminists, who read and use these texts widely in their classes and research. These texts have also become subjects from which a white feminist learns, with which she desires solidarity, which she seeks to serve through representation in her own texts. Unfortunately, as critics both black and white have shown, unself-critical alliances of this sort are likely to re-erase differences among women or reproduce racist hierarchies even as they militate against sexism. I return to these issues directly at the end of this chapter, but my approach to collaboration also presupposes them.

My reading here is one neither of whiteness nor of blackness, but of collaborations between characters in Jacobs's text, and authors in Jacobs's production of her text, who are marked white and black. These two stories—of Jacobs's narrative and of her coauthorship of this narrative—produce their own critiques of black author–white editor/reader interactions. There is tension within and between these stories; where Jacobs's narrative celebrates a collaboration, her correspondence occasionally mourns it, and narrative and correspondence both affirm and interrogate the collaborations in which Jacobs and her pseudonymous protagonist Linda Brent found themselves. The term *collaborate* is itself caught between the dual valences of working together with someone in common cause and colluding with an enemy. Fascinatingly, in Jacobs's case, these dual valences texture both Jacobs's collaborations and her narrative, producing seeming impasses, or catch-22s, where she is damned if she does, damned if she doesn't enter into a collaborative relationship with someone else—someone with whom she shares a common cause but who is also aligned (usually by race, gender, or class, but also by financial or emotional pressure) with the white supremacist, patriarchal systems of her day.

My discussion of Jacobs's text may also be read as an "approximate" conversation with feminist African-Americanists, for although it fails to incorporate a full conversation such as that between bell hooks and Mary Childers,[3] for example, it is overtly engaged with previous critiques of white-black relations in Jacobs's text, particularly with those of Hazel Carby and Alice Deck. Following standard practice, I cite other critics where their remarks influence, support, or notably depart from my discussion of Jacobs, but I also reverse the usual method of critical disagreement in this chapter by offering my evaluation of Jacobs's collaboration before showing how some other critics' readings differ substantively from mine. In this way, although I argue for the desirability of collaboration and for the progress that can be made through (indeed, as a result of) contradiction, I also quote previous critics at the end to remind readers of the ways in which such collaborations have failed to materialize and disparity is repeatedly reproduced.

In arguing that Jacobs's collaboration was ultimately successful, I emphasize that this is not because it was a full, mutual collaboration, but because it was mutually beneficial. The relationship between Jacobs and her editor only approximates coauthorship, yet Jacobs's text itself shows how useful and how necessary for survival an approximate relationship may be.[4] Such relationships—relationships that are temporary and asymmetric, yet not tyrannically hierarchical, and that are mutually but not equivalently rewarding—can move people out of viciously oppressive circumstances into ameliorated ones; this at least, I argue, is the story of and in this autobiography.

I begin by discussing the story of Jacobs's coauthorship as recorded in her correspondence, then turn to the narrative of *Incidents in the Life of a Slave Girl*, which in certain respects parallels the story of her coauthorship. If one assumes that the incidents themselves and their causal links were Jacobs's own (for Child liked the way Jacobs told her own story), then, in retelling the history of her collaboration, I am placing first what came last in the writing of this text. But because Child worked over the narrative, the orderly story told by these incidents owes something to Child as well as to Jacobs. Lacking definitive evidence as to who contributed what to the final order of this autobiography, my decision to deal with the collaboration first is the consequence of a belief not only that a text should be read in the context of its collaborative circumstances, but that a text's narrative partly replicates those circumstances. My account of how *Incidents in the Life of a Slave Girl* came to be and mean is an

entirely new one in its stress on the complex context and frictional effects of collaborative authorship. Collaboration was a mixed bag for Jacobs, but these collaborations cannot be extricated from her progress
toward authorship.

In this case, an intent to collaborate preceded an attempt to author.
The main facts of Jacobs's literary relationships are well known, thanks
to the editorial work of Jean Fagan Yellin, Dorothy Sterling, Milton Meltzer and Patricia Holland, and Alice Deck; however, Yellin and Deck are
the only critics to have considered the evidence in any detail, and both
are concerned with extracting Jacobs's authorship from her influences.[5]
Jacobs became involved in the antislavery movement through her brother,
John. While staying with him in the 1840s, Jacobs met the feminist abolitionist Amy Post, who first urged Jacobs to seek an audience for her story
and to contact Harriet Beecher Stowe as possible author for her story (to
create an "as told to" autobiography). It was the conjunction not only of
potential collaborators, but also of previously disabling conflicting loyalties to others and to herself, loyalties involving issues of both gender
and race, that enabled Jacobs to accede to Post's suggestion.

Jacobs, a proud person determined to act honorably as a woman and
as an African American, initially expressed nervousness about Post's
urging because hers was not "the life of a Heroine with no degradation
associated with it" (Sterling 75). She had earlier avoided the antislavery
movement because she did not want to tell her story without including
the central events of her sexual life, and this seemed to her impossible:
"I had determined to let others think as they pleased but my lips should
be sealed and no one had a right to question me. For this reason, when I
first came North I avoided the antislavery people because I felt I could
not be honest and tell the whole truth. . . . I never would consent to give
my past life to any one without giving the whole truth" (Sterling 75;
Yellin, Correspondence 232). To agree to the publication of her story,
Jacobs had to cross the treacherous border between the (female) private
and the public. This dilemma was by no means merely a personal one (if
anything can ever be only that); it was also political, for Jacobs's story
would break new ground in what was already an extensive set of first-
person slave narratives. There was little or no precedent for the autobiography of a woman's sexual harassment, resistance, and choice. By suggesting that she record her story, and then approaching Stowe as a possible
transcriber for her, Post became Jacobs's first audience. Without the example of her brother's activism and without her own desire to help other women—to "save another from my fate" (Sterling 75)—Jacobs might
still not have overcome her anxieties about "tell[ing] the whole truth."

Unfortunately, this promising linkage of race and sex, texts and women, white and black, male and female, free and enslaved broke on the rock of Stowe's classist racism. When Post contacted Stowe, Stowe thought she might use some of Jacobs's story in her planned *Key to Uncle Tom's Cabin* (a collection of short autobiographies of slaves meant to corroborate and testify to the truth of *Uncle Tom's Cabin*), and she wrote to Jacobs's employer, Mary Stace Willis (whom Jacobs had not entrusted with her story) to verify Jacobs's account and request it for her "key." After Willis discussed this development with Jacobs, Willis wrote to Stowe to say that Jacobs wanted her story published by itself. Stowe did not answer her letters. In addition, in response to Jacobs's suggestion that Stowe take her daughter Louisa with her on a journey to England, where Louisa might be "representative of a Southern Slave" to English abolitionists, Stowe responded that Louisa would be the object of "much petting and patronizing which would be more pleasing to a young Girl than useful," and commented further that she did not like "this class of people" being introduced to the English (Sterling 76–77; Yellin, Correspondence 235).

Stung, Jacobs wrote to Post—"Think dear Amy that a visit to Stafford House would spoil me as Mrs. Stowe thinks petting is more than my race can bear? Well, what a pity we poor blacks can't have the firmness and stability of character that you white people have" (Sterling 77)—and decided to write her story herself. If conflicting feelings about her anomalousness had once restrained her, the sympathy of Post, the antipathy of Stowe, and her desire for a different future for her daughter compelled her finally to take up the pen: "Dont expect much of me dear Amy. . . . God did not give me that gift [of talent] but he gave me a soul that burned for freedom and a heart nerved with determination to suffer even unto death in pursuit of that liberty which without makes life an intolerable burden" (Sterling 79; Yellin, Correspondence 236). This crucial decision, to write her story rather than simply tell it, was thus motivated as much by hatred for her oppressors as by love for others. The history of Jacobs's collaboration—of her narrative itself—is a tissue of split affect and polarized feelings as well as of racial fissure, yet these do not always produce paralysis; indeed, often they result in an astonishing mobility.

As Yellin explains, Jacobs sought publication first through letters sent to the New York *Tribune*, which printed them anonymously. She then requested Post's help with writing (Yellin, Introduction xix–xx). Eventually she devoted herself to composing the entire history of her slavery, which would become *Incidents in the Life of a Slave Girl*. Writing the autobiography while carrying on her duties as a nurse and housemaid in the Nathaniel Willis household was an enormous task. It took seven years to produce the book, and she suffered repeated rejection from publishers. Thayer and Eldridge in Boston finally accepted the manuscript on condition that a preface be solicited from Lydia Maria Child, whose name would help sell the book. Jacobs feared approaching another Stowe, but when Jacobs met Child in the Boston Anti-Slavery Office, she found in her, as in Post, a powerful and sympathetic audience: "Mrs. C is like yourself a whole souled Woman," she told Post (Sterling 82; Yellin, Correspondence 247). Thus, consummating a classic story of enlightenment and liberation, Jacobs found her text finally on the way to publication. Even now, however, Jacobs's road to publication lay not through absolute insistence on self-autonomy, but through collaboration.

Jacobs's comparison of Child with Post is charged with affect more intensely intimate than Jacobs's short sentence suggests. Earlier Jacobs had written to Post that "Your purity of heart and kindly sympathies won me to speak of my children. It is the only words that has [sic] passed my lips since I left my [grand]mothers door" (Sterling 75; Yellin, Correspondence 232). In this formulation, purity and heart, words and lips, speech and passage, grandmother and threshold knit Post (and thus now Child) into a web of memory in which language, moral value, house, and family— the heart(h)—spring into being together, emerging together as a threshold, a place of passage. If Child is like Post, she is kindred; arising from the same matrix as Post and Jacobs, Child is "whole souled." Yet it should also be remembered that this fabric of language, body, maternality—this "literalization," and an instance of what Margaret Homans has identified as a specifically female sociolinguistics[6]—is woven across old wounds in all these spots. Indeed, words, flesh, home, kinship, and morality itself acquire their fierce desirability and efficacy for Jacobs precisely through her recurrent encounter with their impossibility: Southern law prohibited literacy for slaves, regulated their bodies, disowned them of house and home, stripped them of motherhood, sold their families, and denied them "whole souls," obliging them to collaborate with racism.

Child made herself at home, in turn, with Jacobs's narrative. In a letter of 13 August 1860, she found the language "wonderfully good," particularly "for one whose opportunities for education have been so limited"; she praised the narrative as "interesting, and well told"; and she admired the authorial commentary ("The remarks are also good, and to the purpose"). Child willingly took enormous "pains" with the manuscript because it was "unusually interesting" and because she believed it would do "much service to the Anti-Slavery cause." Child became as personally as she was politically interested in and by it. "You know," she said, "I would go through fire and water to help give a blow to Slavery"

(Holland and Meltzer, *Lydia Maria Child* 357; Yellin, Correspondence 244). Child said such things to Jacobs not in a mood of self-preoccupation but in an effort to relieve Jacobs of too much indebtedness to her: "So you need not feel under great personal obligations" (Holland and Meltzer, *Lydia Maria Child* 357; Yellin, Correspondence 244).

To a contemporary ear, much of this has a patronizing sound, but Child would have expected Jacobs to feel obligated, and it was a credit to Child not just that she wanted to free Jacobs of yet another burdensome obligation but that she imagined in the first place the possibility of an equitable and reciprocally rewarding relationship with Jacobs. Child also spoke in modest phrenological terms of her editing: She called it "my bump of mental order" (Holland and Meltzer, *Lydia Maria Child* 357; Yellin, Correspondence 244). There is little glamour, monumentality, or genius to be discovered in the trope of a "bump"; at the same time, she knew Jacobs would want to see and discuss what this bump may have jarred in the manuscript.

These various tributes to Jacobs's work and mind indicate how active Child had become in editing this book. The rest of this letter is devoted to the changes she was making. In a brief, largely overlooked account of this collaboration, Alice Deck points out that Child did far more than copyedit the manuscript; Deck argues, against the text's principal editor, Jean Fagan Yellin, that "transposing sentences and pages goes beyond copy editing to transforming a text" (Deck 39). Yellin quotes a letter that Child sent a friend about her editing, which registers Child's surprise at how little she had to do: "I abridged, and struck out superfluous words sometimes; but I don't think I *altered* fifty words in the whole volume" (Introduction xxii). Yellin persuasively argues for Jacobs's initiative in writing and then promoting her book, before and after she received help from Child. But Yellin's concern is to establish Jacobs's authorship of this text—once thought fictitious and possibly the creation of Child—and this leads Yellin to minimize Child's changes (the extent of which remains unknown).[7] Child reorganized it; she made the story, she thought, "more clear" and more "entertaining"; she solicited Jacobs's observations of the events that ensued from Nat Turner's rebellion; she deleted historical material about John Brown; she decided that the autobiography should end with Jacobs's grandmother's death rather than with Brown; and she fictionalized names (Holland and Meltzer, *Lydia Maria Child* 357; Yellin, Correspondence 244). Who knows what else she may have done in styling the language, adding touches to characters and deleting elements of characterization, or rewriting the story? In altering the manuscript so substantially, Child became its ineradicable coauthor.

Nor did the interaction between these two writers end here, with Child's report on the extensive editing she was undertaking and her request for more material. Although we do not know how Jacobs responded to all of Child's suggestions, we know enough of one of them to see that Jacobs could run with them. In response to the request for more material on the Nat Turner rebellion, Jacobs sent not merely some notes or even paragraphs to insert wherever Child might like (a point that Deck [39] also emphasizes); Jacobs "put the savage cruelties into one chapter, entitled 'Neighboring Planters,' in order that those who shrink from 'supping upon horrors,' might omit them, without interrupting the thread of the story" (Holland and Meltzer, *Collected Correspondence* no. 1282). In responding to Child's request in this way, Jacobs clearly joined with Child in the desire to produce a narrative that would appeal to and persuade readers, for she goes further here than Child in worrying about offending or jarring them. But Jacobs also differed from Child when asked to make this narrative conform to the patterns of a slave narrative. Jacobs recognized that the Nat Turner material constituted a break in the narrative she had produced, which was focused on her personal trials—that is, on the sexual abuse endured by a black woman who enjoyed more "privileges" than most rather than on the violent physical abuse endured by the most oppressed black slaves. Jacobs wanted both to respect the stories of others and to gain respect for her own.

Jacobs saw her primary audience as an audience of women, whose moral fervor was needed in the antislavery cause. These women would be touched by a "sentimental" narrative but would be shocked by the horrors of a slave narrative. Thus, although Child may have tried to change this story, to make it conform to conventionally shaped narratives, Jacobs also attempted to divert its sensationalism away from the violent toward the sentimental. The result was a narrative with doubled threads.[8]

But neither thread—the personalizing sentimental or the melodramatically historical—can be attributed entirely to only one of these women. Both Child's deletion of the John Brown incidents[9] and Jacobs's careful screening of the Nat Turner episode contributed to making the narrative more "sentimental" and less historical. Yet at the same time, Jacobs's original intention to close with John Brown and Child's suggestion that she add Nat Turner indicate a shared desire to link the story to its broader historical context and to make a larger point about the necessity for abolition. On the face of the evidence that remains, the two women joined in each other's interests even at the moments where they most obviously departed from each other. Jacobs and Child both were concerned with the difficult balancing act of strategically politicizing yet cautiously subordinating, sensationally disclosing while morally rationalizing the incidents of Jacobs's sexual life. Together, they eventually produced an elusively contradictory story of one woman's bold partial escape both from slavery and from normative sexual mores.

Best of all in this editor-author relationship, Child sent the manuscript back to Jacobs so that she could respond to it. Although we do not know how Jacobs replied, this crucial step in editing, where an author is invited to interact directly with the editor, is so often omitted that it is striking to see this happen in the nineteenth century between a famous white abolitionist and an unknown former slave. What more could be desired of a collaboration between an author and editor?

Something important was lacking in the end and thus crucially in the entire collaborative process. Jacobs wanted to meet with Child in order to discuss the editing; she wanted to consult together and "compar[e] our views. Although I know that hers are superior to mine yet we could have worked her great Ideas and my small ones together" (Sterling 83). For Jacobs, conversation had not only preceded the writing of her text—as it precedes most collaborations—but had made it possible; Jacobs's text and collaborations took root in her early conversations with Post. She should not have had to miss out on the final conversation. The collaboration between Child and Jacobs ended without Jacobs feeling that they had worked their ideas and themselves together. In this letter Jacobs also shows her sense of a hierarchy between Child's more highly educated, universalized "Ideas" and her own self-educated, particular "ones," between Child's "great" authority (as published writer, well-known editor, famous abolitionist) and her own "small" existence (as victim, example, witness).[10] Jacobs desired a fuller collaboration in the very teeth of presumed differences in status between Child and herself.

She wanted a fuller conversation probably, in part, because she now possessed some "confidence" as an author and wished to assert her "integrity" (Deck 40) but also, as Jacobs herself expressed it, because she saw it as her "business" to participate in the final stages of revision (Sterling 83). She wrote of this failure in terms of exclusion not specifically from autonomous authorship nor even from the family of "whole souled" women, but from a professional partnership in which she had been unable to play her part. As she says in this same letter, although she knows that Child "will strive to do the best she can, more than I can ever repay," discussing the editing was nonetheless "my own business" to which "I should have [attended]" (Sterling 83). The missed conference entails her final exclusion from the ethics as well as economics of literary collaboration. If they had done this final business together, they could have produced a better text, a text that bridged the gaps between them more resolutely.

Responsibility for the fact that Jacobs missed out on this meeting seems to rest not solely on Child, but also on the racial and domestic structures Jacobs inhabited. It is unclear whether Child did as much as she could have to bring about a meeting; what we know is that at the time Child and she were to meet, Jacobs could not excuse herself from the Willis household for such a rendezvous. Mrs. Willis was bedridden for four weeks after losing a child during childbirth, and she needed Jacobs by her side. This is a prominent pattern in the story of Jacobs's life (as told in *Incidents*). Jacobs must serve others' interests first, and these are usually her owners'/employers' interests, but she feels that her first duty and own desire are to serve the people for whom she cares most. These two opposed directives were often merged, as in this case, for she cared deeply for Mrs. Willis and her children. Antithetical constraints (her servitude in the Willis household) and desired ends (her devotion to the Willises) combined in this event to prevent her from completing her business with Child. One set of labors and loves canceled the other.

Yet to describe this event only in terms of Jacobs's interests would be to draw too narrow an outline of what happened. Underlying the final stage of this manuscript's production was a process of objectification and restriction of Jacobs's work by race- and class-marked literacy apparatuses.[11] She did not feel free to talk to the Willises about her writing. Surely they could have found a way to release her to see Child for one discussion. But Nathaniel Willis was "pro-slavery" (Yellin, "Text and Contexts" 265), and she feared the Willises' reaction too much—the "criticism and ridicule" of all such "educated people"—to trust them even with the knowledge that she was writing (Sterling 80). In order to write at all, she secluded herself in private quarters, stealing time from the night after her work was finished just as she had stolen midnight hours to see her children. It is with this recurrent plight of Jacobs—once more unable, except in stealth, to cross from one world into another—that her collaboration with Child came to an end.

Still, the text did not come to an end there. Jacobs's approximated coauthorship with Child enabled publication of her work, and it was a significant accomplishment: Before that time there had been little description of a slave woman's sexual abuse, particularly from her own point of view, little hint that a slave woman's sexual life might be emotionally and ethically complex. Jacobs's text thus became an important participant in the struggle not only against slavery and the Fugitive Act, but also in behalf of women, both black and white, arguing for their ability to reason, their right to make sexual choices, and their distinctive claims to authorship. In publishing this narrative, Jacobs and Child each had something important to gain. For Jacobs it meant taking part in the antislavery movement, which until then she had participated in marginally and without telling her story.[12] For Child it was both a blow against slavery and a blow for women as authors, moral beings, and thinkers.[13]

Although this text marks an important multidimensional moment of struggle, a moment directly benefiting the interests of both its author and its editor, it could not solve any of the problems it describes, and far from presenting its narrative as a teleology whose happy ending (freedom for its heroine and her race) has been achieved, it protests the false freedom that the second Mrs. Willis bought for Jacobs and wonders when freedom will ever come for American slaves. As Brent also says, in the literalist language of domesticity noted before, "I still long for a hearthstone of my own, however humble" (302).

The oscillations in this history of problematic relations between black-white, author-editor, female-female collaborators—Post's encouragement of Jacobs, Stowe's discouragement of her, Child's support, the Willises' unwitting obstructionism, and publication of the final text—replicate defining patterns in Jacobs's life story, as told in *Incidents in the Life of a Slave Girl.* Jacobs's narrative is at least as alive to the ironic impossibilities as to the sentimental possibilities held out to Brent. The narrative sequence of this book thus continually hinges on a complex, contradictory relation between Linda Brent's experience of enslavement, hatred of her abuser, choicelessness, and enforced silence and her experience of self-ownership, love for her family and friends, choice, and outspoken self-assertion. These are not things that she feels separately; they occur simultaneously. They are combined conditions for her as a slave and a woman.

But just as Jacobs came to write her story, Brent gradually finds her way out from under her oppressor through the constellated pressures of rage and love. This text embeds Jacobs's *Bildungsroman* in a web of difficult collaborations. The impasses in which she is caught compel seemingly impossible choices, yet she continually finds a way to choose alternative evils and alternative allies, which the other authority figures in her life (especially, for opposite reasons, her grandmother and her slave master) have forbidden her to choose and thus do not expect, but that yield temporary refuge from her abusers. Brent's agency is severely curtailed by the social system of slavery,[14] yet her partial collaborations with others within this system enable change for her.

The daughter of slaves, Linda Brent was six before she realized she was a slave; when her mother died, she was left in the hands of a kind mistress who taught her to read and write. But while thanking this mistress for her literacy, and ultimately for the book now in readers' hands, Brent must denounce her and does so passionately: Her mistress betrayed her by not freeing her, the first of many such betrayals for Brent and a routine event in the life of a slave (15–16). At the mistress's death, Linda, now twelve years old, is bequeathed to the five-year-old daughter of Dr. Flint, who with his wife exercises tyrannical control over his family's slaves. This introductory chapter sets the stage for subsequent chapters detailing a devastating series of lost alliances and "evil" alternatives.

The fifth chapter (after a curious sequence of two contextualizing chapters not focused on Brent, a pattern that repeats itself several times in this narrative) discloses Brent's sexual education as a slave, her harassment by Dr. Flint, and his temptation and psychological and physical abuse of her, which stops short only of forced rape.[15] The disclosure of chapter 5 in *Incidents in the Life of a Slave Girl*—of the slave girl's sexuality—indicates a "possession" that would have been no less surprising to Northern women than that of her literacy. In fact, they become closely linked: Sexuality and literacy attract worrisome attention to each other in this text and thus to Brent, but they also deflect persecution, producing friction against her persecutors. This first disclosure delineates Brent's central impasse and thus marks the lines along which Brent's affiliations and disaffiliations develop. In the three chapters delineating Brent's sexual enslavement, Jacobs elaborates first "The Trials of Girlhood" to which Dr. Flint subjects her; then, in "The Jealous Mistress," her failed effort to find an ally in her mistress and subsequent position squeezed between the mistress's hatred and the master's lust; and third, the further disclosure of "The Lover," whom Dr. Flint refuses to let her marry and who must leave her behind for life in another state. Denied her lover, Linda Brent has ever fewer options. She must endure in silence as Dr. Flint pours lascivious words into her ears and, delighted at the discovery that she can read, pursues her with love notes. In silence she bends under her mistress's attempts to extract from her the admission of a sexual lapse with Dr. Flint, and she is unable to confide these horrors to any of her proud and morally upright relatives, in part from shame, in part from protectiveness because she is acutely aware of their inability to help her.

Not for long does she have even this luxury of remaining in an inert, self-canceled (and friendless) state. Her first impossible choice is narrated after another two-chapter break, and it involves a greater sexual scandal.[16] (Such two-chapter deferrals make Brent's disclosures no less powerful, serving as much to dramatize breaks in her life and her alliances as to elaborate the wider nets and slave networks in which her story and she are caught.) At the beginning of chapter 10 ("A Perilous Passage in the Slave Girl's Life"), she reveals that Dr. Flint has begun to build a cottage for her at a distance from his estate and from his wife, where he can keep Brent as a concubine.[17] He intends to remove all obstacles to his access to her by distancing her from all potential allies; she is required by law to live where he wishes. But she has found an alternative, and she now reveals it to the reader by means of a lengthy apology, the familiar apology of a sentimental heroine, preparing the reader for her moral fall. She has "chosen" the evil of an illicit lover, yielding to another white man. Mr. Sands is a powerful but benevolent slaveowner and a bachelor who treats her with respect, sympathizes with her in her plight, and, although he writes often to her, does not impose himself as Dr. Flint does. Denied the former slave she loved, under compulsion by the slaveowner she hates, and aroused to sharp awareness of her sexuality by both these men, she submits to attraction to Mr. Sands.

In the lexicon of this sentimental novel, *lapse* would be as appropriate a term as *choice* for this incident in her life: Brent falls along the easiest path in a rocky place. The names of the two slave masters allegorize her choice as a Scylla and Charybdis:[18] Between flint and sand, which is better? One may survive when wrecked on sand, but it is no place on which to build. Mr. Sands is a nonchoice; she may not marry or claim him in any way as her lover. Moreover, her liaison with Mr. Sands and the pregnancy that comes of it immediately alienate her from the one major figure in her life, her grandmother, who, as a freed slave with independent means, has the capacity and desire to shelter her and would have bought her freedom already if Dr. Flint had permitted it. The grandmother's response to Brent's pregnancy makes it clear why Brent has kept her trials and choices to herself. The grandmother is shocked and disappointed by her granddaughter's lapse and does not forgive her.

Nonetheless, Brent has nowhere else to go now that she is pregnant, so after evicting her, her grandmother takes her back in, and Brent thus gains the shelter her grandmother could not otherwise have given her. Dr. Flint, astonished, stymied, and infuriated though he is, leaves her to her confinement. Visiting her, he taunts and heaps scorn on her, but no longer seeks to remove her to a rural cottage. Most important to Brent's eventual escape, the male child who is born becomes, as she says in the chapter 11 title, "The New Tie to Life" for whom she is capable of enduring still greater trials. No longer merely dependent on older relatives for their support, she now supports another generation. The result is the development of an uncanny "canniness" in Brent as love and repugnance combine to foster in her an extraordinary aptitude for living amid impossibilities.

The most pregnant gap in the narrative—the gap that least anticipates what comes next—occurs directly after the birth of her boy, Benny. After "The New Tie to Life," two more chapters unfold in which she again turns away from herself to narrate the atrocities committed against other slaves. The first of these, "Fear of Insurrection," is the chapter in which she narrates the assaults on blacks that followed Nat Turner's rebellion. At the same time, she shows clearly how much better off her family was than other slaves thanks to their residence in town and in the neighborhood of influential white friends, who helped protect them from the marauding gangs. What retrospectively appears still more important to the narrative, however, is the implication that Dr. Flint's behavior cannot be isolated from the worst maraudings of the white lower class. Although there are important exceptions among Brent's own white upper-class friends, the two classes are implicated in, and perpetuate, each other's predatory deeds. At the beginning of chapter 14, we learn that Dr. Flint has developed a new threat, promising to sell her son if she will not have sex with him. But in a surprise for the reader as well as for Dr. Flint, Brent has something new up her sleeve, and despite (in part because of) the contrasts she has just drawn between much of white society's immoral lawlessness and her own ethical behavior, the next disclosure seems not entirely explained: She has conceived a second child, this time a daughter, with Mr. Sands.

Brent's sexual reticence makes this moment of particular interest to the contemporary feminist; it is the untold story at the heart of the told in this narrative.[19] Nowhere does Brent tell us anything of pleasure, but where a first child is readily perceived in sentimental narratives as a regrettable lapse, a second child speaks of desire in action. Apparently Brent has not learned the lesson one might expect of a sentimental heroine, who finds a deepened morality at the heart of her error. Jacobs's silence on this point registers not only inhibition or her certainty of disapproval by others and self-censorship, but also two important features of this narrative. First, as I have already suggested, this and the other gaps in the narrative point to persisting impasses in this narrator's situation, the impasse in particular of her denied existence: Forbidden all rights, she is denied a normative sexual existence as well as liberty. Second, these gaps gesture not only at Brent's unspoken yearning for autonomy, self-ownership, and sexual choice, but also at a different, less easily articulated, but more readily attained possibility and pleasure.

Valerie Smith (among others) describes Jacobs's narrative as producing a subversion of "the more orthodox public plot [in slave narratives] of vulnerability" with a secondary "plot of empowerment" (Smith, Introduction xxxiv; "'Loopholes of Retreat'" 213), yet Brent's power is so subordinated to a network of enmeshing constraints that this narrative is more precisely described not as a doubling of opposite plots (oppression versus empowerment), one of which subverts the other, but as a story of canny, transformative coupling and elusion of dichotomies such as those of master and slave. The possibility—and pleasure—of this narrative dwell as much in its performance of evasion as in its implied arguments for independence, authenticity, or truth, as much in its protagonist's canniness as in its hinted confession of sexual desire. Brent's silences[20] may be read not only as marks of frustration, but as acts of refusal, not only as silent admission, but as success at elusion.

In the conclusion of chapter 3, I return to the process by which an impasse or contradiction can yield alternative possibilities as imaged by a rebus knot. But to use here a metaphor that Jacobs uses in a later chapter (and that other readers have also used), a gap in her narrative is not merely a "hole" but a "loophole"—a path of escape.[21] Where does the loophole lead? Back to the same old circumstances but with a difference, a difference that leads to inverting the hierarchy between slaveowner and slave, that turns this relation inside out, without ever entirely canceling its opposition, and that thus complicates rather than reverses the power structure.

Brent's second pregnancy succeeds better than any of her previous acts at keeping Dr. Flint at bay. Not only does it indicate sexual activity over which he is powerless, it also renders his threat against the son useless because the object of his desire is again bedridden, this time with a convalescent illness as well as with pregnancy. It confronts him with yet "Another Link to Life" (as Jacobs titles chapter 14) for Brent to hold onto if Flint acts on his threat against her son. And its repetition threatens Flint with an indefinite series of further repetitions, frustrating him. The risks Brent has run in becoming pregnant also are made clearer than ever in Flint's brutal reaction, for he now lashes out at her, throwing her down a staircase, and in the next chapter he heaves her four-year-old son across the room into a wall. Terror of Dr. Flint, not only pregnancy, sickens the normally tough Brent, and she nearly dies in this chapter. She attributes her return to life to the new "link" of her baby daughter, Emily.

Another two chapters (chapters 15 and 16) elapse before Brent starts to literalize her escape from Dr. Flint. These two chapters are not directed away from her, however; rather, they detail a new set of conditions devised by Dr. Flint. Her narrative thus begins to resemble more closely the expected pattern of the "melodramatic" slave narrative, yet it also continues to unravel as a series of nonchoices that Brent cannily evades. Dr. Flint places her under greater pressure by lending her to his son to work on his plantation; the son is more sexually and physically aggressive than the father, and Dr. Flint thus expects Brent's fear of the son's predations to throw her back into the father's arms. Moreover, the demands put upon her to manage the son's household prevent her from caring adequately for her baby daughter, who cries almost ceaselessly for her. (At Dr. Flint and his wife's urging, the younger Flint and his wife bring both children to live with Brent because they believe she is less likely to try to escape if she has her children with her.) The Flints' "Continued Persecutions" (as the chapter title names them), when joined with her libidinal anxiety for her children, have the opposite effect from what any of the Flints imagine. The Flint plan, which condemns her children to slavery on the plantation, persuades her to escape.[22]

This section of the narrative is a web of moves and countermoves by the myriad participants in Brent's entrapment. Thus Brent finds a slightly more secure situation when she is removed from a black friend's small house to an attic room in a benevolent white female friend's house—the first successful collaborative venture with a white woman in this book. But this woman's gesture does nothing to alleviate Brent's suffering. Dr. Flint exploits his enormous power as a slaveholder to have Brent's only brother, William, and both her children thrown into jail. Flint has gradually depleted his funds through expenses incurred in pursuing Brent and imprisoning her family, so when he is approached by a slave trader acting secretly on Mr. Sands's behalf with an offer for the children, he sells them. But again, far from yielding simple comfort, these events accompany an increase in misfortune for Brent, whose "New Perils" (chapter 20) result from a tattletale in the white household where she hides. The living tomb in which Brent is ensconced in the friendly white woman's house (in a small upper-story room and occasionally under the kitchen floorboards) anticipates her situation for the next seven years.

Brent escapes from this hiding place to one much like it—one in which she leads her "life" in the bosom of her family but completely hidden from them. This next hiding place is the uninsulated, leaky attic (9 by 7 by 3 feet) of a shed in her grandmother's backyard. In this cell—in the most incredible incident of all in this narrative—Brent spends seven years hidden from her children and prey to freezing cold in the winter, biting red insects in the summer, illness, and her own inertia. She becomes the untold story, the gap, at the center of her family's life, and the best-hidden secret of her narrative. Three chapters (chapters 21 through 23) are devoted to detailing what she endures in her "Loophole of Retreat," her "Christmas Festivities," and her survival "Still in Prison." Fitted as this cell is to her body, there is no heavier irony in her narrative than the naming of her "retreat" a loophole. Yet this most uncanny of Brent's escapes becomes also the most unforgettable moment in the text's protest against slavery: Jacobs willingly endured an absolute enslavement of her body for the sake of eluding enslavement of her children. This incident thereby recontextualizes the earlier events of Jacobs's sexual "choices"; the parallels among these successive nonchoices reconfirm that these are all choices of alternative imprisonments rather than of alternative satisfactions. Brent's pleasure in escape is the minimalist pleasure that can be gotten from what Jacobs herself subsequently calls "cunning" (when she titles chapter 25 "Competition in Cunning").

Brent might have died in this loophole, but what finally enables her to make the more usual kind of escape of slave narratives is yet another intricate set of intolerable pressures. Although she has managed to keep Dr. Flint employed elsewhere hunting her down—by writing misleading letters and arranging for them to be posted from various places in the North—she now fears Mr. Sands's plans. Having briefly resembled the hero of this plot, Mr. Sands betrays his true colors. Elected to Congress, he leaves the children behind and in jeopardy (not having freed them) and takes William with him as his slave; from Washington he writes to Brent's grandmother about his gratification with William for disdaining the temptations of abolitionists. William perceives Mr. Sands's delusion—he is not the happy slave of Mr. Sands's dreams—and makes his escape while he can. Distressed at the possible consequences for her children, Brent tries to learn Mr. Sands's intentions for them. But Mr. Sands is now married, and because the Sandses believe Brent gone forever, possibly dead, Mrs. Sands wants to do something for Emily, possibly having her adopted by an Illinois relative. Complicating this situation further, when questioned by Brent's relatives, Mr. Sands insists that the children are free as far as he is concerned but does not produce the documentation to prove it, and Dr. Flint has found his own legal loophole to renew his claim on Brent's children. Thus, when Mr. Sands proposes the lesser evil of sending Brent's daughter to keep house for a poorer relative in New York, Brent yields to something she had sworn never to do: She sees her daughter go without a document verifying her freedom. He proposes to let her son go north with her Uncle Phillip when he is ready. Brent is "free" at last to follow the standard formula of the slave narrative, seeking escape on a ship headed north.

The narrative that follows is as complex as what precedes it, yet it follows strikingly similar patterns, obsessively reiterating in ever-changing forms the net in which Brent is trapped. Caught between subservience to hateful moral and economic laws and her love for her children and the people who try to help her, Brent struggles on and on, without an end to her personal struggles for freedom for her children and herself or for her people. Yet her circumstances do improve, for at the end of the narrative her daughter is in boarding school, her son is employed with her brother, and she is at last legally (if not economically or ethically) free. In a climactic chapter called "The Confession," Brent, pressured by fear of what her daughter will hear from her schoolmates, confesses her sexual past. Emily, who already knows who her father was, values loyalty more highly that sexual purity, thus rewriting the Christian moral framework under which Brent has partly labored, with its authenticating narrative of sin, confession, and forgiveness. Devoted to her mother and having rejected long ago the father who never loved her, Emily operates according to the more Manichean ethic suggested by this book of inextricably linked love and hate.

Mother and daughter are each other's strongest "approximate" partners at the end of the story, rejoining divided generations, women, and fortunes, knitting over Brent's old wounds even as they prepare to part from each other again. As Claudia Tate stresses, Jacobs "affirm[s] black women's rights to be respected as mothers, rather than being treated as 'brood-sow[s]' to use Nanny's term in Hurston's *Their Eyes Were Watching God*," and "the text asserts political autonomy for maternity with its break from the conventional closure of marriage in sentimental fiction." In two famous sentences at the end of the novel, Brent asserts, "Reader, my story ends with freedom; not in the usual way, with marriage. I and my children are now free!" (302).[23] But at the same time, with her recurrent irony, in the following sentences Jacobs does not permit the reader even the sentimental ending of a reunion with her daughter: "I do not sit with my children in a home of my own. I still long for a hearthstone of my own, however humble" (302).

Two sets of relationships in this narrative bear comparison with Jacobs's subsequent literary collaborations. These are her relationships with Mr. Sands and with older white and black women. Although I have already detailed Mr. Sands's role in Brent's narrative, his relationship to her requires special attention. It is an approximate collaboration in the terms I have already defined. Structured by asymmetric power relations, confined within the larger institutions of slavery that Mr. Sands partly endorses by his inaction, Brent's relationship with Mr. Sands was headed toward betrayal from the first. Brent's commentary is especially critical when it turns to the delusions of "decent" whites such as Mr. Sands. As an owner of slaves, a congressman, and a married man, Mr. Sands is as much to blame for the perpetuation of slavery as Dr. Flint. But he is also a place where change becomes possible. If it had not been for such a compromising, hypocritical figure as Mr. Sands, Brent would have been condemned (so this narrative suggests) to complete sexual degradation by Dr. Flint and to producing Dr. Flint's slave progeny. Like Ursa's female ancestors in Gayl Jones's *Corregidora*, Brent's history would have been a history of generations of women all enslaved, each delivered to sexual concubinage in her turn. If Brent evaded this, it was not through any innate mental genius, moral superiority, or propensity for rebellion; she survived by making unlikely allies and finding unlikely alternatives in sexual availability and physical confinement. Mr. Sands in particular played a pivotal role in moving Brent out of a horrendous situation into a better one, and he makes possible the distinctive lessons that are to be learned from this narrative: that no choice is free in a society regulated by economic, political, racist, and sexist systems and that sexual/appetitive choice is an especially elusive kind of nonchoice.[24]

There were less hypocritical allies than this in Brent's escape, but some of them are far less visible in her narrative than Mr. Sands and most of them played ambiguous roles. Among the most important figures are the most anonymous, whom Jacobs wanted to protect from exposure at the time of publication, such as the black and white women who hid Brent in their houses for a short time. The important second Mrs. Bruce would blur together with the first Mrs. Bruce if the second one weren't distinguished by her decision to buy Brent's freedom. Both women and men helped her at various times—from Brent's grandmother (who feared the very thought of escape) to her Uncle Phillip (who prepared her outhouse cell for her)—but the women, with their Post-like sympathies or Stowe-like condescension, play more frequent roles than the men in the narrative of Brent's sentiments. In addition to those already mentioned, there is a great aunt whom Jacobs barely mentions until her death. In strong contrast to her grandmother, it turns out that this woman had been encouraging Brent all along to escape. We learn this at the same time that we learn about the aunt's funeral, and that occurs, with the narrative neatness that typifies this text, just before the chapter in which Brent finally escapes to the North. Earlier impasses in the text would have seemed less forbidding if Jacobs had let us know about this woman sooner. Instead, Jacobs introduces her at the moment when Brent has lost her but has finally been propelled into the escape she encouraged.

Hovering in the corners of her story, these pivotal women represent sources of comfort and support that were lurking in the wings—as they were later in the form of Post and Child—and could quite suddenly extend shelter to Brent. Distant observers and sympathetic hearers, these absent women anticipate the women readers Jacobs and Child hoped to attain. Jacobs and Child show these anticipated women readers the choices involved between acting like Mrs. Flint or Mrs. Bruce.[25] At the same time, poised at the edges of this narrative, the sheltering women Brent encounters are shielded from the anger and outrage permeating her story; they become contrasting figures whom she discusses briefly in memorial moments rather than complex characters like her grandmother or Mr. Sands.

Despite the marginal status and minimal characterization of such women in this text, do these collaborations, in particular with sympathetic white women such as the second Mrs. Bruce or Amy Post, represent model alliances? Jacobs's narrative—which also became Child's— is a tribute to such women, but it is also a veiled complaint. For example, the white woman who hid her had also to hide their actions and to remain, in a variety of ways, complicit with the slave system. Brent repeatedly shows us, moreover, that the special respect she gained from white allies was due to the fortunate place she held within a system in which some blacks could earn more privileges than others through their acquisition of literacy, special skills, economic advantages, or good looks. In the text's conclusion, Brent bitterly resents the bill of sale with which Mrs. Bruce gained freedom for her and shows herself deeply torn by a gratitude she should never have had to feel:[26]

> So I was *sold* at last! A human being *sold* in the free city of New York! The bill of sale is on record, and future generations will learn from it that women were articles of traffic in New York, late in the nineteenth century of the Christian religion. . . . I well know the value of that bit of paper; but much as I love freedom, I do not like to look upon it. I am deeply grateful to the generous friend who procured it, but I despise the miscreant who demanded payment for what never rightly belonged to him or his. (300–301)

I have characterized Jacobs's collaborations with Post and with Child, and Brent's collaborations with Mr. Sands and the various women who helped her, as approximate achievements, ultimately yielding improved circumstances. But I wish to end this essay with a reminder that various women African-Americanists have seen this text quite differently, and their concerns about the failure of such sisterhoods remain potent.

Writing about the collaboration between Child and Jacobs, Deck goes back to an earlier interview Child published with Charity Bowery, where Deck finds evidence of Child's suppressions and melodramatic aims:

> The sixty-five year old narrator had been living, and died, as a free woman in the north for many years, but she was asked only to recreate her slave identity while telling her story. Her opinions about herself as a free woman were not sought; her new self was not portrayed. The interview format allowed Child to leave her own voice, replete with editorial comments and leading questions, in the printed text. The fact that Child had the first and last word in Charity's narrative, suggests that she frames the former slave in the stereotype of a pious, hymn-singing, Christian woman who was unjustly treated by an avaricious slaveowner. In this guise, Charity was an appealing figure for Child's abolitionist melodrama. (36)

Deck goes on to demonstrate how impressive, by contrast, were Jacobs's efforts to produce and control her narrative, yet even here the relation between "auto" and "bio" tore apart, as Deck explains it, with Child rewriting the "auto" according to her notions of a slave "bio": "The demands of the slave narrative format dictated the shape into which Jacobs, via Child's editing, had to fit her story. This produces a dialogue of authorial and editorial voices in *Incidents* that resembles a debate between a subjective (insider's) and an objective (outsider's) representation of one black woman's life" (40). Focusing on Jacobs's sustained effort to correct the "outsider's" view with the "insider's," Deck concludes that "nevertheless, this demonstrates that Jacobs did not sacrifice completely her 'self' and 'life' in her story in the name of a cause" (40). For Deck, the two narratives—of author and editor—join in debate rather than in agreement, and Jacobs must resist not only submission to another voice but submission to a supposedly shared cause.

Hazel Carby writes in still stronger terms of what Jacobs's narrative tells us about such "sisterhoods":[27]

> This historical account questions those strands of contemporary feminist historiography and literary criticism which seek to establish the

existence of an American sisterhood between black and white women. Considering the history of the failure of any significant political alliances between black and white women in the nineteenth century, I challenge the impulse in the contemporary women's movement to discover a lost sisterhood and to reestablish feminist solidarity. Individual white women helped publish and promote individual black women, but the texts of black women from ex-slave Harriet Jacobs to educator Anna Julia Cooper are testaments to the racist practices of the suffrage and temperance movements and indictments of the ways in which white women allied themselves not with black women but with a racist patriarchal order against all black people. Only by confronting this history of difference can we hope to understand the boundaries that separate white feminists from all women of color. . . . "Sisterhood" between white and black women was realized rarely in the text of *Incidents*. Jacobs's appeal was to a potential rather than an actual bonding between white and black women. . . . Many of the relationships portrayed between Linda Brent and white women involve cruelty and betrayal and place white female readers in the position of having to realize their implication in the oppression of black women, prior to any actual realization of the bonds of "sisterhood."[28]

Carby's charges in this passage, and her reading of Jacobs's text, seem unanswerable except by future change.

It is not unequivocal agreement—"sisterhood" in that sense—between these two analyses and mine that will produce change. On the contrary, while difference divides, difference is as crucial as agreement to producing change. Carby's willingness to disagree with white feminists produces a necessary and elusive "sibling" friction. It is the pressure of contradiction, rather than totalized agreement and harmony or totalizing disagreement and dissension, that breaks impasses, passing by and beyond the limited relationships in which they occur. Before such change can occur, it is also necessary for members of a dominant race and a subordinated gender, like me, to see themselves—and to be seen—perched not exclusively on the white "upperside," nor exclusively on a female "lowerside," but on a nether side of a twisted loop that knots us all.

PART 2

Coupled Women
of Letters

3   Contradictory Legacies:
Michael Field and Feminist Restoration

AFTER 1970, AS H.D. and Gertrude Stein achieved canonical status and numerous turn-of-the-century women and lesbian writers benefited from renewed interest, it seems odd, but not inexplicable, that Michael Field received so little notice.[1] The two women, Katherine Bradley and Edith Cooper, who came together as one author, Michael Field, were each other's primary allies. Although they received important recognition and support from some major figures of their time (Robert Browning, George Meredith, and John Ruskin, among others), they were not elements or operators within a muscular literary circle; they neither systematically patronized (as Stein did) nor were systematically patronized (as H.D. was) by other artists who remain widely recognized today.[2] Moreover, they belonged to an era and ethos of writing that modernism self-consciously supplanted and cast into shadow, and the preferences of many contemporary feminist critics of poetry are still shaped by modernism and its descendants. But the obstacles they faced in finding interested readers in their day and the next were far more complex than those posed merely by aesthetic alliances. As writers who were women, female aesthetes,[3] and an aunt and a niece who lived together as an established couple and wrote together as if they were a single male writer, they seemed eccentric to their contemporaries as well as to the writers and critics of the century to come.

Angela Leighton's 1992 book on Victorian women poets thus marked a major turn in Field's reception by devoting—highly selective as it is— a chapter to Field and, together with pathbreaking articles on Field by

Chris White (1990 and 1996) and Yopie Prins (1995), established a critical context in which Field's texts at last can become widely known.[4] But
Leighton's *Victorian Women Poets: Writing against the Heart,* with its
construction of an alternative history of women writers within which it
frames a biographical portrait of Field and with its primary goal of aesthetic appraisal through exegesis of selected lyrics, fails to address the
contradictory heritage that Field left for their readers:[5] the multiple, subversive challenge to, yet subtly complicit cooperation with, social norms
of literary production and familial relationship. Instructed by the New
Historicism, we have grown accustomed to looking for such contradictions in writers, but Field offers a particularly unusual instance of "lesbian" coauthorship, at once worrisomely hidden, desirably successful, and
emanating from a historical situation close to our own. As Prins explains,
Leighton "assumes that their authorship is defined by lesbian identity
rather than complicating the claim to such an identity—as if the lesbian
signature exists prior to writing rather than being produced by it." Leighton's approach "limits an exploration of this central problem in the poetry of Bradley and Cooper to a form of biographical reading that does not
fully register the multiple textual mediations at work" (Prins, "Metaphorical Field" 139). Prins then turns away from the sociocultural issues that
emerge in a biographically based consideration of Field's struggle for fame
and a name to a nearly exclusive preoccupation with Field's textual and
intertextual self-constructions. Leighton, White, and Prins are all engaged—again in Prins's formulation—in "rediscovering Michael Field as
part of a larger inquiry into the cultural context and literary structures
of women's writing, and more specifically into the history of lesbian
writing" ("Metaphorical Field" 130). But, as I will show, the multiplicity of what is encompassed in Field's (collaborative) relationship threatens the very categories "women's writing" and "lesbian writing."

At the same time, Field anticipated the feminist, historicizing scholar,
she who seeks representations of women and gender in the fracturing
mirror of past texts in order to put the fragments together in her own
documents. Field anticipated not only her struggle with the past—her dual
allegiances to past and present, her quest for utopic alternatives, her criticism of historical oppression—but also her struggle for authority amid
a nagging sense of marginality. There is no explicit sign that Field feared
the effects of professionalization in the obvious ways that today's academic feminist does (although publication of their work in limited editions
militated against a broad middle-class readership). But there is a parallel
between the archival creativity that was the hallmark of Field's career and
that of the contemporary feminist scholar/teacher. Even Field's generic

choices, which seem at first glance peculiarly Victorian—historical and mythological verse drama, fin-de-siècle lyricism—acquire a strange familiarity when we allow ourselves to hear their echoes in contemporary feminist work. The depressing failure of Michael Field to survive their moment, despite their long and rich record of publication, can only make the echoes more disturbing and may suggest the impossibility of surviving our own contradictions, the futility of trying to change anything through writing. The abruptness of their disappearance from literary anthologies and conversation says something else to me: that a frightened retreat from the threat they posed to literary and social norms had occurred, and, despite the efforts of a small number of scholars and friends to enshrine their memory in the early 1920s,[6] a tacit, mutual agreement had been made by the literary world to bury them. For this reason alone, it behooves us to unbury the past and to make it a political point to do so—to persist in our disinterments no matter what this may lead us to discover about our own impossibilities. In many ways, Field appears exemplary for the contemporary feminist literary scholar in search of groundbreaking women writers of the past, yet the history of Field's choices as writers suggests as many questions as alternatives. Enmeshed in the literary politics of their day, Field's example is as monitory as it is exemplary for the feminist aesthetic restorationist of the late twentieth century.

Their pseudonymous authorship, their collaboration, their sexual companionship, and their prolific production of agonistic verse drama and poems that looked backward to legendary figures such as Sappho or the tragic Mary—all merit our attention and constitute their place in history, enabling them to remain, if nothing else, an odd couple on the not-too-distant horizon. Leighton treats Field as a poetic anomaly in their defiant and "pleasure-loving" escape from the "conflict" and "dissociation" of artistic imagination from social conscience evinced by other nineteenth-century women writers (*Writing against the Heart* 3, 209, 225–26), yet she simultaneously treats their masked authorship, collaborative relationship, lesbianism, and historicism as uncontroversial, unanomalous, requiring little discussion beyond simple narration of their career struggles. In reopening the Field controversy, we need to guard against rendering their public—and private—gestures innocuous. As I hope to show, there are conflict and stress in Field's work, but not only between inward imagination and outward social morality (which could be shown in their work). More compellingly, their most public gestures—of publication under one male name, of authorial collaboration, of lifelong marriage with each other, and of archivalist aestheticism in their tragic drama and verse—are themselves divided, or fissured, in effect.

The functioning of Bradley and Cooper's pseudonym is symptomatic of the ambiguous character of their efforts to obtain publicity. The male pseudonym acts most obviously to disguise and protect the female writer from notice and condemnation, but it also plays a more dangerous part. In her early book on female tradition, *A Literature of Their Own*, Elaine Showalter touches on this more subversive aspect of the male pseudonym:

> I have begun with the women born after 1800, who began to publish fiction during the 1840s when the job of the novelist was becoming a recognizable profession. One of the many indications that this generation saw the will to write as a vocation in direct conflict with their status as women is the appearance of the male pseudonym. Like Eve's fig leaf, the male pseudonym signals the loss of innocence. In its radical understanding of the role-playing required by women's effort to participate in the mainstream of literary culture, the pseudonym is a strong marker of the historical shift.[7]

In this description, the male pseudonym becomes a kind of cross-dressing: It signals the abandonment of former sexual innocence/restriction and the conscious adoption of a new sexual role.

Bradley and Cooper chose vaguely androgynous yet heterosexually linked and individualized pseudonyms for their earliest two books: Arran and Isla Leigh. The faintly masculine "Arran Leigh" (Katherine Bradley) wrote *The New Minnesinger* (1875), a book of poems, and the faintly heterosexual couple "Arran and Isla Leigh" wrote *Bellerophôn* (1881), a play. These names also evoke Elizabeth Barrett Browning's famous poet-heroine Aurora Leigh, signaling the dawn of a new woman poet. The writers then shifted to the pen name of an unambiguously singular male; "Michael Field" (used for the first time in the edition of the two plays *Callirrhoë, and Fair Rosamund* [1884]) served better to disguise them and gain them notice in the publishing world.[8] They were anxious that exposure of their actual identities would restrict their freedom as writers, as we know from Bradley's distressed letters to Robert Browning after they were partially revealed as being female: "It is said the *Athenaeum* was taught by you to use the feminine pronoun. . . . The report of lady authorship will dwarf and enfeeble our work at every turn" (*Works and Days* 6). The name Michael Field covered over both their femininity and their collaboration. Unfortunately, this choice also distanced them from potential readers in the twentieth century; at least one set of feminist coauthors in the 1990s has described Field's choice of a male pseudonym as disassociating Field from "women and women's work."[9]

But both sets of names represented Showalter's "radical understanding of the role-playing required" for a woman to get published "in the mainstream." Moreover, the act of role-playing lent itself to radicalism of a more joyous sort. The choice of *Field* in particular came to play a major part in their private as well as public lives. When Michael Field was unveiled as two women, the large potential audience that had seemed theirs to cultivate declined. Although they subsequently published some works anonymously, they also persisted in using the pseudonym. Even when they composed separately, they did so under the signature of Michael Field (for example, Cooper wrote *Poems of Adoration* [1912] and Bradley wrote *Mystic Trees* [1913] almost entirely). They referred to themselves not only publicly but privately as Michael and Field. While they played with various nicknames for each other,[10] *Michael Field* retained its preferred status as their "poet's" name. *Michael Field* was split between the two: Bradley took on the name *Michael* and Cooper acquired the nicknames *Henry* and *Field*. Thus they divided one name between them. But they also shared the same surname, joining themselves in a happily married, albeit now entirely male couple, "Michael and Henry Field." Friends called them "the Fields." The pseudonym clearly enabled them to play a game with sexual as well as literary and gender identities. Like Eve's fig leaf, it became a sign that pointed to even as it concealed their transgressions.[11]

In the angry letter to Browning resenting the revelation of their "lady authorship," Bradley also renews a warning earlier expressed by Cooper against disclosure of the secret of their "dual authorship," which would be "utter ruin" to them (*Works and Days* 6). Their biographer of the 1920s, Mary Sturgeon, called the "neglect" of Field's work that had begun in the 1890s a "boycott" and speculated that it resulted partly from revelation of their "true sex," partly from "something in the fact of a collaboration" seeming "obscurely repellent" (*Michael Field* 29). Greatness in art, which has long been largely contingent on single, identifiable authorship, carries inconsistent but all the more powerful associations both with innate, semidivine genius and with a democratic ideal of noble, free individualism: Although collaboration persisted in the nineteenth and twentieth centuries, despite an increasingly entrenched mythology of solitary authorship, and became more common at the turn of the century, these collaborations rarely have been acclaimed and rarely have earned both partners equal honor. Still more rarely has a collaboration operated as enduringly, as pervasively, or, ultimately, as openly in its authors' lives and careers as did that of Field.[12] Field's collaboration and the very idea of collaboration, as Leighton puts it, must "have threatened some notional sanctity of authorship" (*Writing against the Heart* 203).

Field wished to protect their access not simply to authorship, but to single authorship. Even when their duality was known, they insisted on their essential oneness; as I have previously noted, even when only one of them wrote a work, it was published under their singular writer's name. To Havelock Ellis, who had become curious about their relationship, they asserted righteously, "As to our work, let no man think he can put asunder what God has joined" (Sturgeon 47). Similarly, they repelled Browning's efforts to divide up their contributions: "Spinoza with his fine grasp of unity says: 'If two individuals of exactly the same nature are joined together, they make up a single individual, doubly stronger than each alone,' i.e., Edith and I make a *veritable Michael.* And we humbly fear you are destroying this philosophic truth" (*Works and Days* 6). Bradley subsequently closed off discussion of their collaboration altogether: "I do not care to speak to you again of our relations to our work" (7). They insisted on the "sanctity" of their single authorship, and they wrote their lyrics in the conventional manner, as one person with one voice. Field thus adopted conventions of a single persona and single female object that hemmed in what they could say and even how they would be read. "A Girl," for example, pictures a reciprocity of subjects but not an inseparable interaction between two authors; instead it depicts the separate actions of one author at a time. This poem does allow, as I argue in the Introduction, a simultaneity of different interpretations of the relations between the speaker and "girl." Yet even Wayne Koestenbaum, who takes seriously the possibility of coauthorship of this poem, also says, "The speaker leaves the page half-empty so her lover can complete it" (174). If the speaker does this, then the contributions to such a poem are indeed divisible, and the poem is a product of one rather than of two authors.

The Fields adapted themselves to conventions they seemed to defy. Their impassioned insistence on their oneness suggests that a great deal was at stake—that they not only sought a shield against criticism, but had internalized a sense of the dangers of both divided and multiple authorship. Their insistence is echoed by that of literary collaborators in our own time: Partners in successful collaborations often describe their contributions as ultimately inseparable, merging in complex ways at every stage of composition, so that handwriting itself becomes an unreliable indicator of authorship. So one could readily argue that Field simply reflects, and reflects on, the nature of collaboration. On the other hand, their insistence—and the insistence of their counterparts in the 1980s and 1990s—betrays their intimate knowledge of multiplicity, their acute awareness of its dangers not merely to their reception by readers but also to the accomplishment of a final, finished work.

Field conveys a profound awareness of the push and pull of collaboration. After remarking on their indivisibility, they went on to offer Ellis first an instance of a work (*The Father's Tragedy*) that was almost entirely Cooper's and then a description of their composition process when more fully collaborative: "The work is perfect mosaic: we cross and interlace like a company of dancing summer flies; if one begins a character, his companion seizes and possesses it; if one conceives a scene or situation, the other corrects, completes, or murderously cuts away" (Sturgeon 47). This more detailed description suggests a plurality of ways of interacting, which add up to something more than two. The passage expresses a radically free play like that of their multiple nicknames. But they describe their relationship also as containing its own powers of destruction. Yes, they "dance" together, but each also "seizes and possesses" the work of the other (like a constable? an angry landowner? a rapist?) and at times one of them "murders" what the other has "conceived." Collaboration was indeed treacherous, and not only to a social shibboleth. Collaborators are a species endangered by themselves.

Collaborative authorship has suffered from the skepticism of modern readers and scholars, who equate literary expression with single authorship, who are all too likely to equate collaboration with authorship's opposite—nonauthorship—and who thus try to separate the contributions of one author from another even when collaboration is undeniable. So it should be no surprise to see collaborating authors vacillate in insisting on the plurality of their writing and insisting on their oneness. But this oscillation between extremes affects not only perceptions of Field's collaboration, but also reception of their cohabitation and, in the process, has closed down their "plural" options no less effectively.

In Sturgeon's and their own comments, a source of threat more dangerous than that of collaboration lurked in, and to, the success of their relationship. In calling their collaboration "obscurely repellent" to the public (29), Sturgeon uses a vocabulary that one would not expect in connection with the abstract idea of coauthorship; it suggests rather the public response to the "obscure" possibility of a sexual relationship, a possibility that in other parts of her biography Sturgeon carefully (but, to contemporary eyes, ineffectively) guards Field against. The Fields themselves were bolder than this when they spoke of their collaboration in their private diaries in the phraseology of Christian marriage: "Let no man think he can put asunder what God has joined." Nor was this an accidental or isolated reference. Field repeatedly linked their personal to their authorial relationship rather than hiding one behind the other. Thus they compared themselves favorably to the Brownings: "Those two poets, man and wife, wrote alone; each wrote, but did not bless or quicken one another at their work; *we are closer married*" (*Works and Days* 16; emphasis in original). And an oft-cited published poem declares, "My Love and I took hands and swore, / Against the world, to be / Poets and lovers evermore."[13]

Here is the daring "openness" that so impresses Leighton, as if they needed no disguise from themselves, their friends, or, eventually, the public. But not all critics have been sure of how the Fields expected remarks like these to be read. Sturgeon may strike some of us as disingenuously protective of the Fields in her biography, but an influential contemporary feminist has also seen their relationship as probably nongenital. In a short section of *Surpassing the Love of Men*, Lillian Faderman writes, "They were generally so completely without self-consciousness in their public declarations of mutual love, that from a twentieth-century perspective it is hard to believe that their love was not—as a Victorian would phrase it—innocent. . . . If they saw something unorthodox about their relationship, they would have been more reticent in their poems to each other."[14] These comments provoked sharp debate from Chris White, who sees in Faderman's hesitation a more general error of "desexualizing" female friendship in the effort to obtain acceptance for a too-tame model of "romantic friendship" in Faderman's particular brand of lesbian feminism ("'Poets and Lovers'" 204). White argues that Field had in Greek literature a large vocabulary available for the expression of sexual experience and made ample use of it. But White overstates her case against Faderman, who details painstakingly the sensuality of Field's language and the frankness of their avowals of love to each other. At the same time, Faderman notes the "vagueness" of their treatment of physical manifestations of lesbianism—especially of Sappho, the speaking subject of their important book *Long Ago* (1889; Field's second book of poems)—and she attributes this to the fact that their love would not have been as "clearcut as we would see it today. While Sappho's feeling for Phaon is patently erotic, just as it is in Ovid's poem, her love for women is almost impossible to define given our twentieth-century choices. It is sometimes sensual, but the sensuality is usually mixed with strong maternal emotions."[15] "Lesbianism" was only beginning to be named (and diagnosed) in the 1890s, and so, in Faderman's argument, the possibility of a genitalized relationship may have been submerged within the more open ground of Field's female companionship.

Pitted between the extremes (in our day, obsessively polarized extremes) between sexual love and asexual friendship, however, the terms
of this debate override other important facts about the Fields.[16] The Fad-
erman-White debate represents an important, politically and conceptually strategic moment in an ongoing contemporary struggle over definition
of the lesbian, which should not be minimized. But in dealing here with
the specific case of Field, my object is to extend the discussion beyond yet
another dualistic framework that, in effect, squeezes out the more diverse,
less easily categorized, and contradictory character both of Field's representations and of their enactments of women's relationships. On the one
hand, in hinting at sexual relationships between Sappho's Lesbians and between themselves, Field challenged religious and social taboos against
sexual relations between women (for that matter, against incest, although
it is unlikely that this occurred to them). On the other hand, in Sappho's
desire to conserve the maidens' chastity (also conveyed in *Long Ago*), Field
invoked ancient traditions of "true" marriage—marriages that would be
chaste—and of communities of virginal women. (This last fact—Field's
repeated admiration for "virginal" women's communities—has led White
more recently to modify her position; she now argues that Field is not
necessarily representing a "same-sex sexual relationship" but rather is
"Tiresian": female in experience and sensibility, male in authoritative
name.)[17] Bradley and Cooper's relationship is striking, moreover, for the
many kinds of female-female relationship it bridged in the course of their
lives. Perhaps one of the most obvious risks that they faced (as obvious as
that of their status as women writers or as coauthors) was exposure of
Michael Field as a spinster aunt-and-niece duo. Nothing could have seemed
more quaint or amusingly eccentric than this or less like the single male
author. They risked becoming merely a mild joke in the literary world.

Katherine resided with her mother mostly in the Cooper household
after 1860; Mrs. Cooper was Katherine's older sister (eleven years her senior) and had taken part in raising Katherine. Katherine inherited this role
of older sister-mother (as well as aunt) at the age of fifteen, when Edith
was born in 1862. Edith's mother fell ill after the birth of her second daughter, Amy—probably when Edith was three years old and Katherine eighteen—and Mrs. Cooper became a lifelong invalid; Katherine helped replace
her, accepting Edith as a daughter.[18] Whatever else Katherine and Edith
felt for each other, it included the cross-generational passions and tensions
of parent and child, teacher and student. Thus, in *Underneath the Bough*
(their third cosigned book of poems, 1893), the opening poem to "The
Third Book of Songs" (a section described by Sturgeon [74] as an autobio-

graphical sequence of love lyrics; see also Donoghue 78), presents a new genesis myth that pivots on generational difference. Here is a long excerpt from this mythic genealogy:

When high Zeus first peopled earth,
        As sages say,
All were children of one birth,
Helpless nurselings. Doves and bees
Tended their soft infancies:
Hand to hand they tossed the ball,
And none smiled to see the play,
        Nor stood aside
        In pride
And pleasure of their youthful day.
        All waxed gray,
Mourning in companies the winter dearth
. . .
Zeus at the confusion smiled,
        And said, "From hence
Man by change must be beguiled;
Age with royalties of death,
Childhood, sweeter than its breath,
Will be won, if we provide
Generation's difference."
        Wisely he planned;
        The tiny hand,
In eld's weak palm found providence,
        And each through influence
Of things beholden and not borne grew mild
. . .
Dear, is not the story's truth
        Most manifest?
Had our lives been twinned, forsooth,
We had never had one heart:
By time set a space apart,
We are bound by such close ties
None can tell of either breast
        The native sigh
        Who try
To learn with whom the Muse is guest. (65–66)

True to Field's contradictions, this poem (disregarded thus far in the criticism) conveys the inseparability of the two women's voices—of their "native sigh[s]"—even as it takes the position of Bradley rather than of Cooper, so that it concludes,

> To see and smell the rose of my own youth
> In thee: how pleasant lies
> My life, at rest
> From dream, its hope expressed
> Before mine eyes. (67)

Between themselves, and in the privacy of their own home, nearly everything must have seemed possible. But it was not until Cooper was thirty-six that they lived alone together; even after their mothers had died, they lived with the Coopers, moving away only after James Cooper's death and Amy's marriage. As Edith Cooper aged, Bradley and she rapidly became more like cousins or sisters than aunt and niece or mother and daughter. When Cooper was old enough to matriculate, the two enrolled in University College together as fellow students. They had probably become even more than peers by this time, spending most of their time together, including their nights in one bed. While attending college they also became fellow suffragists and partners in the antivivisectionist movement. They were always fond of their dogs, but later, after setting up house together, they became especially devoted to Whym Chow, for whom they felt nearly as passionately as for each other.

But while several familial relationships were available to the Fields, these were surely productive of complex kinds of friction. As open as they were about their mutual love, they were as markedly discreet about possible inequalities or irritating differences dividing them.[19] And although they had other passions for men and sensual encounters with women, they managed to hedge all this within the walls of a firmly monogamous "marriage," living an increasingly structured domestic life together. When Browning objected to what seemed to him their defiance of "social conventions," Bradley quickly sought to reassure him that while they desired not to be "stifled" (or rendered speechless) by social expectations, they had no desire to challenge the "customs" and "beliefs" of men (*Works and Days* 7–8). Perhaps they were only placating Browning when they said this, but they did so successfully. In this context, their marriage may seem less open or defiant than safe, keeping them from external notice, from intrusions and complicating interactions with others, and even from the ambiguities of their relations to each other. To raise their relationship as an ideal or model of lesbian relationship is not to advocate asexual romance, but to advocate single, domestic partnership. Theirs was not a life of outward social activism; despite their college feminism, for the most part they enclosed their personally lived differences in a world of their own among relatives or close friends and in their masked poetry.

But they sought, above all, an identity as a poet. Though not directed toward reform of particular social institutions (as was the verse of
Elizabeth Barrett Browning or Augusta Webster), verse was nonetheless
their outward field of social action and the woman of letters their public hero. If there is an identity theme to be traced in their writing, that
theme most persistently and explicitly is the name of poet and tragedi-
an; their quest was the aesthete's self-conscious quest for literary fame.
That they succeeded at all—given the precarious business I have just
detailed of aunt-and-niece coauthors masquerading as a single male—is
no mean feat. Yet the name of poet proved fragile, the quest for poetic
fame elusive, and the business of investing themselves in verse had
countervailing effects. Even as it rewarded them with continuous publication—with speech—it exposed them to a vast, fickle, and conventional literary marketplace in which they quickly found themselves at
a competitive disadvantage. If it had not been for their financial independence, as their fathers' inheritors, they could not have continued as
long as they did. But to survive through their fathers' bequests was not
to achieve financial independence, a secure establishment, or poetic
license in the literary world.

Their frequent reliance on historical precursors offered protection
from the identity politics of the turn-of-the-century literary world, but
it also served to submerge them further in obscurity. They pursued their
quest to be poets by imaging not only pagan immortals—undying gods
such as Aphrodite and Apollo or prophets such as Tiresias and the Sibyl—
as the muses of their art, but poets themselves, above all Sappho, as in-
spirational precursors. Rather than imagine or create a new heroine (like
the Princess of Tennyson's poem or Aurora Leigh), they disinterred an
old one. Unlike the Rossettis in their ambitious lyric sequences *The
House of Life* and *Monna Innominata*, Field set themselves and their
own histories aside in order to discover their poetic ambitions in the
blurred mirror of history, legend, and mythology. Rather than claiming
the unencumbered "originality" in which solitary authors so often want
a stake, they repeatedly cited their sources and, in *Long Ago*, presented
their poems as "translations" of the Greek.[20] We have come to think of
this habit of writing of the past and (in cases like Browning's *The Ring
and the Book*) *through* documents from the past rather than the present
as a primary characteristic of Victorian poets. Field is not distinctive in
this regard, yet their choices are telling: Sappho as the subject and speaking voice of an extended poetic sequence had been left alone by others,
even though, as White indicates, "the plurality of depictions and appro-

priations of Sappho indicate the extent to which Sappho [had become] a cultural battleground" ("'Poets and Lovers'" 199). Field thus found a point of entry in Sapphism, but they then faced the prospect of being silenced within it. Twentieth-century writers and critics all too easily buried and eventually forgot these Victorian eulogies to an ancient woman poet. *Long Ago* entered into a history of Sapphism, an unnoticed item in an arcane archive.

This positioning—Field's quiet habitation of library shelves—does allow for recovery. But as feminist historians, we too delude ourselves if we assume that we have only to retrieve a poet for her to be heard or that we have escaped Field's contradictions. The risky, self-compromising, though occasionally thrilling struggle for identity (for name and fame); the still undecided battle with the Romantic myth of single, canonized (male) authorship; the persistent modern compulsion to define an ideal model for relationship amid a bewildering array of conflicting alternatives; the constant public rewriting of history with its very personal consequences, at once productively reconstructive and worrisomely forgetful—all these are problems posed by and, in various ways, faced and negotiated but left unresolved by Field. In seeking to connect politics with literary study of poets such as Field, feminist scholars try to find resonances of their own protest and their own chosen alternatives, to delineate an alternative, ongoing history of feminism. As many critics have shown, however, that history is pocked by holes, rifted by cracks that make the past unlike the present in ultimately unfathomable ways. Even where the echoes are strongest, they carry with them a warning: To speak against social custom is not to speak out forever or ever to obtain understanding—it is not even to be heard in the same way by different people. The parallel I am drawing at this moment between Field's archival creativity and that of the contemporary feminist scholar is problematic, a symptom of my own desire to see myself reflected in the mirroring past.

Equally vexing consequences for a coherent feminist literary scholarship can result, however, when a feminist scholar seeks to honor the complexities of the past, not only in its suspected differences from the present, but in its own contradictoriness. These specificities, these differences (of historical context, of textual details, of literary production), and these contradictions threaten to engulf the scholar in an ideological impasse—not an echo of her desire, but an acknowledgment of her desire's defeat. If acknowledged, such contradictions may, as some theorists believe, produce their own unsettling effect, their own erosive deconstruction of impacted ideologies. As Eve Sedgwick suggests, however, they may merely confront us with an insoluble knot in which we are entrapped, which may be manipulated:

> It is at least premature when Roland Barthes prophesies that "once the paradigm is blurred, utopia begins: meaning and sex become the objects of free play, at the heart of which the (polysemant) forms and the (sensual) practices, liberated from the binary prison, will achieve a state of infinite expansion." To the contrary, a deconstructive understanding of these binarisms makes it possible to identify them as sites that are *peculiarly* densely charged with lasting potentials for powerful manipulation—through precisely the mechanisms of self-contradictory definition or, more succinctly, the double bind. Nor is a deconstructive analysis of such definitional knots, however necessary, at all sufficient to disable them. Quite the opposite: I would suggest that an understanding of their irresolvable instability has been continually available, and has continually lent discursive authority, to antigay as well as to gay cultural forces of this century.[21]

Success in redefining a definitional knot appears to depend almost entirely on the ability of writers such as Sedgwick to persuade others to see— and value—the "knot" in the way that she does: as a complex, deconstructive, yet politicized event in which the heterosexual and the homosexual (and many other associated opposites) are bound up in each other in currently violent but potentially less destructive ways.

In the only essay thus far to treat Field's drama extensively, David Moriarty briefly cites the play *Canute the Great* (1887) for what in Field's drama is an unusual "theme of lesbian love"; this play is "most notable for a rather explicit love scene between two women, which forms the core of the drama."[22] Beyond a cursory plot summary in an endnote, he says no more than this and thus does not explain why he sees act 3, scene 3 as the lesbian "core" of this four-act play; it is not central to the storyline of Canute, and it is a rare reader who would have noticed anything lesbian in it. Moriarty's observation nonetheless offers an unexpected glimpse of the rewards, not only the problems, that may emerge through feminist restorations.

In this scene, a woman named Edith has been driven mad by her husband's use of their young son to murder her brother, Edmund, King of England, and by her son and husband's subsequent deaths. Edith is about to kill herself when she is interrupted by her brother's widow, Elgiva, who yearns only for revenge, but is touched by Edith's agony and

instead chooses to prevent her suicide. At the scene's end, Elgiva cradles
Edith at her breast and says,

> You shall be
> My care, my child, my blessing. We will live
> Thus hand-in-hand, for we are sisters, both
> Beloved of Edmund

and Edith responds,

> I have never
> Known all this joy since I was three years old.
> I go back in your arms through many days
> Till I can find that I lay warm like this,
> Taking no thought, my blood just like a prayer
> They chant to measured harmonies.[23]

Is this regressed three-year-old Edith the "woman-child" (as Elgiva calls
her in the last line of the act) of a past Edith Cooper, whom eighteen-year-
old Katherine Bradley cherished (although, in the year of this play's publication, 1887, Katherine was forty-one and Edith twenty-five)? Perhaps,
although the relations of character to character, of character to author,
of text to reader, and of the text to itself are nothing if not complex.

In the preface to the play (although Moriarty takes no note of it) Field
could indeed be read as encouraging a late twentieth-century reader to find
the Fields in their play, for they write there of parallels between the setting of *Canute the Great* and their experiences of friendship; there is a
"peculiar pleasure in visiting a district of one's native land that has retained
the idiosyncrasies of a province. It is like coming across an unexpected
phase in the character of a familiar friend" (3). This "unexpected phase"
in the countryside of Norfolk—which inspired the writing of *Canute the
Great*—appears in the midst of "the humble landscape, with its clear-cut
outlines on the horizon, its large sky, its penetrating sunshine . . . [its]
absence of mystery and reserve." Field "discovers" here a "secret and se-
clusion of [the landscape's] own": As Field sailed "among the Broads" and
"moored close to the shrouding boundary of the reed-bed," they "seemed
to catch the very heave of the breast of silence." Then, just as suddenly,
from the midst of "one of the loneliest of these rush-girdled meres," Field
is reminded not of the humble, clear, open horizon or penetrating sun of
the surrounding Norfolk countryside, but of the "boom of the ocean"
breaking on the ear, for it is divided by only "a few sand-hills . . . from the
unprotected coast" (3–4). In this uncanny encounter with the unexpected in a familiar friend, what is unexpected? Is it the open landscape of

Norfolk itself with its penetrating sun (an unanticipated "district of one's native land," England), is it Norfolk's own "secret" and secluded "reed-bed" with its heaving "breast," or is it the "boom of the ocean" from which the reed-bed is not, after all, entirely secluded? It is surely each of these things in turn: The unguarded Norfolk is unexpected, but so too is the hidden reed-bed, which in its turn is divided by practically nothing at all from the "unprotected coast." The familiar is made uncanny by strangeness, the strange made familiar by danger. A shrouding (both dangerous and protective) "reed-bed" reappears only once in the play, in act 3, scene 3: in the orchard of a nunnery where Edith has been protectively garbed as a penitent, where she means to drown herself in a mere, where Elgiva guards her from suicide, and where the two women embrace each other for the sake of their own and each other's survival.

Field's landscape curiously anticipates Diana Fuss's description of sexual identity in her theoretical introduction to *Inside/Out: Lesbian Theories, Gay Theories* (which, like Sedgwick's discussion, also invokes the imagery of the knot). The knot of the Norfolk landscape, with the odd interchangeability of its open "outside" and hidden "inside" (the character of a familiar friend who is suddenly unfamiliar), acts much like Fuss's knot: "visualiz[ing] for us, in the very simplicity of its openings and closures, its overs and unders, its ins and outs, the contortions and convolutions of any sexual identity formation."[24] So too, I would suggest, the feminist historian may indeed "discover" or recover the familiar face of a friend in an unexpected place, the buried past, but she will inevitably become herself one end of a still more complex knot, in which it is impossible to separate in any absolute way what is inside a historical moment and what is out, what is the same and what different, when we are daring to be different and when we are not, where the safety of an embrace may be found and where danger lies, where obscurity ends and openness begins. Yet for all their intractability, it remains at least possible for the feminist critic to unearth, remap, and rhetorically revalue such knots.

4 Uncanny Couplings: Anglo-Irish Big House Gothic in Somerville and Ross

THE TWO TURN-OF-THE-CENTURY couples in this study—
Michael Field and Somerville and Ross—were prolific contemporaries.
Katherine Bradley was born fifteen years before the other three women,
but Edith Cooper, Edith Somerville, and Martin Ross were all born between
1858 and 1862; Cooper and Ross share almost identical lifespans. Yet there
is no evidence that these couples ever read each other's work, that they
ever met, or that they would have been glad if they had. The two facts that
link them and have brought them together in previous studies (in Koestenbaum's *Double Talk* and Lillian Faderman's study of women's romantic friendships in *Surpassing the Love of Men*) are lifelong mutual devotion and lifelong literary collaboration. The vast differences between them,
however, suggest that for collaborative pairs of women writers, parallels
in lifestyle are few and far between. This fact will become increasingly
salient in the course of this book: Involved as these collaborative writers
are with comparable aesthetic projects, no single set of circumstances
appears more conducive than another to a career of coauthorship.

To the few facts from Bradley and Cooper's lives I have offered in
previous chapters, I now add more, in order to elaborate the contrasts with
E. Œ. Somerville and Martin Ross—the names under which Edith Somerville and Violet Martin wrote their works—and to set the stage for the
particular problems I explore in Somerville and Ross's work.[1] In posses-

sion of independent means inherited from their fathers, successful British merchants, Bradley (1846–1914) and Cooper (1862–1913) were able to travel to the continent and own their own house. They spent most of their lives quietly together and with their small family (Bradley's mother and older sister, Cooper's father and younger sister, and a few maids), eventually living alone together at Richmond, where their male friends Charles Ricketts and Charles Shannon (editors of *The Dial*) found them a place to live.[2] Especially in their later years in Richmond, theirs was a disciplined and formal life; although they often collaborated at every stage of composition, they also began their days by working solo, laboring from 9:00 A.M. to 1:00 P.M. without speaking to each other, in separate studies. They received guests for dinner in evening dress, entertaining their occasional visitors in an assiduously formal way. Writing nothing for the popular press, they aspired instead to produce literature in its highest traditional forms: lyrics, verse dramas, and one masque in elegant, limited editions. This writing was not tame; inspired by Greek drama and by Sappho, befriended by Pater and Browning, they wrote of Bacchic tragedy and bliss and portrayed themselves in their writing as oracular women, ravished by the Muse. But their three chief delights were domestic: their collection of aesthetic objects, their garden, and their dogs. Only the dogs had a disruptive effect on their normal routines or seemed out of place (and unseemly) to visitors.[3]

Field eventually became isolated from most of the outside world, and after college they took no part in politics. One of their dogs, Whym Chow, played the part of a child (or even third partner) in their lives, and Chow's death produced a major crisis, alienating them from many of their friends. Their grief also brought them into the Roman Catholic church. Both its ritual and discipline probably attracted Field, as they had attracted other aesthetes before them, but Bradley and Cooper were drawn, above all, by the belief that conversion would ensure their eternal partnership in the afterlife. Their deaths from cancer within nine months of each other consummated a life lived as if they shared a single self between them.

The bustling, heterogeneous clans in which Somerville and Ross lived differed sharply from the tiny nuclear family of Field and Whym Chow. Somerville and Ross grew up enveloped in large families and conducted much of their collaboration amid the hectic daily life of the Somerville estate of Drishane. They were second cousins (great-granddaughters of the Lord Chief Justice of Ireland at the time of the Union, Charles Kendal Bushe [1767–1843]), and they were only four years apart in age. They probably experienced greater parity than did Bradley and Cooper, but there was also greater distance between them because they did not meet until they were grown women in their twenties. Moreover, Somerville and Ross fit their writing into crowded schedules—writing on the run—among numerous responsibilities in estate management, bookkeeping, gardening, housekeeping, maintaining vigorous social schedules (including occasions when they danced into the night), hunting, and riding. They loved dogs, too; they were surrounded by packs of dogs, as well as cats, horses, and cows.

Like Bradley and Cooper, Somerville (1858–1949) and Ross (1862–1915) delighted in each other's company from the time they met in 1886.[4] Somerville called her partner Martin (much as Bradley and Cooper called each other Michael and Field): "Perhaps I ought to begin by saying that I have always called her 'Martin'; I propose to do so still. I cannot think of her by any other name. To her own family, and to certain of her friends, she is Violet; to many others she is best known as Martin Ross. But I shall write of her as I think of her" (*Irish Memories* 1). Somerville then proceeds in this memoir to write a sensual eulogy of Martin: "A colour like a wild rose—a simile that should be revered on account of its long service to mankind, and must be forgiven since none other meets the case—and a figure of the lightest and slightest" (121). But romantic though Somerville's description is of their sudden attachment to each other in the 1880s, they never publicly called themselves "poets and lovers" (*Underneath the Bough* 79).

They avowed an intense, lifelong love: In Somerville's words after Ross's death, "For most boys and girls the varying, yet invariable, flirtations, and emotional episodes of youth, are resolved and composed by marriage. To Martin and to me was opened another way, and the flowering of both our lives was when we met each other" (*Irish Memories* 125). But their self-representations are particularly obscure on this question of the "flowering" of their lives. Somerville was reportedly "reticent and reserved about all physical contacts," and she was inclined to "change the subject" after tersely asserting a view against "sexual immorality."[5] "Controversy," she writes in *Irish Memories*, "and especially controversy of this complexion"—that is, on the subject of women's friendships—"is a bore" (326). As a result, a fierce dispute has flowered among Somerville and Ross's biographers and critics.

Somerville and Ross's apologists are often unpersuasive in their insistence on these collaborators' chastity. Prone to special pleading and eager to assure readers that "while their love and respect for each other could hardly have been greater, it never transgressed the bounds set by Christianity," Hilary Robinson goes on to claim that they "hardly knew" that "sexual liberation" and the "lesbianism advocated by so many of [their] social equals in London . . . existed."[6] Robinson repeats the gesture of numerous previous biographers (without any indication of her sources) when she cites as evidence for sexual abstinence an incident in which, after Ross's death, Somerville was "shocked and horrified" by the outspokenly bisexual Dame Ethel Smyth's invitation to a physical relationship (Robinson 19). But we do not know what Somerville said or wrote to Smyth; we have only Somerville's nephew's word for it because her replies to Smyth's letters are lost.[7] It is as likely as not that Somerville and Ross abstained from sexual intercourse, whether on principle or unconsciously. The ongoing dispute among scholars about their relationship is thus a register of the changing definitions and seesawing climates of acceptance of lesbianism in this century.[8]

It is precisely the attitude of "shock" and "horror" that I find notable in Somerville and Ross's early novels and to which I return later. The public lives Somerville and Ross led made it difficult to obtain privacy of any kind (including, of course, that required for writing), and the kinds of families to which they belonged were fertile ground for suppression of both family secrets and latent desires. Their novels repeatedly uncover scandal and often cover it over again. Sexual desire between women could well have counted among the more deeply concealed of such secrets—a secret they kept even from themselves and thus found uncannily horrific when disclosed by Ethel Smyth.

Somerville and Ross were as embedded in social contradictions as Field, if not more so.[9] They were public activists, Somerville in particular speaking her mind far more freely than Field about national and gender politics in Ireland and politely defying their families' initial discouragement of their work as writers. To write at home was in itself a quiet act of rebellion. But they were by no means political or sexual radicals. Deeply engaged in the politics of turn-of-the-century Anglo-Ireland, they (Somerville especially) sympathized with—and knew intimately—what concerned the Irish lower classes, but they were proud members of the Irish gentry, with family trees that stretched far back through Anglo-Irish gentry and aristocracy. Yet they were keenly aware of the economics of the modern bourgeoisie and more negatively affected by social changes attendant on its dominance than were, obviously, the merchant-class Bradley and Cooper. Making money became for them not only an embarrassing imperative of their social circles, but one of their most compelling motives for writing, repeatedly dictating what they wrote—the short stories, travel sketches, short novels with which they supplemented their incomes. Indeed, critics often call them "Somerville & Ross," as if, in keeping with metaphors Somerville sometimes used, they constituted a two-person company, a commercial as well as literary partnership (Robinson 3). They began by writing novels, but they rarely had time and energy enough for anything more than short stories, travel literature, and journalism, for which they received more encouragement from publishers, and the economic motive became a recurrent theme of their fiction. Even so, while working entirely within the range of popular forms, they aspired in their novels and stories to great art.

Their writing differs from Field's in being often boldly realistic, but although this social realism insists on an openness about Irish social and family problems that worried their own families, it does not court transgressive alternatives such as those one glimpses in Field's writing. They wrote comic stories about Anglo-Irish life in the country, focused on both the denizens of the Big Houses and the rural folk, and intended to capture the dialects of all walks of life. Romance rarely touches these stories; they are sharp satiric portrayals of the interactions between the different classes and, to a lesser extent, the sexes in Anglo-Irish society. This meant that although their collaboration with each other was successful, they devoted themselves to portraying failed relationships. Though antiromantic, the skeptical realism of their work is allied to an implicit mourning for the Ascendancy and a nostalgic critique of its decadence.[10]

In their writing, Somerville and Ross seem skeptical about dogma of all kinds, but unlike the late-converting Field (who earlier had been first Anglicans, then atheists, then self-nominated Pagans), they were conscientious Protestants throughout their lives. Far more interesting than this religious difference, however, are the different kinds of mysticism that shaped these two couples' lives and deaths. Like many others of their time, Somerville and Ross and their families practiced spiritualism. If Bradley and Cooper believed that they would be reunited after death in a Roman Catholic heaven, Somerville was certain when Ross died that Ross's spirit had survived death and remained still with her. Death did not prevent them, Somerville claimed, from collaborating after Ross's death. From then on Somerville saw most of her work as the product of a kind of automatic writing. Nearly all their works, from 1886 until Somerville's death in 1949, bear both their signatures. Spiritualist belief hovers behind and in their texts from the start of their careers, and the faint mysticism in even their most realistic narratives opens up a space (a loophole) for other potentialities, other border crossings, other desires.

Like my chapter on Field, this chapter could readily be devoted to the contradictions in Somerville and Ross's most public gestures. But these are sufficiently obvious even from the brief biographical sketch I have already given. In turning to Somerville and Ross, I wish instead to shift the focus from the problematic of contradiction to the "horror" of boundary confusion—in particular the unstable, frangible borders marked by gender, kinship structure, class, sexuality, and ontological belief. Contradiction itself may be reconceived as two sides of a socially constructed border (or loop or knot). In Somerville and Ross's novels, the carefully observed divisions between genders, classes, lines of kinship, and so forth often are marked by closely held secrets where these boundaries have been (or may have been) crossed and by uncanny "others" and "doubles" who threaten or embody boundary confusion. By looking closely at two of their novels—their first novel, *An Irish Cousin* (1889), and their most highly regarded novel, *The Real Charlotte* (1894)[11]—as representations of impassable but often blurred borders, a reader may occasionally infer the difference it might have made for these borders to be conceived as passable. This does not mean that I see Somerville and Ross's fiction as yielding more hope for social relations than Field's, however. Somerville and Ross's vision was consistently ironic and often pessimistic. They collaborated fruitfully as authors, but the tales they told concern comic limitations in their short stories and scandalous relationships that result in familial tragedy in their novels. Nonetheless, as I suggest at the end of this chapter, their sense of impossibility indicates contrary possibilities, which, as I show in the following chapters, manifested themselves in the writings of subsequent pairs of coauthors, particularly Peter Redgrove and Penelope Shuttle and Daphne Marlatt and Betsy Warland. As a wedge for this discussion, I focus on the boundary between cousin and lover because cousinship is the primary familial relationship that existed between Somerville and Ross and because this particular boundary was crucial to the writing of their first novel together.

Somerville and Ross have been called "the Irish cousins," and they gave their first novel the title *An Irish Cousin*, but no critic has confused their cousinship with that of their first novel. Why would one identify the solid, public women writers with the Irish cousins of this novel, a romantic heterosexual couple?[12] Still more important in occluding any parallelism is the melodrama in which the protagonists find themselves: a male heir's unrequited passion for his female cousin, the secret shame they unknowingly share of their fathers' divisive, Cain-and-Abel history, and the mystery of Mad Moll that unravels around them. (As far as we know, no madwomen inhabited Somerville or Ross's attics.) Nonetheless, I intend in this chapter to make just this mistake of confusing Somerville and Ross with their fictional cousins, nicknamed Theo and Willy.[13] (Theo, short for Theodora, and Willy both appear to be named after their paternal grandfather, Theodore William Sarsfield.) The novel itself vexes multiple boundaries—between male and female, lover and kin (in this case cousin), upper class and lower, experience (especially sexual experience) and innocence, the economic motive and other kinds of motives (of love, family, inherited title, or greatness in art), natural and supernatural. All of these are structuring distinctions biographers have used in their accounts of the collaboration of Somerville and Ross, but the characters in their fiction find these distinctions difficult to maintain.

One previous critic's account of this novel begins at its end, treating *An Irish Cousin* simply as a thriller whose interest is in the outcome, where "some of the sins" of the narrative are uncloseted but remain "so secret" that "the reader is never quite sure of the truth" (Robinson 57).[14] To the extent that these secrets are revealed and are the final "meaning" or essential story of this novel, they become so only in its last pages and remain partially cloaked.[15] The cloaking and uncloaking that occurs in this conclusion is crucial not for the dramatic closure it gives to a well-made plot (a task this novel does not perform as tidily as it might), but for its function as an exciting threshold, momentarily treading the "thrilling" borders merely hinted at thus far in its narrative.

What becomes clear at the end, as Robinson explains, is that years ago, with the help of his female servant, Mad Moll, Theo's Uncle Dominick Sarsfield (Willy's father) plotted successfully to seize his elder brother's (Theo's father's) inherited estate by murdering him. This is the Big House, Durrus, where Dominick lives with Willy and which Theo is visiting after having been brought up by an aunt in Canada. What is less clear is the "true" identity and ancestry of Mad Moll, a housekeeper who is unable to speak (possessed by a "dumb madness")[16] but who, before her madness, claimed descent from the Sarsfield family as the illegitimate child of one of Dominick's uncles, a claim that Dominick's father honored by allowing her to live in the house. Moll, then, would be Dominick's cousin. Now married to a tenant on the estate, Michael Brian, Moll still goes by the name Moll Hourihane. Although Theo is told early in the novel that women in Ireland generally keep their last names after marriage, we do not encounter another married woman who does so. Moll Hourihane thus becomes a subtle sign of gender crossing[17] as well as of class-crossing, Anglo-Irish decadence.

Moll is hinted to have been Dominick's mistress, abandoned when he married but restored to the household upon the death of Dominick's wife. As housekeeper and nurse, she is a kind of foster mother to Willy, although the reader never sees her in a maternal role. Moll's madness began at the time of Theodore Sarsfield's death, when she married Michael Brian, and her senses were entirely gone a year or so later when she gave birth herself. Given Moll's closeness to Dominick and her reported desire to be more than a servant ("'twasn't thrusting to being a servant at all she was!" [210–11]), Moll's child—a girl named Anstice, or Anstey, Brian—could be Dominick's illegitimate offspring, although this too is left unclear.[18] Dominick often expresses what to Theo seems a surprisingly "violent" distaste (103) for "people in that class of life" who "presume" when "taken out of their proper place" (24). Anstey Brian, a servant in the Big House, has fallen in love with Willy, and before he met Theo, he obviously sought her interest in him. Willy insists that he has not taken Anstey Brian to bed, but he marries her at the end, so if Moll's claim to family membership is to be believed, this is the second generation, at least, of intrafamilial marriage.

As I suggested at the outset, this involved plot is fully revealed only toward the end; it informs the narrative (particularly in retrospect) and intermittently rises to its surface: Moll's relationship to Dominick and their conspiracy to murder is the story's "shocking" mystery,[19] hinted at as the narrative proceeds and half-revealed at the end. Moll's uncanny sudden appearances in particular gesture toward this mystery, and her ghostly behavior thus adds a hint of the supernatural to the narrative. But the plot in which Theo, like the reader, is most overtly involved is a conventional romance story in which Theo learns to love a stiff, austere upper-class Oxford-educated man and must choose between him and the more vital, conversational, and countrified, though less dignified and educated Willy. The reader (but not Theo) quickly becomes aware of Willy's prior liaison with Anstey. These aspects of the novel develop as if in conscientious ignorance of the novel's gothic subplot.

Yet, in a curious twist of the romance plot, Theo must outwit not a female rival, but Willy himself, in order to capture Nugent O'Neill's attention. The narrative thwarts any expectations its romantic intrigue raises for the success of the more interesting and passionate Willy, who, though continually represented as lacking in etiquette and education and unusually at ease with country folk and slovenly environments, is of the same class as Theo. As Powell comments, "These surroundings are symbolical of Willie's handicaps, but the story comes to life whenever he is present. Even Theo is always more interested in him than in the blameless Nugent, who lacks any characteristic beyond an unattractive tendency to make fun of his neighbours' primitive habits."[20] Once we become aware of the family history at Durrus, the involved illegitimacies both of property and birth, and the cross-class coupling of cousins, however, this primary plot becomes secondary and must be read as a story of Theo's moral triumph in avoiding, even without clear knowledge of her danger, the tainted ancestry and inheritance that her cousin offers. Theo's cautious, rational manner sets the tone for much of the narrative of *An Irish Cousin*, vying with the violent, irrational gothic. Romance in this narrative, as in much of Somerville and Ross's work, is a potentially dangerous liaison covertly linked to the horror of collapsed social boundaries.

But despite her ingenuous virtue throughout the novel, the subplot does implicate Theo. Because Willy loves Theo, a lineage of illegitimacy has been complicated by triangulation not with a foreign element, but vaguely incestuously with another family member, Theo herself.[21] Theo's arrival intervenes at first between Willy and Anstey, but she also potentially extends the chain of intrafamilial marriage. Later, after arousing Willy's jealousy, she seeks a reconciliation, and she comments, "I went to bed feeling that I had more than regained the position I had held in Willy's esteem, and a little flurried by the difficulties of so ambiguous a relationship as that of first cousins" (91). We are given many more opportunities to imagine Theo as Willy's wife than to imagine her as Nugent's, and everyone except the Brians on the estate of Durrus clearly hopes for their union. Theo eventually offers to marry Willy, even after learning of his relations with Anstey, although she offers not out of love but out of the desire to rescue him from the despair caused by her rejection of him.[22] Meanwhile, sure of her rejection, he has done what he considers the right thing and has married Anstey Brian against his uncle's wishes. The narrative invites our sympathy for Willy, and, beyond his close family relation to Theo and his rusticity, no compelling reason is offered for Theo's unresponsiveness to him before she learns of his father's deeds.[23]

Moreover, because endings of novels point toward the alternatives they do not play out as well as toward the option they choose, we are left imagining Theo's marriage to Willy even at the end. This particular novel does more than many others to remind us of that alternative. In two final paragraphs, which set the main story of the novel in a vaguely distant time and place, Nugent and Theo teasingly converse.

> "I believe you cared a great deal more for Willy than you did for me," Nugent said to me one evening when the hawthorn was in blossom, and the Clashmore woods were green.
> "I don't know why I didn't," I answered, "but somehow, I always liked you best." (306)

Nugent here invokes the rivalry with Willy that has occupied the romance plot, and Theo responds in kind: Nugent was always the one she "liked best" "somehow." The casual and sane manner of this bit of dialogue clashes with the reader's still vivid memories of the novel's scandalous passion and thus does as much to undermine as to reinforce the credibility of the romance between Nugent and Theo.

Nowhere is it suggested that Theo is another of Willy's half-sisters, and this possibility is implicitly discounted by Theo's and her dead father's apparent impeccability of character. But "sisterliness" describes the way Theo feels toward Willy when she is feeling fond of him. She claims a sibling's companionship, which she missed when young and is therefore all the more delighted to recapture as an adult. After Willy's announcement of his marriage to Anstey and of their planned emigration to Australia, she reflects on what she will lose in never seeing him again: "Willy, the trusty companion of many a day's careless pleasuring; who had taken me out schooling and ferreting, and had ransacked every hedge to cut for me superfluous members of the flattest of blackthorns, and the straightest of ash plants—Willy, with whom I used to gossip and wrangle and chaff in the easiest of intimacy; who had been, as he himself would have expressed it, the 'best play-boy' I had ever known" (286). In other words, she feels something not unlike what Violet Martin and Edith Somerville felt when they met in their twenties.

Early in the novel, a character comments on Theo's "great likeness" to Willy (8). Theo is perhaps as much like a brother as a sister to Willy. Most of the pursuits in which she engages with him are rough ones—the hunt, long walks in the muddy countryside, romps with dogs, ferreting—and she looks boyish, closely resembling her father, especially when she wears a riding cap (or Willy's own cap). Somerville and Ross engaged constantly in these and similar activities together. They inhabited a world—the hyphenated world of the Anglo-Irish and of country-estate living—in which women could cross those kinds of gender boundaries. Willy, for his part, has pronounced feminine qualities: Theo finds something "half amusing and half touching in the anxiety of his little housewifely attentions to me" (34), and she soon "discovered that Willy possessed in a high degree the feminine faculty of sitting over a fire and talking about nothing in particular" (43).

Sibling relationships go badly wrong in this novel, however; the deadly rivalry of unequal brothers becomes Theo's primary inheritance. The novel's climax occurs when Theo discovers her uncle in the woods, and, maddened by rage and despair at his son's elopement with Anstey, Dominick mistakes her for her father, Owen, returned from the dead. In terror at the apparition, he doubts, Macbeth-like, the success of his murder, then rushes off to his own death by drowning. With the boundary-breaking disclosure of Dominick's misalliance with Moll and treachery against his brother, the loss of Dominick's son and heir to Anstey, and the recognition of his brother's ghost in his niece, of the supernatural in the natural, *An Irish Cousin* reaches its catastrophic conclusion.

This novel's primary secrets—of familial inbreeding, cross-class relationship, a dissolute patriarchy,[24] and even fratricide—were not unimaginable occurrences in Anglo-Irish families. Cross-class romantic involvements by patriarchs or their heirs were matters of semipublic knowledge in Somerville and Ross's circles, and several of their novels directly address these, including *The Big House at Inver* (published after Ross's death). According to Somerville and Ross, however, a single event, rather than a general cultural pattern, lay behind not only *An Irish Cousin* but their collaborative efforts more generally. In analyzing Somerville and Ross's description of this episode—compared by one critic to Stephen Dedalus's "epiphany" on the beach in *A Portrait of the Artist as a Young Man*[25]—and its replication in the narrative of *An Irish Cousin,* I turn from discussion of the kinds of borders broken in *An Irish Cousin* to more direct consideration of the ways these authors linked the "horror" of collapsed borders to the specter of antithetical others, uncanny doubles, and unsuitable cousins.

Somerville's record in *Irish Memories* of the experience with which *An Irish Cousin* originated is reticent, yet it is also richly suggestive of the secrets disclosed and hinted at in the novel. Somerville and Ross's "epiphany"—what it was that made the story they were to tell suddenly "real"—was a vision of a mad person in an attic. As they said goodbye to an acquaintance whom they had been visiting in a decaying Big House and rode toward home, they looked back and saw in the house's upper window a "white face":

> The sunset was red in the west when our horses were brought round to the door, and it was at that precise moment that into *The Irish Cousin* some thrill of genuineness was breathed. In the darkened façade of the long grey house, a window, just over the hall-door, caught our attention. In it, for an instant, was a white face. Trails of ivy hung over the panes, but we saw the face glimmer there for an instant and vanish.
>
> As we rode home along the side of the hills, and watched the fires of the sunset sink into the sea, and met the crescent moon coming with faint light to lead us home, we could talk and think only of that pres-

ence at the window. We had been warned of certain subjects not to be approached, and we knew enough of the history of that old house to realise what we had seen. An old stock, isolated from the world at large, wearing itself out in those excesses that are a protest of human nature against unnatural conditions, dies at last with its victims round its death-bed. Half-acknowledged, half-witted, wholly horrifying; living ghosts, haunting the house that gave them but half their share of life, yet withheld from them with half-hearted guardianship, the boon of death. (*Irish Memories* 130–31)

Somerville and Ross had initially intended to write a "Shocker,"[26] a "Penny Dreadful," until this uncanny experience compelled them to cast off "the insincere ambition . . . [as] realities asserted themselves, and the faked 'thrills' that were to make our fortunes were repudiated for ever." Their intention shifted from a project "begun in idleness and without conviction" to their "first genuine literary impulse" (*Irish Memories* 131, 129). (At issue here also are the distinctions between popular and "genuine literary" writing, or writing "to make our fortunes" as opposed to writing out of "sincerity," "conviction," and without care for their "fortunes"—a set of distinctions that seems especially soft in relation to this first gothic-romance novel.)[27]

Virginia Beards and John Cronin correctly note that this vision offered Somerville and Ross an epiphanic "quotidian" detail (Beards xiii),[28] something particularized, an elucidating image that could operate as a Jamesian "slice of life." This accords with the general modernist, aestheticist notion of the epiphany. But this detail also gave them access to, in their own phrasing, "subjects not to be approached" (*Irish Memories* 130). For a detail to be recognized as intensely important or illuminating, it must have psychological resonance, a charged touch of psychic ambivalence and transformation. Dedalus's vision of a nearly naked girl is such a moment, but, though less artfully expressed, Somerville and Ross's epiphany is in some ways more interesting than a boy's revelation of female sexuality—more interesting because it beckons toward a more deeply hidden and complex subject. In addition, contrary to Somerville and Ross's suggestion, I argue that their epiphany retains the form of a "shocker" or a penny thriller as Joyce's does not, yet this adds to rather than diminishes its interest for a reader.

Joyce's epiphany extends permission to men to look at women as sexy and spiritual at the same time (presumably healing Joyce's Madonna/whore split), but it also reproduces the age-old situation of a man gazing at a woman and transforming her into an object for use in his art, and it has wound up being a classic instance in which nineteenth-century aesthetic norms about relations between men and women were readapted for use as twentieth-century literary norms. The form Joyce's epiphany takes is that of the conventional Petrarchan love lyric translated into poetic prose: He comes upon a girl and sees her as radiant.

In contrast, Somerville and Ross's description is itself a kind of horror tale with its own "half-acknowledged" secrets. It suggests the topic Beards pithily summarizes as "Anglo-Irish Big House decadence" (xiv). But what exactly are the "excesses," what are the "unnatural conditions"? The passage suggests, as critics preoccupied with its epiphanic status have not noticed or at any rate not said, the horrors of inbreeding, of a family's self-propagation. As the passage proceeds, Somerville and Ross speak of the horrific spectacle of people given "but half their share of life," who are perhaps constrained by social convention or dementia from having a "full" life, or who are forcibly prevented from acting out whatever desires they may have, or who *have* acted something out and must be isolated in solitary imprisonment for the trespass. There is the suggested horror in this passage of "old stock," of family incest, of solitary existence, of desire, and of the wages of sexual sin—the multiple whammy of existence in a decayed Anglo-Irish Big House. From two writers, who were not at all writers of fin-de-siècle "decadence," this epiphany nonetheless surfeits on the decadent. Not least, the genderlessness of the white face intensifies its effects: If it is female, then this is a portrait also of Somerville and Ross's own uncanny "other."

The details of language in this passage are telling: The person is both "half-witted" and "wholly horrifying." Things that go by halves (the mind, the secret, the sister or brother, the share of life, the self) are "wholly horrifying." It is not quite accurate, then, for Beards to call this epiphany, as she does, "less spectacular than Stephen Dedalus's vision of the ivory-legged seaweed-splotched birdlike girl in *A Portrait of the Artist*" (xiv); it is surely more spectacular, more sensational, more emotionally charged. Somerville and Ross produce less of a spectacle in not permitting us to gaze at the female figure, but they show us something more ambiguously intriguing: an aging person's face whose thoughts, identity, and meaning—his or her secrets—can only be guessed.

This moment recollected under the "crescent moon," and the "realities" to which Somerville and Ross gained access from it, are recaptured in the novel in the figure of Mad Moll, and knowledge of the passage thus resolicits our attention to Moll's half-revealed secrets. In chapter 6, as Theo gazes at the moonlit scene outside her window, she first loses "the sense" of the "reality" of the trees and shrubbery, then "at length [is] aroused to realities by a sound . . . of some stealthy advance in the wet grass under the trees. . . . A woman's figure slid into the dim light" (44–45).

Like Bertha Mason in *Jane Eyre*, Moll's obscure character is a pivot on which this plot turns; for the feminist reader, she may seem its buried protagonist. Much as Elaine Showalter and Sandra Gilbert and Susan Gubar once saw Bertha Mason as the figure of Jane Eyre's own fear and rage, we could think of Mad Moll as Theo's (and Somerville and Ross's) dreaded other.[29] When Moll first sees Theo, it is with a look of "concentrated, half-terrified intentness"; "There had been something in [her eyes'] expression which, beneath the oblivion of insanity, seemed almost to struggle into recognition" (56).

Like Bertha Mason, Moll does not speak, she does not participate in any of the activities of everyday life, and she never leaves the estate.[30] She is an illegitimate daughter without a legitimate inheritance whom people refuse to recognize as part of the Sarsfield family. She is now old, half-witted, shrugged off by everyone. Compounding the evil for female denizens of Anglo-Irish society, Moll's "Master" is an alcoholic who once used and then rejected her, and she is married to a tenant who is himself subject to the Big House master's will. As it transpires, she is also the murderer of Theo's father, for which she is living out her lonely punishment; she is indeed, as Theo sees her, a living "ghost" (47). Moll haunts the estate and especially Theo's bedroom, appearing and disappearing unpredictably.

But unlike *Jane Eyre*, *An Irish Cousin* by no means sups full on horrors with one madwoman. Moll is not the only spectral figure in this novel, nor the only possible *Doppelgänger*. Theo's Uncle Dominick also is spectral, ghastly in appearance, wavering between sanity and insanity, between excessively controlled politeness and uncontrolled anger, and he is thoroughly mad by the end of the novel. The "white face" seen in the Big House could readily have been his in this novel rather than Moll's. Together but apart, Dominick and Moll haunt the estate with their fatal, failed relationship. If Willy marries Theo, Moll's daughter Anstey is likely to follow the same path as her mother. Anstey also appears at unexpected moments and draws Theo's attention; as a rival for Willy's affections and as, possibly, Anstey's cousin, Theo finds herself doubled potentially by Anstey (and wishing her "hair would curl as attractively as" Anstey's [55]). Although the novel at first appears to present a real choice for Willy in Anstey and Theo, it may not matter in this cross-class, faintly incestuous lineage which woman he marries: With either Anstey or Theo, he will be doubling back the line.

There seems to be no possibility of a friendship between women in

An Irish Cousin, and there are no legitimate female cousins to support, work with, or provide companionship for Theo. Two possible female peers are available in Nugent's sisters, but both are introduced as antitheses to her—"others" who, though not feared as Moll is, also threaten Theo, and whom she resists with equal determination. Posed as extremes between which Theo navigates, Henrietta—though more admirable than Connie—is too independent, aloofly sure of herself, and preoccupied with progressive ideas, whereas Connie—though more playful and accessible to Theo than Henrietta—is too flirtatious, feminine, and preoccupied with romance. This avoidance of the female options available leaves little space, if any, for Theo to occupy. The sole alternative to her minimal alliances with Henrietta and Connie as well as to the dangerous friendliness of Willy is Nugent, the standard romantic option (an option neither Somerville nor Ross chose for herself). Only if we see Mad Moll as Theo's Bertha Mason–like double is there a serious female-female relationship at the heart of this novel, a relationship of unconscious, scandalous affiliation.

Interestingly, however, some of the most crucial moments in the novel in which Theo feels intense horror are episodes connected not to Moll or Anstey, but to her cousin Willy. Horror, prominent among the few intense feelings expressed in this novel, is also among Theo's rare intensities. One of the striking characteristics of this narrative is Theo's frequent lack of affect; as she herself describes it, "I had always taken my life as it came, without much introspective thought of its effect upon me. . . . I had taken for granted that I must be a hard-headed, hard-hearted person" (226). Although she experiences "enjoyment" in what later seems like "one long *tête-à-tête* with Willy" (110) and occasional dread or depression when left alone at Durrus, she generally glides along on the surface of her new life in Ireland, concerned primarily with fitting into the family and the local society and cultivating a mixture of mild feelings with regard to her cousin: "Willy certainly had many attractive points, but, although he was a pleasant companion, he could not be said to be either very cultured or refined" (94). Yet her reaction to Willy's affection for her is instant and complete repulsion: She snatches away her hand when he first takes it in his (127), and, when his lips touch her hair, she stumbles both literally and metaphorically into the "deepest of the quagmire" of a muddy field they are crossing (148).

For Theo to be attached to Willy—or even to come close to him—is to be drawn into messy places, bogs, muddy ditches, and dirty yards. Her deepest feeling about Willy is horror and repeated horror; when Willy kissed her, she "stood in a kind of horror of passive endurance while he kissed [her] over and over again" (199). After this display of affection, the kiss she gives one of the dogs brings back a flood of difficult memories of Willy in which pleasure is turned to pathos and revulsion:

> As I stooped over and kissed his little white and tan head, a crowd of insistent memories rushed into my mind. In every one Willy's was the leading figure; his look, his laugh, his voice pervaded them all, but with a new meaning that made pathos of the pleasantest of them. I wondered, with perhaps some insincerity, why I had not liked him as well as he liked me. He had said that, if I were to try, I might some day; but though I should have been glad for his sake to believe it, every feeling in me rose in sudden revolt at the idea with a violence that astonished myself. (206)

As it happens, the first passage in which she expresses this combination of the pathetic and the revolting occurs in the opening chapter of the novel when she is seasick: "For me [seasickness] has only two aspects—the pathetic and the revolting" (3). Theo and Willy each do try to espouse the other (out of the different motives of Theo's "sane" compassion and Willy's "insane" passion); what intervenes between them throughout the novel is Theo's horror of intimacy with Willy.

Although it is unclear what precisely is the "revelation" that causes Theo's horror when Dominick reveals Willy's involvement with Anstey, certainly part of it is her uncle's effort to persuade Theo to marry Willy:

> "The thought that Willy might be led on into doing anything to lower the family preyed upon me more than I can tell you, and it gave me the greatest pleasure to see what his feelings for you were."
> What could I say? Horror at this revelation, pity for Anstey, bitter, sick disappointment in Willy, together with the knowledge of what my uncle so obviously expected of me, were pursuing each other through my mind. (235)

In addition, horror in this passage and in many others is inspired by class disdain. Nugent's mother is "horrified" (181) at a country ball that Theo, Nugent, and Willy attend (and enjoy). Dominick evinces his own "horror" (234) at Anstey's involvement with his son. A country funeral with its shrilly keening women impresses Theo as "so barbaric and so despairing" (208). And much as Theo fears Moll and Dominick, she increasingly fears Willy and "laugh[s] servilely" when she endeavors to remind him of an impending visit from Nugent (141).

Theo gradually does become attached to Nugent, who is introduced to us as a man completely detached—unattainable, cold, without feeling (as well as not related to her). When he begins to disclose his love for her, she experiences "a strange sensation for a moment," which deepens into "foolish enjoyment," a "strange pang of delight" when he takes her hand, and finally "dizziness" at the "certainty that he loved me" (184, 221, 223, 227). Discovery of her feeling for this unlikely romantic object occurs as a sudden surprise to her; it is quickly mixed with guilt toward Willy, and she cannot find any anticipation of her tenderness for Nugent in her diaries. What she embarrassingly finds instead is "one pithy entry after the first day's hunting": "Mr. O'Neill piloted me [during her first day's hunting]. Dull and conceited" (227). It is almost as if love had been imposed on her, made a condition of her life without her agency in it. Theo's happiness soon is deflected and dissipated by guilt toward Willy and by Nugent's belief that she means to marry her cousin. It thus seems more than coincidental that, not long before Nugent first reveals his interest in her, Theo has linked Nugent with Willy in her mind as partners in a kind of border-breaking horror: "I was very unfortunate. . . . I first got wet through, and then one cross young man after another dragged me over these horrible wet stone walls" (151).

There are a few glimpses of comedy in *An Irish Cousin* (as in the ending) that hint at the possibility of socialized reconciliations. But on the whole, before its abrupt happy ending, this novel says "no" to nearly every affect except those associated with horror, and at the end Theo finally identifies this horror with herself, internalizing it, seeing herself as its ultimate cause: After Dominick's death, "all that remained for me was to drag myself back to the desolate house on which I had brought ruin" (304–5). She has become her own most dreaded "other."

Yet *An Irish Cousin* also says "no," through Theo, to horror, and sends the things she avoids underground in the novel's murky conclusion and artificially happy ending. Somerville and Ross continued to write about the Anglo-Irish Big House in a number of stories and novels, but they never returned quite so directly to the Big House's potential for the uncanny or to their half-expressed, hydra-headed "epiphany." Their most famous novel, *The Real Charlotte*—a novel that contemporary critics consider not only their greatest achievement, but among the outstanding novels of modern Ireland—took shape in the very different genre of tragicomic realistic fiction. Nonetheless, it is in this novel more than in any other that they once again returned to some of the horrors hinted at in *An Irish Cousin* and, in particular, to the problematic kinship of cousins.

It is on the eponymous protagonist Charlotte Mullen's affiliations and the uncanny element in the otherwise realistic mode of *The Real Charlotte* that I will focus, but first it is important to consider this new protagonist herself. In addition to setting aside the murder mystery mode of *An Irish Cousin, The Real Charlotte* shifts attention from the cautious and conventionally minded Theo to an impassioned, independent woman. Because this shift first occurs in the novel Somerville and Ross wrote between *An Irish Cousin* and *The Real Charlotte,* it is useful to look briefly at it. Their second novel, *Naboth's Vineyard* (1891), reads in some ways like a trial run for *The Real Charlotte.*[31] *Naboth's Vineyard* is as lightly written as *An Irish Cousin,* containing none of the thick description, sociological and psychological background, or dense linguistic texture and conversation of *The Real Charlotte.* But their second novel's protagonist, Harriet, is a too-passionate, too-independent woman making her way among conventional options for women. Harriet is attracted to a man whom she had spurned in order to marry another man of higher financial and social standing. She thinks that she can go on loving her first suitor when he returns from enriching himself abroad and is so preoccupied with her manipulation of events that she does not notice his new love for another woman. Harriet discovers her failure with her first lover only after she has let her husband fall to his death. Although the secret of this novel is hidden only from the heroine's husband—the reader and she are both very aware of her passion—it drives and ruins her in the way Dominick's secret ruins the Sarsfields. Somerville and Ross have thus turned away from the quagmire of familial and class slippage with its horrific mysteries, in order, surprisingly, to turn a cold eye on a strong woman.

The heroine of *Naboth's Vineyard* is a thinly drawn caricature, but when recast in "the real Charlotte," now a spinster and literally "ugly," this new "realism" seems courageous: A fierce, plain woman had rarely, if ever, been the central focus of a novel. But this does not make strong women attractive.[32] The *femme fatale* here becomes literally fatal and not at all beautiful, reinforcing old stereotypes of women rather than undoing them. Charlotte is not presented entirely unsympathetically or without rational explanation and could easily be reread by a contemporary feminist reader, but few of her machinations are presented for the reader's admiration. She is depicted, above all, as an agent of upward mobility for herself and downward mobility for her enemies; she is as demonically active in undermining others as in promoting herself. The primary secrets in this novel are, as in *Naboth's Vineyard,* all shared with the reader: They are Charlotte's secret plots against others. To these others, meanwhile, she seems like someone with nothing to "conceal" (*Real Charlotte* 222). Thus, although its realism proved to be both less conventional and less popular than the sensationalist *An Irish Cousin* and its protagonist is neither a Theo nor a Mad Moll but a fully functioning public figure, *The Real Charlotte* nonetheless shrinks from women's secret passions, ambitions, and affiliations. When Charlotte upsets gender roles, she seems to represent a distortion of femininity and an inversion of the social order. (Even her male cat is misnamed "Susan" by Charlotte's cousin Francie.)

Like Dominick, Charlotte becomes a victim of the situation she maneuvers. Despite her manipulations, including allowing the wife of the man she loves to die, she unwittingly loses him to the attractions of her beautiful young cousin. Charlotte herself becomes ever more deeply thwarted by, and entwined in, the destinies of those she seeks to control. At the end, she seems a puppet in a theater of uncanny coincidences.[33] In the process of entrapping Charlotte in her own plots, however, the novel also suggests an alternative to demonization of Charlotte and to its own insistent realism. In the uncanny events of the novel, one discovers what Somerville and Ross would have called a "spiritualist" propensity, or what I describe in this study as an affirmation of unlooked-for affinities between people of opposed status interests, kinship and class positions, financial situations, gendered spheres, and "realities" or worldviews. The novel turns both its protagonist and its "realism" in on themselves, so that they too collapse into their polarized opposites.

Somerville and Ross at first called their third novel *The Welsh Aunt*, a title that positioned it as a sequel to *An Irish Cousin*. In contrast to the dangerously close relation and mirroring of cousins, the aunt is typically an isolate, fringe figure. She is often stereotypically a spinster woman, a woman who has failed to become, or resisted becoming, a wife and mother. Whether she is evil (like a stepmother) or negligible (as a nonmother), the life and opportunities of this kind of aunt are behind her. The Machiavellian protagonist of *The Real Charlotte* refuses *not* to have a life of her own: She seeks not only returned passion from, but equality with, the man she admires; she successfully pursues her own financial independence; at times, she practically runs the community of Lismoyle. But in the end, as she fails to find her love requited, all these pursuits seem as empty as the stereotype predicts: "She saw herself helpless, and broken, and aimless for the rest of her life" (229–30). Her sole aim after this is revenge, and, when accomplished, revenge itself turns back against her.

We learn early in the novel that *this* aunt considers herself to be no more an aunt than she is Welsh. She corrects several men in turn who refer to Francie as her niece, but with little success. Francie Fitzpatrick, she insists, is her cousin. Painstakingly, she explains, "whereas my first cousin, Isabella Mullen, married Johnny Fitzpatrick, who was no relation of mine, good, bad, or indifferent, their child is my first cousin once removed, and *not* my niece!" To this, Roderick Lambert—the man she loves—replies, "You're a nailer at pedigrees, Charlotte . . . but as far as I can make out the position, it comes to mighty near the same thing; you're what they call her Welsh aunt, anyhow" (14). Hard as she tries to nail down the distinction between aunt and cousin, she can do nothing to eradicate the generation gap that is obvious to all the men present—a gap figured further here as the divide between rivalrous nation-races (wherein Charlotte is also denied her Irishness).[34] Moreover, this cousinship lacks mutual regard and affection: Francie, with her tendency to drift, her social ineptitude and naivety, her flirtatiousness and beauty, is represented as the antithesis of the fiercely controlling, socially apt and cynical, commonsensical and mannish Charlotte, and no love is lost between them. Readers often see Francie as a co-protagonist. If Charlotte and Francie are alter egos for Somerville and Ross, they are far less attractive doubles than Theo and Willy.[35]

In renaming the novel *The Real Charlotte,* Somerville and Ross diverted attention from Charlotte's familial status to Charlotte alone and to the vexed question of Charlotte's reality. This title invites the reader to expect a drama of appearances and reality, and to a considerable extent the novel fulfills such an expectation through reenacting Charlotte's deceptive plots against others while showing the reader her true motives. But this novel also begs the question of a distinction or distance between appearances and realities, truth and falsehood, mask and self by showing us—what it does not, until the end, show most of the other characters—that Charlotte's literally ugly appearance matches an ugly reality. The real Charlotte really is ugly, as she appears to be.

One of the most interesting questions thus posed by this novel is how we are to read the term *real:* We might see Charlotte's "reality" as an expression of an inner essential self, a demonstration of the biopsychological claim that anatomy is destiny,[36] a symptomatic figuration of the female as lack, an internalization of the social construct of the independent woman as malevolent, or a signifier for an arbitrarily designated signified of woman as (feared) other. The novel's late-nineteenth-century vocabulary provides its own multiple possibilities, which are comparably contradictory. In addition to referring simply to Charlotte's actual inner thoughts about and plots against others, which are known to the reader and only belatedly known to the other characters, the "real" appears to refer both to a rounded realistic character whom the reader gets to know and to a foundational, essential character, or hidden "soul," possessed by Charlotte. Despite the dense detailing of her thoughts and feelings in the present-time of the novel, nothing is said about Charlotte's childhood years, experiences, or relationships before her adulthood, so that her deeper nature is far less fully explained than it might be. In addition, like many of the characters, she is sometimes caricatured (as in her appellation "Welsh aunt") so that she then becomes less a sociopsychologically realistic personage than a slightly ridiculous, *sui generis* social type—a social exemplum. The "real" thus oscillates in complex ways in this novel between social constructionism and essentialism.

The phrase "the real Charlotte" makes its first two appearances in the language of the narrative at moments when Charlotte uncovers *others'* secret betrayals. At these instants, she reveals her own hidden character: her raging passion, her immoral unkindness, and her domineering aggressiveness. The "real" seems on these occasions to point to an essentially bad Charlotte. To her supposed friend, the antithetical Mrs. Lambert—who is naive, sedate, docile, and harmless—the "real Charlotte" discloses Roderick's assiduous flirtation with Francie, "quelling [Mrs. Lambert's] feeble" effort to believe the best of her husband. This Charlotte has "a dangerous look about her jaw" (173). "The real Charlotte" uncovers herself to Francie at the moment when Charlotte discovers her cousin's betrayal of Charlotte's plans for her. Charlotte is enraged by Francie's refusal of love from the aristocratic Christopher Dysart, a love at which Charlotte has been conniving (Charlotte wanted to be able to call the highly positioned and wealthy Christopher her "cousin," 150). Francie's initially benign view of Charlotte as "queer" but "kind and jolly" becomes increasingly mixed with fear, for which she "could hardly have given a reason. . . . It must have been by that measuring and crossing of weapons that takes place unwittingly and yet surely in the consciousness of everyone who lives in intimate connection with another, . . . she had learned, like her great-aunt before her, the weight of the real Charlotte's will, and the terror of her personality" (191–92). In close proximity, amid the daily conscious and unconscious competitive struggle—"that measuring and crossing of weapons"—that occurs in intimate relations, Francie discovers a Charlotte not at all "kind and jolly"; this Charlotte is malevolent and possesses an overweening will. She is a dominatrix.

The narrator eventually offers a constructivist account of Charlotte's behavior. With the third and last occurrence of the phrase "the real Charlotte," the narrator offers a causational account of Charlotte's "many evil[s]":

> It is hard to ask pity for Charlotte, whose many evil qualities have with-
> out pity been set down, but the seal of ignoble tragedy had been set on
> her life; she had not asked for love, but it had come to her, twisted to
> burlesque by the malign hand of fate. There is pathos as well as humil-
> iation in the thought that such a thing as a soul can be stunted by the
> trivialities of personal appearance, and it is a fact not beyond the reach
> of sympathy that each time Charlotte stood before her glass her ugliness
> spoke to her of failure, and goaded her to revenge. (236)

The explanation for Charlotte's evils, then, is that her love has been
thwarted by society's trivial categorizations. The arbitrary social deval-
uation of her appearance is internalized as failure and hatred. Charlotte
has learned to wreak havoc in others' lives by manipulating appearances,
especially by appearing generous.

This third and final explanation of Charlotte's "real" ugliness—that
she is "stunted by the trivialities of personal appearance"—may also
express a feminist protest against society's insistence on the feminine for
women, including conventions of female beauty, passive charm, dependency, and frivolity. All this is embodied in Francie. On the strength of
what this narrative shows us, one might indeed argue (although the narrator does not go this far) that Charlotte's duplicity itself—her superficial kindness, calm, flexibility, and ethics, disguising her "real" unkindness, passion, domineering character, and amorality—is predefined by the
double-facedness of a society that polarizes the world into good and evil,
beautiful and ugly, human and animal.

But there is no room in the world of this novel for a rational alternative.[37] *The Real Charlotte* is repressive rather than overtly reformative,
and it is here that the uncanny emerges: The novel's psychological and
causational explanation is contradicted by so many vivid passages portraying Charlotte merely as succumbing to a repressed "other" side of
herself that her "terrible" character finally seems overdetermined and,
paradoxically, inexplicable. In several passages, moreover, Charlotte is
nearly archetypal in her behavior, no longer an individual at all. It is not
only serenity, rationality, and morality that fail her, but civility and hu-
manness:

> A human soul when it has broken away from its diviner part, and is left
> to the anarchy of the lower passions, is a poor and humiliating specta-
> cle, and it is unfortunate that in its animal want of self-control it is sel-
> dom without a ludicrous aspect. The weak side of Charlotte's nature was
> her ready abandonment of herself to fury that was, as often as not, wholly
> incompatible with its cause, and now that she had been dealt the hard-
> est blow that life could give her, there were a few minutes in which rage,

and hatred, and thwarted passion took her in their fierce hands, and made her, for the time, a wild beast. When she came to herself she was standing by the chimney-piece, panting and trembling; the letter lay in pieces on the rug, torn by her teeth, and stamped here and there with the semi-circle of her heel; a chair was lying on its side on the floor, and [the cat] Mrs. Bruff was crouching aghast under the sideboard, looking out at her mistress with terrified inquiry. (229)

The "malign influence" of Charlotte's "many bad fairies" at birth (260) produces something in Charlotte more than "wild," more than "animal"; she becomes ghastly, demonic. As Beards suggests, she reanimates folk mythology of the witch (Introduction xvi). This "real Charlotte" is surreal.

To restate the novel's complex characterization of Charlotte in terms of my larger argument in this book, Charlotte is (like two cousins) both like and different from herself, but, as in *An Irish Cousin*, where health and sanity depend on keeping likenesses apart, it is in her likeness to herself—her both superficial and "real" ugliness—that the horror lies. The circularity of Francie's thoughts about Charlotte—that she fears "the terror of her personality"—thus seems more than accidental. Charlotte and Francie are caught in a closed circle in which all distinctions return to the same calamitous and inexplicable, undifferentiated point of origin, to a "malign fate," a circle in which distinctions, especially absolute distinctions, must crumble calamitously, annihilating both Charlotte's enemies and her own purpose in life. The novel continually gestures toward a moral universe that none of the characters, especially Charlotte, ever occupy, belying the "reality" of a universe in which "truth," "beauty," "goodness," and "reality" itself have any solid or separate grounding. Charlotte is caught in her own mirror, and so also are her antagonists. In the end, what is "real" uncannily comprises what is conventionally considered "unreal."

The uncanny operates more surreptitiously in this novel than in *An Irish Cousin*.[38] The "realities" of Charlotte's power plays are explicit, placed on display for the reader, so that the text appears to have no secrets with which to horrify us. On the contrary, the device with which the novel closes is, as Robinson argues, the "shared-secret" (116), shared between reader and writer but withheld from the man Charlotte desires (Roderick Lambert) and from Charlotte herself: Francie has been killed in a riding accident caused by the funeral cortege of a woman Charlotte has previously outwitted, Julia Duffy. Francie's death destroys not only

Lambert's last hope in life, but also Charlotte's; she has revealed all her plots to Lambert and thus lost any chance she would have had to attract him with Francie gone. But although none of Charlotte's secret "reality" is hidden from the reader, this text does have some secrets even from the reader that are only half-revealed in the course of the narrative, and the Big House is once again a climactic site of disclosed horrors. The "uncanny" itself—the very possibility of a spirit world inhabiting, haunting, even controlling the ordinary world—is (as in Charlotte's own double character) half-acknowledged, then repressed again. The narrative voice in *The Real Charlotte* is far more assiduously skeptical than in *An Irish Cousin.* It is a voice of enlightenment, rational to the point of cynicism about what human moral good intentions are worth when confronted with the worldly incentives of love, money, or power, and often satiric, as on the occasions when it notes the superstitions of the characters. But the plot depends on a series of foreshadowings, uncanny doublings, ghastly madwomen, and coincidences ending in disaster, so that *The Real Charlotte* seems, finally, as two-sided as its titular character.

The novel represses but also yields to its uncanny side, much as Charlotte both represses and yields to superstition. Charlotte is skeptical of others' superstitions, but she is also superstitious, and at the moments of her own superstition, she is herself demonic. In the early chapter introducing Charlotte's cousinship, we learn also about her knowledge of spiritualism, but this latter fact is treated far more casually than the former, as if her spiritualism were not significant (12). We discover Charlotte's superstitiousness similarly in a realistic context, but Charlotte herself is transformed in this passage into an irrational hellion. When Charlotte has forced Mrs. Lambert to uncover her husband's letters from Francie, and Mrs. Lambert has died from a heart attack, Mrs. Lambert's dog

> crept from under the table to snuff with uncanny curiosity at his mistress's livid face, and as Charlotte approached, he put his tail between his legs and yapped shrilly at her.
> "Get out, ye damned cur!" she exclaimed, the coarse, superstitious side of her nature coming uppermost now that the absorbing stress of those acts of self-preservation was over. Her big foot lifted the dog and sent him flying across the room. (178)

Like the dog, Francie evinces a similarly "unreasoning" and "uncanny" fear of Charlotte at a moment when it is too late to act on her suspicion (275).

Charlotte's superstition takes a turn for the worse when she throws Francie out of the house. Charlotte now fears losing her sense of the boundary between the natural and the supernatural, but Charlotte is at this instant acting monstrously by usurping the property of her neighbor, Julia Duffy:

> Since her aunt's death, she had never liked Tally Ho. There was a strain of superstition in her that, like her love of land, showed how strongly the blood of the Irish peasant ran in her veins; since she had turned Francie out of the house she had not liked to think of the empty room facing her own, in which Mrs. Mullen's feeble voice had laid upon her the charge that she had not kept; her dealings with table-turning and spirit-writing had expanded for her the boundaries of the possible, and made her the more accessible to terror of the supernatural. (223)

Eventually Charlotte's best-laid plans are undone, as if indeed she labored under a curse, but she is the terrifying "other" who has cursed herself. So too the omniscient narrator registers skepticism toward the uncanny, never losing track of the realistic contexts in which it emerges yet tracing uncanny coincidences as carefully as if they were not coincidental. *The Real Charlotte* thus "deals" with "table-turning" in a simultaneously literal and supernatural sense.

In *The Real Charlotte,* the madwoman elbows her way onto center stage alongside the more rational women of the novel (Charlotte is described as "a madman who is just sane enough to fear his own madness" [194]), and there is not only one such woman. The second chapter, in which Charlotte first appears, begins by depicting an eerie scene at Tally Ho, Charlotte's home: The east wind is "crying" "inconsolably," and Norry the Boat (who works for Charlotte) is inspired by it to think of the Banshee (7). In general, Norry seems like yet another Charlotte: a no-nonsense, hard-working, information-gathering tyro. But this fringe character plays an important and uncanny role in the closing funeral scene. Norry is the cousin of the dead woman, Julia Duffy. As Francie passes by the cortege on her skittish horse, the keening Norry rises and raises her arms; in her cape, she looks exactly like a vulture, and it is this gesture that terrifies Francie's horse into throwing its rider.

Charlotte is doubled most obviously by Julia Duffy, whom the rivalrous, money-hungry Charlotte outdoes and indirectly drives to her death. Charlotte and Julia's Anglo-Irish "Ascendancy" pedigree, unattractiveness, spinsterhood, maverick independence, and fierce willfulness make them nearly identical. They even share skills in the occasionally indistinguishable medical and "occult" herbal arts: As the narrator says of Julia, people "called her Miss Duffy, in deference to a now impalpable difference in rank as well as in recognition of her occult powers, and they kept as clear of her as they conveniently could" (34). Julia has declined in health, wealth, and circumstances sufficiently for Charlotte to pry her out of the legacy of the Duffy Big House, Gurthnamuckla. By the end of the novel, Charlotte has moved from her own familial home, Tally Ho,[39] to Gurthnamuckla, and Julia—after a short stay in a mental asylum—is dead. But the event of Julia's funeral at the novel's close deprives Charlotte of the satisfactions both of property and revenge against Roderick Lambert, so Julia has her own Charlotte-like revenge.

Both superstitious practices and a lack of etiquette are predictably associated primarily with the illiterate working class throughout this novel, but the working poor become ascendant in this closing scene while the gentry crash down among them. Norry the Boat is not the only uncanny figure of working-class uprising in this episode; the impoverished Billy Grainy, whom Julia Duffy had employed and who has been a threatening figure for Francie from the first, begins the disastrous sequence of events when he vengefully hails Francie and grabs her horse's bridle. While the fashionable Francie literally plunges to her death, her husband Roderick is approaching Charlotte—looking like he has "been at [his] own funeral" (290)—to seek and be refused her help for the financial and social destruction she has brought upon him. As in *An Irish Cousin,* the horror facing the reader at the end of this novel involves not only "table-turning" but the collapse of all social and "natural" distinctions.

The novel's plot is dense with foreshadowing, particularly of Francie's fatal fall.[40] Time and again, Francie gets recklessly involved in a mad chase involving a horse (or boat or even a tricycle), in which her hat and often Francie herself fall off (5, 21, 39, 62, 89, and 254). When Francie's horse is startled at the funeral, first her hat falls, then Francie is thrown headfirst onto the pavement and killed (288). The funeral itself is highly reminiscent of the funeral in *An Irish Cousin,* which horrified Theo. Like Theo, Francie "felt a superstitious thrill as she saw it; a country funeral, with its barbarous and yet fitting crudity, always seemed to bring death nearer to her than the plumed conventionalities of the hearses and mourning coaches that she was accustomed to" (287). But it is Francie—described elsewhere as a soulless Undine (90)—who "barbarously" breaks "convention" on this occasion when, "heedless of the etiquette that required" that she stop her horse until the funeral went by, she hit her horse and "passed by . . . at a quickened pace" (288). Francie—like Charlotte—brings her tragedy upon herself.

———————

As Freud points out in his essay on the uncanny, in German the various meanings of the adjectival form of the uncanny, *unheimlich,* are with one notable exception opposed to *heimlich*. In addition to meaning "uneasy, eerie, blood-curdling" (as in "an *unheimlich* horror"), *unheimlich* is defined as the antithesis of *heimlich*, whose primary meanings are listed as "belonging to the house or family" (an obsolete meaning), "tame" as opposed to wild (for animals), and "friendly, intimate, homelike." The exception to these terms' opposition is that both *unheimlich* and *heimlich* also mean "concealed, kept from sight, so that others do not get to know about it" (as in a "*heimlich* love, love-affair, sin"). The *heimlich* crosses or becomes the *unheimlich* in the "secret."[41] The uncanny, then, is the secret place or moment in which the homelike, familiar, and tame become horrifyingly untame, unfamiliar, and alien. For Somerville and Ross, this is a quite literal process in which one's "familiar" acquires all its ambiguity, to mean both familial relative and otherworldly spirit, and in which the home—whether in the Big House or the low, dark Tally Ho—turns out to harbor all that threatens social distinctions.

Freud sees the "double" and eerie coincidence in particular as frequent features of the uncanny and attributes this to the repetition compulsion and the process by which something repressed recurs (391, 394). But to become civilized, Freud suggests, repression of primitive beliefs and anxieties was necessary. It is no surprise, then, that the *Heimlichkeit* should become identical to the *Unheimlichkeit* in their shared meaning of "concealment." "Many people," he argues further, "experience the feeling [of the uncanny] in the highest degree in relation to death and dead bodies, to the return of the dead, and to spirits and ghosts" because modern people have "ceased to believe, officially at any rate, that the dead can become visible as spirits," thus repressing a forgotten belief, and fear, in the continuation of life after death (395, 396). The apparition of witchcraft in particular is among the major factors that "turn something fearful into an uncanny thing" (396). Similarly, the phenomenon of the double is a "harking-back to particular phases in the evolution of the self-regarding feeling, a regression to a time when the ego was not yet sharply differentiated from the external world and from other persons" (389)—or, we might add, to a time or phase, in which none of the distinctions on which social structures depend were sharply differentiated.

Freud goes on to describe the way in which the self-controlled, highly evolved modern mind responds when it reads a realistic novel that pivots on some uncanny event. Readers are far more likely to experience the uncanny in the context of realism than in a fantasy genre, which takes the incredible as its realm and thus invites the reader to suspend disbelief from the outset. In contrast, a realistic fiction reproduces the conditions in which "primitive" feelings and associations are repressed and so also creates the opportunity for intense experiences of the uncanny. But because such fiction seems intended to represent our own (rational) world, the reader is also likely to begrudge the author's deceit upon discovery of the author's hand shaping an uncanny event:

> He takes advantage, as it were, of our supposedly surmounted superstitiousness; he deceives us into thinking that he is giving us the sober truth, and then after all oversteps the bounds of possibility. We react to his inventions as we should have reacted to real experiences; by the time we have seen through his trick it is already too late and the author has achieved his object; but it must be added that his success is not unalloyed. We retain a feeling of dissatisfaction, a kind of grudge against the attempted deceit. (405)

Repelled by the uncanny itself, we are naturally repelled by fiction that reproduces an uncanny moment, and we blame it on the fictionist.

There are many such moments in *The Real Charlotte* when the authors' hands obtrude, shaping uncanny coincidences. These occur primarily in the sequence of deaths that dictate the course of the narrative, from Charlotte's Aunt Mullen's death with which the novel opens, through Mrs. Lambert and Christopher's father's sudden deaths, which are necessary to the plot's development, and finally to Julia Duffy's death and Francie's freak accident with the horse. The tragic ending, in particular, is as sudden, as inexplicable, as contrived as the comic one that ended *An Irish Cousin*. It is also obviously uncanny. Its saving grace for lovers of realism is its irony (Robinson 117) because it enables Charlotte to be defeated moments after she has defeated both Francie and Lambert.

But what is a contrived incident in this novel, and what is not? Both its (comic) realism and its (tragic) pathos are, after all, as inventive as its uncanny events. Moreover, this novel's uncanny coincidences are inextricable from its narrative texture, which not only uncovers eerie likenesses (between women, genders, and classes) in the midst of the differences it continually displays but also allows the possibility of a spirit life beyond that of the "real" even as it hedges this with skepticism.

In his theory of the uncanny, Freud essentially grounds all experience of a spirit world in the psyche, and in so doing brings spiritualism firmly under the aegis of psychoanalytic rationalism. But although *The Real Charlotte* is comparably cautious in its rationalism, neither the novel nor Somerville and Ross themselves entirely subordinated the surreal to the rational. For Somerville especially, the spirit world became ever more possible and not finally separable from the real world.

Nothing demonstrated the kinship of a "spirit" and a "real" world more firmly for Somerville and Ross than two events, the first occurring during the writing of *The Real Charlotte,* the second after its publication. The character Charlotte was modelled on a real woman, Emily Herbert, who was an enemy of the Somerville family; she had grasped an inheritance meant for them. She was long dead (and had been much disliked by all) when Somerville and Ross set about their novel, and so they felt uninhibited in writing about her. But while they were writing the novel, Herbert spoke to them through one of Somerville's sisters: Herbert communicated a message that, in Powell's words, "breath[ed] bitter hatred."[42] Somerville's reaction took form in an adage about women, suggesting that Somerville did not take the incident terribly seriously: "Hell holds no fury like a woman scorned" (*Irish Memories* 231). But then, two years after the novel was published, an old lady who had been intimate with Herbert asked Somerville how she had known about Emily Herbert's love affair, which had been a deeply held secret (*Irish Memories* 230–31). Critics generally offer this kind of story as a bit of casual amusement (as, for example, Robinson does [88–89]), electing not to comment, analyze, or inquire into it.[43]

Yet these uncanny occurrences are a critical component of the stories Somerville and Ross wrote and lived, as they continued to write together long after Ross's death.[44] The fact of their collaboration itself counted among the more uncanny of their stories. Continually asked (often "not without a certain violence") to explain and expose the "mystery" of their "Joint Authorship," Somerville made one last attempt in 1946 in her essay "Two of a Trade," but she prefaces this account by saying, "Unfortunately, much as I should enjoy giving away a secret, there is none to tell" (80).[45] There is no "secret" in that there is no special trick and, above all, no hidden reality of separate authorship; they simply "do it" (in Ross's words [80]). But their collaboration thus remains mysterious and secret. Indeed, they write of themselves as having a nearly religious faith in each other as well as in their writing together: "The two *Shockers* have a very strange belief in each other joined to a critical faculty" (Ross, qtd. on 80–81). Their postmortem collaboration is merely the last of a series of uncanny spiritual phenomena in the story they told of themselves. (Like all their previous works, "Two of a Trade" is cosigned.)

The various "mysteries" of Somerville and Ross—from their sexuality to their spiritualist intercourse to their collaboration—become oddly linked to one another in biographers' and critics' accounts. In defense of Somerville, Cummins slides seamlessly from countering suggestions of "sexual immorality" to describing Edith's "'defiant implacable faith' in the survival of human personality after death": "She greatly shocked some members of the younger generation with her extremely unconventional belief in the power of certain sensitive people to receive communications from departed souls."[46] Even while biographers and critics attempt to account for these three scandals separately, they explain both Somerville and Ross's ability to write together and Somerville's belief that they remained in communication beyond the grave by attributing these things to the intense love the writers had for each other. Meanwhile, contradictorily, their love is deemed unfathomable. Like the first novel Somerville and Ross wrote, these three inextricably intertwined features of their relationship were (and remain to this day) ghoulish "shockers."

The uncanny is the place where the imagined or the denied becomes real and where rationally opposed or socially differentiated "realities" coincide. Both imagined and denied affinities haunt the reader who involves herself with Somerville and Ross. Although the "spirit" may well be only another name for our own repressed psychological realities and doubles, as Freud believed it to be, if admitted (as I show in the next chapter) the uncanny need not be—as it is to Freud's modern man—either a place of inadmissible horror or a negligible joke. But if unadmitted, hell holds no fury like a secret affinity that has been scorned.

PART 3

*Revisionary
Collaborations*

5 Rewriting the Uncanny: H.D., Redgrove and Shuttle

WAYNE KOESTENBAUM'S STUDY of men's collaborations, *Double Talk*, begins with two chapters on "men of science," who turn out to be men of psychoanalysis and sexology—above all, Sigmund Freud and Josef Breuer, John Addington Symonds and Havelock Ellis—and with the argument that psychoanalysis originated in and as homosocial collaboration. It is Koestenbaum's argument about Freud that concerns me here.[1] As Koestenbaum describes it, psychoanalysis is not the creation of a solitary genius in an armchair, but derived rather from the playful clinical and linguistic congress of loving and competing men.

As Koestenbaum further suggests, this playful teamwork functioned to objectify and disempower the female patient, daughter, wife, and mother. All these became female "hysterics," a construction of male doctors. Moreover, Koestenbaum indicates, the search for the origins of the adult psyche was a process of appropriation of women's procreative power: Her literal ability to conceive and produce a child was erased and rewritten as man's psychological power to conceive and originate. The latter replaced the former as the primordial origin of distinctively human life as well as of individuality. In this account, Freud's effort to produce in psychoanalysis a metascience—a science that would hold the key to all human mythologies—was founded on the conceptual murder of the mother, the elimination of subjectivity in the daughter, the subordination of the female patient, and the redefinition of the female as hysteric.

Koestenbaum focuses in particular on the story of Anna O. because Freud's first close collaboration—with Breuer—developed around this client, and Anna O.'s case became the pivotal study in Freud's coauthored work with Breuer, *Studies in Hysteria,* which both Breuer and Freud saw as inaugurating the new science of psychoanalysis.[2] Anna O.'s case resulted in two particularly important discoveries. The first was the process of the "talking cure," which Breuer credited Anna O. with "inventing." The second was something about which he spoke almost exclusively to Freud (and even then not fully) but that led Freud eventually to reappropriate the curative power in talk for the male doctor. As Koestenbaum relates, Breuer's published account suppressed a secret, and it was this secret rather than any empirically observed or fully documented case study that formed the key to Freud's relationship to Breuer and to Freud's belief in the unconscious. (Anna O.'s case became famous in the history of psychoanalysis, but her case was conveyed first through oral exchange, then through gradual and partial disclosures in print.) The secret was that when, as a result of Breuer's wife's jealousy, Breuer ended his therapy with Anna O., Anna O. went into labor with an imagined baby of Breuer's. The story of this psychic labor—despite its secret character and the resulting barriers to any faithful transcription of the case's facts—persuaded Freud of the power of the psyche. In his playful conversations with Breuer, Koestenbaum argues, Freud jokingly made the still more radical suggestion that literal conception might have its roots in the insemination of the female psyche by the male analytic mind. In his jokes, Freud transferred the power of conception not only from body to psyche and from female hysteric to male mind, but from the power of conversation between a man and a woman to the power generated by two male minds in intercourse with each other.

This complex case history and Koestenbaum's argument about it (which I have necessarily simplified) are relevant here for the portrait they offer of psychoanalysis as homosocial collaboration. Feminist psychoanalytic theorists, in partial contrast, have sought not only to expose the not-so-secret misogyny of patriarchal institutions, including psychoanalysis, whose collaborations exclude women and whose arguments are premised on women's inferiority, but also to reform the contexts in which psychological development occurs and women's cultural denigration is internalized or reproduced. One method they have used is to offer (with varying success) models of productive, equitable sociopsychological collaboration.

My aim here, however, is not to review the large role played by psychoanalysis in feminist work by such theorists as Gilbert and Gubar,

Susan Stanford Friedman, Juliet Mitchell, Nancy Chodorow, Jacqueline Rose, Jane Gallop, Hélène Cixous, Catherine Clément, Luce Irigaray, and Julia Kristeva, nor to present comprehensive discussions of the various kinds of psychoanalytic theory. Rather, taking it for granted that psycho-analysis has become a central contemporary discourse, that it has devel-oped an ineradicable history in modernity and in modern feminism, and that feminist goals both conflict with and build upon standard psycho-analytic assumptions, my concern in this chapter is with two literary collaborations that put the retheorization of psychoanalysis in relation to the processes of collaborative writing. In discussing H.D.'s partial col-laboration with Freud and Bryher and Penelope Shuttle's full coauthor-ship with Peter Redgrove, this chapter also returns to chapter 4's concern with the uncanny. In scrutinizing these literary collaborations I exam-ine uses not only of Freud, but of Jung, whose theories often are ignored by feminist literary theorists but who is central to the work of at least one set of collaborators and whose contention with Freud pivoted on the opposition between the rational and the spiritual—an opposition that the feminist collaborators discussed in this chapter seek to undo.

The uncanny is one of Freud's most literary and aesthetically based theories, so it has seemed to literary critics a particularly friendly Freud-ian concept to apply to literature. Furthermore, it is a theory that com-patibly engages with and allows literature's structures of disclosure and concealment rather than treating texts as passive bodies to dissect for their "true" psychological purport. This theory is as commonly invoked by feminist critics as any of the more widely discussed theories (wheth-er of the Oedipus complex, the imaginary and the symbolic modes, the archetypal, or the pre-Oedipal mother-daughter bond), yet there has been little effort to revise the theory of the uncanny for specifically feminist purposes. A feminist revision of the uncanny could provide a very differ-ent way to talk not only about how social structures and structures of the psyche interact, how politics and psyches reproduce each other, but how political activism and psychic release may interact.[3] The uncanny entails scandal: It derives from unspoken secrets, from the possibility that some uncrossed border may be about to be crossed, from the thought that walls might come down. The uncanny thus also marks places where, for the feminist, previously trapped political and repressed psychic energy might be unleashed. In chapter 4 I developed a conventional analysis of the uncanny, showing the ways in which uncanny moments point to taboo secrets and treacherous borders in their texts. In this chapter I dis-cuss what texts look like when the uncanny marks the threshold of a permitted secret, when it marks a trespassable boundary, even while retaining the uncloseted secret's powerful otherness, the threshold's ethos of mysterious impenetrability.

Anna O. produced such a secret. Her psychic labor was a tantalizing double of actual childbirth. To Breuer's horror, it opened two boundaries he wanted closed: that between the psychological and the physical and that between scientific examination and sexual interest. At the same time there was something attractively revelatory about this event. For Freud it had an aura of mystery rather than horror. The uncanny often marks the desirable as well as what one has been taught must be undesirable, and thus marks the most mysterious objects of intense attraction, not only those of greatest repulsion. Whereas Breuer wished to conceal his complicity in a woman's hysterical childbirth and to prevent sexual gossip from reaching his wife and the scientific community, Freud wished to reveal this childbirth in order to claim coauthorship with Breuer of the discovery that the psyche could operate autonomously. He would hence cure Breuer and the scientific community of slander by cathartically explaining the false pregnancy and turning it into a familiar, neutral fact.

But Freud's way of using this revelation, in Koestenbaum's account of it, covers over something else. It renders again unfamiliar, alien, and secret the possibility that the female "patient" could in fact actively conceive, in mind as well as in body, without the aid of a male body or the immediate support of a male mind—that she possessed not merely potent flesh, but a procreative imagination. It is this latter possibility that the feminist collaborators discussed in this chapter reexpose, but in doing so they seek not to cure an ill or to rationalize an irrational event, but paradoxically to reallow the mysterious otherness of creativity—whether textual or psychological, male or female—and to reanimate or reauthorize the uncanny possibility of a spiritual realm.

H.D.'s Admissions

Tribute to Freud is what H.D. called her memoir upon its first publication as a book, a retitling urged by Norman Holmes Pearson, but the text itself reveals no passive deference to Freud's (or any man's) commands. The protagonist of this text—which H.D. originally, more ambiguously titled "Writing on the Wall"[4]—turns out to be not Freud, but H.D. as thinker and writer, prophet and priestess. Yet she does not acquire these roles at much expense to her "tribute," nor does she assert her own autonomy or superiority of thought. H.D. depicts herself as occasionally not conforming to Freud's expectations and eliciting his frustration, but she also reveals his interest in her and respect, and in so doing she pays tribute to their mutual participation in what Susan Stanford Friedman persuasively describes in a 1987 essay as a "reciprocal" rather than "hierarchical" (nonauthorial) "collaboration" with each other. H.D. presents us with a Freud so little like the standard portrait of the properly impersonal psychoanalyst that a reader might wonder whether this is an anomalous Freud, momentarily appearing in therapy with H.D., or even a Freud H.D. made up. Friedman argues that this Freud existed, yet that he became possible only through collaborative interaction with "students" who not only were receptive to his guidance, but also stimulated and resisted him, who were willing to take leadership into their own hands, transforming the traditional hierarchy between (male) doctor and (female) patient.[5]

H.D.'s work with Freud has been central to discussion of H.D. in contemporary criticism, beginning with Norman Holland's psychoanalytic interpretation of *Tribute to Freud* and Friedman's rebuttal of its unconsciously misogynistic assumptions as well as those of an essay by Joseph Riddel.[6] Indeed, many critics see H.D.'s work with Freud either as pivotal to, or the most useful entry into, reading her work more generally. H.D. has thus become an important factor in feminist revaluations of Freud. Claire Buck notes that "H.D.'s writing is exemplary of the question which psychoanalysis has posed both women and feminism since the 1970s. The early stages of the feminist debate which surrounded Freud's account of the making of the woman and his analysis of the vicissitudes of that process coincides with, and marks, the feminist revaluation of H.D.'s work."[7] Following Friedman's critique of Holland, most critics have interested themselves in and valued the ways H.D. resists Freud's direction and ideas. But they disagree widely about the extent of her resistance.[8] Friedman is nearly alone in describing their work as "collaboration."[9] H.D.'s success in representing her therapy as a collaboration is nonetheless measured by the extent to which critics tend to take her citations of Freud literally as "Freud's words" and to speak of her memoir as recording actual, recollected "conversation" between Freud and H.D. rather than as a text she constructed. *Tribute to Freud* is thus described by one critic as having "at least two authors, and two analysts, and dialogically project[ing] itself as a 'writing on the wall.'"[10]

But H.D. is in obvious ways the single author of this text. She has the last word about her analysis, which she reframes not as a doctor's diagnosis and cure of a patient but as spiritual reciprocity. This is another version of what I have called an "approximate collaboration": an asymmetric exchange of benefits. Freud remains the master to whom H.D. pays tribute; his preeminence as thinker, father figure, teacher, and analyst are continually reasserted in her memoir. Yet in writing her testimonial, H.D.

set aside Freud's requests not to take notes during analysis and not to defend him after his death; although her *Tribute to Freud* did nothing when published to alter the direction of the field of psychoanalysis or to transform Freud's projected self-image in his own writing as dispassionate scientist, her memoir remains behind to challenge that image.[11]

In the course of representing the relationship between analyst and analysand as collaboration, H.D. rewrites a number of Freud's psychoanalytic premises; other feminist critics, notably Friedman, have dwelt in particular on her corrective response to his theory of women's lack. With the important exceptions of (again) Friedman and Adalaide Morris, however, both feminist and nonfeminist critics tend to deemphasize or gloss over, diagnose or seek apologies for what in *Tribute to Freud* she herself claimed as a primary realm of disagreement with Freud: spiritualism.[12] H.D. diverges from Freud's idea of the uncanny, and this proves to be a major and multidimensional swerve from his thought that leads to a manifold admission of traditionally preserved "secrets" and to an opening up of several kinds of supposedly closed borders, including those between teacher and student, this world and another world, one mind and another.[13] H.D. held herself aloof from Freud's rival, Jung, but in *Tribute to Freud*, admission of the uncanny becomes a Jungian site of psychic renewal and mystery, a wellspring of desire and creativity.[14]

For H.D., the uncanny is decidedly not a place of inadmissible horror or even marked discomfort. H.D. denied few of the border-crossing "realities" that plagued Somerville and Ross, as readers of H.D. well know: She admits to her capacity for "madness," as the world defines it; she admits to love for women; she admits her implication in psychologically incestuous relationships[15] with various surrogate fathers, mothers, siblings; she admits to her recurrent sense of people as doubles. The relations between antitheses of *The Real Charlotte*—between sanity and insanity, masters and subordinates, the man of the world and the dependent female, lovers and kin—are replaced by relations of fluidly interpenetrating yet mutually resistant duos.[16] But H.D. not only treats as permeable the boundaries most fear to cross yet recognize as "real"; she also admits supranormal phenomena in her writing.

The uncanny is the place where—in phrasing that H.D. recalls repeatedly and approvingly from Freud in her memoir—"the childhood of the individual" intersects with "the childhood of the race" (and vice versa [12, 38]). Thus in "The 'Uncanny,'" Freud writes,

> Our analysis of instances of the uncanny has led us back to the old, animistic conception of the universe, which was characterized by the idea

that the world was peopled with the spirits of human beings, and by the narcissistic overestimation of subjective mental processes (such as the belief in the omnipotence of thoughts). . . . It would seem as though each one of us has been through a phase of individual development corresponding to that animistic stage in primitive men [during which man "strove to withstand the inexorable laws of reality"] . . . and that everything which now strikes us as "uncanny" fulfils the condition of stirring those vestiges of animistic mental activity within us and bringing them to expression. (393–94)

But therapy works in defiance of "the inexorable laws of reality" to suggest that what is coincidence is as significant as what can be explained logically or causatively. What is imagined becomes real. Moreover, the uncanny regains an application in *Tribute to Freud* that Freud passes over without discussion in his catalogue of usages and definitions of *unheimlich* ("'To veil the divine, to surround it with a certain *Unheimlichkeit*'" [375]). What is "primitive" for Freud proves for H.D. to be redemptive.

In the process of avowing both her personal "trespasses" and experiences of an unknown spiritual realm, H.D. crucially recalls a second, more radical collaboration with her lover, friend, and patron Bryher (Winifred Ellerman), and this collaboration is the "Writing on the Wall" to which H.D.'s original title refers. This title primarily denotes neither some vague future doom (a world war) produced by men's treachery and violence nor the mysterious inscription at Belshazzar's feast in Daniel (although these remain suggestive connotations of her title), but an actual event in which Bryher and H.D. mysteriously experienced a prophetic, hallucinatory vision on the walls of H.D.'s room. When H.D. began to struggle with the agony of seeing images on a wall, Bryher encouraged her to go on, then completed the vision for her after H.D. stopped short in exhaustion.

Whether or not the reader agrees with Freud's concern that this event (as H.D. records it) constituted her single "dangerous 'symptom'" (41),[17] this act of visionary collaboration ironizes H.D.'s "tribute to Freud" and proposes a dramatically different view from Freud's of the potential of "conversation" in psychic work. As in the case of Somerville and Ross's uncanny telepathic experiences and their spiritualist "coauthorship," the role this paranormal "cowriting" plays in H.D.'s text has gone practically undiscussed by feminist and psychoanalytic critics alike. Bryher's participation is routinely recorded by critics as the last event in the "writing on the wall," but then becomes the blind spot in their analyses as they subsequently ignore its occurrence.[18] As toward much other occultist experimentation among writers of this period, critics generally adopt an apologetic stance toward these phenomena, treating them as eccentric, temporary lapses in authors and redescribing them as waking dreams whose primary function was to provide metaphors for poetry. In doing so, however, they fail to account for the ways writers such as H.D. explore the possibility of the spiritual.

The uncanny remains a place also of shadow for H.D.,[19] of secrecy and terrors that may emerge or reemerge: a place where memories of childhood trauma resurface, where she is betrayed and denigrated by husbands and lovers, where her own art fails her, where her children are stillborn, where illness may seize her at any time, where brothers, fathers, mothers, and therapists die, where violence and world wars break out.[20] It was largely H.D.'s effort not to deny these experiences, but rather to face their most emotional forms, that took her into and through therapy. In *Tribute to Freud*, H.D. remembers the analysis she undertook with Freud as a preparation in particular for the horrors of war that lay behind and before her.

Friedman and Barbara Guest's documentation of H.D.'s letters to Bryher are especially relevant to a discussion of what happens to secrecy in *Tribute to Freud* because the letters leak the secret processes of therapy, which Freud had asked H.D. not to share with others or to write about. Her therapy did not involve an uncanny and scandalous event like the one Breuer sought to hide; H.D. never imagined herself in labor with Freud's children.[21] But their intimacy, if disclosed and taken seriously enough, might have been detrimental to the emerging image of "classic" psychoanalysis. H.D.'s letters uncover a subjective Freud who takes a personal interest in her, a Freud whose curiosity—for example, about H.D.'s innovative family life or about the latest gossip[22]—H.D. knows how to cultivate, and a Freud caught up in countertransference (in resemblances between H.D.'s life and that of his dead daughter, Sophie).[23]

This mutual personal interest enabled H.D. paradoxically to allow Freud's power in her mind even while allowing her own. She is no less preoccupied with her self-analysis than with Freud's analysis of her, and while reliving Anna O.'s "talking cure," she reinvents Freud rather than suffering reinvention by him. At the end of her sessions, Guest reports, H.D. believed she had graduated from being a student, that Freud had released her to take on patients (Guest, *Herself Defined* 217). "Writing on the Wall" consists of neither the notes nor the letters about her therapy that Freud forbade her to write, yet it calls upon her recollection of both these sources as it works with fresh memories and impressions to produce a profoundly moving narrative and retheorization of Freud: a secret disclosed.

Friedman and other feminist critics focus on an important possible secret of this text, not explicitly shared with her reader or with Freud; they claim that H.D. secretly disagreed sharply with Freud's estimate of women, with his theory of woman as a castrated man, and with his assumption that women need men and "man-strength."[24] In the terms of a poem written about Freud, "The Master," which often is cited in this context, *Tribute to Freud* substitutes for "man" and "man-strength" a "flower / that in itself had power over the whole earth."[25] Although H.D. never disagrees directly with Freud about woman's castration in her memoir, even this secret is not deeply buried under its surface.

The opening passage of "Writing on the Wall" includes references to the Frau Professor (whom H.D. never meets) and the professor's patriarchal household, both of which are set at a safe distance from Freud's office; to the hall porter of her Vienna hotel, H.D. makes this possibly ironic statement, "I said I had not met the Frau Professor but had heard that she was the perfect wife for him and there couldn't be—could there?—a greater possible compliment" (3). Later, as the text reaches its central paean to Freud (43), she suddenly registers intense disappointment in his inability to see his future as contained in anything except his grandsons: "It was so tribal, so conventionally Mosaic" (62). Framed between these recognitions are, first, H.D.'s description of their relationship as a meeting of minds and of arts, not of a lordly male analyzing a submissive female, and, second, her portrait of the writing on the wall in which a woman (H.D.) is "strengthened" by another woman.

Encompassing this drama of a battle between genders and sexualities[26] is the equally deliberate and radical departure from Freud of H.D.'s spiritualist vision. H.D. presents herself in the first three sections of this text as (in Freud's words) "tak[ing] the place of" Freud's deceased former "student" and client Dr. J. J. Van der Leeuw, a scholar of the occult who had come to Freud because he "wanted to apply the laws of spiritual being to the acute problems of today" (5–6). Pervading H.D.'s tribute, especially in her mythologizing of Freud as spiritual forerunner and in her revelation of the uncanny writing on the wall, her interest in laws of spiritual being is no secret either, but it clearly was something she kept partially cloaked from Freud: "About the greater transcendental issues, we never argued. But there was an argument implicit in our very bones. We had come together in order to substantiate something. . . . The great forest of the unknown, the supernormal or supernatural, was all around and about us" (13). Of course, Freud was accustomed to discourse of the occult, which was widely prevalent among intellectuals, artists, and many others in his day, and so was undisturbed by his clients' interest in it, but he was also anxious to separate his "science" from it and indeed to absorb and explain the occult with psychoanalysis. Correcting what H.D. sees as Freud's failure of vision, H.D. projects in these pages a future for him that he would not have foreseen for himself, one that overwrites his rationalism with her irrationalism.

Writing of her distress at Freud's "tribalism," for example, H.D. feels as if "a chasm or a schism in consciousness" had opened up that she had "tried to conceal from him," and this chasm is caused by Freud's inability to imagine an afterlife beyond a kind of Biblical genealogy: "I knew the Professor would move on somewhere else, before so very long, but it seemed the eternal life he visualized was in the old Judaic tradition. He would live forever like Abraham, Isaac, and Jacob, in his children's children, multiplied like the sands of the sea" (62). When first speaking of the gulf between their attitudes toward the afterlife, she is more explicit about the alternative she sees:

> I am also concerned, though I do not openly admit this, about the Professor's attitude to a future life. . . . There was a more imminent, a more immediate future to consider [than that of Freud's grandchildren and his books]. It worried me to feel that he had no idea—it seemed impossible—really no idea that he would "wake up" when he shed the frail locust-husk of his years, and find himself alive. . . .
>
> I did not say this to him. I did not really realize how deeply it concerned me. It was a *fact*, but a fact that I had not personally or concretely resolved. I had accepted as part of my racial, my religious inheritance, the abstract idea of immortality, of the personal soul's existence in some form or other, after it has shed the outworn or outgrown body. (43)

This vision of rebirth—as opposed to the material support Freud receives from his wealthy benefactress and friend, "the Princess"—is what H.D. feels she has uniquely to give him and to future assessments of him. It is a vision of resurrection: "I wanted something different or I wanted to give the Professor something different. Princess George of Greece [Marie Bonaparte] . . . was 'our Princess' in the world, devoted and influential. But is it possible that I sensed another world, another Princess? Is it possible that I (leaping over every sort of intellectual impediment and obstacle) not wished only, but *knew*, the Professor would be born again?" (39).

H.D.'s vision of Freud as spiritual leader is not something that, as she repeatedly points out, he would ever claim or wish to claim for himself, so their half-secret "argument in our bones" is an argument also over the precise nature of her tribute. According to H.D., Freud recognizes himself as a philosopher—"My discoveries are a basis for a very grave philosophy" (18)—but she projects for him the far bolder roles of seer, church founder, and, ultimately, "god" who will be reborn. H.D.'s deification of Freud is not unusual in her texts; she recurrently found divinity in people and things. But Freud is more immortal than most.

When Freud interprets the baby Moses in an important dream H.D. has of "the Princess" (Marie Bonaparte, as well as the biblical Princess of Egypt) as manifesting "a hidden desire" to "found a new religion" or, as she elaborates, "a suppressed desire to be a Prophetess" (51), H.D. quarrels with him: "Obviously it was he, who was that light out of Egypt" (119). Freud "insisted I [H.D.] myself wanted to be Moses" (120), however; indeed, in her repeated identification of Freud with Moses, she approaches the role of church maker. In *Tribute to Freud*, Freud becomes "Leader of the Dead" (101). Years after her analysis, she is still arguing: In an incident to which she alludes throughout "Writing on the Wall," she sends Freud gardenias with an anonymous note that read, "To greet the return of the Gods" (11). This time, although others to whom Freud shows the note misread it as saying "goods," he himself reads it as "Gods" and guesses correctly it was sent by H.D. "The Professor knew, he must have known," she writes triumphantly, that "by implication, he himself was included in the number of those Gods. He himself already counted as immortal" (63). Whatever this incident shows about Freud, it certainly reveals H.D.'s own desire, as Freud had seen it, to found a religion, in which Freud would play a central part.

H.D. thus plays the roles of prophetic Sibyl and interpretive priestess, of the watchful Miriam and the founding mother of a new messianic religion. She does this not merely through revisiting the religious mythology of Miriam and Moses in her dream of the princess (the only dream experienced during analysis that she fully elaborates in this memoir), but through positioning herself and her writing on the wall in the midst of the new mythos being developed. At one point, H.D. suggests that the primary confidence she wished to entrust to Freud in therapy may have been not any trauma of childhood or adulthood, but rather her various occult experiences.[27] Opening the section immediately following her first assertion that she knew Freud would be reborn, she continues,

> For things had happened in my life, pictures, "real dreams," actual psychic or occult experiences that were superficially, at least, outside the province of established psychoanalysis. But I am working with the old Professor himself; I want his opinion on a series of events. It is true, I had not discussed these experiences openly, but I had sought help from one or two (to my mind) extremely wise and gifted people in the past and they

had not helped me. At least, they had not been able to lay, as it were, the ghost. If the Professor could not do this, I thought, nobody could. . . . He was more than the world thought him—that I well knew. If he could not "tell my fortune," nobody else could. He would not call it telling fortunes—heaven forbid! But we would lead up to the occult phenomena, we would show him how it happened. (39–40)

Occupying nearly ten sections and located structurally in the middle of "Writing on the Wall," the narrative of her vision or hallucination moves as seamlessly and suspensefully as any of the other memories recounted (if not more so). It directly follows her meditation on her definitional dream of the baby Moses and the princess and a section in which she asserts her belief in the soul's immortality (43). It anticipates and precedes her descriptions of the rise of fascism at Freud's door in Austria. There can be no skirting of its (reconstructed) prophecy of the coming war if we focus on its position in this text's main narrative: "The picture now seemed to be something to do with another war, but even at that there would be Victory" (56). The event itself took place on the island of Corfu during a frustrated effort to visit the oracular site at Delphi.

The images H.D. saw successively projected on the wall of her hotel room were these: the face of a soldier or airman (or dead brother or lost friend); a goblet or chalice; a spirit-lamp or Delphic tripod, the tripod surrounded at its base by a mob of annoying, insectlike creatures or people; a Jacob's ladder; and finally the figure of Niké, Victory, who floats up the ladder, then brushes past a series of inverted "S" shapes (like scrollwork or question marks) to move into and through several tentlike triangles. Early in this succession of images, H.D. told her companion Bryher of the vision, and Bryher urged her to go on with it although she had not seen the images herself; but at this point, H.D. silently yielded to exhaustion and Bryher began to see the images herself, completing the vision: "a circle like the sun-disk and a figure within the disk; a man, she thought, was reaching out to draw the image of a woman (my Niké) into the sun beside him" (56).

One might readily see in the climax of H.D.'s "Writing on the Wall" a woman's Delphic vision of a woman warrior and goddess: Niké, a figure of female victory, a goddess before whom, as H.D. says in her poem "The Master,"

> all men will kneel,
> no man will be potent,
> important,
> yet all men will feel
> what it is to be a woman,

will yearn,
burn,
turn from easy pleasure
to hardship
of the spirit,

men will see how long they have been blind.[28]

In such a vision, H.D. and Bryher acquire not only the positions of prophetess, priestess, sister, and mother, but also the god-role that H.D. had claimed for Freud.

But extending this feminist vision, *Tribute to Freud* resists merely reversing the polarization of male/female, heterosexual/homosexual, god/worshipper. Gendered attributes are deconstructively crossed and crisscrossed in H.D. and Bryher's writing on the wall. What might be called the feminophallic imagery of the triumphant Niké is framed and "perfected" by "male-concentric" symbolism in H.D.'s initial visions of a soldier's quarter-turned face and goblet and in Bryher's concluding vision of a sun god, drawing Niké into his circle.[29] Despite its Michelangelesque quality, Freud himself, on H.D.'s account, analyzed this final vision in part as an expression of a "desire for union" with her mother (44). Then, too, H.D.'s conceptualization of herself crossed genders and sexualities, as did Freud's of her: In "Advent," the posthumously published record in which she reconstructed her original notes of her sessions, she writes that Freud insisted that "I [i.e., H.D.] want to be a boy" (120). She conceives of Freud also as harboring cross-gendered desire when she makes him into the androgynous Theseus in *Helen in Egypt*.[30]

Coincidentally, earlier in her sessions (according to the recorded sequence in "Advent"), Freud led H.D. through his treasured collection of figures from antiquity and pointed to a statue of Pallas Athene—"she whose winged attribute was Niké, Victory," writes H.D.—as his "favorite" of the "Gods (or the Goods) on his table" (68–69, 118). Freud's further comment that "She is perfect, . . . *only she has lost her spear*" (69) has been persuasively read as betraying his assumption of woman's lack (especially by DuPlessis and Friedman), but it also leads H.D. to meditate specifically on his materialism and his "Jewish" focus on a "pound of flesh," against which (racist) portrait she opposes her own spiritual revaluation:[31] "But this pound of flesh was a *pound of spirit* between us, something tangible, to be weighed and measured, to be weighed in the balance and—pray God—not to be found wanting!" (70). In "Writing on the Wall," H.D. narrates this episode *after* discussion of her hallucinatory vision, where it functions to remind us of an earlier comment by

H.D.—"But the Professor was not always right" (18)—even while under-lining the uncanny coincidence of their minds.

In the text itself, of course, such coincidences occur so often as to seem, eventually, far from coincidental. It is thus no accident that, for example, H.D. should enjoy discovering among the primary associations with "Sieg-mund" Freud's name that of the "victorious voice or utter-ance" (105). Niké is both Victory and Athene; Athene is H.D. and victo-rious; Athene is Freud's favorite figurine; Freud is "victorious." "Coin-cidence" transforms Freud and H.D. into enlarging mirrors of (or icons for) each other. Writing itself becomes both Freud's and hers in a passage in which it is difficult to tell not only what and whose writing H.D. means (it could also be the "writing" of Freud and H.D.'s associative talking cure or H.D. and Bryher's writing on the wall): "There was Victory, our sign on the wall, our hieroglyph, our writing" (88). In this sentence, it no longer matters what belongs to whom.

————————

Tribute to Freud foils the skeptic not by "insisting" on the "super-normal," but by stopping short of ever taking vision and prophecy entirely literally and instead offering an "other" world as a possibility among multiple possibilities. It is this openness that has allowed previous read-ers to see the spiritualist themes chiefly as Yeatsian metaphors for poet-ry. But in doing so (for Yeats as well as for H.D.), they have failed to see the extent to which spiritualism is entertained as a "real" possibility in this text—so much so that, as I have suggested, it acquires considerable explanatory power in deciphering H.D.'s argument with Freud and in guiding a reader through the impressionistic sequence of her narrative. To entertain the paranormal, however, is to entertain the unknowable and thus, for H.D., to refuse monological dogmatisms of any kind, wheth-er Christian or Judaic, psychoanalytic or psychic, rationalist or irratio-nalist. The supranormal acquires a decentering rather than a centering or a synthesizing function in this text.

H.D. offers an array of possible interpretations for her writing on the wall:

> We can read my writing, the fact that there was writing, in two ways or in more than two ways. We can read or translate it as a suppressed desire for forbidden "signs and wonders," breaking bounds, a suppressed desire to be a Prophetess, to be important anyway, megalomania they call it—a hidden desire to "found a new religion" which the Professor ferreted out in the later Moses picture. Or this writing-on-the-wall is merely an ex-tension of the artist's mind, a *picture* or an illustrated poem, taken out of

the actual dream or daydream content and projected from within (though apparently from outside), really a high-powered *idea*, simply over-stressed, *over-thought*, you might say, an echo of an idea, a reflection of a reflection, a "freak" thought that had got out of hand, gone too far, a "dangerous symptom." (51)

In the course of relating these multiple possibilities, they circle back, repeat, and overstate each other, confounding meaning. As H.D. tells us in "Advent," Freud is "puzzled" by her "writing on the wall" vision, and there is no indication that he ever settles upon a final explanation (173). Meanwhile, as she proceeds to say in "Writing on the Wall," this picture-writing nonetheless happened, opening another set of options, the paranormal: "But symptom or inspiration, the writing continues to write itself or be written. . . . The original or basic image . . . is common to the whole race" (51).

At an earlier point, she ascribes an intermediate status to her vision, neither conceding that it is merely psychological, nor asserting that it is psychic, nor suggesting that it is an intense version of poetic inspiration (an "illustrated poem" "projected from within"), but allowing it to partake of all these things: "For myself I consider this sort of dream or projected picture or vision as a sort of halfway state between ordinary dream and the vision of those who, for lack of a more definite term, we must call psychics or clairvoyants" (41). Although other critics have quoted this to make the rationalist argument that her hallucinations were a form of poetry, one could as easily make the irrationalist argument that her writing on the wall was a form of shamanism,[32] mediating between the ordinary and the extraordinary.

In either case, H.D. refuses to polarize or hierarchize her explanations. And when she finally completes her narration of the writing on the wall, she offers no further interpretation at all. After Bryher's vision of the sun disk in section 41 (quoted earlier), the text breaks and begins again in section 42 with an account of the period approaching the war. She thus leaves her hallucination an unexplained, inexplicable event—an *aporia*—testimony perhaps of impasse, but also of something beyond what "the world thought" or is capable of thinking.

As noted earlier, Friedman and Morris are nearly alone among critics in taking seriously and considering closely H.D.'s claims about the supernormal in *Tribute to Freud*.[33] Morris, however, sees H.D. as offering only two choices as to how to read her visions—as "merely an extension of the artist's mind" (*Tribute to Freud* 51) or as "projected from outside" (*Tribute to Freud* 46), messages from another world—and she believes H.D. "clearly prefers" the latter interpretation of the "writing on the wall" as a psychic phenomenon.[34] But H.D. offers at least two choices, neither of which she ultimately prefers over the other: "We can read my writing, the fact that there was writing, in two ways or in more than two ways" (51). Friedman argues that "the luminous sight from the dream, the vision, or occult experience had, for H.D., to be balanced by the rational perception of the conscious mind" and, quoting H.D., that "we must not step right over into the transcendental . . . or the brain itself, can be unhinged by dissociation." Friedman sees H.D. as striving ultimately for "synthesis of intellect and vision, science and religion" and argues that "what H.D. hoped to do was to apprehend the whole, transcend the dualism," quoting H.D. as saying that "science and art must beget a new creative medium"—namely, H.D.'s poetry.[35] But it is precisely this passage that then concludes, "Yet we must not step right over into the transcendental," as if the "medium" H.D. projected were that of the occult rather than of poetry. I agree that H.D. did not jettison the rational and, of course, her "professional" vocation was that of "poet" (although this was to a large degree defined for her by her peers and, retrospectively, by critics). But in addition, as I have argued, the outcome of the text of *Tribute to Freud* is neither Morris's "two choices" nor Friedman's transcendent "synthesis," but rather multiple possibilities for reading, multiple ways of writing, which are permitted simultaneous play and enlargement of each other. H.D.'s dualisms themselves multiply, shift, change, and become exchangeable in the course of her writing. "To grow nearer or to blend, even," as H.D. puts it in a passage about "twins" (32), is not to achieve complete synthesis or transcendence, let alone to "choose" between options: It is only to *approximate* oneness.

While admitting the kinds of secret realities that Somerville and Ross could only half-admit, while admitting the kinds of possibilities that modern civilization had repressed, H.D. never claims that everything can be understood or made explicit. The modernist (or is it postmodernist?) language of her text is itself a tissue of openings and closings, of public acknowledgment and private allusion, of disclosures and secrets. However coherent the narrative of her spiritualist argument with Freud might be (in my description of it), her playful language and section breaks continually interrupt, refute, and mock such coherence. She herself applied the fluid, fragmentary, and subjectivist term *impressions* to her memoir, not desiring careful coherence for it: "I do not want to become involved in the strictly historical sequence. . . . Let the impressions come in their own way, make their own sequence" (*Tribute to Freud* 14). Although her language is thus also analogous to the therapeutic process of "free association" she had explored and developed with Freud (as various critics have noted),[36] her impressions are not "rambling" or "irreducibly" multiple.[37] Contrasting her mode of knowledge with Freud's, she writes,

> I was swifter in some intuitive instances, and sometimes a small tendril of a root from that great common Tree of Knowledge went deeper into the sub-soil. His were the great giant roots of that tree, but mine, with hair-like almost invisible feelers, sometimes quivered a warning or resolved a problem, as for instance at the impact of that word *stranger.* "We'll show him," retorts the invisible intuitive rootlet. . . . "Show him that you have ways of finding out things about people, other than looking at their mere outward ordinary appearance." (98–99)

The "hair-like almost invisible feelers" that "quiver a warning or resolve a problem" in the dark "sub-soil" do more than contest the ancient "giant roots" of the "tree of knowledge"; they undermine, outwit, elude, and entangle, and in so doing altogether reshape what psychoanalytic knowledge, creativity, and writing can look like.

H.D.'s text is not a coauthored work, except where H.D. willingly admits recollected words, thoughts, and influences from Freud and Bryher. But in important respects, it represents a kind of collaboration from which its female writer benefited more than could, say, Jacobs in *Incidents in the Life of a Slave Girl.* Whereas *Incidents* is the result of an approximate collaboration between Jacobs and her editor, a mutually beneficial collaboration, but also one for which Jacobs paid a price and from which she was excluded in the last stages, H.D.'s text reflects the results of approximately collaborative conversations that she survived to reenact in her own writing. By conversing with Freud, in particular, by both accepting his views and resisting them, H.D. moved beyond her role as disciple to become a successor.

At the same time, H.D.'s argument with Freud is quite unlike the struggles to the death that Koestenbaum records in his chapter on Freud's collaborations with men, in that she never publicly broke with Freud or changed her "tribute" to denunciation. Rather, she struck a difficult, ever-shifting balance between utter reverence and utter transformation of the patriarchal Freud: "I was a student, working under the direction of the greatest mind of this and of perhaps many succeeding generations. But the Professor was not always right" (18). She affirmed for herself as well as for him a second birth in her work amid psychologically pregnant, mythopoetic, spiritualist figures such as that of the "frail lavender flower / hidden in the grass," so that "all men will feel / what it is to be a woman," "will see how long they have been blind," and "shall see woman / perfect."[38] In the concluding paragraph of the tribute, H.D. writes that, paraphrasing a poem by Goethe, despite the "scattered rocks and ruins [lying] about us and the threatening roar of the cataract . . . still echoing in our ears," "in the end," Goethe's Mignon "does not ask if she may go; or exclaim, if only we could go; but there is the simple affirmation, with the white roses—or the still whiter gardenias, as it happened—of uttermost veneration" (111).

Authorship itself becomes transformatively recycled in this text: As Bryher's completion of H.D.'s vision prefigures, permits, indeed justifies H.D.'s completion of Freud's vision, two kinds of "writing," two kinds of "vision" (or "more than two") intertwine.[39] Bryher's contribution to the writing on the wall and thus to *Tribute to Freud*, though peculiarly unexplored by critics, is the more intriguing of these two collaborative relationships. What Freud saw in the picture writing "as a desire for union with [H.D.'s] mother" (44) I would be inclined to call a "satisfaction " of such desire, for the vision was not H.D.'s alone, but produced by two women working together. H.D. herself saw Bryher's contribution as "determinative": "She saw what I did not see. It was the last section of the series, or the last concluding symbol—perhaps that 'determinative' that is used in the actual hieroglyph, the picture that contains the whole series of pictures in itself or helps clarify or explain them" (56). Earlier in the text, H.D. writes, "Here is this hieroglyph of the unconscious or subconscious of the Professor's discovery and life-study . . . and there is my friend Bryher who has brought me to Greece. I can turn now to her, though I do not budge an inch," and when Bryher says, "Go on," H.D. can do so, "discovering" for Bryher and herself the agency of the unconscious long before either woman met Freud (47).

Her tribute to Bryher does not end there, however, as she proceeds,

> I had known such extraordinarily gifted and charming people. . . . And yet, so oddly, I knew that this experience, this writing-on-the-wall before me, could not be shared with them—could not be shared with anyone except the girl who stood so bravely there beside me. This girl had said without hesitation, "Go on." It was she really who had the detachment and the integrity of the Pythoness of Delphi. But it was I, battered and disassociated from my American family and my English friends, who was seeing the pictures, who was reading the writing or who was granted the inner vision. Or perhaps in some sense, we were "seeing" it together, for without her, admittedly, I could not have gone on. (48–49)

Bryher in this passage is oracle, prophetess, and finally coseer with H.D. At this juncture, a section break occurs as H.D. makes room to tell of how Bryher took her on the trip to Delphi to help H.D. "get well" after her traumatic experiences of 1914–19: "Travel was difficult, the country itself in a state of political upheaval; chance hotel acquaintances expressed surprise that two women alone had been allowed to come at all at that time. We were always 'two people alone' or 'two ladies alone,' but we were not alone" (50). With Bryher, H.D. could recover vision along with her health.

This is not to say that this relationship was without tension or dissension. As Guest reports, Bryher's arrival on the scene in Vienna during H.D.'s work with Freud seems to have caused the first set of sessions to break off.[40] Guest and Katherine Arens also stress H.D.'s financial dependence on Bryher, who paid for her analysis.[41] Arens sees both women as eager to exploit their "contacts," citing Kenneth Macpherson's comment that H.D. "has got in [with Freud], hasn't she. She'll be unbearable. A pupil of Freud. She'll live on that till she dies."[42] Meanwhile, Bryher got to learn "some of the tricks of the trade" from H.D.[43] "Contact with Freud in 1933," says Arens, "meant much more than just treatment for an individual's mental health: it meant admission into an inner circle, a cultural legend of its own, with its attendant publicity."[44]

But H.D.'s argument in the text itself is explicitly with Freud, not Bryher. The scandalous relation of "two women alone" and their co-writing-on-the-wall are offered as possibilities that even the great Freud could not fully interpret or explain away and that pose, to this day, a challenge to readers.

Collaborative Menstruation

Penelope Shuttle and Peter Redgrove[45] are virtually unprecedented in their achievement of a coequal literary collaboration between a man and a woman and their production of cosigned texts in poetry, the novel, and nonfiction. Furthermore, theirs is an unabashedly feminist collaboration that, although it invites feminist critique in some respects, has contributed an important and complex argument to contemporary feminism. This contribution has received scant notice from feminist cultural theorists in the United States, partly because Shuttle and Redgrove do not promote themselves as theorists or make any great effort to take up a position in international academic feminism. In England, where cultural feminism has developed in a more dispersed way, in alignment with other theoretical developments (for example, with Marxism), they are more widely known. Redgrove and Shuttle see themselves primarily as writers of literature with important insights and knowledge to impart. Nonetheless, as coauthors of the nonfictional study *The Wise Wound* (1978), one of the earliest psychological studies and political revaluations of menstruation, they are feminist pioneers. Their work on menstruation forms a point of departure for rethinking gender, sex, sexuality, and modern spirituality. "Something kept secret and feared by all men," menstruation "nevertheless insists on returning time and again."[46]

Like H.D., they are interested in a revisionary mythology that will honor women and women's poetry, prophecy, and sexualities. They interrogate, criticize, and transform the conventional oppositions of the menstrual cycle to male linearity, to ovulatory (procreative) sexuality, and, more controversially, to meditational spiritualism. They insist on a circulatory linkage of all these things, suggesting that in an improved world, the cycles of the moon, the cycles of woman, the ups and downs of psychic life, and the journeys of spiritual life would be perceived as different levels of the same process. Not surprisingly, their theorizing embraces an ecofeminist vision of the relations between the human species and its environment.

Their collaboration, and their arguments and anecdotes about gender and sex, are rooted in the psychoanalytic theories of prominent male theorists, particularly of Jung and his follower John Layard, a psychologist and anthropologist also associated with Auden and his circle for a time in Berlin in the 1920s. These therapeutic beliefs and practices set them quite apart from H.D., who, in her loyalty to Freud, ignored Jung's thought. Yet in *The Wise Wound* Redgrove and Shuttle see themselves as taking up a subject either unglimpsed or treated prejudicially by these Jungian precursors as well as by Freud. They critique their antecedents, often finding more to credit to prior women psychologists than to male predecessors (including Emma Jung, Barbara Hannah, Marie-Louise Von Franz, Ann Ulanov, and Esther Harding, 105). Thus, though like H.D. in other ways, they go further than she in their resistant collaboration with traditional psychoanalysis.

Redgrove and Shuttle are not only absent from North American feminists' "mattering map," they are also rather difficult to place on it. Through *The Wise Wound* they took an active part in the women's liberation movement, and, in tune with the late 1960s and 1970s, they conceived this as a dual liberation of women and of sexuality. But although they do not avoid the word *emancipation* in their study, their emphasis on the alternative worlds of myth, dream, and the unconscious allies them more closely with the cultural mythic revisionism of H.D., Monique Wittig, Mary Daly, Judy Grahn,[47] and the feminist Jungian Annis Pratt, or even with Hélène Cixous and Luce Irigaray, than with the critical analyses of modern social arrangements and of literary assumptions inaugurated by Betty Friedan and Kate Millett. But their thought is embedded in Anglo-American empiricism and personalism rather than in the French philosophical tradition, and this can be seen most obviously in the kind of feminism they practice: They take as premises the argument that the personal is political, their approach to menstruation in *The Wise Wound* works empirically with accumulated data, their work involves them in consciousness raising as a political and personal strategy, women's health issues are central to their thought, and they celebrate female difference. All this opens them up, as it has many early American and some French feminists, to charges of essentialism, biologism, and ahistoricism.

Yet their work does not sit easily even with early Anglo-American woman-centered feminist empiricism. For one thing, they are not both women: The coauthored work of a heterosexual married couple obviously resists placement within a gynocritical tradition. If Shuttle had produced *The Wise Wound, The Hermaphrodite Album,* and *The Terrors of Dr Treviles* by herself, this work probably would have drawn more attention from American feminist critics. For another thing, despite Redgrove's purported neoromanticism, Shuttle and Redgrove's collaborative novels are postmodern, moving and speaking like a hermaphroditic Coover.[48] Predictably, reviewers were unnerved by this literary collaboration: *The Hermaphrodite Album* "infuriated" critics, "who wanted to know whether it was a man or a woman who had written a given poem."[49] The problem of what it means for collaborating heterosexual poets to label themselves hermaphroditic carries over to gender relations in their nonfiction and fiction as well, for although the subject of their nonfictional work is women's menstruation, their texts are as preoccupied with masculinity as with femininity. *The Wise Wound* is concerned with men's place in feminism and with the "new man," and one could readily argue (although I will argue otherwise) that their novel, *The Terrors of Dr Treviles,* with its *ménage à trois,* is centered around its male protagonist.

These complications in placing their work—their hermaphrodism and their postmodernism—are allied to each other within their work itself. Their collaboration has two effects in particular. First, as if reenacting their collaborative relationship, their fiction conjures multiple worlds and intertextual and metatextual relationships, as in many postmodern texts; second, their anecdotes and verbal puns often bend the gender difference, and their fiction experiments with gender inversion, gender multiplication, transvestitism, performativity, and cross-grafting of bodies. Seen in these ways, their work looks like neither Anglo-American feminist empiricism nor like visionary neoromanticism, but like feminist postmodernism. Even *The Wise Wound*, which appears as a straightforward argument about gender difference, throws some curves; like H.D., Redgrove and Shuttle challenge the borders between the rational and the irrational, the scientific and the artistic. Though persuasive, there is also something elusive, irritating to a rationalist, dismissible by the strict scientist in *The Wise Wound*, with its juxtapositions of science and myth, of the "hard" physical sciences and the "soft" sciences of psychology, of empirical accumulation of anthropological data and playful interpretative etymology, even of divergent objects of study, which include both female menstruation and ancient and popular culture.[50]

The questions Redgrove and Shuttle raise in their fiction, whether for a feminist or nonfeminist reader, do not end there, moreover. Like scientist and ritualist Robyn Treviles (a protagonist of *The Terrors of Dr Treviles*), they practice in their fiction "the simplest form of taboo-breaking"[51] by probing the improper: improper sexual and gender relations, scandalous spiritual practices, uncanny supernatural phenomena. In *The Terrors of Dr Treviles*—which, as their sole fully coauthored and cosigned novel, is my primary focus of analysis in this chapter—they permit not only, as H.D. does, such things as lesbian and bisexual sexuality, visionary trances, and theologization of psychological practices, but also the more disconcerting practices of father-daughter incestual relations and the *ménage à trois*,[52] the paranormal phenomena of ESP and "orthomolecular psychology" (the study of molecular change caused in a person by someone else's voice [5–6]), and Satanism.[53] From its first scene, this novel is the reader's own closet of terrors, or an uncloseting of social taboo and of the horrorhouse of the unconscious. The name "Treviles" is etymologized in the novel as "horrorhouse" (136).

The novel's playfulness could in itself make it objectionable to an ethical or political critic, raising the kinds of concerns that postmodern work has raised generally (for feminist critics, for example). It may seem to avoid practical, ethical determinations. But as I have already suggested, *The Terrors of Dr Treviles* belongs to what feminist, African-American, and multicultural postmodern critics have described in the past decade as political postmodernism;[54] although a reader could construe its scandals in any way he or she wished, when read either in its historical context or, formally, in the context of the choices its characters make, this is a novel with a political argument, one that tallies closely with the arguments of *The Wise Wound*. Its set of political assumptions includes an antipatriarchal approach to gender, sex, and sexuality; an antirationalist approach to the psyche; an antifoundationalist and antienlightenment approach to truth and logic; and an anti-Western approach to the connections between mind and body, body and spirit, spirit and cosmos.

My closer analysis of Redgrove and Shuttle's collaboration begins not with the novel, but with the authors' stories about their collaborative relationship and with their arguments about gender relationships. It is useful to look at what they have said, in particular, about the beginnings of their relationship in the 1970s, not only in order to contextualize their writing, nor only because they introduce themselves as characters into the narratives of their books, but because some of the problems raised by their fiction can be discerned in their autobiographical anecdotes. One may read these anecdotes in various ways. Particularly in regard to what they say about their relations as a man and a woman, their story could be seen as a familiar patriarchal narrative, as a radically revisionary story, or, as I will argue, necessarily something of both. Because they developed their complex arguments about gender and sexual relations over time, mostly after getting to know each other, and because their autobiographical anecdotes say as much about their views as do their explicit arguments, the stories they tell about their collaborative relationship, not just the arguments they frame around it, should be examined.

My discussion starts with what might seem most problematic about this relationship from a feminist viewpoint (especially in Redgrove's version of their story), proceeds through Shuttle's version to their larger justifications and arguments, and concludes with a discussion of some of the taboos they break (the borders they cross) and those they only flirt with. My treatment of their various arguments, anecdotes, and texts is longer than that in any previous chapter, not merely because I am introducing these writers to audiences among whom they are nearly unknown, but because I see them as innovative collaborators, interesting feminist thinkers, and complex artists.

Like a romance heroine, Shuttle caught Redgrove's eye while absorbed in reading. In a 1986 interview with Erika Duncan in which they discuss their first meeting, it is male writers' literary spaces that are explicitly recalled. They met in a farmhouse near the cottage in Zennor where D. H. Lawrence and his wife, Frieda, lived during World War I; Shuttle was reading Hardy. Redgrove saw her "reading a book of verse with a quality of attention I never saw before." It was "attraction" at first sight, but then terror: "because Penny was a novelist. She showed me a very French piece of work, and I fled to Ireland where for three weeks I lived on nothing but Guinness. I didn't eat anything."[55] In a short 1992 essay on their relationship, Redgrove adds that her novel reminded him of Rimbaud.[56]

In Shuttle, Redgrove discovers not merely a woman reader, not merely a Jane Eyre to the bachelor Rochester, but a Brontë, a woman writer, and a writer of sexy, avant-garde fiction (a Colette or Sarraute)—"a very French piece of work." Shuttle was in her early twenties at the time she met Redgrove in 1969, but had begun to write at the age of fourteen and had already published two novels, which had received serious critical notice. Confronted by a candidate muse-competitor, the frightened male poet fled overseas and attempted to drown and simultaneously starve his embryonic passion with an all-Guinness diet: "My turds resembled the graphite of pencils" (*We Two* 135–36). He felt "very unholy," and then he remembered "Penny had been wearing crosses in her ears." When he returned to her, he "never left" (Duncan 22).

One could easily interpret this episode—about which Shuttle says nothing in the interview except that she was reading Hardy—as a reenactment of a standard heterosexual romance convention. It's love at first sight, and the hero both starves and feeds upon his desire, but then seizes/surrenders himself to the desired object when he realizes she is Cornish angel rather than Parisian demon. Redgrove was married, but his marriage was "breaking up"; the romance with a younger woman involves infidelity to an older one and the abandonment of an older life (Shuttle is fifteen years younger than Redgrove).[57] Finally, Redgrove's story indicates an attempt to reassert his vocation, to conquer the female threat, not preeminently in this case by making her the object of his own creativity, but—as I will show—by recruiting Shuttle as a collaborator.

In describing their method of collaboration, Duncan makes it sound full and exemplary (although as in the story of the meeting, some hyperbole may be narrated as fact by the interviewer):

> For fifteen years or more there has hardly been a day in which they did not exchange notebooks detailing works in progress. Indeed, over the years their notebooks have taken on an almost identical form. In the particular way that new ideas are entered and complete prose drafts precede each roughing of a poem, one has the distinct impression that these notebooks are written for an intimate, that even as they are working out the solitary riddles of composition, Penelope Shuttle and Peter Redgrove are talking to one another.

Over the years they have learned to take lines and ideas from each other's notebooks, and to recognize which of their own ideas might be better suited to elaboration by the other. (18)

In these notebooks, there is apparently no such thing as authorial ownership with its fenced-off territories: The borders are open. As Shuttle and Redgrove said in response to questions posed by Michelene Wandor, "If scholars should ever be interested in the generation of our work, it would become a small industry for them, since we exchange and use for our individual purposes each other's ideas and images so freely. They will have a well-nigh impossible task untangling which was whose!" (145).

But later in the interview with Duncan, in the midst of a series of responses to how Redgrove and Shuttle are influenced by each other's acceptance and rejection of their ongoing work, Redgrove talks "of a time when 'Penny did not like [his] taking her phrases and making poems of them.'" For the most part, they talked about "the excitement of finding ideas for each other . . . happily sharing and 'stealing'" (21).[58] Redgrove appears to have initiated this practice of mutual theft, one that Shuttle disliked when she first encountered it. In Duncan's report, the story of Redgrove and Shuttle's first meeting emerges more distinctly from Redgrove's point of view than from the mostly silent Shuttle's. Yet, as I will later show, Shuttle also resists and enlarges Duncan's portrait and so does Redgrove.

Better known than the story of their first encounter is the tale of how they developed their menstrual theories and practices, as presented in the opening pages of *The Wise Wound*. At the time they met, Shuttle was enduring "deep and suicidal depressions" connected with menstrual distress (Duncan, 18). From a mystical convergence of two writers in love, the relationship progressed into a therapeutic collaboration: Shuttle brought her feelings and physical pain to Redgrove and he brought Shuttle his knowledge of psychology and experience of dream analysis. This classic psychiatric pattern of female body with male mind, female patient with male therapist became foundational in their lives together and in their careers. After several months of work with Shuttle's dreams, "the depressions were no longer severe, and the pains had eased," and Shuttle "had found a fresh attitude to her period, which enabled her to enjoy that time for its particular qualities, and no longer reject it." In addition, "there were subsidiary effects, such as a radical improvement of eyesight, and an enhancement of her creative abilities" (*Wise Wound* 14–15). This experience fed directly into their next novels and poems (both cosigned and not).

In the prologue to the cosigned *The Wise Wound*, they become submerged together in an omniscient narrator of a third-person narrative, but the narrative nonetheless delineates conventional roles for them:

> During early 1971 Penelope Shuttle was suffering bad pre-menstrual de-
> pressions, and menstrual pain when the period came. Peter Redgrove had
> studied analytical psychology and dream analysis for many years, and in
> particular had spent 1968–9 as a pupil of the famous analyst Dr John
> Layard, who himself had studied with Homer Lane, C. G. Jung and oth-
> ers and had published many distinguished contributions to psychology
> and anthropology. With the help of Layard's methods, Redgrove enabled
> Shuttle to draw pictures of the depressions, and then to dream vividly as
> a consequence. She dreamed every night for five months, and the dreams
> were analysed every day, in sessions often lasting many hours. (14)

What could sound more patriarchal than this? The decontextualized
Shuttle suffers emotionally and physically; Redgrove studies, and has
done so for many years, with a lineage of famous male psychologists, and
he ministers to Shuttle by directing and analyzing her dreams.

Yet if Shuttle and Redgrove aligned themselves with traditions of
great men in psychology as well as in literature, they were also quick to
admit their entrapment in a patriarchal structure. Not only in *The Wise
Wound*, which is dedicated to dismantling this trap, but throughout their
writing, they seek to elude and erode hierarchical gender norms. Preceding Redgrove's 1992 essay (appearing in tandem with it) is an essay by
Shuttle. The concluding paragraph to its first section deals with their
work on her menstrual dreams and begins in this way: "Both of us were
wounded, as who is not, by the strictures of over-masculinized society;
of living by its wrong rhythms; and it was through work on patterns of
feminine identity and body/spirit experiences that we drew closer together" (*We Two* 125).[59] Shuttle's narrative is an account of coequal need, of
the suffering exacted from both of them by patriarchal mandates, and of
healing that came not through "masculine" means, but through openness to "feminine" experience. Whereas Shuttle records the "release"
from patriarchal structures that they both experienced as a result of their
therapeutic work together (*We Two* 125), Redgrove records the antifem-
inist backlash against his work with Shuttle: "Of course I have blotted
my copybook irretrievably red for danger by collaborating in a book on
menstruation, and have received many insults from the masculinist establishment as a result" (*We Two* 140). In their dream work, they removed
themselves from further possible influences: "We determined that we
should not consult any book on the psychology of menstruation until the
initial phases of the analysis were over, in case it prejudiced our observations" (*Wise Wound* 14). When they had completed their work with
the dreams, they discovered that no tradition existed for what they were
doing: "THERE WERE NO SUCH BOOKS!" (*Wise Wound* 15).[60]

Shuttle and Redgrove's resistance to the "masculinized" social structures enmeshing them and to stereotypes of their heterosexual relationship are not and probably could not be completely successful; they can never escape such structures altogether. In addition, like Irigaray and Cixous, Shuttle and Redgrove believe in differences; they criticize modern culture for attending to, and exalting, only one side of the sexual difference. What is feminist, then, in their narratives and arguments is the shift of balance from exclusively valuing the masculine to revaluing the feminine, the revisionary description of characteristics such as "listening" and "receiving" as active rather than passive qualities and as signs of "intensity" rather than of nonexistence (Duncan 21).

One could read it as a sign both of gender difference and of resistance to the "man's story" that Shuttle's most extensive account of their first meeting (in her 1992 essay) begins neither with the sudden first sight of the beloved nor with allusions to (male) writers—and certainly not with a terrified recognition of Redgrove's writerly potency (and subjecthood)—but with a landscape. The passage begins with a literality—pointing to each and every thing she recalls with words whose textures evince the babble of sensations—which recalls Margaret Homans's theory of women writers' literal language. This language of the pre-Oedipal and of the Lacanian "imaginary" (where the borders between mother and child are experienced as fluidly permeable, and a child feels its mother's physical and verbal caress as its own) is opposed to the distancing oedipalized and socially constructed "symbolic."[61]

> West Penwith is high moorland: gorse; heather; bracken; some cultivated tracts of land; rocky outcrops, ancient stones, ever-changing shades and shadows of sea, sky and land. I'd been living for some months in Somerset, having moved from urban Middlesex, but this was more than countryside; this was not England! It was a different land, having a profound stillness of earth, of stone, and a glittering lurching light from sea and sky; an enclave agitated yet peaceful, simmering yet stable; changing and changing, a place of second and third and fourth thoughts, on to infinity. The very names, the last living traces of the lost Cornish language, were speaking their poetry. (*We Two* 123)

Shuttle never gazes upon Redgrove at all in this account. He appears by name alone, suddenly and abruptly there: "In this strange beautiful magical and auspicious place, of barrows, standing stones, cromlechs, carns, little fields, moors and stone hedges, Peter and I met. We realized almost at once that we shared the same reality." By "reality" she means "a three-fold reality: of poetry; of love erotic, spiritual (and, later, parental); and of Cornwall (not England), weather and landscape and separateness." So she turns at last in this passage to what Redgrove feels he has in common with her and even lists these things, "poetry," "love erotic," in the same order in which we find them in his story. Yet adding and insisting on landscape, she ends this paragraph meditating again on Cornwall, "not the least powerful of the three" (123).

Cornwall, which she experiences as "embracing," even "seizing," nonetheless also permits "separateness." So too she describes merging with Redgrove as bringing her back to her own separateness: "Through the contagiousness of love and writing-enthusiasm we exchanged hats as it were"; quite literally, for he began to write novels and she to write poetry, "we were beginning to become one another. And becoming one another we became more our ownselves" (*We Two* 124). Her account of her menstrual work with Redgrove also differs from the narrative of *The Wise Wound*, for she makes no attempt to distribute the contributions each made to her therapy, and, as I have noted, she presents both of them as suffering at the time of their meeting. Moreover, the emphasis is on a mutuality that permits separateness, rather than on a separateness that threatens and must be "stolen" back: "So Cornwall and writing brought us together. But we were also brought together by adversity and unhappiness. At this time I was struggling with the deep and paralysing depressions that later opened out into the dreams and the releasing work between us that led to the writing of *The Wise Wound*, and new visions of writing for us both. Also when we met Peter was deep in the painful disintegration of his first marriage. So we were both at crisis point; and in need of healing" (124).

The arguments that Redgrove and Shuttle make about gender difference are as open as the stories they tell about meeting each other to a variety of interpretations. In their response to a question posed by Wandor,[62] Redgrove and Shuttle acknowledge the differential roles they played during their early dream-work, but in commenting on that work in the context of their arguments about gender, they treat these gender roles as exceptional rather than normal:

> A variation of the usually-accepted masculine-feminine roles became important during the preliminary dream-work for *The Wise Wound*, our book about menstruation. Penelope dreamed the menstrual dreams, and Peter, by analysing them, reflected them back to her to stimulate the development of the dream-story. Thus, instead of our usual flexible situation, Penelope was the Sybil and Peter her Scribe. However, since that time, in the majority of our work, either of us may be the visionary, and either one of us the critic or analyser; the circulation between us is at

the heart of the work, but who takes which role is not important. (Wandor, 143)

Redgrove and Shuttle here see traditional gender role-playing as exceptional in their collaboration, but they also see the sexual difference between them as essential in their lives together. Carefully separating sexual from gender difference, which they believe can be "unlearned," they see "an inclination towards different kinds of life-experience brought about by the two kinds of [anatomical, sexual] endowment, as man or woman," and they take the empirical position that "it is not yet known how far sex differences can be unlearned also" (Wandor 141–42).[63]

They insist on crossing and recrossing the gap, both socially constructed and anatomically given, that vexes feminist theorists even now. But Redgrove and Shuttle do this not only by treating the problem of gender difference as a problem of value but also by treating the sex difference as bridgeable, possibly even provisional. That is, although they focus on sexual and gender differences as these observably exist, they refuse to see sex difference as absolute, refuse to split it not only from the socially constructed category of gender, but also (more importantly perhaps) from mind and spirit, and they leave all these things speculatively open to exchange and change, as in their equivocally open-ended assertion that it is not known how far sex differences can be unlearned.

Thus they interpret the sexual difference they posit as a question of value by arguing, first, that contravening men's historical valuation of themselves as the superior sex in their possession of a penis, women possess superior access to a greater range of sexual experience. It is in fearful reaction to this, they argue, that men have attempted to set a greater value on themselves. Women enjoy special access to all the physical processes of the menstrual cycle, childbearing, and multiple orgasm. Although men's fear and repugnance have traditionally repressed women's feelings during menstruation, Redgrove and Shuttle argue also that women desire sex and have heightened sexual sensitivity during menstruation. Such physical tendencies further appear (to fearful men, at least) to incline women to a more direct relation to their environments, in particular to the changes in the moon as well as in the sun, to seasonal as well as diurnal changes, all of which, in ancient cultures, promoted greater mystification and mythologization of women's powers—a more direct link with the gods but also more reason for fear.[64]

Masculinity, they argue further, is alterable in a revised culture, and men can and should "work" to "redress" the "balance" that is "due" to women (Wandor 144). Redgrove and Shuttle express this "work" as "bending," and this becomes a literal, physical trope, not only an abstraction in *The Wise Wound*. Men's "work" can and should be a literal bending of the body—by no means only of the mind—of the male toward the female. This gender bending takes on plural signification of hailing, bowing, honoring, permitting, and, above all, yielding of privilege to the (female) body heretofore granted nearly exclusively to the (male) mind: "If the men do not bend, as the women have to," they argue, "then they will break, and carry our world down with them" (*Wise Wound* 79). They are nearly silent about penile "experience"—which in Western culture traditionally has dominated sexual description—but it is the bending not only of the inner man and mind but also of the literal penis that enables the male to share a woman's experience.[65]

Thus, in addition to sharing a woman's menstrual sexuality through respecting and yielding to her desires and moods, through listening to, reflecting back, and vicariously experiencing for himself the dreams that come during menstruation, men may "bend" toward her experience through sexual intercourse. As Shuttle and Redgrove restate this in their 1983 interview with Wandor,

> It is possible for a man to participate deeply in the menstrual rhythm, so that his whole body responds, even to the sympathetic accumulation of fluid during the pre-menstrual week, and the pattern of dreaming, with some creative resolution arrived at with the period arriving in his female partner; however, he is still experiencing this through that partner, and she is the source of this, not him. . . . Tantric tradition tells how a man by becoming the sexual and spiritual student of the woman may learn multi-orgasm, may learn to follow the flux and reflux of energies patterned in her fertility cycle, and in partnership with her may learn to produce his own children: but they are spiritual children, ideas, works of art that have the tinge of both partners, discoveries that have the quality of both genders. (Wandor 142–43)

During Shuttle's pregnancy, Redgrove "caught the glow" from Shuttle even without making love, but in addition, "the deeper or 'uterine' orgasms were very strong indeed while she was carrying, and Zoe in the womb seemed to participate in our love-making"; "This creative 'afterglow' appears to be a state mediated to Peter by sex predominantly. . . . Lovemaking and sex . . . restores the fluidity of personality" for him (146–47). Their arguments thus intersect with especially vivid moments in their autobiographical anecdotes in breaking paths across borders generally considered uncrossable or taboo.

Just after first mentioning "Peter's vicarious anal bleedings and his nosebleeds that accompanied Penny's menstrual bleeding during the most intense period of their research into her dreams," Duncan abruptly admits a sense of deep discomfort, "as if I too were walking into the realm of a deep taboo," and she finds herself wondering why (22).[66] What exactly was the source of the taboo?

> Was it the merging of the menstrual material and focus on the sexual act that I found jarring? Or was it the degree of the merging of the couple, the attunedness so few will dare, out of which both had made their finest art? And how did I as a woman react to Peter's insistence that the men in a household feel women's menstruation as keenly as women themselves, and must learn to take energy out of the powers released by it, his descriptions of how, as a boy he had smelled his mother's menstruations, and had waited eagerly for them, hoping that his mother would not be pregnant with another baby? How safe the penises and noses in *Tristram Shandy* seemed compared to all of this! (22)

It was probably all these things: the taboo sexual border erected between menstruation and sexual intercourse, the taboo gender border that this couple was crossing, the taboo psychological border that they insisted on ignoring periodically (valuing "merging" in addition to the "separation" of traditional psychoanalysis), and not only these but the feminist borders between male and female, child and parent more recently developed to protect female experience and childhood from predatory men. In comparison, Sterne's masculinist erotic play on penises and noses seems mild and safe. But as Shuttle and Redgrove argue in *The Wise Wound*, the "taboo" itself was once held "sacred" and may trace its roots to menstruation: "'Taboo' or 'sacred' in Polynesian and Siouan is the same word as 'menstruating.' In Dakotan, 'Wakan' means 'spiritual, wonderful, menstrual'" (65).

Another crossed border deserving mention in this context is only implied in Duncan's series of questions: Redgrove and Shuttle cross the deep line that Western rationalist societies have drawn between physical and mental experiences. In Redgrove and Shuttle's relation to each other and in their writing, bodies are directly linked to intellectual endeavor for both women and men (*Wise Wound* 152–53). Hence writing itself is as intense as any other kind of experience and enjoys no less priority than other realms shared between them. As Shuttle says, sharing their work has "the effect that 'touch has on the person who returns the touch'" (Duncan 22).

Of course, Duncan's comparison to *Tristram Shandy* evokes quite another possible response to Redgrove and Shuttle's arguments: One might simply find Shuttle and Redgrove's "collaborative menstruation" ridiculous, not to be taken any more seriously than Redgrove's self-dra-

matizing account of his Guinness binge. Their frankness can verge on
sexual boasting. But if we find it risible, our amusement may mix incredulity with standard Freudian displacement of our own repressed sexual
tendencies.

Meanwhile, their collaborative relationship has lasted not only through
exploring taboo areas—a process they experience, not surprisingly, primarily as an exciting adventure—but also because it has worked, enabling their
ideas and literature as well as their lives, proving to be profitable. Redgrove
and Shuttle, husband and wife, act not only as a two-person emotional dyad
but as a two-person literary movement, supporting each other at every level
in their life and writing. In the course of a seven-year preparation for *The
Wise Wound* in 1978 (the last of their cosigned books until *Alchemy for
Women* appeared in 1995), they coauthored and cosigned a book of poems,
The Hermaphrodite Album, and a novel, *The Terrors of Dr Treviles;* Redgrove authored "with" Shuttle (this way of signing their work marking it
as a partial collaboration) a second novel, *The Glass Cottage.* In addition,
in this period Redgrove published four books of poems (*Dr. Faust's Sea-Spi-
ral Spirit and Other Poems, Three Pieces for Voices, Sons of my Skin: Selected Poems 1954–1974,* and *From Every Chink of the Ark: New Poems
American and English*) and his novel *In the Country of the Skin,* while
Shuttle published two novels (*Wailing Monkey Embracing a Tree* and
Rainsplitter in the Zodiac Garden). Their productivity is impressive, and
it was a thoroughly collaborative engagement, for (like most of the collaborative work of Louise Erdrich and Michael Dorris), even their single-signed
works are produced collaboratively.

Creative "concentration" (of their sexual, creative, and social powers)
is produced, they claim, by a monogamous relationship.[67] This is something about which they have a lot to say. Shuttle explains it this way: "Our
relationship is monogamous because it is difficult to tell the truth otherwise. Lying is not a good training for poetry. The mutual illumination sex
brings us is of a poetic nature. Everyone of us experiences this sometimes
but perhaps not enough people concentrate on it and open the way for it
to increase" (*We Two* 127). And Redgrove writes, "In sexual alchemy—
which is to say an artists' relationship that is erotic—you cannot hop from
partner to sexual partner. The Work is a long process, and the Soror and
Frater Alchymica work on each other and the work works on them for as
long as it takes, which may be a lifetime. . . . Concentration is needed, an
accustomed temenos or laboratory" (*We Two* 138). In other words, monog-
amy creates a safe, stable arena for exploring the relations between sex and
poetry, menstruation and sex, themselves and poetry. Perhaps they enjoy
the security with which they may explore the interplay between sex, po-

etry, environment, and themselves too much to improvise further. Indeed, there may be some practical psychological value to the notion of the monogamous relationship as a "temenos," that only within such a relationship are psychosexual healing and psychosexual risk-taking simultaneously available. Theirs are the rewards, as for Field and Elbrecht and Fakundiny, of a long "durée" rather than only of romantic "love at first sight" or, for that matter, of the experimental one-nighter.

For all this concentration on their own heterosexual relation, however, there is something "queer" about the ways the gender distinction operates in Redgrove and Shuttle's stories and arguments, as in the moment when Redgrove and Shuttle consider the possibility that one might "unlearn" the sex difference. In his 1992 essay on their collaborative relationship, Redgrove offers the same story of their first encounter that Duncan does except that he provides more detail, and in the detail are some differences. When he opened Shuttle's novel, which was lying on the table next to her,

> I had seen nothing like it before: it was the story of three people in a sexual triangle and though they were almost entirely caught up in their jealousies they moved through a clairvoyant world that sparkled and hummed with awareness that the characters only intermittently shared. As in Wallace Stevens, they were unhappy people in a happy world. Shuttle's sentences slid over each other, chatoyant, exposing layers of texture, sound, scent, abrasion, silkiness, sentences of every kind that explored the spaces they created like fighting ants and bejewelled leopards establishing domiciles. I was reminded of Rimbaud, extended. I have since heard celebrated by the French feminists of the 1980s "the feminine sentence" and the quality of *jouissance* in writing. (135)

A sexual triangle, a "humming" and "sparkling" "clairvoyant world," and sentences in erotic relations to each other, exposing and rubbing their sounds, smells, and textures, a feminist, "feminine" *jouissance* preempting the earlier references to Stevens and Rimbaud—all this suggests an enchantment with Shuttle that has little in spirit to do with the prospects she might open up for a proprietary, monogamous, heterosexual relationship.

When Redgrove reencounters Shuttle after his Irish interlude, these alternative worlds continue to multiply as he discovers her "dresses": "the sartorial equivalent of the feminine sentences [Shuttle] constructed: 'her wonder-awakening dresses, star-rays combed into a shaggy dress, bone-flounce skirt, turbinal blouse.'" But he concludes that although all this was "quite an eyeful," he "could not wear the dresses" and could only "do my best to allow the feminine sentence to write through me, and for a while I became the novelist" (136). Thus gender begins to bend, the transvestite moment surfaces, only to be pressed back underground in favor of the now-disguising rather than "exposing" sentences.

Whereas Shuttle and Redgrove appear happy to offer interpretations of their lives together and to avow shared beliefs, their novel, *The Terrors of Dr Treviles*, avows nothing. As it mixes dream, ritual, fantasy, psychodrama, flashback, myth, and ordinary narrative, borders among these realms of experience often blur both in the minds of the protagonists and in that of the reader. Any given moment in the novel seems a performance, and this further disrupts the traditional representational and ethical functions of the novel. Yet the novel's fantasies dovetail with Redgrove and Shuttle's arguments about male-female sexual collaboration and about menstruation; these form a thematic center to a postmodern psychological romance–thriller.

Like *An Irish Cousin*, *The Terrors of Dr Treviles* combines psychological realism with conventions of a popular genre, indeed two popular genres in this case: the romance and the horror movie. Its playful excursion into the uncanny comes complete with a gothic house and female ghost; a mad male occupant who obsesses over the death of a younger brother and former wife; a technically incestuous relation to his stepdaughter; the stepdaughter herself, a white-clad younger woman who practices satanic rituals; a bisexual *ménage à trois* augmenting this odd couple with a second woman; constant erotic fantasies; and continual hints of an impending catastrophe. But it does not end in catastrophe; on the contrary, although its ending is not a simple one, its protagonists, both living and dead, appear to be at peace by the end. Unlike the sensationalism of *An Irish Cousin*, the horrors of this novel emerge from articulated thoughts, memories, and fantasies rather than from half-admitted secrets; its "terrors" are excitements to be imagined or guilts to be evaluated. Redgrove and Shuttle thus offer an alternative both to the conventional sexual situations of romance and to the usual structure of the horror film, which depends on buried social secrets. In *The Wise Wound*, Redgrove and Shuttle point out that in such films,

> one is watching something that, normally, is concealed, now extravagantly revealed. It may be, however, that the revelation is a further concealment. . . . One usually finds that the "horror" is worse in the anticipation than in the revelation. . . . It is reasonable to suppose that horror films, which have probably been seen by more people than have read

the Bible, might have a similar function at least to detective-stories. Freud said in his essay that the "Uncanny" is "that class of the terrifying which leads back to something long known to us, once very familiar." (239)

The uncanny facts here awaiting detection have to do with menstruation and the various borders that may be breached in male-female relations. Like works by Coetzee, Kundera, or Wittig, *The Terrors of Dr Treviles* is partly a political fable, anticipating the issues canvassed in *The Wise Wound*, focusing in graphic detail on a physical process rarely described in the novel before the 1970s. *The Terrors of Dr Treviles* plausibly records the events and fantasies that occur to Robyn Treviles and to her stepfather and lover, Gregory, in the course of her menstrual period, offering a feminist fable of menstruation.

Complicating and obscuring this politicized theme is the fact that both female and male characters often experience graphic masculinist fantasies. But again, read in the context of *The Wise Wound*, with its revisionary feminization of male mythologies, the obviously male imagery in these fantasies carries, in its turn, intriguing female subtexts. If the novel is enhanced by knowledge of the mythological project of *The Wise Wound*, so also *The Wise Wound* is extended by *The Terrors of Dr Treviles*. For the nonfictional study goes no further than to outline an alternative interpretation of conventional cultural imagery, whereas the novel acts out the implications of this interpretation and explores an alternative culture, mobilizing a cross-gendered imagery of menstruation in the context of characters living a life cross-cut with those of the authors. (Both Shuttle and Redgrove are named within the novel, and Redgrove is a minor character.)

The title *The Terrors of Dr Treviles* hints at the doctor's equivocal status as, like Frankenstein, maker of the horror, the horror's victim, and the horrific monster itself. The title also suggests, again like its classic precursors, a cultural allegory of the relations between science and nature, a religious fable of the relations between nature and the supernatural, and a psychological story about the relations between the unconscious and conscious self. These multiple purposes anticipate *The Wise Wound*, where Redgrove and Shuttle argue that modern science, religion, and culture must be revised by informed sensitivity to psychological processes accompanying women's bleeding, that nature and the unconscious are made horrific by the lopsided overemphasis of the analytic and "pure," and indeed that the impulse to control and devalue buried energies is suicidal, wounding men, women, and the world's ecosystem. *The Terrors of Dr Treviles* itself makes no such argument; instead, in keeping with the themes of *The Wise Wound,* scientific, psychic, sexual, and spiritual exploration intertwine inseparably in the minds of the characters and in the narrative.

On the face of it, the title and title character focus this novel on a male paradigm and lead a reader to expect a story in which a male doctor, Dr. Gregory Treviles, plays the central role. But like the imagery of this novel, the name "Treviles" becomes caught up and revised in the fantasies of the women characters and in a narrative structure that juxtaposes the "terrors of Dr Treviles" with the interwoven tales of three women: his stepdaughter/lover (possibly wife), Robyn Treviles, who in addition to practicing occult rituals while menstruating is a molecular biologist whose professional name may also be Dr. Treviles; of Robyn's and Gregory's lover, Brid Hare, who in addition to being a Jungian psychologist and colleague of Gregory is a sculptor, a maker of mythic images; and of Mamie Treviles, the ghost in this story who was Gregory's first wife and Robyn's mother. The juxtapositions of science with women's experience, of science and spiritualism, and of the conscious self with its psychic horrors are no less important in the narratives of Robyn and Brid than in that of the doctor-poet Gregory. So Gregory Treviles becomes, in a multivalent phrase Brid Hare uses, "one man among three" (133), and the cultural narrative he rewrites of science's encounter with other modes of knowledge is only one story among four. In what follows I begin with Gregory's narrative, but gradually interleave with this an account of the ways his story is not only juxtaposed and interwoven with, but framed and contested by the women's.

As the novel develops, the interrelatedness of Treviles with terrors is thematized, first through playful but nightmarish associations that occur in Gregory's fantasies, and then through etymologization of the name "Treviles." "Alone in Treviles Towers, the great mansion that has grown into the garden, that obstructs Fentonluna Lane, Gregory Horrorhouse weeps hot tears" (87). House and name merge twice in this sentence—in Treviles Towers and Gregory Horrorhouse—and together make explicit what is usually implied in the horror story: the convergence or collapse of the internal and the external and, more specifically, the identification, which is so essential to the workings of the uncanny, of self with house.[68]

"Treviles" undergoes further deconstructive transformation, this time in gender formation, in the fantasies of Brid Hare.[69] Her meditation on the name begins with a Manichean—or Jungian—double-pronged apprehension, for even as she "adores" Treviles, she recollects the name's origin in the "vile." She then gradually develops these associations by retracing the name's complex roots in a history of patriarchal culture and in the distorted relations between the sexes:

> Adoration of the name "Treviles." "Reviles," Brid mused to herself, "Treviles. From the Latin, vilus, vile. French, vil." Clearly the Treviles were an old Huguenot family who emigrated from Brittany immediately before the St. Bartholomew Day's [sic] Massacre and settled in Cornwall. Très, the French word for "very."
> . . . a very vile fellow. A family closely associated with all sorts of vileness, named and unnamed, vileness worn as a badge of honour. The Vile Ones. Worshippers of Satan. Yoni soit qui mal y pense. Gentlemen of the Moon. Trevires. One man among three. The man in the Moon. An old witch family fleeing church persecution and burnings and tortures. Fleeing to Albion, the land of the Goddess, and its noble Order of the Garter. Order of the Jam-Rag. Lady Salisbury, dancing, dropped a garter, a witch-cord: honi soit qui mal y pense, said Edward, evil to him who evil thinks, and founded the most noble Order of the Garter. Or she had the curse, dancing, and dropped her towel from between her legs: yoni soit qui mal y pense. Cunt to him who evil thinks. Ye shall honour that whence ye emerged. (133–34)

This same set of stories is told in *The Wise Wound* (183). First there is the story of men and families who wore "vileness" as a "badge of honour," that is, men and families who deliberately allied themselves with women during their menstrual periods. Then they tell the story of women *and* a few men who were perceived as witches because of the special connections they maintained with each other and the cycles of the moon. They tell also of women who, in ancient menstrual ritual practice, turned to their "other husband"—figured by the man in the moon, refigured in modern psychology as the Jungian shadowy "animus"—and followed the direction of "darker" desires, independent of monogamous attachment or the reproductive function.[70] (A man becomes one of three possibilities for a woman who, when aroused by her menstrual flow, loves a second husband, loves herself, and loves other women who join her in the menstrual cycle.) Finally, they narrate their revisionary version of the moment in English history when Edward founded the Order of the Garter in order to honor his wife, who had accidentally dropped her rag in public. The citation "Yoni" (cunt) "is evil to him who evil thinks" becomes, for Redgrove and Shuttle as for Brid Hare in this passage, the motto of all these stories of menstruation. The cunt too, of course, is a "house": ancient, ancestral, seemingly original "first home" through which all pass.

Even as verbal play disrupts the gender distinction, producing uncanny crossings of male with female, however, tension about sex roles surfaces in the dialogue between Gregory and the women characters. Gregory apparently disagrees with Brid Hare's set of associations with his name: "No," he says at breakfast, "Treviles is the same word as travail, meaning to labour, and it derives from the Cornish word 'trevas,' meaning tillage, crop, produce, harbour. We Treviles are a family of harvesters, people employed at harvest" (134). Gregory's monothematic imagery of labor implicitly appropriates female "travail" for a happy "family of harvesters," of which Gregory would be the chief male descendant and head. Brid's response to his correction superficially indicates acquiescence, but it also resists its puritanism and male emphasis by reinfusing his imagery with sexuality and by uncovering the male paradigm behind the harvester figure: "You ploughed me . . . will you harvest?" (134). We might rephrase this (in a manner reminiscent of Redgrove and Shuttle in *The Wise Wound*) as "You seem to think you can be both plow and harvest—sole maker—will you absorb me too?" Brid is described as "aghast at the coincidence" (134) of his terminology with their sexual intercourse, but the use of the words "aghast" and "coincidence" is not accidental: This novel's language and narrative are permeated with ghostly coincidences and coincidental ghosts. Gregory's Horrorhouse is haunted, in particular, by ghosts of buried women and by the uncanny coincidences of one (male) way of seeing things with a buried (female) way.

In this same section (part 3, section 3), independently of Gregory and Brid, Robyn becomes curious about the name *Treviles* as she is waiting for books in the library, and she looks up related terms in a dictionary. As if in response to Gregory's confident declaration of "harvest labor" as the sole meaning of his name, Robyn demonstrates its more multiple and duplicitous history, which goes back not only to "travail" but to "torture-chamber" and to "horror house":

> "Trestle, tret, treve, trews." A treve, she read, was a roof-beam, and the term was usually reserved for a particularly stable construction of three beams cut from the same tree that was resistant to the stresses of storms, flaws and winds. It was important to lay these beams with the grain of the wood in certain directions. She flipped over a few pages. "Traumatism, traumato, travail . . ." she was surprised to learn the derivation from old French "travailler" meaning to torment—she had no idea the feeling was so strong—and as it went back it got stronger, back through the vulgar latin "trepaliare" meaning "torture," and "trepalium" which meant torture-chamber, and, literally and originally, an instrument of torture with three stakes. Her mind moved slowly back over her lifelong mem-

ories of Gregory. She found the Cornish dictionary, which told her that the prefix "tre" meant a dwelling-place, and "vyl" meant horror. Thus through two languages, the name Treviles meant Horrorhouse. Gregory Horrorhouse. (135–36)

So we are returned to the masculine figuration of the novel's title: It might as well be called "The Terrors of Gregory, Gregory the Terrible." As Robyn meditates on the name, her mind goes back over memories of Gregory, and then her dictionary discoveries give way to fantasies of a man impaled on a stake and strung across beams of wood; of a notice tacked above his head, "Death to the Midianite Witches"; and of a woman in labor and a midwife who, resembling a butcher, seizes the baby to be circumcised by a young doctor, all of which occurs in a house on a cliff named "Treviles." In this set of fantasies, Gregory begins as a man-witch under torture and only at the end is associated with an emergent modern science and its cruel surgical methods. Whereas Brid's long meditation on Gregory's name emphasizes its female antecedents, Robyn's fantasy includes the tortured and the torturers, acknowledging a history in which men have allied themselves with women while other men (and women) have cut themselves off from women.

Though less elaborately than *Treviles*, terrors acquires a life of its own in this novel, and in almost every case it is associated with the narrative of Gregory Treviles's psyche. In the poetry seminar he attends (led by "Peter Redgrove"), a woman who is studying to be a nun is irritated by the poem he has written, sees it as nothing but an unadmitted expression of guilt about his brother's death, and angrily renames all his poems: "This poem is misnamed, all the poems of this author are misnamed. The title of these works should be 'The Terrors of Dr Treviles!'" (110). As it happens, Gregory does not entirely disagree with her, but he sees "terror" as a condition to be allowed and explored rather than a sign of guilt to be repented and repressed. Later, applying the term to Robyn's description of their "exciting walks" together, Gregory sees "the Terrors" as (in her words) "like a change-over, a transition, like changing trains at a station" (140).

As if taking the would-be nun up on her challenge, the "first of his terrors" turns out to be a vision of his brother's face, "softly and cheerfully looking in [the window] at him out of the blossom" (115). When his "terrors began again," he sees a "sturdy infant"—his brother again—watching him, and "slowly Treviles is turning into that dead person" (139). Gregory's memories of his brother hinge on an opposition between the lively and lovely boy, Jonathan, who adored physical sport and the older, rigid Gregory with his chemistry set. One could describe his changed, recollected relationship to his brother as a replay of the deconstruction of male and female in this novel. Gregory seeks to recover the lovely boy he earlier rejected and thus to become a poet-scientist. As Al Bodkin says, "in writing [the poem, Gregory] was determined to become more like the brother he envied" (111).

While confronting his guilt and permitting his love, he seeks also to exorcise the "malice" of the seminar participants and of Christian repression. He thinks of the "burning desert of disappointed stubborn people" in the seminar, and although he does not consider himself "exempt," he feels "fairly free from malice" precisely because he is so aware of the terrifying "things his imagination told him could happen to people" (116). Similarly, meditating on Augustine, he sees the founder of Christianity as a man who "hated and repressed his infancy" and "expunged the earlier doctrine: that 'Jesus saw children who were being suckled'" (139). In contrast, the child is, for Gregory, an erotic being, who brings us back to the womb: "The child speaks to us; it is the womb speaking . . . my cock goes in there, into any womb, to listen to and love her" (139–40). Nowhere in the novel are Gregory's (and Shuttle and Redgrove's) psychological interpretations clearer: As if providing allegorical tags for the fabulistic episodes of the novel, he explains his fantasies in terms entirely compatible with *The Wise Wound*, first as psychic terrors that will not turn into actual horrors as long as he is willing to face them, and second as signposts to a forgotten ecstatic communion of child with mother that he may recover by "listening" to woman and womb.

In the novel's conclusion, this explanation of the "terrors" and of Gregory's method of coping turns out not to be so simple, however; its psychological realism is supplanted first by a surreal event, then by a highly realistic and rationalist deflation, then again by yet another psychological event, finally by a religious sentiment. Among these variant endings, no matter how neat or conclusive any of them is, the reader is left in doubt as to a definitive interpretation of Gregory's narrative; all of these conclusions are somehow equally possible, even though several are, by normal logical standards, incompatible.

The penultimate section of the novel begins with someone asking, "And whom do these terrors serve?" and someone else answers, "The dead, I think." The first voice then says, "You'll not bring that back. You said it would unmake you. We have met it enough times even in our peaceful lives without asking it in. We have seen enough messengers breaking into our love with their tidings. . . . You ignore your doctor's training" (149). We are never told whose these voices are, but subsequent clues in this section suggest that this is a dialogue between Gregory and his dead wife, Mamie. She is warning him against deliberately seeking out the dead and reminding him of the necessity of professional detachment, his "doctor's training." Yet if she is warning him, then he is already deeply submerged in his courtship of death; indeed, we soon discover that, while this dialogue has gone on, Gregory has been engaged in laying out a ritual anniversary supper for himself and his dead wife in the attempt to commune with her. The named "terrors" in Gregory's narrative here are deaths, which he has tried to meet through poems, fantasies, and psychodramas.[71] The boundaries between the ordinary and the spirit world are overridden not only in Gregory's mind but in the narrative collapse into dialogue that, like a set of floating signifiers, is dislodged from clear reference to specific speakers.

But then this uncanny and disjunctive scene is abruptly undercut by this section's ending and by the opening to the next (and last) section. At this section's end, the door "open[s] slowly," and a woman "glide[s] swiftly into the room." The lights go on, and it is Robyn, "now the same age as her mother was when she died" (155). Leaving the reader little room for doubt, the supranormal apparition of the dead Mamie ghost is instantly replaced with the terribly normal appearance of her real-life, living daughter, and in the novel's final section, Gregory's fantastical vision is, with precise scientific efficiency, deflated: "It was as though he had come to the end of a long road that something in him, which had died as the big lights in the overhead chandelier came on, had made interesting, every inch of it. This 'something' was his jewel, his imagination . . . his invention which he had allowed to surround him. . . . It was dead, this thing in him, and the dead were dead also, and did not come back, except in their children. What kind of survival was that, without memory! Nature had no memory" (155). To Gregory, the thought that the dead do not come back except in their children is no more attractive a method for coping with death than it was for H.D.

Yet in a moment of Wordsworthian psychological renewal, his imagination flickers forth once more, as he feels waxy masks begin to fall from his face. He offers a romanticist hermeneutic for these masks: "All his terrors . . . in visions" (156). We are also now told specifically what his visionary "terrors" have been. They include not only the memories of his dead brother and wife, but also a conference he attended at the opening, his first encounters with Brid Hare, his madness in the train home from the conference, and his ritual feast; these all "pass by him in visions like masks" (156). The explanations of the "terrors" now seem to be complete. Moreover, in a clinical therapist's dream ending, after these "masks" have dropped away (only "visions," after all, and his own "faces"), he is finally able to see his own, actual face in the mirror above the sink where he puts the anniversary dishes to be washed. This passage implies a neat, if elaborate, opposition between a plural, deceptive, temporary, apparitional, performative, and false identity and a single, undisguised, stable, actual, real, and true identity.

But once again, the novel does not leave it at that. Instead of offering this essentially secular, humanist conclusion, the narrative keeps moving; for Gregory, in giving up his self-questioning quest, also gives up the belief that full, rational understanding is possible. After "his own face greets him in the mirror" above the kitchen sink, "he believes he will allow God to choose his face for him" (156). In such a novel, who is God? And is this a sudden Christian thought, a nondoctrinal opening up to mystery (and to any god), or merely an offhand remark ("leave it to God")? The last possibility might be most acceptable to the postmodern reader who views all logocentric statements as themselves mere "faces," provisional ideologies, or identity tags, which will pass as quickly as Gregory's other "terrors." But without narratological help as to how to take it, the word *God* comes as a shock to the reader of this novel, especially in the mouth of Gregory, who has shown himself indifferent to orthodox notions of God, whether Christian or anything else. If we are led to expect something in this novel, it would be an open ending or a catastrophe (or both).

The significance of Gregory's resignation to God resides, I argue, in its effect: in the fact that it is unexpected by the reader and thus productive of doubt. As if anticipating doubt about whether this really is the ending and seeking to eliminate it, Redgrove and Shuttle baldly state at the end of this last section, "THE END OF THE TERRORS OF DR TREVILES"; in fact, the text does not end even there, but with verse by Robyn.

A second, more disconcerting effect is achieved by this ending, for although the appearance of Robyn at the end of the penultimate section deflates Gregory's vision of Mamie, it has the reverse impact on a reader, confronting us directly, without any narrative mediation, with a spectacle that has not been broached since early in the novel: the identification of Robyn with her mother, Mamie, and Gregory's successive loving relations to mother and daughter. What are we to think about Robyn? What are we to think about her quasi-incestuous relation to Gregory? Robyn has her own narrative in this book, and her narrative ends not with her appearance at Gregory's ghost supper, but with the "Appendix" of "Robyn's Candle Poems," placed after Redgrove and Shuttle's deceptive closing statement "The End of the Terrors of Dr Treviles." The novel's difficulty emerges less from Gregory's "terrors" than from the parallel narratives: What are we to make of Robyn's menstrual rituals, her psychic communion with Gregory, her creation of a *ménage à trois*, her creative scientism?

———————

Rather than attempting to summarize the many parallel and mininarratives, in what follows I focus on a few of the more incredible and antinormative occurrences in Robyn's narrative. This is a deliberately troubling, not only a playful, novel; in analysis of Robyn's stories, I consider what is most problematic about these narratives alongside their challenges to a reader.

The novel begins with Robyn. The reader is presented with a vivid catachresis of thoughts and images: "There are three pulses, and a trough." We soon learn that this is a description of the tortions (and distortions) of physical tension, specifically of premenstrual tension: "There are three pulses, and a trough. All day, her thumbs have been on backwards. This wave will not break. She wishes to break into the trough. As the cavern grows greater, the head bends straining, wishing to break. The neck and shoulders which should be green and cool, streak with white pains. The head contemplates that cavern, where the current reverses" (3). Dropped throughout this and the following sections are images glossed in *The Wise Wound* as figures for the intense physical and sexual changes that occur during menstruation, images that have circulated for centuries through myth and legend. For example, bloody cuts to a limb, wineglasses, and butcher blocks are figures for menstruation; in her premenstrual awkwardness, Robyn "bark[s] her shin" on the bedcorner, "cut[s] her hand on one of the old wineglasses," and watches the blood swell on the "breadboard . . . like a butcher's block of headsman's wood" (3).

Read in conjunction with *The Wise Wound*, the imagery of the opening passage is particularly notable for its reapplication of male figuration to a woman. In the nonfictional study, it is men's heads that, having become too devoted (in modern, Western patriarchal societies) to abstract reasoning, need to "bend" toward women's experience.[72] In *The Terrors of Dr Treviles* "heads" belong to both women and men, and they are physical, not merely mental; they may strain and break just as shoulders, backs, or wombs do. This passage thus substitutes for the dualism man/

head/contemplation and woman/cavern/pain, a punning set of interchangeable terms: "Head," "pulse," "trough," "cavern," and "current"
are all dual male/female, mind/body, penetrative/receptive phenomena.

The breaking of rigid dualisms, the tortuous passage across taboos—
the physical, mental, moral, and emotional struggles involved in "being
on backwards" in a "forwards" society—become thematized in the rest
of Robyn's narrative: in her officiation at her own mildly Satanic ritual;
in her mirror imaging both of Gregory's therapeutic methods ("Gregory
loved to bring the dream into waking life. She loved to use objects and
actions of waking life to bring herself closer to the dream. She loved
magic" [4]) and of his fantasies (she participates psychically in his nightmarish fantasies while he is away at a conference); in her own nightmarish realization that a lock of her mother's hair has been plastered onto a
skull in a painting portraying a Hamlet-like Gregory with a skull in his
hands; in her macho lovemaking with Gregory and its hints of sadomas-
ochism; and in her lovemaking with Brid Hare, after which Robyn imagines herself with "the head of Treviles" on her shoulders looking down
at her own breasts (98), and Brid is ecstatically astonished at Robyn's
lovemaking "as if [she] were a man" (100). These "cross[ings] of [the]
bridge," as Shuttle and Redgrove might call them (*Wise Wound* 70), occasionally become horrific not only for the common reader (for whom
the book is an ideological workout), but also for the feminist in search
of alternatives to masculine, heterosexual discourse. Not all of Robyn's
exploits look like alternatives.

Some are "simpl[e] form[s] of taboo-breaking," which she acts out
(just as Gregory dreams or fantasizes) in order to turn taboos "inside-out,"
that is, in an act of confrontation, exorcism, and renewal (24). Robyn's
rituals revalue Satanism; indeed, these might better be called "candle
rites" because they are structured around the lighting and extinguishing
of candles and nowhere does Robyn use the word *Satanic*. They also turn
her mind and body "inside-out," allowing her to confront physical pain
through demonic fantasy and, ultimately, conjure herself to begin her
menstruation, to bleed. At a climactic moment as she recites the Lord's
Prayer backward, just before her menstruation starts, she sees seven
black-armored knights approach her, while she is decked in lily-white
armor: They hack off her helmet and breastplate, reveal a naked girl child,
and swing the child's head like a bursting melon against a tree (13–14).
Later, we are told she has been following a guide book, which tells her
these rites will release her from "the shalts" and "shalt nots," and "something will happen," "who knows . . . what" (16). In fact breaking few of

the ten commandments, Robyn performs this ritual to invoke her period to come, which it does after the third backward prayer.

At first, the incidents in Robyn's narrative might seem to trespass
not only against the shibboleths of Christian, rationalist, and patriarchal
socialization, but also against standard feminist arguments about gender
norms. Thus the basic feminist principle that one should not privilege
male constructs over female is not observed in the novel. As Robyn's
menstrual ritual develops, she invokes "the branching blood within herself, and . . . this perhaps was like a separate person within herself . . . He!
certainly it was a He . . . [though] not the Lord of the Christian Lord's
Prayer whose apostle St Paul so despised and feared women" (17). Although "he" is not the Christian Lord, he is "he" nonetheless—the "he"
of the stag with its branching antlers in Gregory's fantasies, the "he" of
the "other husband" Redgrove and Shuttle describe in *The Wise Wound*
and of the Jungian "animus" (63, 223, 225). What is feminist about a process so embedded in male traditions and figures—in the "Christian Lord,"
in a "He" within, in Satanism? But just after identifying the "branching
blood within herself" as "he" rather than "she," Robyn angrily denounces
the "Mother Church" as "a dummy made in the likeness of a woman,
just as the Japanese masturbatory dummies are so made," and adds, "No
Church changed in itself week by week within the month, no Church
bled each month." She wonders "where were the Sayings of St. Mary, to
tell what a woman might expect from within herself? Who split wom-
ankind up into the virgin and the whore. . . . 'Noli me tangere,' said the
risen Jesus. . . . Robyn could think of a good whore's reply to that—'Go
Fuck Yourself!'" (17). Robyn's narrative undermines any construction of
her identity in the image of only one gender or another, and it does so in
juxtaposition with a critique of patriarchal institutions such as that of
the "Mother Church."[73]

More worrisome (to this reader) than Robyn's cross-gendered figures
and violent exorcist fantasies are the glancing associations in her narrative of sex with domestic and child abuse. One of these moments is nightmarish for Robyn herself: When she sees a hank of her dead mother's red
hair plastered to the skull in a painting (primarily a portrait of the live
Gregory), she wonders whether the portrait expresses the painter's—Gregory's friend the Reverend Al Bodkin's[74]—homosocial jealousy or whether
it "spell[s] out some necessary message or warning about her father-lov-
er" (31). While worrying, she remembers Gregory slapping her mother's
face three times before the Christmas fireplace. She never explains or
mentions this memory a second time. Neither is the lock of hair fully

explained or explicitly justified, but she believes that Bodkin plastered the hair on the portrait: "Yes, the hank of red hair was really there . . . for the very first time in her recollection she was uneasy in the . . . house. Then her anger began. 'The bastard! that shit-sipping bastard Al.' She thought how the clean virtue of the priest of an extinct religion cast a very dirty shadow. Then the anger which was coloured like whips and iron turned inside out and . . . she wept at the macabre insult to her dead mother, Mamie" (28). She does not ask Bodkin why he did this, letting the incident slide when she encounters his cheerful presence again, "not a trace of guilt or guile" in his face (66). It is enough for her to have analyzed his act as an unconscious, ghastly "casting" of the priest's shadow.

Similarly, though with more narrative detail devoted to it, Robyn comes to accept Gregory's current preoccupation with Mamie. Robyn wishes Mamie not out of the portrait, but rather repainted as a live nude, either sitting in Gregory's hand or, preferably, with a tiny Gregory standing in her palm. Later in the novel, becoming even more clinical than Gregory, she thinks,

> It was distressing . . . that he spoke so much of Mamie, Robyn's mother, but she concealed her distaste of this dwelling on past things, deciding that Gregory was entitled to ransack his past. As for her, she was more interested in what she was going to accomplish, not what had passed. She thought that Gregory's present interests were natural; as Jung had said, it is normal for a man in the second half of life to wish to relate himself to his inevitable end, and to consider the fate of those who had gone before him. A refusal to face up to the fact of death was the root cause of all neurosis. (135)

This passage goes as far as anything in Gregory's narrative to provide a psychological explanation for his fantasies. But it leaves the compelling question of Gregory's current relations to his first wife's daughter untouched.

Yet the narrative itself is designed to tease a reader with just this fact of Gregory and Robyn's relationship. It is directly after her candle ritual has come to an end and her menstruation has begun and before she notices the hank of hair on the painting that the narrative begins to indicate the status of their relations. Not yet admitting everything, the narrative discloses only the fact that Robyn is Gregory's stepdaughter and does this in the context of a joke about Christian thought: Section 12 of part 1 begins, "Robyn is Gregory's stepdaughter, which is not allowed in the degrees of kinship listed at the back of the book of common prayer" (24). For Anglicans, such a marriage is disallowed as incestuous. Gregory and Robyn's relation emerges as another unpermitted matter that Robyn and Gregory (and Redgrove and Shuttle) are working to permit, on a par with menstruation, sex during menstruation, and female difference.

We are introduced to the possibility, never fully established, that Robyn may be Gregory's current wife even more coyly. In the section before the announcement that Robyn is Gregory's stepdaughter, Gregory is thinking about how many books have been written, and without authorial comment he includes in his list "The Bride of Treviles (a Gothic Romance)" (23). This title is a metatextual joke on the novel's title and its horrific contents; arguably, it is a more fitting name for this novel. Two sections later, immediately before Robyn notices the hank of red hair, this metatextual joke resurfaces—in a gothic moment much like that in which Gregory first associates himself with the "horror-house"—and Robyn is finally named as the "bride of Treviles." Section 14 begins, "Robyn, the bride of Treviles, contemplated the bridegroom's portrait done in oils by Al Bodkin" (27). Is this just another fantasy, a horror to be aired and exorcised, as Gregory's horrific memories of death are aired, so that at the same moment that Robyn enters into her nightmarish thoughts of Gregory, the reader will do so as well, for different (more horrific) reasons?

As it turns out, Robyn's relation to Gregory at least as his stepdaughter-mistress is, like the hank of hair, all too true (in the context of this narrative), and it is a truth with which the novel taunts us. But it leaves us with not much meat to gnaw, for, as with the hank of hair and Gregory slapping his wife, no explanation or justification is ever attempted for their relationship. Robyn's nightmare—"To paint a man holding his wife's skull!" (31)—dissipates almost as rapidly, as she concludes either that Bodkin is jealous or that Gregory is a kind of Hamlet, presiding over death rather than life. Two more sections later, she lets her mind travel over childhood memories of her stepfather, and although she remembers quarreling with Gregory about her desire to be financially independent in her first year at Cambridge, there is nothing nightmarish for her in these memories. There is also no hint of sexual relations between the married stepfather and young girl ("She had been a very young child when her mother had met Gregory in the Army Hospital," 39). As if entirely nonchalant about this issue, or intentionally defying the reader, the novel says nothing about when and how Gregory and Robyn became lovers.

Perhaps such a relationship should not be held to a subsequent feminist standard or made subject to a concern of the 1980s and 1990s with cross-generational, intrafamilial relationship. What is particularly provocative about this novel, however, is its simultaneously teasing awareness and bland indifference to such appearances. Unlike Redgrove's accounts of his own sexual history and theories, there is no psychologist's explanation of Robyn and Gregory's relationship as itself either a fantasy or a psychodrama of daughter-father, son-mother desire. As far as they and their peers and neighbors (including the Reverend Al Bodkin) are concerned, Robyn and Gregory's relationship gives no cause for scandal.

It is soon after we learn of their possible marriage, and in a similarly offhand way, that we learn, incidentally, that Robyn and Gregory are lovers, when her experience of the candlelit occult atmosphere she has created reminds her (among many nonsexual impressions) of "a webwork of nerve cells twinkling with messages . . . [including] a sudden excitement like an interesting sexual suggestion, as though Gregory had taken out a whip and then kissed her navel, kissed her ear" (10). Pieced into a "webwork" of sensuous images, this one is not singled out for the reader as deserving special notice. Ignoring modern society's charged associations of the whip with sexual and patriarchal brutality, the narrative offers this tactile "suggestion" as just another concatenated image, like Brid Hare's recognition of "Treviles" as both adorable and "vile": another fantasy that permits a memory (and shadow) of pain along with pleasure, not separating "good" from "bad."

In the single scene in which the reader is invited, as D. H. Lawrence once put it, to witness "the whole act," Robyn and Gregory again cast sex in patriarchal terms. Like the ungrounded dialogue between Gregory and Mamie, this section begins with a dialogue whose participants are identified only retrospectively:

> "Your father was a Mason."
> "Yes."
> "I bet he could build a tower better than you, otherwise you'd not be here."
> "Bitch!"
> "Here it comes."
> "Rose-croix bitch!"
> "That's better. Now let me . . ."
> "Blood-bath! Countess Dracula!"
> "It's good for you. Hormones. Make you grow."
> And astride him she leant back sliding her hips with a full look about her closed eyelids and red hair quiet in the darkened bedroom. Her lips went tight and her cheeks drawn for a moment, then she relaxed and looked down at him.

"That's twice."

"I'm good at it." (77)

The easiest way to read this is as a conversation in which she taunts him into a stronger erection with the allegedly greater sexual prowess of his father, and he responds in kind by calling her a "bitch." Taking the "male" part (as, in *The Wise Wound*, Redgrove and Shuttle suggest women are particularly keen to do during menstruation [89]), she directs their intercourse and its masculinist vocabulary, and because she is menstruating, she not only invokes the occult male club of Masonry but subjects Gregory to an arousing "bloodbath" which he likens to vampirism. Robyn and Gregory collaborate in activating the energies of male aggression and competition as fodder for the rising sexual tension between them, culminating in her second orgasm (for which he—or is it she?—takes credit, saying "I'm good at it").

This emphasis on stereotypical male behavior then suddenly yields to its opposite, for the dialogue does not end here. It goes on, after the climax and another bout of lovemaking (this time side-to-side, where Gregory climaxes too) to the "calm" aftermath during which Gregory notes how many more orgasms she has had than he ("my once to your how many") and recounts his fantasies as they made love, walking by the river among the willows and seeing "a graceful slim vase with handles." Asking her for direction as to what this means, she tells him, "I know what you saw. Me," and "You had a womb-flash, my darling" (77–78).[75] This episode insists once again on mixing things up—male aggression with female reception, male rivalry with female sexuality, male orgasm with female womb-flash.

A more drastic cross-gendering and gender-transplanting occurs during a fantasy of Robyn's that unwinds while Brid is recounting her difficult life decisions:

Transplants. Cosmetic surgery. Cosmic surgery. Bravura surgical feats done by the dream doctor in the locked attic bedroom. Avenues of moon stood on the river. Avenues of dawn-mist stood on the river. The head of Treviles on the slim body of Robyn, gazing down at her slight pale breasts. Brid's scalp on Treviles's chest, her long hair cascades through the front of romantic Treviles's ruffled shirt. The horns of Himself fastened to the scalp of Brid; she is the horned bride and her white head-dress looms monstrously like a sheer mountain or a glacier walking. The foetus of Robyn's baby transplanted to Gregory's thigh; the baby is born with tiny horns like rosebuds: "Give me milk, Mummy," he cries in Russian as he emerges. Treviles's penis transplanted to Brid's *fossa navicularis*, long enough for her to get up her own true self. Brid's tit grafted to Gregory's scrotum, to milk the horned babe. (98–99)

This long passage goes on and on with comparable graftings, which end in the thought that "Robyn's hand is fastened to the cervix of Brid's womb and Treviles's glans has been replaced with Brid's hand so that the two women shake hands in friendly intercourse and refuse to let go" (99). Robyn has not yet invited Brid to live with her and with Gregory (although when she does, she is confident Gregory will agree to the arrangement, and so he does), yet she is already mixing them up together in elaborate transsexual combinations.

Although Brid has no idea what Robyn is thinking, she is grateful for the sudden trespass across gender that she feels has occurred:

> "Dr Ronda told me that my chief fear was of not being a woman. Surgery made me mad because I wanted to give myself a man's body. I could not stop the metamorphoses. He taught me to hate the magic, to settle for a one reality, the reality accepted among folk like me. Existence was bearable that way. Otherwise it was as though somebody constantly swung the handle and changed the plots. . . . But now you, a woman, have made love to me as if you were a man. What have you done to me Robyn?" . . . "Didn't you like it, Brid?" "It was *lovely.*" (99–100)

Trouncing assumptions that her therapist suggested she should live by, Brid Hare discovers in this episode that a woman does not have to settle, after all, with "being a woman," and that she, a woman, does not have to settle for or repress "envy" of men. Instead, women and men may metamorphose into each other and back again through same-sex intercourse. Robyn meanwhile feels "justly proud of the natural force Brid had elicited from her" and that she will no longer need to perform any other kind of magic, "though perhaps all the magic she had ever done was only natural" (100).

Once Brid Hare moves into the Treviles household—literally, not only imaginatively—the threesome quickly falls into shape: "The arrangement was working, since Gregory loved and was interested in both women all the time, and each woman was relieved of the necessity of loving and being interested in Gregory every day of the month, as in an ordinary marriage arrangement. Robyn had found a crystallization of her individuality taking place. She had given her first lectures at Ruan Minor and attended Endenberg's seminars at Tintagel College, and she was deep into her vision of things as woman and scientist" (134). What appears on the face of it a sexist arrangement—where a man is free to move between more than one woman while each woman shares a single man—is Robyn's antisexist means for permitting her lesbian love of Brid to go on without excluding her ongoing marriage with Gregory and, more radically still, for allowing the two women their "periods" of indifference to men.

All this has not occurred as easily as Robyn seems to think for Gregory, who in fact—like Robyn's backward thumbs—feels he has been "cracked across" by this new arrangement, his "heart" broken, "like a great funerary slab . . . cracked across between Robyn and Brid and between you both at nights gestures the red-haired Mamie-ghost I do not believe in." Yet in a Lawrentian metamorphosis, out of the cracks "grow new plants, new flowers" (137–38). As Redgrove and Shuttle argue in *The Wise Wound*, "The men who were not so afraid might have been allowed to wear the horns of the Devil on their head, the sexual man with womb-horn knowledge, horns which the institution of marriage considered the mark of a cuckold: a sad deterioration when that may mean that the man does not (as in marriage) treat the woman as a possession like breeding stock, but a person with her own varying sexuality that may demand more than one partner" (223).

Not only sexual and gender borders are crossed, rewritten, and interwoven in this novel; psychic and physical borders dissolve in the course of Robyn's narrative. Throughout part one, the phenomena passing through Robyn and Gregory's minds and in their physical experiences echo and respond to each another, even though the two people are physically separated, with Robyn remaining at home while Gregory attends his conference. While Robyn is approaching menstruation, Gregory sees the conference participants unconsciously "catch" a sneeze from the lecturer, Endenberg, and wipe their noses; nasal activity (as I noted earlier) is a male version of female menstruation. More overtly in the narrative, complementary images enter Robyn and Gregory's minds simultaneously: As she thinks about Bodkin's painting, Gregory dreams of himself as Bodkin conceiving of the painting (31–39). While she thinks about a waterfall, which she calls The Force, he is reading a book of poems called *The Force* (52–54). Soon after (or perhaps at the same time that) he sees some scarecrows outside his train window, she too sees scarecrows in the distance (51, 55). Their mutual sightings and fantasies continue until at last she sees Gregory staring out the window of the train she is meeting. It becomes increasingly difficult for the reader to tell when Gregory and Robyn have actually seen something and when they have fantasized it and who has first seen or fantasized what.

The novel does not hesitate to allow its characters psychic power. Indeed, it goes further than this to suggest—and, through Gregory, to argue under the name of "Orthomolecular Psychiatry" (5)—that physical changes may be wrought by psychic influences. As a child, Robyn asked Gregory,

> "Greggy, was your hair always red?"
> "No dear, it went red shortly after I met your mother. Before that it was brown, like the cushion here."
> "Oh. Why did it go red when you met Mamie?"
> "Because I loved her."
> "Why?"
> "The colour of love is red."
> "Why?"
> "Don't just say Why ducky. Try to think what I said."
> "Why?"
> "I love you." (40)

She asked him again as a teenager, and his response was, "Well Robyn, you may not believe this, but my hair went this colour shortly after I met your mother. . . . My ideas crystallised at that time, and I began planning my thesis for the D. P. M." (41, 43). Gregory (and the scientist Endenberg) believe that molecular change is produced through psychic influence, and Gregory's head bears living proof. Many visionary fantasies—utopic as well as dystopic—play out this idea in the course of the narrative, disputing some fundamental modern, "rational" assumptions about the universe.

Do they challenge also the reader's? They are as likely to add to what seems the inconsequential, postmodern playfulness of the narrative as to produce any kind of paradigm shift. But perhaps to accept the premises of such a narrative—its floating signifiers, ungrounded meditations, unreferenced dialogues, cross-over fantasies—is to undergo just such a paradigm shift, at least for as long as the novel lasts. This novel also offers something more than a thrill (unlike, for example, a vampire film): It offers provisional theories, possible alternatives, and political critiques of the status quo.

This is a novel as problematic as it is challenging. Although, to borrow a now-famous phrase of Judith Butler, there is a lot of "gender trouble" in this novel, there is not as much trouble for some normative relations as many feminist, multicultural, and poststructural theorists would like. In their cosigned works, Redgrove and Shuttle proceed as if the politics of ethnicity and racial identity do not pertain, they do not discuss or portray gay male relations, and in *Alchemy for Women*, they distance themselves from transsexualism.[76] Yet the questions they do raise in defiance of Freudian psychoanalysis, of single-author writing, of single-sex and heterosexual worldviews, of fundamentalisms of science, philosophy, and religion, and of Western binaristic thinking, make their work well worth the trouble. And when this novel closes, it presents itself as the distinctive fruit of a male-female collaboration: The last page is blank except for these words:

PETER REDGROVE PENELOPE SHUTTLE

THE END OF OUR BOOK[.]

6 *Rewriting Writing: Stein and Toklas, Marlatt and Warland*

ALTHOUGH I OCCASIONALLY use the now-common term *deconstruction* in discussing literary collaborators selected for this study, few of them write deconstructively and still fewer—only Elbrecht and Fakundiny, Marlatt and Warland—have absorbed poststructuralist theory directly into their texts. Yet aspects of both the theory (or antitheory) and the practice of Derridean deconstruction fit coauthorship well. The moves from speech to writing, from author to intertext acknowledge the systemically collaborative aspects of language and thought. When two writers come together to produce a text, they cannot be the single center of intention that critics have often taken writers to be, and the texts thus produced are inevitably intertextual. At the same time, collaborations neither dissolve nor bracket bodily identity, but instead draw attention to the permeable borders between orality and textuality, between authors and texts, between one sex and another, at times between one body and another.

In this chapter, I discuss two sets of writers whose texts act upon and enact a decentered premise; one of these sets, Marlatt and Warland, invokes poststructuralist theory explicitly. Indeed, Marlatt and Warland seem to mark the climax of this study, for they have produced the most exhaustive and generative theory of feminist literary collaboration thus far offered by writers and scholars, and their theory is simultaneously literature, or prose poetry. In their texts, (anti)theory and practice, fiction and nonfiction become interdependent activities. To "rewrite writing" (as my chapter title proclaims) is to develop a Derridean *écriture*, or perhaps *écriture collaborée:* writings that continually, overtly rewrite themselves.

However, I do not consider the writing or theory of the collaborators in this chapter more innovative than that of others in this study. Indeed, I expect the poststructuralist ideas played out in the texts discussed here to be familiar to readers, particularly to readers in the academy (thus my discussion of Marlatt and Warland is shorter than that of Redgrove and Shuttle's less familiar linkage between feminism and spiritualism in chapter 5). What makes the writers in this chapter distinctive is the way they introduce—whether implicitly in the case of Stein and Toklas or deliberately in the case of Marlatt and Warland—the issue of collaboration into modernism and postmodernism.[1]

Explicit coauthorship of literary narratives or poems is unusual in modern times (from the nineteenth century to the present), and it is extraordinarily rare among the high modernist writers; the fact that so few readers have thought even to ask whether "*The Autobiography of Alice B. Toklas* by Gertrude Stein" was coauthored is a symptom of the larger construction of aestheticist modernism. What does it mean to reintroduce the possibility of collaboration into this context? In a coauthored, biographical study of modernist women writers, *Writing for Their Lives: The Modernist Women 1910–1940* (whose introductory chapters focus on H.D. and Bryher, Stein and Toklas), Gillian Hanscombe and Virginia L. Smyers connect the experimentalism of these writers' texts with their experimental lifestyles and with their cooperative networking, yet they ignore entirely the ways these writers' texts may have been, occasionally or in part, coauthored.[2] The issue of collaboration reopens the questions of where life ends and art begins in the modernist text, unsettling the paradoxically linked concepts of the solitary creative genius (loftily paring his fingernails) and the self-contained, autonomous text (the well-wrought urn).

In contrast to modernist writers, contemporary feminist scholars and theorists, including poststructuralist and postmodern writer/thinkers such as Hélène Cixous and Catherine Clément, Monique Wittig and Sande Zeig, Sara Maitland and Michelene Wandor,[3] often coauthor their texts. But again, coauthorship enters minimally, if at all, into their subject and their discourse. Thanks to the well-known French feminist theorists (especially Cixous, Luce Irigaray, and Julia Kristeva) who work under the influence of Derrida, Lacan, and other European theorists; to the cultural translators and summarizers of these theories (such as Gayatri Spivak, Ann Rosalind Jones, and Toril Moi); and to the American feminist theorists who first picked up on European influences (for example, Barbara Johnson, Shoshana Felman, and Peggy Kamuf), deconstruction and feminism seem no longer an odd but an old couple.[4] Certain French feminist concepts— for instance, *l'écriture féminine, jouissance,* or a pre-Oedipal linguistic *chora*—have been so widely used and debated as to have become clichéd; they have been largely absorbed in the American academy into a materialist new historicism and into postcolonial cultural studies. But what happens when the question of coauthorship is introduced into the poststructuralist context? This issue could not emerge when authorship was set under erasure, yet like authorship it haunts the margins of these theories and thus also of cultural studies, as evidenced by standard lists of the theorists who have produced these theories. *Les écrivains,* the self-multiplying chain of (co)writers—writers who know and, to a large extent, work with each other—are these theories' open secrets.

The open secret is a useful point of departure for analyzing the texts in this chapter, particularly Stein and Toklas's *Autobiography.* It was developed by D. A. Miller in *The Novel and the Police,* but I use it differently here to emphasize not, as he does, the ways in which subjectivity becomes self-policing and society depends on a spurious difference between inner and outer for social maintenance,[5] but rather how the structure of the open secret enables a writer (or writing) to toy with the false borders between writers and writing, speech and text, texts and subtexts (including the subtexts of the unconscious and the body), one writer and another. The structure of the open secret also involves the uncanny: Rather than building suspense around social taboos, as do Somerville and Ross, H.D., and Shuttle and Redgrove, the open secret is an uncanny function of language. The open secret operates through and within linguistic binarisms in language: Springing from imposed hierarchies, such as those of man and wife, genius and ordinariness, the private suppressed term enters into buoyant interchange with the public open term. Because the open secret is both open and secret, public but not blazoned, it is neither thrilling nor frightening. Though amusing in being half-uncloseted, it produces no great mystery or great revelation. Nonetheless, like the texts of H.D. and Shuttle and Redgrove, the texts discussed in this chapter place themselves at the mobile, uncanny threshold of a number of half-buried secrets that underlie and undergird, and— when half-disclosed—relax and playfully undo modern social taboos.

The Open Secret of "The Autobiography of Alice B. Toklas *by Gertrude Stein*"

Like "bronze by gold" at the head of *Ulysses'* "Sirens" episode,[6] two women share the narrative of a single autobiography, seductively veiling their proximity to each other in a shifting "I" and, on the title page of most editions, a teasing "by."[7] Although the original edition of this text appeared simply as *The Autobiography of Alice B. Toklas,* generations of publishers, booksellers, librarians, critics, and scholars have designated Stein the author and Toklas the subject of *"The Autobiography of Alice B. Toklas* by Gertrude Stein." Stein and Toklas were the first to do this in the narrative of Stein's authorship of Toklas's autobiography with which the text concludes.[8] The question this text prompts of "Who Really Wrote *The Autobiography of Alice B. Toklas?"*[9] has shifted its valence over time: For its first readers, the open secret was that Stein had written this text, but for some contemporary readers, Stein's asserted authorship masks the haunting possibility that Toklas wrote it. Oddly, only one scholar has advanced a third possibility—that they wrote it together—and even this critic, Richard Bridgman, submerges this possibility under the more radical and less likely suggestion that Toklas "composed her own autobiography."[10] Readers and scholars have repeatedly responded to the question of the autobiography's authorship by seeing it as a choice between Toklas and Stein.

Both title and text are a tease, deliberately violating the conventional distinction between autobiography and biography, even while invoking the distinction between subject and author, thus sending the reader on a wild-goose chase for the "real author." In the same way that the narrative of this autobiography treats Toklas's status as Stein's wife as a mere diversion (in both senses, as both joke and side issue) from the more serious topic of Stein's genius, thereby distracting attention from their companionship, the autobiography teasingly veils Toklas's status not as author, but as *co*author, by diverting attention to Stein's designation as the text's final authority.

As the narrator explains at the end of chapter 1, to meet Stein was to meet a genius: "I may say that only three times in my life have I met a genius . . . Gertrude Stein, Pablo Picasso and Alfred Whitehead. . . . I have only known three first class geniuses. . . . In no one of the three cases have I been mistaken" (5). What is Toklas's position in relation to a first-class genius? In chapter 2, the narrator "Toklas" tells us in passing of a moment, early in the narrated history of Stein and Toklas's relationship, when Stein assigned Toklas the position of hostess to wives: "Miss Stein

told me to sit with Fernande [Picasso's wife]. . . . I sat, it was my first sitting with a wife of a genius" (14). Because this moment occurs when
Toklas is enjoyably occupied conversing with the probably lesbian "Miss
Mars" (who, along with "Miss Squires," is a prototype of the characters
"immortalised" in Stein's story "Miss Furr and Miss Skeene" [14]),[11]
Stein's seat assignment diverts Toklas and simultaneously draws attention to their lesbian and all-but-married status. But Toklas, designated
"wife of a genius," toys with these categories, for she "sits" not only with
nonwives as well as with wives, but with wives of geniuses "who were
not real geniuses" as well as with wives of "real geniuses": "I had often
said that I would write, The wives of geniuses I have sat with. I have sat
with so many. I have sat with wives who were not wives, of geniuses who
were real geniuses. I have sat with real wives of geniuses who were not
real geniuses. I have sat with wives of geniuses, of near geniuses, of would
be geniuses, in short I have sat very often and very long with many wives
and wives of many geniuses" (14). That Toklas as well as Stein might
write (like a genius) a memoir (like this passage)—"The wives of geniuses I have sat with"—is, like their lesbian marriage, an open secret of this
autobiography.[12]

Unlike the two barmaids whom Joyce embodies metaphorically in
"Sirens" for a reader's voyeuristic pleasure, Toklas and Stein operate not
merely as sexual signifiers in this text, but as coauthorities and cosub-
jects: Although Stein appears only as an absence on the first edition's title
page, she appears everywhere in Toklas's narration as this "autobiography's" biographical subject.[13] Indeed, like bookends, Toklas's name gives
the text its title and Stein's title as author gives the text its conclusion.
The text's teasing thus occurs less at Toklas's expense than at the expense
of solitary genius and of rigid, traditional distinctions between the artist and his or her life, between author and subject, between the conscious
author and the "unconscious" text, between written text and oral speech,
and between one artist and another competing for ascendancy (as, for
example, Picasso and Matisse do in this narrative [64–65]). *The Autobiography of Alice B. Toklas* acknowledges such distinctions and their hierarchies only to question, mock, and upset them (much as Stein's placement of her luncheon guests each in front of his own painting mocks the
men's desire to be noticed). This autobiography performs a kind of Derridean writing, at once interrogating and putting into play conventional
divisions of writing and, not incidentally alongside these, the socially
embedded oppositions of male genius and female helpmate, marriage and
homosociality, heterosexual and gay, and, on the other hand, between the
solitary artist and art group, the individual agent and aesthetic move-

ment, the art work and aesthetic theory, and the text and its context. Vexed as each of these sets of oppositions is in itself, my concern here is with their intersection in the controversial question of Stein and Toklas's collaboration.

To focus my analysis of this much-discussed text and to facilitate comparison with earlier collaborators in this study, I begin by reconsidering the theme of the previous chapter—the role of the uncanny—in the context of Stein's dismissal of an unconscious and her loudly publicized emphasis on sentences. This theme introduces several of the autobiography's open secrets, which in this text are closely linked: of the life behind the writing, of the gossipy women behind the modernist art movement in turn-of-the-century Paris (along with the quarrelsome men behind their abstract paintings), and of the wife, autobiographical subject, and cowriter Toklas behind the solitary genius Stein. Along the way, it is useful to note the parallels between Stein/Toklas's writing and Derrida's relevant essay "The End of the Book and the Beginning of Writing."

Of all the aesthetic issues that generally concern an autobiographer, the possibility of an "unconscious" is the one to which Stein and Toklas[14] give least credence; this is an issue on which they are particularly likely to differ in their concerns and strategies from H.D. and Shuttle and Redgrove, but they differ less than their professed disregard for the unconscious/subconscious would suggest. In the *Autobiography* Stein and Toklas describe Stein's writing as without such a feature: "She had come to like posing, the long still hours followed by a long dark walk intensified the concentration with which she was creating her sentences. The sentences of which Marcel Brion, the french critic has written, by exactitude, austerity, absence of variety in light and shade, by refusal of the use of the subconscious Gertrude Stein achieves a symmetry which has a close analogy to the symmetry of the musical fugue of Bach" (50). Later they contradictorily acknowledge that other critics have said Stein's work appeals to the subconscious, as music does: "Music she only cared for during her adolescence. She finds it difficult to listen to it, it does not hold her attention. All of which of course may seem strange because it has been so often said that the appeal of her work is to the ear and to the subconscious. Actually it is her eyes and mind that are active and important and concerned in choosing" (75). One must not count on Stein not to contradict herself, however; contradiction is a figure of speech that held no terror for her.[15] At the same time, Stein and Toklas concede this "appeal . . . to the subconscious" only to dismiss it in favor of the mind's (presumably conscious) choices. The appeal to the subconscious would in that case be an accidental effect of the overriding concern with creating sentences. Or is it accidental? Perhaps the subconscious is achieved precisely through conscious indifference to it.

Both of these passages imply an absence of interest in depth effects more broadly. Depth itself is merely an effect. For Stein and Toklas, to be true is to be exact; to imitate music is to produce not hidden meanings, but symmetry; to write is not to produce a vicariously inviting illusion of verisimilar realities, but to choose words. As D. A. Miller says of Dickens's *David Copperfield*, "Writing the self, then, would be consistently ruled by the paradoxical proposition that the self is most itself at the moment when its defining inwardness is most secret, most withheld from writing—with the equally paradoxical consequence that autobiography is most successful only where *it has been abandoned for the Novel*" (emphasis in original).[16] Toklas describes Stein not so much as making her "defining inwardness . . . most secret" as seeking exactitude in rendering the inner as well as the outer—as being, again oxymoronically, "possessed by the *intellectual passion* for exactitude" (211; emphasis added).

All this makes the *Autobiography* unrelentingly uncanny. In its refusal of depths, the language of the *Autobiography* evokes the eeriness of the women and dolls in the story of "The Sand-Man," central examples in Freud's essay of the literary uncanny: "A particularly favourable condition for awakening uncanny sensations is created when there is intellectual uncertainty whether an object is alive or not, and when an inanimate object becomes too much like an animate one" (385). In Stein and Toklas's autobiography, it is sentences rather than dolls that seem curiously both animate and inanimate: at once so colloquial as to seem spoken, so simple as to seem flat, and yet vivid with wit. Her texts are especially famous for phrases and sentences that mirror and repeat each other like doubles,[17] as if previous thoughts were undergoing continual disinterment and reanimation: "Anyway in no time they were knowing each other and knowing each other very well" (35).

In addition to language—which becomes odd, both like and unlike itself—what is uncanny in this narrative are the many aspects of conventional autobiography that haunt it through their absences: Not only is the text more biographical (about Stein) than autobiographical (about Toklas), but the conventional childhood, education, and personal maturation of the *Künstlerroman* are marginalized for both Stein and Toklas, restricted to the brief first chapter for Toklas and to chapter 4 for Stein. In their place is the *Bildung* of modern art, yet this also, despite the turbulence of its personalities, rivalries, and public reception, is observed as if through peripheral vision. Rarely does the text linger with grand events; even an important exhibition or biographical portrait is the occasion for casual recollection, digressive anecdotalism, and bits of mildly vicious gossip. The text thus becomes more memoir than either biography or autobiography.[18] Meanwhile, the development of Stein's artistry and career is treated in brief allusions, dropped intermittently among descriptions of the male painters, and her career seems never to change even as it is unfolding: One Stein text after another is the true "beginning" of modern writing (57, 82, 215), practically none published until the autobiography nears its end. Missing from this autobiography, above all, are the more personal details of Toklas's relationship to Stein, so public in some ways in this narrative, so shielded from scrutiny in others.

The two most obviously uncanny aspects of this narrative—its language and its autobiographical erasures—coalesce in the presence of the ghostwriter Stein just behind the gossip Toklas, the ghost coworker Toklas just behind the genius Stein.[19] As I show later, the text does not altogether determine who wields the pen, who is the "real" subject of this "auto," who is "I." As Toklas narrates Stein's story and Stein nominally authors Toklas's story, the two of them double for each other as author, narrator, and subject. Moreover, the questions raised by this teasing narrative reopen the question of the relation between artist and art group, solitary writer and writers' collective, text and context: Perhaps the modernist art movement is the "real" author or subject of this text, producing Toklas and Stein even as they endeavor to (re)produce it. Who owes more: the "independent" artists who depend so obviously in this memoir on the energetic patronage of Stein and Toklas (the "two americans [who] happened to be in the heart of an art movement of which the outside world at that time knew nothing" [28]) or the unknown Stein and Toklas who owe so much of their reputation to this art movement?[20] Like "the real Charlotte," Stein and Toklas appear to be caught in a fate much larger than themselves yet at the same time are represented as the agents of that fate.

But the narrative does not work toward some horrific encounter with the uncanny, as do Somerville and Ross. This autobiography offers neither a climax of horror nor a deflationary anticlimax. Nor does it court tabooed thresholds whose uncanny borders are turned into numinous moments, as does H.D.—nothing is visionary in this text. The emphasis is on writing itself and on the way the "writing is written," as if it were a kind of automatic writing without a spirit world (or, as H.D. said of the "writing on the wall," as if it wrote itself [*Tribute to Freud* 51]).[21]

For New Critics, Stein became an emblem of the modernist preoccupation with method over meaning, of "making it new" for its own sake.
Stein became a standard example of this aesthetic philosophy (especially for those who did not read her) and her writing was cited for its repetitions rather than its meanings. But was it method she propounded, or
was it something still more radical than that about writing?

When Stein wrote about her purposes in writing, the standard aesthetic vocabulary opposed form to content, method to message, word
sound to word meaning. Modernists (Pound perhaps foremost among
them) responded to such anti-aesthetic binaries—where content was
valued above form—by polemically reversing the emphasis, to stress
word over meaning, form over content, method over message. Scholars
of modernism followed Pound's lead, particularly in their treatment of
Stein. Yet Stein's writing does not itself privilege what we might now
prefer to call signifier over signified, but rather plays upon their arbitrary
relations to each other. And Stein's choice of terms often is defter and
more ambiguous than the standard dichotomies: She emphasizes the
sentence rather than word or image, for example, value[22] rather than form
or design, and particular methods such as repetition and variation (which
are meaningfully dual)[23] rather than generalized method or strategy. In
reading Derrida, one may feel that philosophy finally caught up with her;
the post-Saussurean, antimetaphysical theory of Derrida approximates
more closely what Stein was attempting than does a standardized modernist aesthetic.

As Derrida writes in "The End of the Book and the Beginning of
Writing," "What writing itself, in its nonphonetic moment, betrays, is
life. It menaces at once the breath, the spirit, and history as the spirit's
relationship with itself. It is their end, their finitude, their paralysis.
Cutting breath short, sterilizing or immobilizing spiritual creation in the
repetition of the letter, in the commentary or the *exegesis,* confined in a
narrow space, reserved for a minority, it is the principle of death and of
difference in the becoming of being."[24] Writing does not reveal life; it
betrays it. Like the trace, its marks elude the presence of beings. In so
doing, writing does not exactly destroy something that can at best only
be alluded to in language, but "menaces . . . the breath, the spirit, and
history."

To menace is also to accost, as if life, spirit, and the history of these
things somehow formed a boundary to language and were constantly held
at bay by its menace, so that writing thus betrays a life of its own. History is no longer the "spirit's relationship with itself" but its finitude; the
diachronic mediations of writing impose a paralyzing limit beyond which

spirit cannot go. So too breath fails within the "repetition of the letter." But if writing is "the principle of death," it is also the principle of "difference in the becoming of being"; that is, language is a place where being becomes different from itself. That difference is nothing less than the death of being (that is, of "being" as mistakenly conceived by philosophers), but the word *difference* is a particularly resonant one for Derrida,[25] as is *becoming*, suggestive of a different kind of life in language: a bracketed and deferred life, yet also a life that depends (playfully) for its definition on death. Although this passage may open itself to an erroneous death-centered reading, it insists no more on death than on life. Writing repeats and differs from itself and all that it menaces at its borders, but it is itself a process of becoming rather than a thing of death.

For Stein and Toklas the available terminology included (in addition to *form* and *content* and associated dichotomies) *beauty* and *ugliness*, *realism* and *abstraction*, and in these cases Stein gave new emphasis to the latter terms in those pairs (*ugliness* and *abstraction*), just as Derrida appears to choose *end*, *paralysis*, and *death* over *life*, *breath*, and *spirit*. Unlike Derrida, this autobiography seems at first only to have shifted from one side of these polarities to the other. In ambiguous words such as *betray*, *menace*, and *difference*, Derrida puns on the exchange of *being* for *writing* rather than presenting an either-or of *being* and *nothingness*. But Stein and Toklas similarly refuse the oppositions between the natural and the abstract, between the beautiful and the ugly object of art. Thus when, at the first autumn salon in Paris, people "were roaring with laughter at the picture [Matisse's *La Femme au Chapeau*] and scratching at it," "Gertrude Stein could not understand why, the picture seemed to her perfectly natural . . . just as later she did not understand why since the writing was all so clear and natural they mocked at and were enraged by her work" (35). Yet at the same time her own "impulse" toward "abstraction" often is registered in the autobiography (64). In addition to questioning such oppositions, this text renders them less absolute: "As Pablo once remarked, when you make a thing, it is so complicated making it that it is bound to be ugly, but those that do it after you they don't have to worry about making it and they can make it pretty, and so everybody can like it when the others make it" (23). In this case, it is the unfamiliarity of an image that renders it ugly, and this changes when the new idea becomes familiar.

The distinction offered in this last passage is, further, between making something new as opposed to reproducing something old, and, like Derrida's "becoming," the "making" is a Wilde-like process in which art produces a new reality. Later Stein and Toklas recall the scene in which

Picasso and they first saw cannon that had been painted in camouflage: "Pablo stopped, he was spell-bound. C'est nous qui avons fait ça, he said, it is we that have created that, he said. And he was right, he had. From Cézanne through him they had come to that. His forethought was justified" (90).

But what kind of a justification is it for Picasso to have "forethought" military camouflage? Such an analogy appears to open Stein's writings to Umberto Eco's postmodern charge that the modernist avant-garde premised its art self-defeatingly on destruction of the past.

> The historic avant-garde (but here I would also consider avant-garde a metahistorical category) tries to settle scores with the past. "Down with moonlight"—a futurist slogan—is a platform typical of every avant-garde; you have only to replace "moonlight" with whatever noun is suitable. The avant-garde destroys, defaces the past: *Les Demoiselles d'Avignon* is a typical avant-garde act. Then the avant-garde goes further, destroys the figure, cancels it, arrives at the abstract, the informal, the white canvas, the slashed canvas, the charred canvas. In architecture and the visual arts, it will be the curtain wall, the building as stele, pure parallelepiped, minimal art; in literature, the destruction of the flow of discourse, the Burroughs-like collage, silence, the white page; in music, the passage from atonality to noise to absolute silence (in this sense, the early Cage is modern).
>
> But the moment comes when the avant-garde (the modern) can go no further, because it has produced a metalanguage that speaks of its impossible texts (conceptual art). The postmodern reply to the modern consists of recognizing that the past, since it cannot really be destroyed, because its destruction leads to silence, must be revisited: but with irony, not innocently.[26]

To the eye of her audiences, Stein indeed (like Picasso) "destroy[ed], deface[d] the past." Consider the discussion in the *Autobiography* of national difference:

> That cubism is a purely spanish conception and only spaniards can be cubists. . . .
>   . . . that americans can understand spaniards. That they are the only two western nations that can realise abstraction. That in americans it expresses itself by disembodiedness, in literature and machinery, in Spain by ritual so abstract that it does not connect itself with anything but ritual.
>   I always remember Picasso saying disgustedly apropos of some germans who said they liked bull-fights, they would, he said angrily, they like bloodshed. To a spaniard it is not bloodshed, it is ritual.
>   Americans, so Gertrude Stein says, are like spaniards, they are abstract

and cruel. They are not brutal they are cruel. They have no close contact with the earth such as most europeans have. (91)

In this case, to be abstract is to be cruel.

But while such racially and nationalistically based distinctions are
worrisomely dichotomizing in themselves, Eco's account does not fit
Stein and Toklas's avant-gardism perfectly. One might cite the way Stein
and Picasso attended to actualities of national identity, not only to art
(even while those actualities are "betrayed" rather than realistically represented), and note that the irony in modernist art, as Eco would wish,
"revisits" rather than destroys the past. As in *Tribute to Freud*, moreover,
narration of an actual war is central to this autobiography, and Stein and
Toklas took sides in it by enlisting as drivers in the American Fund for
the Wounded. In this context, the opposition of Germans to Americans
is overdetermined by history rather than ahistorical. Moreover, the opposition presented is not the sentimental and patriotic one of right versus wrong, of life versus death, but of bloodshed and brutality versus
abstraction and cruelty. This distinction enacts, again like Derrida's vocabulary of betrayal, not the usual binarism, but instead a kind of Derridean deferral in signification. As in Derrida's description of the way
writing menaces life, this autobiography's cruelty and abstraction hold
bloodshed at bay, putting an end to it.

Camouflage elegantly figures an art (like Stein's writing) that beguiles
or betrays the eye with its motley by undermining the historic military
uniform (whether uniformly light or uniformly dark), supplanting this
with a play of difference, of light against dark.[27] This tactical art bears
comparison with Derrida's guerrilla relation to the history of philosophy
and to binaristic constructions such as those of being and nothingness,
presence and absence. But this is not a metaphysic or aesthetic sheerly
of destruction of the past.

It is in breaking down the notion of authorship that Stein and Toklas go furthest in producing a postmodern writing. Both the autobiography's frame and its narrative play on the interchangeability of the text's
inside and outside, the exchangeability of its biographical subjects and
autobiographical authors. I suggested earlier the ways in which the title
does this, and in analyzing the function of the uncanny in this autobiography, I further suggested the ways in which author, subject, and narrator double each other. But the narrative itself has many metatextual episodes concerning the making of storytellers, authors, and writers.

Toklas tells us how she began as a writer, writing to a famous author,
how she continued (as a writer) by scribbling out the words of her conver-

sational partner, how she proceeded as an editor and an agent, then went on as a publisher, scheming what to produce and publicize—scheming essentially how to make Stein into an author in the literary marketplace. Toklas stops short only of calling herself an author. It was "difficult," she says, "to add [to her other jobs as housekeeper, gardener, needleworker, secretary, editor, and veterinary for the dogs] being a pretty good author" (251–52)—difficult, but not impossible. The possibility of her authorship is embedded in this sentence's own disclaimer.

In the fourth paragraph of her auto/biography, she explains how, falteringly, she tried writing at the age of nineteen. The occasion is her writing to a famous author, Henry James, about her desire to transpose one of his novels into a play: "When I was about nineteen years of age I was a great admirer of Henry James. I felt that The Awkward Age would make a very remarkable play and I wrote to Henry James suggesting that I dramatise it. I had from him a delightful letter on the subject and then, when I felt my inadequacy, rather blushed for myself and did not keep the letter. Perhaps at that time I did not feel that I was justified in preserving it, at any rate it no longer exists" (4). The greatest event of this first chapter turns out to be a reprise, successful this time, of this correspondence with James. At the end of the chapter, Toklas tells us that the return of "the elder brother of Gertrude Stein and his wife" from Paris inspired Toklas to go to Europe and meet Gertrude Stein (4). Five chapters later, Toklas explains that when she came to Paris, she visited Stein and "helped Gertrude Stein" with her writing:[28]

> Then my friend went back to California and I joined Gertrude Stein in the rue de Fleurus.
> I had been at the rue de Fleurus every Saturday evening and I was there a great deal beside. I helped Gertrude Stein with the proofs of Three Lives and then I began to typewrite The Making of Americans. (86)

In this passage, the "help" Toklas gives Stein coincides exactly with the occasion of their first "joining."

Toklas's role as secretary produces both occasion and opportunity for a much larger role. Who knows what writing may occur when a typist (particularly the typist of a writer who specializes in "exactitude") transcribes a handwritten script or the speech of a writer? As Toklas puts this, "I always say that you cannot tell what a picture really is or what an object really is until you dust it every day and you cannot tell what a book is until you type it or proof-read it" (113). Toklas analogizes daily dusting to typewriting and to "really" "tell[ing] what a book is" much as, earlier, she explained Matisse's painting by comparison to cooking: "He used his distorted drawing as a dissonance is used in music or as vinegar or lemons are used in cooking or egg shells in coffee to clarify" (41). For Toklas, who finds it imperative to introduce the reader to an extended portrait of Stein and Toklas's cook Hélène before introducing us to the various geniuses who visited the rue de Fleurus (7–8), and who is herself wife and housekeeper for a female "real genius," the "female" occupations of cookery and typewriting are less distant from the "male" vocation of art than they would be for any of the visiting male painters whose wives took care of all that.[29]

The image of amanuensis is a common image—or, as Stein and Toklas might call it, "device" (138)—of the woman writer, appearing frequently in the descriptions of "solitary" women writers as well in as those of coauthors. Thus, for example, Rachel Blau DuPlessis describes H.D.'s relation to Freud: When H.D. writes, "In my dream, I am *salting* my typewriter. So I presume I would salt my savorless writing with the salt of the earth, Sigmund Freud's least utterance" ("Advent," *Tribute to Freud* 148), DuPlessis sees H.D. "imagining herself . . . as amanuensis, not writer."[30] Like other amanuenses of her time, Toklas not only typed for Stein, but wrote for her—as evidenced by the fact that Toklas's handwriting appears in various texts by Stein.[31] This is evidence that can be, and has been, used for her role either as author or as amanuensis.[32] I argue that it is most obviously evidence for the kind of coauthorship I am describing.

It is at an early stage in Stein's career in the autobiography that her first biographical portrait was produced—of Toklas. "Ada" is based on the story, retold in the autobiography's first chapter, of what Toklas's life was like when her mother had died, when she had not yet met Stein (when "there was no real interest that led me on" [4]), and then again when she had met Stein (when "She came to be happier than anybody else who was living then. . . . She was telling some one, who was loving every story that was charming").[33] Stein compels Toklas to read the story just before dinner (although the time sense also is uncertain here):[34] "In spite of my protests and the food cooling I had to read. I can still see the little tiny pages of the note-book written forward and back. It was the portrait called Ada, the first in Geography and Plays. I began it and I thought she was making fun of me and I protested, she says I protest now about my autobiography. Finally I read it all and was terribly pleased with it. . . . Ada was followed by portraits of Matisse and Picasso" (114). To read this autobiography is admittedly not to write it, and to protest someone else's writing is not to rewrite it, except perhaps in the postmodern practices of collaboration described and theorized by cowriters such as Elbrecht and Fakundiny, Marlatt and Warland. But if Toklas was able to read Stein's handwriting when Stein could not, as their text claims, then reading approached still more precipitously the threshold of writing: "As a matter of fact her handwriting has always been illegible and I am very often able to read it when she is not" (76).

Soon enough Toklas is revealing a business sense in the autobiography that indicates her ever more important role not only in cultivating Stein's career but in marketing Stein: creating Stein's public image as an author. In chapter 5, Toklas asks Stein "to let me subscribe to Romeike's clipping bureau . . . one of the romances of my childhood," so as to follow the "newspapers that noticed" *Three Lives* (112). Moreover, Toklas is credited with finding "the device of rose is a rose is a rose . . . in one of Gertrude Stein's manuscripts and insist[ing] upon putting it as a device on the letter paper, on the table linen and anywhere that she would permit that I would put it. I am very pleased with myself for having done so" (138).[35] She is pleased because this action (crossing the borders between private manuscript and public forum even as it crosses those also again between writing and eating, between writing paper and table linen) went a long way to define and disseminate the public image of Stein as a writer.

Near the end of the autobiography Toklas further discloses the extent of her role in producing/creating "Gertrude Stein" amid "all her [still] unpublished manuscripts" (197), when Toklas "began to think about publishing the work of Gertrude Stein":

> I asked her to invent a name for my edition and she laughed and said, call it Plain Edition. And Plain Edition it is.
> All that I knew about what I would have to do was that I would have to get the book printed and then to get it distributed, that is sold. (242)

This final chapter of the autobiography stresses the considerable debt that Gertrude Stein's making as an author owes to Toklas's efforts as publisher, distributor, publicist, and popularizer (242–45). As Toklas had once arranged for Stein and Toklas's contribution to the war effort—advising Stein to learn to drive a car "and I will do the rest" (168)—she now again did "the rest."

The account of the writing of the autobiography itself is reserved for the culmination of this text, occurring in the final two pages. Various people and publishers had been asking Stein to write her autobiography, and she had replied, "not possibly," but eventually she turned to Toklas to write one (for them both):

> She began to tease me and say that I should write my autobiography. Just think, she would say, what a lot of money you would make. She then

began to invent titles for my autobiography. My Life With The Great, Wives of Geniuses I Have Sat With, My Twenty-five Years With Gertrude Stein.

Then she began to get serious and say, but really seriously you ought to write your autobiography. Finally I promised that if during the summer I could find time I would write my autobiography. (251)

Like Ford Madox Ford, who once found it "difficult" to be "a pretty good writer and a pretty good editor and a pretty good business man" all at once (251), Toklas finds it "difficult to add being a pretty good author" (252) to being "pretty good" at all "the rest." But Toklas's long list of everything she is "pretty good" at fails to include everything she does (like Ford, she is a "pretty good business man" and, additionally, a pretty good publisher), and, as noted earlier, the passage does as much to raise as to settle the question of whether she could be pretty good at one more thing. The inclusion of "pretty good editor" in the long list of what she can do suggests a more important role than any previous term she had used in this text—for example, "proof-reader" and "typist"—pushing her across the brink (as Stillinger argues generally of extended author-editor relationships)[36] into coauthorship. Toklas, of course, wrote and signed *What Is Remembered*, an autobiography and memoir, after Stein's death, thus giving the lie to the earlier denial of Toklas's ability to be an autobiography's author.[37]

In what has been taken by most readers as the definitive statement of authorship in this autobiography, Stein reportedly says, "it does not look to me as if you were ever going to write that autobiography," and she decides, "I am going to write it for you." Toklas concludes (in the last sentence of the book), "And she has and this is it" (252).[38] In this passage, "I" becomes a shifting signifier, as it slides (without quotation marks that might register shifts between the speakers/writers) from belonging to Toklas to belonging to Stein.[39] The joke in this famous passage (both at and between Stein and Toklas)[40] is that "it" and "this" are Toklas's (or is it Stein's?) autobiography for which Stein is being credited by Toklas with authorship. In the original edition, the book ends with a photograph of the first page of the manuscript—in Richard Bridgman's words—"Like a serpent with its tail in its mouth . . . returning the reader to its beginning,"[41] thence back to the "I" of Alice B. Toklas.

In an interview, Toklas once claimed that she had, after all, written this autobiography,[42] and a few readers have believed this rather than various other statements (made by both Stein and Toklas) to the contrary.[43] It is written (so these readers sometimes argue) in the colloquial, gossipy style of Toklas's conversation[44] rather than in Stein's allegedly more neutral, writerly manner. Others see Stein as a genius quite able to capture and reproduce Toklas's style. But in both these discriminations of Stein from Toklas, Stein is credited with textuality and Toklas with orality, a distinction that, as I suggest often in this study, is difficult to sustain. The text itself opens up not only the question of coauthorship—becoming most laughable at the moment when it purports to answer this question most definitively—but also the question of the allocation of vocations between spouses. Thus the text disturbs the neat division of Stein and Toklas as writer versus gossip: "Gertrude Stein enjoyed all these complications immensely. Matisse was a good gossip and so was she and at this time they delighted in telling tales to each other" (67). Perhaps Stein's relationship with Toklas was more democratic than most of her audience has been able to imagine. In one typically oxymoronic statement, Stein is reported by Toklas to believe that "you must have deep down as the deepest thing in you a sense of equality. Then anybody will do anything for you" (174). The relationship between them could possibly have been even more "equal" than this, so that at times they both did "anything" for each other.[45]

Borrowing a formulation from Oscar Wilde, D. A. Miller writes, "A character in Oscar Wilde . . . observes of secrecy that 'it is the one thing that can make modern life mysterious and marvellous. The commonest thing is delightful if one only hides it.' More precisely, secrecy would seem to be a mode whose ultimate meaning lies in the subject's formal insistence that he is radically inaccessible to the culture that would otherwise entirely determine him."[46] To restate Miller's point about Wilde's delightfully flagrant secrecy in the less constrained terms that, I have argued, suit this autobiography, Stein and Toklas openly hide behind each other's personae and authorities in this text and thereby both elude and make themselves and their "secrets" available to the culture circumscribing them, a culture that was itself changing and subject to change.

Can two writers write a single autobiography? Can one writer write another writer's autobiography? Stein and Toklas do as much as any other set of collaborators to answer "yes" to both those questions. If writing is what writing does, of course, it does not matter who is writing whose autobiography, and it does not matter whether there is one writer or two (or more). But, as this study argues, it does matter that in writing, there *can* be more than one and that they could mockingly protest each other's status, coordinating their different kinds of authority, coauthoring each other.

Reading with Marlatt and Warland between the Lines

Like Shuttle and Redgrove, Daphne Marlatt and Betsy Warland[47] see the irrational not as a dimension to be shunned or suppressed, but as a site of revolutionary transformation:

> thought is reading one another's min(e)ds, stumbling onto unexpected gaps, holes, wait, explosive devices—this is not enemy territory we're speaking of or in, though each entry can be for the other a dark side of the moon, its sudden craters, its dry seas or season . . .
> . . . so let's talk about the dark side as it rises dimly behind the lit rooms of our intentions variously engaged.[48]

They are more like Stein and Toklas[49] than like Redgrove and Shuttle, however, in situating these transformations within language. In their representations of the uncanny—the uncanny relations between the familiar and the unfamiliar, between public and private—we reencounter Sedgwick and Fuss's "knot" twisting in and out of itself. The rational and the irrational, the admitted and unadmitted, the heterosexual and the homosexual—ultimately, sameness and difference—become alternate sides of the same coin.[50] Whereas this appears an accidental operation of turn-of-the-century feminist texts, such as those of Michael Field, it is a central and deliberate strategy for Marlatt and Warland. Binarized opposites are entangled in each other, and their knottiness is seen as valuable, even inevitable. Thus in the terminology of her anthology, *InVersions*, Warland writes, "*Invert, To turn, bend.* Shape-changers. The turn of a phrase, the page, the mind. *Inside-out and upside-down.* Coming out turning us inside-out revealing the world upside-down: things aren't what they seem."[51]

Coming out as female and lesbian in particular turns them inside-out and reveals a "world upside-down" where "things aren't what they seem." One passage in Marlatt and Warland's *Double Negative* bears striking resemblance to a moment in *Tribute to Freud* when H.D. recalls her invisibility with Bryher, as they journey together toward Delphi: "We were always 'two women alone' or 'two ladies alone,' but we were not alone" (50). Questioning their invisibility, Marlatt and Warland are forced to observe themselves as "not what they seem" in a "world upside-down":

> walking into the diner
> "are you two ladies alone"
>   "no"
>   "we're together"

i look out the window
déjà vu:
        nothing looking at nothing

two women outback
down under
add it up—two negatives make a positive[52]

My concern in this section on Marlatt and Warland is less with the structure of the open secret in their language than with their own verse-theorizations of such (naughty) knottiness. Marlatt and Warland's fictions and poetry intertwine with theory, producing metapoetic and metafictional texts that insist, above all, on deconstructing this generic opposition. "InVersion" may be observed in Redgrove and Shuttle's writing and certainly in Stein's, but Marlatt and Warland's texts involve a direct encounter with contemporary feminist theorizing, in France and North America in particular.

There is a lot of theory even in *Double Negative*, Marlatt and Warland's first cosigned text, and the theory on which it does a double-take is mostly poststructuralist. As I have already suggested, their texts also make no secret of their feminist-lesbian politics.[53] The neologism *InVersion* itself revises (re-versions) and revalues (re-verses) Havelock Ellis's term for the homosexual, the "invert," and its subtitle is a bold, 1990s reestimation of traditionally devalued terms for female homosexuals: "Writing by Dykes, Queers, and Lesbians."[54] Both the practice and politics of their deconstructionism are thus no less complex, yet in these respects more legible within American academic feminism, than is Shuttle and Redgrove's writing.

Lesbian feminism and poststructuralist thought provide a discourse not only for the politics of Marlatt and Warland, but for many of the writers with whom they claim solidarity. Marlatt and Warland thus are unlike Shuttle and Redgrove in affiliating themselves with specific political groups. Rather than looking primarily to each other for support, as Shuttle and Redgrove did in their rediscovery of monogamous heterosexual marriage, Marlatt and Warland found each other and themselves as a lesbian couple within the alternative community of Canadian feminist writers and theorists.[55] Not only in the debts they express, in the conferences they attend, and in the friendships they cultivate, but in their publications, they ally themselves with other women's words and thought.[56] Thus Warland's anthology *InVersions: Writing by Dykes, Queers and Lesbians* collects feminist-lesbian writers' texts on writing (including one by Marlatt), many of whom have influenced and been influenced by Marlatt. Essays and poems by Marlatt and Warland appear in like-minded anthologies and journals, bringing this cohort greater visibility, as in *Collaboration in the Feminine: Writings on Women and Culture from "Tessera,"* edited by Barbara Godard (founding coeditor with Marlatt and others of the feminist Canadian bilingual journal *Tessera*); *In the Feminine: Women and Words (Conference Proceedings 1983)*, coedited by five women including Marlatt and Warland; and *Sp/Elles: Poetry by Canadian Women*, edited by Judith Fitzgerald, a title inspired by an early discussion of possible names for *Tessera*.[57] In addition, the editors of *Tessera* arranged for publication in their journal not only of an important piece by Marlatt and Warland on collaboration, but of an accompanying article on Marlatt and Warland by a sympathetic critic, Brenda Carr. Marlatt and Warland thus appear as one couple, linked indefinitely to each other, among a much larger group of activist writers, trying to make something different happen in and with their writing.

In addition to the female, lesbian, and feminist "dark side" of language, their texts concern themselves with national difference. Like Shuttle and Redgrove, Marlatt and Warland are also ecofeminists, and they interrogate colonialism as a global political condition, a state of mental subjection, and a language, all of which call for "InVersion."[58] In *Double Negative*, as they ride a train through Australia, they interrogate their own privileged positions as white tourists in a neocolonial age, consumers whose purchase of seats in a train erases other differences, and voyeurs whose ocular distance from the sights passing their train window entraps them within a masculinist, imperialist relation to the Australian. Their linguistic playfulness could arouse the charge (which has attached itself to other poststructural thinkers, from Derrida to Gallop) that their critique merely reproduces the status quo as a stage on which to dance, that they fail to (wo)man "real" barricades. For this reader, however, the linguistic and metaphysical front is a real one, not to be denigrated by comparison to the social or political, and Marlatt and Warland are thoroughly engaged in sociolinguistic skirmishes.

Upon publication, however, *Double Negative* (1988) evidently elicited almost no response at all from contemporary critics, probably because it was coauthored: "Perhaps one of the most remarkable things about *Double Negative* thus far is that it has received practically no reviews," wrote Warland in 1991; "collaborative writing seems to be a radical and unnerving approach for the North American critical mind which champions individualism."[59] Stymied as usual by the spectacle of collabora-

tive writing, reviewers failed to pay any attention to it. Rather than re-
treating into their separate studies, however, Marlatt and Warland responded to this loud silence by turning to the "secret" itself of collaboration and making a public spectacle of it. Adopting a "presyntactic,
postlexical"[60] feminist approach not only to the issues of difference raised
by *Double Negative,* but also to the business of collaborating, they went
on to publish a theoretical essay-poem on collaboration, "Reading and
Writing between the Lines," then composed a collaborative prose-poem
sequence on the way their collaboration works, "Subject to Change," and
then published this along with reprintings of *Double Negative* and the
first poetic sequences they had written (separately) for each other, *Touch
to My Tongue* (Marlatt) and *open is broken* (Warland),[61] in a single cosigned collection titled *Two Women in a Birth.*

Theirs may be the most far-reaching theorizing of feminist collaboration to be found today, and it is difficult to sum up. They mobilize the
idea of collaboration into a postmodern feminist discourse (though, like
Shuttle and Redgrove, without using the term *postmodern* itself):[62] producing writing that encompasses a philosophical critique of foundation-
alist ideas of authorship, a political critique of collaborationism (meaning complicity with the dominant), and a playful deconstruction and
reconstructive transformation of collaboration. They offer not slogans or
a doctrine, but *l'écriture.* My concern, in particular, is with their pathbreaking essay-poem on collaboration, "Reading and Writing between the
Lines."

At the head of their 1988 verse-essay on collaboration appears an editorial abstract, describing their subject in this way: "Dans ce texte écrit
en collaboration portant justement sur leur pratique de l'écriture en collaboration, Betsy Warland et Daphne Marlatt analysent la nature du
procédé d'écriture qu'elles partagent" (80; "In this text, written collaboratively and pertaining, precisely, to their practice of writing in collaboration, Warland and Marlatt analyze the nature of the process of writing that they share"; although the abstract is in French, the essay appears
in English). Warland and Marlatt refrain from analysis of their collaborative writing in the usual sense of that word; they refuse to take a distanced, third-person stance toward what they do. They create not only
a collaborative text on collaborative writing, as the editors state, but a
collaborative writing, a Derridean writing both about and embedded in
the process of writing collaboratively.

From the outset, they acknowledge the regularizing, patriarchal rules encoded into language, such as those governing analytic discourse, and they tease, prod, and disconcert those codes by, for example, undercutting the opposition between persons, that is, between *i* (almost always lowercase in their writing) and *it, us* and *them,* and *you* and *i:*

> Collaboration is a specious term for the writing you and i do together . . . here, even here, hovering between third person and second person pronoun, to choose second with its intimacy seems to me indicative of how i write with and to you. you my co-writer and co-reader, the one up close i address as you and you others i cannot foresee but imagine "you" reading in for. and then there's the you in me, the you's you address in me, writing too. not the same so much as reciprocal, moving back and forth between our sameness and differences. (80)

Collaboration is a "hovering between third person and second person pronoun" and a reciprocal exchange of first and second, of "i's" and "you's," an oscillation of "sameness and differences." Summing up these thoughts in the next verse paragraph, they call themselves not merely a "doubleness," but a "plurality" and "polylogue" of "i's" and "you's."

But *collaboration* implies militaristic conspiracy, and they confront that association not merely by dismissing it as specious—a case of deceptive and faulty logic—but by directly addressing (in the third verse paragraph) the flaws in its logic:

> which is why i find it difficult to use the word collaboration with its military censure, its damning in the patriot's eyes (the Father appears here with his defining gaze, his language of the law). collaboration implies that who we are collaborating with holds all the power. the lines are drawn. but perhaps it's the very subversion implicit in collaboration that i might see in our favour were we to move between the lines. when i see us as working together reciprocally, then what i see us working at is this subversion of the definitive. running on together (how I love prose). (80–81)

Drawing on the terminology of Lacanian theory ("the law of the Father") and of feminist film theory ("his defining gaze"), Marlatt and Warland theorize that collaboration is defined by language according to a binary system in which the "lines are drawn" and one side "holds all the power."[63] The collaborator is reified as a kind of *femme fatale:* The collaborator is specularized and "damned" in the "patriot's eyes" as she who colludes with the powerful. Warland and Marlatt theorize further (in this resembling Koestenbaum) that if the patriarchal concepts of the "patriot" and "military censure" are embedded in the term *collaboration,* then the resistance fighter may be she who can find *double talk* in "collaboration," its "implied" "subversion"; she can "move between the lines" drawn by the law.

Yet in so doing, she also moves beyond this Koestenbaum-like "double talk" to work "together reciprocally" with her partner ("reciprocity" is not a concept emphasized by Koestenbaum or Stillinger). Moreover, the term *collaboration* does not appear in the title of Marlatt and Warland's essay, and in this passage they show why they refer instead to what they do as "Reading and Writing between the Lines." They sabotage enemy lines (as defined by the law of the Father no matter which side he is on) by reading between the lines (that is, locating what is subversive in collaboration), writing between the lines (that is, deconstructively transforming the opposition between collaboration and resistance into exchangeable terms), and by moving back and forth between the lines (that is, transforming the binary opposition between "i" and the "other" into reciprocity between "you" and "i").

They do not see themselves as moving between enemy lines only. In the rest of this essay they go on to show the ways in which they also move between each other's lines, both of them reading between the other's lines, writing new lines between the other's, moving back and forth in an intertextual reciprocity between each other's words. *Double* itself acquires a variable signification here: They "double" the activities of reading and writing, for both of them read and write each other. They "double" for each other, mirroring each other's samenesses and differences. And they double back on each other's writing, *re*writing themselves and the other, making their text a "polylogue."[64] In addition, of course, "you" is the reader, or readers, not only each author's coauthor, and so the "you's" extend to include us as well in a polylogue that extends indefinitely in time and space.

Having thus deconstructed collaboration, inserting themselves into and thence breaking up its enemy lines of good versus bad into proliferating lines of communication, they end the first section of this essay by transforming "co-labor" into col-laborative play: "the holes we make in such a definite body leak meaning we splash each other with, not so much working as playing in all this super-fluity, wetting ourselves with delight even, whetting our tongues, a mutual stimulation we aid and abet (entice) in each other" (81). For playmates, excess in meaning, "super-fluity," is a "cohabitable" space between the lines. To "aid and abet" one's intimate enemy is to "entice" her to run out and play.

A comparison with the way Benveniste describes the shifting signifier *I* clarifies what Marlatt and Warland are doing with personal pronouns in this essay. For Benveniste, although the personal pronoun *I* is "unstable," denoting not a stable concept (like that of *tree*)[65] but a subjectivity that shifts from speaker to speaker, the *I* nonetheless stands, in his view, in fixed opposition to, and prior to, a subordinate *you:*

> It is the condition of dialogue that is constitutive of *person,* for it implies that reciprocally *I* becomes *you* in the address of the one who in his turn designates himself as *I.* . . . *I* posits another person, the one who, being, as he is, completely exterior to "me," becomes my echo to whom I say *you* and who says *you* to me. This polarity of persons is the fundamental condition in language, of which the process of communication, in which we share, is only a mere pragmatic consequence. . . . This polarity does not mean either equality or symmetry: "ego" always has a position of transcendence with regard to *you.* Nevertheless, neither of the terms can be conceived of without the other.[66]

Even though Benveniste admits that *I* and *you* become exchanged by speaking subjects in dialogue with each other, he theorizes *you* as a hierarchically polarized opposite. *I* and *you* can never meet in language. But because *I* and *you* are exchangeable, their linguistic relation might be better described, using Marlatt and Warland's term, as intimate. The *I* continually drops into syntagmatic constructions in which not only *I* and *you* but *you* and *me* are identified with each other: "then there's the you in me, the you's you address in me" (80). For Marlatt and Warland, *you* and an insubordinate, resistantly nondominant, lowercase *i* operate as in a dance rather than in battle lines drawn between each other.

If it is possible to write this distinction differently, to rewrite, reinscribe the traditional capital *I* as a lowercase *i* on the same level as *you,* then language itself does not enforce its capitalizations on the linguistic agent. Marlatt and Warland's text parallels those of Monique Wittig, for example, in *The Lesbian Body,* where Wittig briefly produces a subjective signifier that slides within itself, a *"J/e"* and *"j/e"* ("I/i" and "i/i"). Wittig thereby rewrites the *I* to remind the reader of the way the *I* has been constructed in a monolithic, capitalized, and male form, which may barely be uncovered to betray the "other" diminished, buried female *i:*

> The fascination for writing the never previously written and the fascination for the unattained body proceed from the same desire. The desire to bring the real body violently to life in the words of the book (everything that is written exists), the desire to do violence by writing to the language which I [*j/e*] can enter only by force. "I" [*Je*] as a generic feminine subject can *only* enter by force into a language which is foreign to it, for all that is human (masculine) is foreign to it, the human not being feminine grammatically speaking but he [*il*] or they [*ils*]. "I" [*Je*] conceals the sexual differences of the verbal persons while specifying them in

verbal interchange. . . . The "I" [*Je*] who writes is alien to her own writing at every word because this "I" [*Je*] uses a language alien to her. . . . *J/e* is the symbol of the lived, rending experience which is m/y writing, of this cutting in two which throughout literature is the exercise of a language which does not constitute m/e as subject. *J/e* poses the ideological and historic question of feminine subjects.[67]

For Marlatt and Warland, such rewriting is even more possible than Wittig suggests here and may not only symbolize the rending of the (presumptively male discursive) *I* from the (covered-over female bodily) *me*, but may also enact the less dichotomized, playful possibility of linguistic motility: the capacity of language, and thus of its inscribed assumptions, to change and be changed.

Poststructuralists have privileged writing, "graphein," and textuality over oral speech, but orality is as clearly an issue as rewriting in collaboration. When we remember that *I* and *you* operate within the context of speech acts, whether simulated on paper or spoken out loud, it is obvious that they behave not only as unstable, shifting signifiers, but also as conversational companions. The opposition Benveniste proposes between *I* and *you* imposes an artificial straitjacket not only on the Derridean slippery slide of language, but also on the reciprocal activity of conversation. Later in the essay, Marlatt and Warland ask, "what about the talking we do that underlies or underlines (between the lines) what gets written on the page" and "the talking we do that underlies the underwriting?" (86, 87). Their writing does not happen at all without such "underwriting."

After their discussion of reciprocal "splash[ing]" and play, the next act of their essay, heading their second section, captures a bit of "talk," seemingly spontaneous or accidental: "let me slip into something more comfortable" (82). The oral and the textual, the improvised and the planned intertwine in this moment. In the reprinted version of "Reading and Writing between the Lines" the first three words, "let me slip," become the title of this section (the sections are unnumbered) and thus reinforce a process in the text whereby various phrases such as "let me slip" become non-Arnoldian touchstones to which the authors continually return in varied usages and playful elaborative rewritings. (This second section takes shape not as poetic prose paragraphs, as in the first section, but as a free verse poem.)

In the lines that follow the first one, the speaker acts upon her words. The speaker could be either of the authors or neither. *She, you,* and *i* never require precise referents in this poem, gesturing instead in various directions:

> she glides across the
> room
> *lābi, to glide, to slip*
>
> *(labile; lābilis:*
> *labia; labialis)*
>   la la la
> "my labyl mynde . . ."
> *lābilis, labour, belabour, collaborate, elaborate*
>
> "The Hebrews named their letters, some guttural . . . others
> dental . . . and so they call others, labial, that is letter of the lips"
>
> slip of the tongue. (82)

Marlatt and Warland play with two forms of representational embodiments simultaneously here: with narrative realism, "she glides across the / room," and with visual verbal mimesis, such that this declarative statement "glides" across the page and then "slips" onto the third line. But soon Marlatt and Warland are sliding out of representational forms into associative linguistic play, as they explore the etymological roots of "glide" in "lābi" and, in exploring these roots, reroute "glide" and "lābi" into further word play, which eventually embraces and recontextualizes *collaborate*. To "collaborate" is now both to "glide" *and* "labour," to "labour" *and* "belabour," to "belabour" *and* "elaborate." By hinting at (rather than belaboring) the regularizing antitheses marked by these words, they enable "collaboration" to span its own contradictions. Antitheses loosen into a kind of thesaurus of "like" rather than inexorably "unlike" meanings. In this poem, they thereby span the distances not only between speech and text, but between the performative body and the performed text and between mimetic representation and self-reflexive word play.[68]

    This passage treats the phonic "'labial, that is letter of the lips' / . . . / slip of the tongue," as a classic instance of the way the "chain" (or, rather, in their terminology, "slide") of dually voiced and unvoiced signifiers works: Double talk and double texts alike operate like a slip of the tongue. A "slip of the tongue" produces many phonic differences, in fact; as obvious a phone as the labial *p* of *lips* is the alveolar *l* of *letter.* The slip of the tongue against the gums in *l* is doubled in *col-laborate,* where one *l* slides against and into the second. Amid the slide of signifiers in this poem, *collaborate* becomes a mere splash in a pond of plural sound associations: "to slip," "to glide," "to labor," to "belabor," to "elaborate," and so forth. Warland and Marlatt thus slide *parole* (the speech act of the

labial and alveolar) into *langue* (coded language), speech act into phono-
logical rule (and back again).

The word play with which this poem begins becomes a kind of verbal foreplay; in the next lines, Marlatt and Warland proceed to link linguistic slippage with female (lesbian) sexuality, the "labial" with the
"labium / 'any of the four folds of tissue of the female external genitalia'" (82). Like the *con* and *cunt* Gallop finds in metonymic *contiguity*
smelling up the language despite its invisibility—in contrast to the more
visible Lacanian figure of the phallus[69]—the sounds of *labia* haunt the
language of this essay, folded into, unfolding within even the word *col-
lab-oration*. Any word can of course become the point of departure for
free play; "the four folds of tissue" remind Marlatt and Warland further
of mythopoetic geometries, "four corners of the earth / four gates of Eden"
(82). As in H.D.'s texts, phonic and semantic play here produce a remy-
thologization of earth and heaven. The biological referent acquires no
special priority; rather, it becomes one among numerous sites for pleasurable rewriting and for phonic teasing.

Returning to elaboration of the sounds and meanings of *labia*, Marlatt and Warland next open their poem up to other speech acts, singing
and teasing: "la la la." The musical signification of *la*, the status of *la* as
the feminine article in French, and its phonic association here with female genitalia produce not just a harmony of associations, but a joking
reappropriation of the feminine for female pleasure:

> labia majora (the "greater lips")
> la la la
>   and
>   labia minora
> (the "lesser lips")
> not two mouths but three!
> slipping one over on polarity[.] (82)

Even while echoing an informal but also formal element of song, they
carefully yet playfully translate and define *labia majora* and *labia mi-
nora* as the "greater lips" and the "lesser," then close this stanza with at
least one theoretical reference that overturns hierarchical definitions such
as these. The final lines of this stanza allude overtly to (and laugh at)
structuralist polarization: "not two mouths but three!" In giving free rein
to word play, they do not merely uncover the deconstructive slide between binary opposites, but deceive, elude, transgress such oppositions:
"slipping one over on polarity." There may be an overt allusion here as
well in the counting of the "labia" (one, two, three, "la la la") to Iriga-

ray's theory, in "This Sex Which Is Not One," of "two lips" at play within women's sexuality. Not only is "labial" sexuality "not one," but it is also "not two." Yet this metamorphic multiplication of associations has much in common with Irigarayan play.

In a kind of reprise, Marlatt and Warland now return to their text and to each other, which for the reader, as they continually remind us, are indistinguishable: "slippage in the text / you & me *collābi, (to slip together) / labialization!*" Parodically summing up their word play and cementing the primary associations they interweave throughout this poem—between textual, interpersonal, collaborative, and sexual slippage—they end by exclaiming the latinate abstraction: "labialization!" Yet they do not in fact end this section here; they continue to "slip(ing)page(es) / like notes in class," and they begin again to revise poststructuralist theory by interpellating the Derridean concept of the "graph-" in language (its written character):[70] "o labilism o letter of the lips / o *grafting* of our slips" (82). The "written" and "graphic" character of language is, in its turn, diverted into the inventive crossings and purposeful agency possible in "creative writing," the "grafting of our slips."

In addition, following both H.D.'s and Irigaray's interest in the kind of metaphorics science may provide, "labile lovers" are "'prone to undergo displacement in position or change in nature, / form, chemical composition; unstable'" (83). As an alternative to classical psychoanalysis, which defines "love" as a misogynist, Oedipal opposition between males who possess phallic privilege and females who are defined as lack, science labels the "labile" in nongendered terms as "unstable," and "give[s] the one authoritative version of the slip / *graft, graphium, graphein, to write* / . . . / slippery lines" (83).

Scientific and grammatical definitions alike yield to "slippery lines." Slippage occurs not only between the lines of language, speech, and writing, but in thought itself, as Marlatt and Warland suggest when they end this poem with one final grafting of associations: "slippery lines / . . . / thought is collaboration." The poem's last line, "thought is collaboration" (83), is the first line in which *thought* appears in this essay, and they go on to elaborate it in the next section, "or thought is" (84). Nonetheless, in the context of this second section, the final line might be read as the result of its opening: "let me slip into something more comfortable. . . . thought is collaboration."

Moreover, these women's bodies have "slipped" into "something" else. If we read the first line as a colloquial expression, one of these women has asked a kind of permission to "slip into something more comfortable" (a standard verbal prelude to sexual seduction, partly parodic here): more comfortable clothes, a casual dress, robe, or negligee (in the next section, they suggest "you'd slip into something more comfortable / . . . / negligible and large, in which we are complicit and inter-ested together to be in this body at sea with one another" [84], and the essay ends with the two of them brushing their teeth in the bathroom [89–90]). If we read that line thematically in the context of this section, these women's bodies have slipped into language and thought. Their bodies cannot be separated from the texts they graft between them. Finally, their collaboration itself slips into the final comfortable, comforting thought that—as I would paraphrase it—no prior theory, definition, linguistic code, or material form is unalterable, unrevisable, ungraftable, or "one." No thought is indivisible. Every thought is connected with its others and with others' thoughts: "thought is collaboration."

Each of the eight sections introduces new linguistic elaborations and suggestive topics and each focuses on new aspects of collaboration. Yet the first two sections illustrate the general strategies and playfulness of the essay as a whole. Rather than look exhaustively at every section, I turn at this point to a more selective discussion of key moments in their developing discussion of collaboration. In so doing, I may misleadingly abstract an analytic essay from within this verse experiment, but I do not intend this account as a definitive account of their slippery prose poem. Marlatt and Warland themselves anticipate such selectivity not only in their readers but in each other, and, as with much else in this essay, they redescribe selectivity as a sign of "the unruliness of our selective minds / we read each other's entries so differently" (90). Contrary to the association (within a rationalist/positivist tradition) of selectivity with organized, analytic thought, Marlatt and Warland point out that to be "selective" is also to be "unruly" because selectivity rewrites the rules, picks and chooses among language's gifts, plays havoc with what has already been chosen. "The mind," they note parenthetically, "only tak[es] in 10% of stimulation at any given moment" (87). I will mention two developments in particular in the essay: first, of the signification of collaboration as a simultaneously political, theoretical, and playful concept and, second, of the performance of collaboration as a simultaneously intimate, dialogical, and "communographic" activity between the *yous, i's, we,* and *u/s* of this text.

The third section reopens the question of the political power dynamic involved in collaboration, this time between the two of them rather than between phallic signifiers and themselves. They take up the *thought* with which the second section left off and revise it in this way: "or thought is reading one another's min(e)ds, stumbling onto unexpected gaps, holes, wait, explosive devices—this is not enemy territory we're speaking of or in, though each entry can be for the other a dark side of the moon, its sudden craters, its dry seas or season" (84). Each other's mind (and again, whom they mean here remains unspecified) is a kind of minefield, a "no man's land," although they never use that phrase. They refer to the faces/texts they present to each other as "a dark side of the moon." For Redgrove and Shuttle or for Judy Grahn, the moon's dark side is a trope of female sexuality, and it is reminiscent of Elaine Showalter's "wild zone," the unexplored, muted place inhabited by women.[71] Yet Marlatt and Warland avoid connecting this with one gender or another; it is instead a metaphor that replaces the notion of an alien other with the notion of spatial adventure, or "mooning" (84). Even before that trope, they do a double-take on "one another's mind," which becomes each other's "mine," meaning not only "explosive device" nor only each other's exfoliated "gap" or "hole," but also each other's possession, as in, "you are mine." To possess the other is to recognize that one cannot possess her: She is unexpected, unexplored territory. Moreover, they follow up on their innuendoes of word warfare by returning almost immediately to "slippage." Even "reading one another's min(e)ds," "stumbling onto unexpected . . . explosive devices" is a process of "slippery words this slippery body we tongue between us comes between us in the ways a word can sound" (84).

Proceeding in this same section to define "collaboration then as power play where we breaks down into you and i," Marlatt and Warland restage the power play explicitly in terms of desire: "us desiring yes this third body we go chasing after and jealousy moves in." But what is "this third body"? Is it the creative act, "the dark side as it rises dimly behind the lit rooms of our intentions variously engaged" (84)? Two sections later, they write of "the page" rather than of their "intentions" as the "lit room," and their "doubling" becomes its dark side, "as if the page were a lit room read from outside while we go on doubling behind the scene" (86). The "third body" is thus the thing they form when working together as a body, "when *together* to be in a body" (84). Then again their "body" is their text, with its slippage and grafting, "this body at sea with one another in the slippage of meaning" (84). The term *body* shifts in and out of their prose poem, giving the reader "the slip." The spectral third body they "go chasing after" is the "dark side" of their collaboration; it is their textual "mooning (we wander aimlessly)" and leakage (84); it is, as Redgrove and Shuttle would describe it, the bleeding that comes as they work together.

In the fourth section, this textual "mooning" emerges again like a third party to their power play: "playing with each other's logic like a dream dark side of the moon right brain conversation the erotic zones of a word we're both attracted to stroke *arousing* our enigmatic ménage à trois one nearly always on the outside edge of two" (85). Whereas earlier their theorization of not two, but three staged a deconstructive rupture of polarity, here they both confront and, in confronting, permit the power play produced by the third: a play of jealousy and desire. But unlike the "homosocial" triangles described by Eve Sedgwick in *Between Men*,[72] Marlatt and Warland describe a "*ménage à trois*" in which "one" (any one of the three) is "nearly always on the outside edge of two a living on it sharpening our semantic shifts slips *yā*." Although the erotic lubricity of this threesome is anticipated in the literal *ménage à trois* of *The Terrors of Dr Treviles*, it is a less simple, less easy or "comfortable" arrangement. No couple within the variations possible in this *ménage*— whether of Marlatt with the text, of Warland with the text, or of Marlatt with Warland—holds priority over any other, and for each of these three parties, the other two present together a "dark side" against which one "sharpens" oneself and against which one "slips."

In this same passage, as Marlatt and Warland move more and more deeply into the way their threesomes work, they also return to the intimacy with which the essay began and elaborate its signifying. "A language intimate" (first hinted at, in their opening section, as an alternative to patriotism and to the law of the Father) derives from "*intimāre, to put in, publish, from intimus, inmost deepest*," that is, it evokes the (male) active verb, "to put in," as well as the (female) doubled superlative adjectives, "inmost deepest" (85). Moreover, its associations have to do with the public as well as the private, with both "publishing" and "inmost." They are able to admit the enemy—to allow penetration of and from within their collaboration—precisely by enclosing it in the "inmost." They conclude this passage by recapitulating the place of jealousy in their collaboration: Jealousy is the erotic risk they take for the sake of erotic reward, "we risk *jealousy* the fear of losing our voice and the afterglow of finding we haven't" (85).

In the seventh section, language is the elusive third: "you and me and language makes three, no baby she, *la langue.* she'll shift the rhythm on you, bend your sense, slam you into difference while you're still stumbling over your intent" (88). She's no baby in the sense that she's not a reproductive product, a dependent, partly malleable potentiality, nor is she a mere "babe" some man may toy with. She is powerfully mobilized, a thing to be reckoned with, shifting the rhythm, the rock and roll, bending sense, "slam[ming] you into difference." As Jacqueline Rose points out, Lacan modified Saussure's term *langue* by emphasizing its definite article *la* and redefined this as operating not according to structured binary opposition but according to unstable difference.[73] For Marlatt and Warland, the "la la-" enacts further the dual process of linguistic repetition and change, the coupled operations of sameness and difference. Then too, "she" is the shifting presence (and absence) of the collaborating writer and reader: "my co-labial writer writing me in we while we are three and you is reading away with us— / . . . / . . . you and you (not we) in me and all of us reading" (88).

As that last passage implies, collaboration is still more than a matter of "three." Marlatt and Warland continually remind us that their text interacts also with readers: "(out in the dark with other readers-in who are also us party to the parts we play in the game, apart and not)" (section five, 86). Their readers are both "in the dark" and "in" the text, both "party to the parts we play" and "apart." Enlarging on this suggestion in section six, they expose "the writer's sleight of hand which tricks the reader into believing in a voice in the wilderness singularly inspired," thus in a line disposing of the myth of solitary genius. Rather than being "singularly inspired," their text is "the embodiment the doubling of the chance of language" (87). Moreover, they move in this section to a kind of declaration of intent or of war, as they claim that no writing is "solitary," all writing is a kind of "double *solitaire*." In fact, it takes part in an innumerable "collectivity of conversation": "here we acknowledge that all writing is collaboration here we question the delineation between the collectivity of conversation and the individual's ownership" (87). Thus questioning the Western capitalist assumption of texts as private property and the notion that any language can be individually owned, they deploy their text as an explosive device in the minefield of capitalist property rights/writes.

In the seventh section, they subvert ownership further by discovering in the word *keep*, as in both *own* and *prevent*, a third, implied meaning of mutual trust: It is not possible "to keep your word/s from running away with sense," but in "eroticizing collaboration we've moved from treason into trust" (88).[74] In addition, as they implied earlier in the phrase "collectivity of conversation" (87), the larger network of writer/speakers dwelling behind and intersecting with the written page opens authorship up to a trust between more than two or three. Overtly acknowledging some textual debts here, they locate themselves within recent discussion of women's autobiography and within Carol Gilligan's theory of the way women communicate with each other: "what is 'self' writing here? when you leave space for your readers who may not read you in the same way the autobiographical becomes communal even communographic in its contextual and narrative (Carol Gilligan) women's way of thinking—and collaborating?" (88).

Picking up on the reference to autobiography, the eighth section (which, like the second, is formatted as a poem) takes as its occasion a meeting "at the bathroom sink" (89)—which constitutes the title and first line of this last section. Throughout the essay they have provided occasional practical autobiographical details of the kind other collaborators tend to foreground when describing their working relationships, but Marlatt and Warland do so always within the same shape-shifting linguistic texture, so that theorizing and autobiography slip together in the slide of signifiers. In the fourth section, for example, they explain, "there are challenges backings up required words we graft from each other's texts that can't be later edited out / . . . / . . . rewrites re you re me" (85). Such autobiographical moments offer the reader a handle, which the next moment slips from grasp into the play of signifiers. Moreover, throughout this essay Marlatt and Warland refer back to the first phrase of the second section, "let me slip," reminding us of its double entendres. They echo "let me slip" in the third section specifically to explore its duplicity. What does the speaker of that phrase mean, after all, by "more comfortable"? Is it the dress one of them slips into? Or the text they both have slipped into? Or is this phrase phatic rather than referential or subjunctive? Rather than referring to an action that is taking place, rather than requesting/inviting a change of circumstances, perhaps it signifies a gesture of elusion whereby the speaker avoids rather than joins the other: "you gave me the slip suggesting you'd slip into something more comfortable" (84). To "give the slip" is to begin the power play, slipping something into or out of the text, something either more "comfortable" or less so—or somehow both at once.

In the last section, they return once more to "giving the slip," and they enumerate its senses, creating "between the lines" a subtextual feminist manifesto for collaborative cohabitation. For a moment, in the opening lines of this last section, Marlatt and Warland might seem to stand before our eyes, reenacting a nightly event in their lives, a snatch of dialogue between writers, and the "wandering" thought this dialogue slips into:

> at the bathroom sink
> "so, do you think it's a good collaboration?"
>
> "yes. do you?"
>
> "yes . . . i don't know what others will think of it—"

i continue to brush my teeth thinking about the word *euphemism*
eu-, good + phēmē, speech   u-feminisms
all our yous (u/s) and all the others'

the words & sayings we're taught as children
so as to avoid embarrassing adults[.] (89)

This final section invites us to glimpse momentarily a peculiarly intimate scene between adult women. Furthermore, it reinvents and retheorizes a peculiarly adult word, *euphemism,* by (as usual) superfluously playing upon it, subverting, transforming it into "u-feminisms"—"all our yous (u/s)."

What tends to be repressed and covered over by adults are not only the eliminative events of the bathroom—"for u it was 'fooze' / for me 'results'"—but the gaminess of bathroom talk itself, with its double talk, sensual explicitness, and affective playfulness. Yet all of this is elusively *permitted* by familial euphemisms. Such euphemisms, when permitted free play, turn out to be a *"gift* of the *ghabh-."* Warland and Marlatt go on to suggest that collaboration has provoked a similar cover up from those who don't think of it as "good." But these two poets gleefully half-expose it, make it explicit and personal, by treating it as if it were a bathroom scene brought into their text (89).

Their collaboration has itself been a kind of euphemism, enacting an onomatopoeic substitution for their more literal cohabitation. Analogously, in this case conjunctively, female collaboration and lesbian cohabitation have both been banned by social law, but in truth merely covered over; they may be resurgently recalled, indeed enacted through the "gift of the gab." And so (as Marlatt and Warland close this section and their essay), "when we interwrite / we call each other's u-phonies out of the dark out of the blue out of / the glare of white."

———————

Mutually disruptive though this text on/in collaboration is, however, only occasionally does it represent the friction between these two writers or catch them in the act of their "interwriting." Such moments appear briefly as recollected interludes ("'where are you going with this?' / 'you didn't go deep enough'" or "'you've written it all; there's nothing left for me to say' / 'you gave me the slip'") whose internal quotations immediately yield to more distanced syntheses of the way they write together: "rewrites re you re me losing the rhythm . . . the tension necessary" or "the elation sparking the provoking each other beyond our endings" (85). The next text these writers produced, "Subject to Change," dwells precisely on these interactions and thus the antagonisms between them, so much so that the poetry they create together in this text seems often like a broken facade to the more animated reconstructed drama going on behind, through, and all around it. This text marks their separate writing through different fonts (roman and italic), which alternate either within a single section or from one section to the next and which are organized by means of diarylike entries titled by dates, from 4 March through 19 March 1991. The reader is invited to listen in on the various "private" ways they provoke, annoy, entice, and resist each other. But what is especially striking in this text, and stands in contrast to their previous texts, is the friction between them.

To gain greater exposure than in their previous texts of their collaborative process, they make use not only of different fonts but of varying formats, and then argue about the formats themselves. Thus, on 4 March through 7 March, a poem in altering fonts on the left-hand page faces a right-hand page of marginal notes (also in altering fonts and broken by asterisks into separate sections). In a second set of entries on 7 March, one of them (in italic) worries about the divergence that has developed in their understanding of these marginalia: "*i thought we were writing a poem together with documentary asides in the margin. you thought we were documenting our writing together.*"[75] In this second set of entries on 7 March, instead of marginalia, the left-hand side appears in roman font, whereas the right-hand side is in italic, thus marking a greater splitting of their writing from each other, as they spell out their disagreement.

Brackets in their marginalia previously marked moments of narrative action (for example, "[repeated searching through dictionary]" [157]), which permit the couple to record everything that happens between them. But in the second set of 7 March entries, one of them objects to too much formless "blather" and notes that, despite her partner's contrary objections to formal selectivity, her partner retains the concept of the "significant" when she chooses to record their "body-shifts" in brackets:

> *you want to document the struggle our wandering, our mind-blather makes along with the flights when we soar together. . . . nothing insignificant. although you still use the word "significant" when you talk about the actions, the body-shifts you choose to record in the margin. you say i want to write a perfect poem. we have a different understanding of form & process—form is more organic for you, what happens. for me form is something we make in collaboration with the poem, a 3rd entity which develops its own process as we continue. for you the poem is the trace of our collaboration, the record of our ins & outs. for me the poem is something we collaborate with.* (159)

This passage, with its record of profound disagreement about how to write their text, responds to a previous entry in roman, where her partner argues,

> i felt betrayed as your impatience increased. felt it as early as when i wrote "where's mine"? why i wrote it. and then felt angry when you began writing, on another page. you left. i accuse you of wanting a "perfect poem," and of not wanting to make yourself vulnerable to the reader." you say it "isn't working." it's "blather."
>
> i say it's being true to the process. i don't only want to present the reader with "perfect poems" but also the back & forth. the struggle for mine *and* the relaxing into, moving with each other into, something more than mine. . . .
>
> you say it's not poetry. i'm ok with that. don't want to feel controlled by form. "But people will look at lines on the page and expect poetry." i suggest we could write about this, these short lines, these unpredictable spaces—our riding the currents of one another's associative and symbolic thought. (158)

This disagreement about form—where the writer-in-italic argues for "poetry" as a "3rd entity" and the writer-in-roman argues for "present[ing] the reader" with "the process"—registers disagreement also about theory. The writer-in-italic complains that *"we talk angrily. you accuse me of leaving the collaboration because it isn't going the way i want it to. i accuse you of judgement when you say i'm getting too theoretical"* (159). There appears to be little left for them to agree about, as the generic interlace they have previously managed and celebrated, an interlace of poetry and theory, poetry and prose, processive writing and textual product, unravels at the exposed seams.

Most disconcertingly in the context of two writers who have thus far persuaded the reader that—however much they disagree—they manage nonetheless to write together, in the following entry "March 7: afterthoughts," the writer-in-italic suggests that they have not cowritten any texts with each other, but rather have joined separate texts: *"up till now when we've collaborated we've each had individual control of our individual pieces so we could shape them according to our own sense of form. it's not surprising that we should have difficulty collaborating on such a microscopic level—it's the first time our senses of form have collided with each other and we've had to give up individual control"* (160). Just as they move "back & forth" between different fonts, they alternate between "individual control" of "individual pieces." It is the decision to "collaborat[e] . . . on a microscopic level" that defeats them. Both methods of collaboration offer opportunities for them to diverge from each other because even full collaboration results in collision.

In the last entries of the poem, "March 16 & 17" (in roman) and "March 19" (in italic), the gap of a day suggests also the gap between them as writers, and the writer-in-italic confirms this as an essential physical gap both of bodies and texts: *"so, letters (safe on the other side). you write downstairs on your computer. i type upstairs. we pass the pages back and forth in the kitchen. not the same as sitting at the same table, writing on one page. we are not the same, not one, sitting side by side, **sam,** together. not is where desire enters"* (169). Subscribing here not only to a practice of separate writing but to an unmodified Lacanian model of desire based on absence and lack, these collaborators appear to expose at the end the failure of collaborative reciprocity as an alternative process of writing and feeling.

Yet this text is even more complex in its enactment than their previous collaborative texts, operating on several narrative and linguistic levels simultaneously and opening up all declarative statements such as these by juxtaposing them with alternative or opposed statements and by leaving their referents undecidable. Which of them, after all—Marlatt or Warland—authored the italic script as opposed to the roman, and did they not (as forewarned) return to these entries to edit, revise, and collaboratively rewrite them: "i want to edit this after & just write freely now / . . . / *you know how hard it is to edit a collaboration—you can't rewrite what you say without affecting what i say in response*" (151)? Individual entries and fonts remain unsigned, so that a reader can only guess who is who. When the 11 March entry (entirely in roman) says, "when we did break away and write our own statements, our writing kept us in close contact, pulled us back to the same meditative page once again" (164), is this entry the product of one writer (as the font suggests) or of two (as the theme and plural person suggest)?

As the writer-in-italic goes on to say in the 19 March entry, their writing together is a *"knotting . . . together,"* a *"combatting [of] old habits,"* in which they learn to *"shift[] ground where we meet"* and thus leave their relation open to change and to each other: *"quick tongue, sweet wit, cl-: not closing it. / . . . / each the other to each in our reach together. oxymoronic no doubt, in excess. yet, yes"* (169). As the writer-in-roman predicts at the end of her prose entry on 7 March, both of their styles of writing "are equally of interest. both have the potential for meaning" (158). On 7 March also, the writer-in-roman does not even try to answer the question of whether they can or should agree or disagree: *"can we agree? or do we have to?"* (159). After the crisis explored in their 7 March entries, the two writers become resolved in their "oxymoronic" sameness-in-difference and in their sense of themselves as simultaneously "subject to change" and "changing the subject": As the writer-in-italic notes, they are *"not we but i + i. starting off on different sides (of the same coin),"* and *"everything entered subject to change"* ("March 12" 165). The writer-in-roman responds, "yes, i + i. . . . double ambiguity. doubled possibility. / . . . / changing the subject—our feminist project. yet, the subject is always subject to change" ("March 16" 166).

As in "Reading and Writing between the Lines," the multivalent text of "Subject to Change" calls for close reading and rereading beyond simple analysis of its collaborative friction (such as I have presented here); as the writer-in-italic reminds the reader, *"everything entered subject to change, subject to transformation in the reader's imaginary, the reader being she, after all, who constructs meaning"* (165). The writer-in-roman describes this opening out of "i" and "i" as "relief, delight of i being only part of (i)t all. the very real difference in this from how we are absented by the dominators" (166). Earlier, the writer-in-roman explains their "collaboration" as necessarily also "a form of mediation," which has traditionally been defined as "'an intervention between two disputing parties in order to effect a peaceful settlement or compromise through the benevolent intervention of *a neutral power,'*" which definition she then disputes, considering it impossible in "form and language": "as lesbians and feminists, we know form and language are not neutral, and when up against the wall—they vie even more fiercely than we. there is no neutral, benevolent mediator—we must also assume this role. after fear and fight, there is our love. there is our paired flight" (164). In place of "settlement or compromise" and "benevolent" "neutrality," their "mediation" is a process and activity of relationship and of mutual writing and reading between interested persons. Rather than a single, fixed structure or comprehensive system for collaboration, they offer instead their active interaction: their enacted movements and shiftings of fear, fight, love, and flight, all of which are always subject to change.

Against the determinedly impersonal voice of most poststructuralist theorizing, including that of Derrida in texts such as *Of Grammatology*, Marlatt and Warland allow the plurality of personal pronouns to animate their theory, breaking down the dichotomies between the various twentieth-century discursive genres as well as between author and reader, speech and text, body and language, one person and another. Rewriting writing, they reauthorize what in poststructuralist writing has become another mildly taboo secret: personal agency in writing. They explore the possibility for creative graftings between the lines of a "ruled" patriarchal language. Collaboration does more than enable this reseeing of theory and of language: Collaboration is exposed as what writing already does, oppressively as "collusion" when it is subordinated and organized by warfare metaphors, excitingly as "col-laboration" when language is released back into dialogical interplay between its different (not unequal) parties—its different dialects, multiple authors, and their various readers.

In exploring the intricate labors of Marlatt and Warland's collaborative texts on collaboration, I have noted few limitations. "Reading and Writing between the Lines" could possibly be critiqued for suggesting at times a special relation between *l'écriture féminine* and women's sexual bodies, which various critics have seen as re-essentializing both writing and the female.[76] Marlatt and Warland's collaborative writing might be further accused of a fallacious feminocentrism and impracticably abstract theorizing. Keith Green and Jill LeBihan counter such a critique (of a novel by Marlatt)[77] by arguing, persuasively, that such writers and theorists take for granted that any comprehension or production of a female existence or writing takes place from within a social and linguistic predisposition to privilege the masculine, that female vantage points are plural, not singular, and that a patriarchal language is undone through the construction of an alternative cultural syntax that is neither strictly male nor female, but rather dialogical as opposed to monological. Marlatt and Warland, I would add, are like Irigaray in undoing abstract theoretical discourse both by rendering a playfully associative discourse in their texts and by measuring the theories of male precursors such as Freud and Lacan against the pragmatic consideration of male/female, heterosexual/lesbian differences. Marlatt and Warland arguably go further than some of their French feminist counterparts in foregrounding each other in their dialogic writing rather than only other (usually male) theorists and writers.

At the same time, Marlatt and Warland emphasize the female gender over and against the male and evoke a lesbian "utopia"[78] that appears to be separatist in impulse not only from defensively male and "straight" postures, but from alternative sexual perspectives (gay male, bisexual, transsexual, "queer"). In addition, although their collaborative writing takes up issues of racial politics, their collaboration does not cross boundaries of race. Warland notes this as she ponders the absence of reviews for *Double Negative:* "It is likely that reviewers' analytical processes have been disturbed by the fact that our individual authorships are not clearly marked in the text. In *Flesh and Paper,* although Namjoshi's and Hanscombe's individual poetry entries are not specified, the reader can identify their individual voices in relation to their differences of race, culture and country."[79] Here Marlatt and Warland's relative lack of racial, cultural, and national differentiation serves indirectly as an advantage in preventing critics from identifying the different authors and from dissecting their collaboration. As Warland says elsewhere, nonetheless, her lesbian difference is one category of difference among many—"as a lesbian i do not speak Universese. few people do. we (collective not universal) come from different cultures, classes, ages, lifestyles, bodies, belief and educational systems. conflict in the world has been largely due to the desire 'to stamp' out difference or at least have authority over it"—and she describes the evolution of her writing from metaphor to a "deconstruct[ed]" writing as a project to embody "difference."[80]

In the next chapter, where I address several sets of mixed-race couples, differences of race, culture, and country (and also of economic status) are inescapably enmeshing terms, and "utopias" among or despite such differences are not easily attained. At the same time, not even collaboration between two writers of mixed ethnicities can produce a comprehensive representation of social differences. There is no such thing as an unlimited collaborative posture or perspective. What I would call for is thus not a singular kind of collaboration, but a collaborative reading of collaborations: Just as various stories of difference by single-author writers of different colors and places have been juxtaposed in multicultural anthologies in recent years, so may collaborative stories and writers be gathered in collections and collectivities. In this last regard, Marlatt and Warland could be seen as notable once again, for, as I mentioned at the outset of this section, they have collaboratively done much in their country to bring authors together in writers' conferences and in editorial collectives as well as gathering the writings of various authors in collections. In the words of a reviewer of *InVersions*, "While all of the essays/texts in this volume are interesting and insightful, to my mind it is the final section, 'Questions Beyond Queer,' that has the most impact," for it "articulate[s] other significant aspects of the writers and their work (like race, class, and belief systems) that often go unnoticed in lesbian/feminist interpretations."[81] Such differences, lesbian or feminist, racial, national, or economic—as I discuss further in the next chapter—are challenges more readily met in larger coalitions of "u/s."

7 *Rewriting America: Erdrich and Dorris, the Delany Sisters, and Ossie Guffy*

THE THREE APPROXIMATE collaborations discussed in this two-part chapter—between two mixed-blood Native American writers, Louise Erdrich and Michael Dorris, and between African-American women oral storytellers, Ossie Guffy and the Delany sisters, and their white interviewer/narrators—write or rewrite American history. Whereas Erdrich and Dorris represent encounters among descendants of European settlers and descendants of indigenous Native Americans in well-known books of the last two decades, the others focus on the civil rights struggle: Ossie Guffy in *Ossie* by Ossie Guffy as told to Caryl Ledner, a book collaborated on in the 1970s, and the Delanys in *Having Our Say* by A. Elizabeth and Sarah L. Delany with Amy Hill Hearth, a bestseller of the early 1990s. These collaborative texts concern themselves with intraracial relations and the ways in which the American inscribes itself as a dissonance in and across racially marked divides. They reproduce some of the hard lessons that have partly replaced the American ideal of the melting pot with a more fractious multiculturalism.

These texts thus produce arguments about social democracy, much as the collaborators of the previous two chapters confront, respectively, the institutions of psychoanalysis and of writing. Michael Dorris in particular argues eloquently for "rewriting history" in relation to issues of ethnocentricity, cultural diversity, and the complex trail of treaties with Native Americans. For Dorris, "colliding" diversities are a defining fact of the American past as well as of the present: "The mosaic of human possibility and potential, the laboratory of cultural experiment" that is America promotes diversity, "that multifaceted reflection of human ingenuity," and for human beings, "as a species, [diversity] has always been our salvation."[1] Dorris was a full professor of anthropology and founder of the pioneering Native American Studies Program at Dartmouth before devoting himself to a career as a writer, and so he initially developed his thinking in part within this academic context. But Erdrich and he,[2] like the Delanys and Guffy, enter the debates about America not through scholarship or theory, but by writing about what they perceive as important in American culture generally and in their own ethnic, class-based, gendered, and professional backgrounds specifically. My own emphasis in this chapter is on these writers as collaborators and on how literary collaboration informs their treatments of national identity, cultural difference, and social inequality.

Literary collaborations across racial and ethnic differences enact and test American social democracy. The distrust of American democracy that is so evident in contemporary cultural and literary criticism attaches mostly to economic individualism and bases much of its critique on the idea that official American positions on the nature of the subject not only are philosophically naive but also, in their focus on individuality and opportunity, condone an unacceptable degree of social inequality. The literary collaborations in this chapter proceed neither exclusively as indictments of the American dominant nor as demonstrations that American society is less riven than it seems, but as both indictments and reconciliations. In addition, as Erdrich and Dorris recognize, to coauthor texts is quietly to challenge the individualistic copyright system even while potentially democratizing it because collaboration promotes writers both through the solidarity and support system thus accomplished and through the greater equity achievable within a collaboration. At the same time, however, it seems nearly impossible to manage long-term, equitable coauthorships in today's literary marketplace in the United States or to achieve wide visibility and acceptance for such collaborations.

Beyond their ethnic differences, the most obvious differences between the collaborators in the two sections of this chapter are the literary markets in which their texts are found (or, more precisely, their reception in those markets by book reviewers and academic literary critics) and their differing kinds of collaborations: primarily textual for Erdrich and Dorris, as opposed to oral for the Delanys and Ossie Guffy and their coauthors. Erdrich and Dorris have been generally received as writers of "serious" literature, whereas the Delany sisters and Ossie Guffy did not write their work at all but rather relied on journalists for transmission of their life stories. Predictably, the texts of these collaborators differ markedly in complexity: Erdrich and Dorris produced semiexperimental narratives that have been called postmodern by some critics, whereas the Delanys and Ossie Guffy are represented by realistic, linear narratives.

But these distinctions make less difference, I argue, than they seem, and despite what seems a significant difference to academics, the market for these writers is largely the same. It is the educated middle class (rather than the smaller avant-garde circles of Marlatt and Warland or the enormous distribution circles of commercial film):[3] a middlebrow market that in the United States is increasingly becoming the only available print market in which to succeed (with the upsurge of superstores such as Barnes & Noble and Borders, the changes in tax law affecting the warehousing of books, and the rise of the Internet). Moreover, although Erdrich and Dorris certainly have produced more difficult texts to read than those of the Delanys and Ossie Guffy, through their writer/narrator, Amy Hill Hearth, the Delanys use some of the same complexities of multiple storytelling and juxtaposed parallel narratives as do Erdrich and Dorris, and Ledner and Guffy produce the multiple layering of narrative irony—what Erdrich and Dorris call "survival humor."[4] Erdrich and Dorris, for their part, see the method and impulses of their writing as emanating from an oral culture of storytelling.

What will matter more than how Erdrich and Dorris's texts compare with those of the Delanys and Guffy in my presentation of them—how "high" or "low," "complex" or "simple," "difficult" or "accessible" these texts seem—are the relative successes of the collaborations (in terms of their avowed satisfactions, public visibility, and longevity), their specific representations of multicultural collaboration, and the varying ways in which they celebrate or problematize collaboration across and among cultural differences in their texts. In this context, Ossie Guffy's autobiography is as interesting as the Delanys', and Erdrich and Dorris's collaboration falls short in some ways of both these others. Nonetheless, whether persuasive or not, enduring or not, problematizing or reconciliatory, each of these collaborations is intriguing in its representation as well as in its reproduction of the problems of a multicultural society, and all deserve to retain a place (which Guffy has nearly lost) in literary history.

Blood Is Always Crossed: The Marriage of Erdrich and Dorris

Before Michael Dorris's suicide in 1997, Louise Erdrich and Dorris[5] were the best-known collaborators in the United States. Their work together competed more successfully than that of any other contemporary coauthors, both in the book trade and in the academic marketplace. They reached a wide audience and won the respect of contemporary critics and teachers. They were successful as writers not only of novels and poetry, but also of children's stories and nonfiction narratives. They presented themselves as having achieved an equitable collaboration. Their single cosigned novel, *The Crown of Columbus,* is a comic romance about a relationship between two academics who become coparents—a highly fictionalized, mildly satirical reenactment of Erdrich and Dorris's courtship and marriage. By the end of the novel, both parents work happily as scholar/writers, both writers parent, and both the work and the parenting are handled collaboratively. One might have supposed that with Erdrich and Dorris we had reached a conventional happy ending to the modern story about feminist literary collaboration.[6] But Dorris and Erdrich embraced coauthorship less fully than a number of the other collaborations treated here, and their collaboration is no less problematic than the others, in part precisely because their resolution to the possibilities and problems of coauthorship reinforces a new myth of the happy, professional supercouple.[7]

Erdrich and Dorris claimed in public interviews to collaborate on nearly all their work together, but they cosigned only one of their novels, one nonfictional narrative, and some nonfictional op-ed pieces.[8] Almost everything they wrote appeared over one signature or the other, and Erdrich describes the act of writing—the hours when a writer literally puts pen to paper—as a solo act (Bonetti 82).[9] In their interviews, they said they had not crossed that last border; they did not meet in the place where what is in one's head turns into the object of writing, where the orality of collaborators' conversations is textualized, and conversation becomes a script. Even in composing *The Crown of Columbus,* each writer produced preliminary drafts of different sections or parts of the same section.[10] The consequences of all this for their reception are obvious: They continued to be seen and discussed as individual writers, solitary authors who helped each other more overtly and more routinely than others.

At the same time, they presented their collaboration as inextricable from their marriage. In their essay on feminist collaboration, Kaplan and Rose perceive Dorris and Erdrich's marriage (before their separation and

Dorris's death) as reinscribing conventional gender differences, with Michael Dorris more dominant and more vocal and Louise Erdrich more passive, quieter. (*Lesbian* in the following passage is intended figuratively by Kaplan and Rose as a radical metaphor for feminist collaboration.)

> Another example that disquiets us and is at variance with our notion of lesbian collaboration is the heterosexual model of Louise Erdrich and Michael Dorris, which has been lauded in written and visual media. When we see it in action—Erdrich and Dorris's PBS interview with Bill Moyers, Erdrich's foreword to Dorris's *The Broken Cord* (1989) . . . —it appears hierarchical. Erdrich, who in her single-author novels has a rich, original, personal voice, becomes a parrot for Dorris's ideas in the foreword and, in the PBS interview, a nearly silent but conspicuously adoring spouse. This "collaboration," which seems literally to embody domination, violates our vision utterly.[11]

Erdrich's novels are not in fact "single-author novels," nor is the novels' "rich, original, personal voice" hers alone, and Dorris and Erdrich's differing personality styles, as disclosed in the Bill Moyers interview, apparently facilitated their development of a highly collaborative relationship rather than the reverse.[12] Their collaboration operated (as evidenced in their interviews and writing about themselves) as a complex balance of powers. Nonetheless, like their cosigned novel, their self-descriptions cultivate the romance of heterosexual marriage. The terrible irony of the way their marriage actually ended—with news stories confirming Erdrich and Dorris's separation and pending divorce at the time of Dorris's suicide, with confirmation also of a failed legal suit brought earlier by Dorris and Erdrich against one of their adopted sons who had threatened them (another of whom died in an accident), and with Dorris allegedly accused of sexual harassment by one or two of his daughters[13]—has demolished that romance in the public eye and with it the image of a successful collaboration.[14]

That the marriage of high achievers should fail in such circumstances is less of a surprise than that their collaboration should have succeeded as long and as spectacularly as it did. From 1985 to 1997, Erdrich and Dorris published one book, sometimes more than one, and several nonfiction articles almost every year, while raising three adopted children (with serious disabilities) and three biological children, amid the endless demands of managing their own careers (including continual requests for interviews, readings, lectures, guest teaching, correspondence, and so on).[15] Dorris and Erdrich's collaborative successes arose not sheerly through their skill or imagination (many less widely read writers have plenty of both), but also through their meeting conventional contemporary expectations for both seriousness and entertainment in literature. Their novels satisfy reviewers and scholars who value complexity and ingenuity in narrative structures, densely textured and thought-provoking plots, and multiple perspectives, and they appeal to teachers who want to introduce students to multicultural literature that does all these things. Yet they also satisfy the broader literary marketplace that finds sex and violence, eccentric characters, and exotic cultures entertaining. Some reviewers criticized them for catering to commercial interests in writing *The Crown of Columbus* in time for the quincentenary of Columbus's encounter with America and receiving a $1.5 million advance for it from HarperCollins (then Harper & Row).[16] The novel also courts popularity in its adventure plot, in its use of glamorous locations (at Dartmouth and on a Bahamian vacation island), and (unlike their previous fictions) in leaving its central protagonists all happy at the end. But *The Crown of Columbus* does not in these respects represent an aberration in their career: Like most "serious" writers of the past, they sought to gain both respectful criticism and a wide readership.[17]

Yet to describe their work together as conformist would not do justice to what Erdrich and Dorris accomplished in and with their coauthorship. Although conflict often arises between the aims of seriousness and popularity, this dual purpose is nearly unavoidable. Without the respect of well-known writers and reviewers, it is difficult to launch a career. Without a wide readership, it is difficult to maintain a career or even to maintain respectful reviewers. In making Dorris and Erdrich more widely known than, for example, the avant-garde Marlatt and Warland, the forms and conventions they chose guaranteed them a wider field for and potentially greater impact on the way in which their books—and Native American writing more generally—are perceived and valued.[18]

Moreover, their narrative strategies have been described accurately as a form of political postmodernism, and like other postmodern writing, theirs flouts both middlebrow and academic distinctions between "high" and "low" ways of rewriting American history.[19] They may be seen—as some critics have indeed seen them—as foremost exemplars of Native American postmodernism, for their narratives are centrally concerned with the difficult specificities by and through which Native American cultures and people collaborate (in both senses of that term) with mainstream, Western culture, often self-destructively.[20] Their fictions produce a plural understanding of modern descendants of Chippewa and Modoc Indians and of mixed-blood people. (Although they present less sexual than ethnic diversity, sympathetic gay characters appear, for example, in *The Beet Queen, A Yellow Raft on Blue Water,* and *Cloud Chamber; Tales of Burning Love* presents a more diverse portrait of women's sexual existence, no longer focusing exclusively on women's heterosexual relations.)[21] They should be seen, on the endlessly proliferating and shifting scale between revolutionary transformation and conservative nostalgia that characterizes the U.S. political scene (especially within academia itself), as reformist progressives.

In what follows I focus first on three important, closely related aspects of their collaboration—on their representations of their ethnic identity, their coauthorship, and their marriage—in order to describe the intricate, often elusive, sometimes self-promoting ways in which they negotiated differences. In all three areas, they argue or enact several things at once. They deliberately particularize and refuse, multiply and problematize identity labels. Thus there is nothing ordained about the way they describe the creation of their writing, for it occurs both in solitude and in collaboration; it is directed toward both literary greatness and commercial success; it is, in their view, both Native American and not, American and universal. At the same time, their self-descriptions promote their mythologization as a late-twentieth-century literary romance comparable to that of the Brownings in the nineteenth.

In sharp contrast, as any reader of their fiction rapidly discovers, their novels represent not only social identity constructions (including gender, sexuality, familial position, and generation as well as ethnicity), but social and familial relationships as profoundly, tortuously at odds with each other.[22] There is little that is natural about being a woman, a man, or a Chippewa in the contemporary America of their fiction. Women vie with men in destructive contests of power, and blood is always mixed. Each successive generation becomes ever more mixed, ever more broken from both the tribal and familial patterns preceding it. Nature itself is not natural in the sense of following fixed, incontrovertible laws; it is full of unexpected deconstructions and shattering conjunctions. Even the uncanny spirit world, so alive in some of the tribal traditions that populate these novels yet so completely nonexistent for a number of its characters, operates as a form of arbitrary disruption in the material world.

But Erdrich and Dorris also effect something more reconstructive and less obvious than this unraveling and clashing of differences in their fiction—and, after looking at their discussions of their collaboration, this will be my second focus in this section. Their fictional writing indicates ways in which affiliations or "affinities" (in Donna Haraway's use of that term) may be developed among differences, "coalitional" bonds (to borrow from Adalaide Morris) may be produced between the unlike.[23] At sporadic moments, agreeing to cross such acknowledged differences, to experience brief merging, may yield a transient ecstasy. Such glimpses of comic or romantic relief appear fiercely contradictory: Bonds are forged in the midst of severe disjunction.

Quirky, incomplete, temporary, provisional, highly contingent, and never free of social structures that divide and oppress, affinities may nonetheless be forged across the gaps between authors, sexes, generations, tribes, and cultures. If readers and critics now begin to devalue these writings by reading into them (consciously or not) their writers' failed marriage, if they begin to see their collaboration primarily as suppressing secrets about their writers' lives, this will not do justice to the ways in which Dorris and Erdrich themselves, while still both alive and striving, saw and wrote about the seeming impossibilities of cross-cultural and intracultural relationships, yet also occasionally suggested how these relationships could briefly work despite and within even the most unworkable situations.

When, in their published interviews, Dorris and Erdrich are asked about whether they consider themselves Native American writers, they routinely both acknowledge it as "simply a fact" and shrug it off, pointing to how useless such generalizations are. "Native American" is, as they often point out, so multitudinous a category as to make an all-encompassing ethnic identity category of this sort fruitless. They write, as Dorris says, out of the traditions of a "particular tribe or reservation" belonging to their specific historical backgrounds, especially the Chippewa and Modoc, and would not "presume or even dare to speak for or write about themes that were important for Navajos or for Iroquois" (Wong 198). But they then go on to prefer to these labels the designation "writer" or "American writer." "I prefer to simply be a writer," Erdrich says early in their interview with Hertha Wong, and then immediately adds, "although I like to be known as having been from the Turtle Mountain Chippewa and from North Dakota" (197). (Erdrich claims German-American as well as Turtle Mountain Chippewa descent, whereas Dorris's ancestors are principally Modoc and Irish-American.) In their interview with Kay Bonetti, after saying, "Well, I think it's simply a fact, but I don't think it's right to put everything off in a separate category," Erdrich then says, "All of the ethnic writing done in the United States is American writing, and should be called American writing" (95).[24] But if they eat their different cakes and have them too, they also make it more difficult for readers to pigeonhole

them. Moreover, they occasionally expose the social discriminations behind labels: "Any label," says Erdrich, is "both true and a product of a kind
of chauvinistic society because obviously male writers are not labeled
'white male writers'" (Wong 197), and Dorris adds, "Native American
literature is about as descriptive a term as non-Native American literature. . . . [It] doesn't tell you a great deal" (Wong 198).

The facts of their collaboration raise comparable issues of identity
for them. Interestingly, the issues emerging from their identities as collaborators not only parallel but become interwoven with their identities
as (Native) American writers. And they reply to questions about their
collaboration in similarly evasive and strategically contradictory ways.
Wong links the Native American to their collaboration, asking whether
they agree with "people [who] like to think of your collaboration as one
of the examples of why this is a Native American novel," or, she suggests
alternatively, "is it just because you two work well together and you like
each other?" They respond at first by seizing upon the latter option, "And
we trust each other's judgment." Implied in Wong's question as to whether they see their collaboration as Native American (202) is the suggestion that Native Americans cultivate communal rather than individualistic traditions, and Erdrich and Dorris reject this in favor of Wong's
second suggestion that they merely have a good relationship. Asked by
Bonetti, "Have you thought about yourself in the context of other couples who write together?" however, Dorris rejects this category as well.
Indeed, he rejects any kind of categorization at this point: "I don't think
we think of ourselves as in a category; we're pretty surprised to find ourselves who we are, and doing what we're doing." After he has refused to
be categorized even as a "couple" who "writes together," Erdrich then
refuses also the notion of solitary authorship for them: "There's this very
romantic and often very true notion of the writer's struggling with his
or her destiny, alone, in some small, painted room. . . . We think of that
sometimes, as our children are cavorting or careening about. We don't
have that kind of life" (Bonetti 86).

But while laughingly rejecting all authorial categories, including the
Woolfian "romance" of a room of one's own, Dorris and Erdrich nonetheless offer a counterromance of the writing relationship, for Dorris
proceeds to describe "one great advantage" of their collaboration: "When
writing about both male and female characters, it is a distinct advantage
to have an absolutely trusted and equitable input from someone of the
other gender who shares the same vision, almost as an opposite-gender
version of yourself." Moreover, they turn out to accept the idea of a connection between collaboration and Native American communal tradi-

tions: When Bonetti asks a question similar to Wong's, as to whether "your comfort with this kind of relationship is in any way related to your Native American roots," they agree that (in Dorris's words) "we both came from specific family traditions, which are probably microcosms of tribal traditions in some respects, of people sitting around and telling stories and embellishing and adding to and participating. It's as though the story evolves out of a set of shared memories" (86–87).

Then again, in publishing most of their novels under only one signature at a time, they subscribe neither to a communal nor to a relational concept, but to an individualist concept of authorship. Against the public knowledge (conveyed through interviews such as these) that they write together, they assert in their title pages their allegiance to modern Western conventions of single authorship. They occasionally describe their collaboration itself as a matter of reading each other's work rather than of cowriting, and see it as making them simply more American. In their interview with Wong, they conclude the discussion prompted by her question about whether they see their collaboration as specifically Native American with Dorris saying (and Erdrich concurring) that because their work is better when they have both agreed to it, "we may just be the common denominator American reader" (203). American as apple pie, or as funnel bread? Not only in their fiction, but in an interview such as this, Erdrich and Dorris have preempted the possibility of discovering a single common denominator for the American, yet they prove themselves unabashedly able to invoke it.[25]

Like most collaborators when asked about their collaboration, they stress its more practical logistics, emphasizing—in the face of its "mysteriousness"—the fact that it works. The result is again a multiply paradoxical representation of coauthorship as both explicable and mysterious, subversive and ordinary, and, again, individualistic and consensual. In response to Wong, who says, "Collaboration is an idea that makes many writers who emphasize individual creativity uneasy. . . . Would you describe your collaborative process?" Erdrich answers, "It's not very mysterious," a reply that seeks to demystify and defang a process that seems both mysterious and threatening to those who cherish belief in solitary creativity. Yet collaboration, as Dorris and Erdrich reinvent it for the public imagination, adds to the mystique of creativity the seductive mystery of their marital relationship. In presenting their collaboration as a partnership, they become not merely American writers but the utopian American working couple.

What emerges in Dorris's longer answer to Wong is the paradoxicality of a process based on individual rights and hierarchically established authority but also on diplomatic exchange and democratic consensus. In his description of how they write, nearly every word they write is both the product of collaboration and not:

> We'll start talking about something a long time in advance of it—the germ of a plot, or a story that has occurred to us, or an observation that we've seen. . . . After we talk, one of us, whoever thought of it probably, will write a draft. It might be a paragraph; it might be ten pages; it might be something in between. We then share that draft with the other person. Shortly thereafter they will sit down with a pencil and make comments about what works and what doesn't work, what needs expanding and what might be overwritten. Then they give that draft with their suggestions back to the person who wrote it who has the option of taking or leaving them, but almost always taking them. Then that person does a new draft, gives it back to the other, and goes through the process again. This exchange takes place five or six times. The final say clearly rests with the person who wrote the piece initially, but we virtually reach consensus on all words before they go out, on a word by word basis. There is not a thing that has gone out from either one of us that has not been through at least six rewrites, *major* rewrites. (201)

A little later, Dorris says, "we both have a real proprietary sense of all the books. We *both* have that sense regardless of whose name is on them. We take a lot of pride and feel very personal about them and the characters" (202). These passages embrace the contradictions of their working both as individual originators and as "us" who come up with "the germ of a plot" (201); of both a hierarchically ordered relationship in which the originator not only begins a manuscript but "has the final say" and a consensual process in which the "author" practically never overrules his or her coauthor; of a procedure of dual ownership, dual sets of proprietary rights. In the interview with Bonetti, the two of them become more specific: Dorris says, "There hasn't been a word from *Love Medicine,* or *The Beet Queen,* or *Yellow Raft* which has not been concurred upon," and Erdrich says, "There was one word we didn't agree on in *Love Medicine*" (79). They achieve consensus at times through horsetrading: "There came a moment in which there was a phrase that I really liked in *Yellow Raft* and a phrase that Louise didn't, and a phrase that she really liked in *The Beet Queen* that I didn't and we traded, we got rid of each other's phrases" (Bonetti 79–80).

Thus far I have suggested that, when they consigned themselves to the published, printed page, Dorris and Erdrich adhered to a copyright system that confers ownership and authority on legal names and signatures. This is certainly how they are known to the general public, but they have written not only as Erdrich or Dorris. They tried out most of the forms in which their coauthorship could be publicly presented, most often through dedications and acknowledgements to their single-signed novels, occasionally through cosigning texts, but also, in some of their earliest work, through a fictitious single pseudonym. "Milou North" is the author of several short stories published in *Redbook* and *Woman*. The use of the pseudonym occurred "early in [their] literary relationship," when they wrote deliberately sentimental stories to "sell." When Wong asks them, "Other than the obvious union of names [*Mi*chael and *Lou*ise], why did you publish under a pseudonym?" Erdrich replies that "it's mysterious. You really think that's probably a female, but you don't know. It's one person. I think that when readers read a story they want to read one by one person. But we liked having the romance of it." As for "North," "we were in New Hampshire. It sort of sounded literary" (203). Erdrich again emphasizes the contradictory duality of their choices, in this case of a pseudonym that presents them as at once a single author and a romantically united couple, mysterious and unthreatening, regional and literary.

Although for Erdrich, as for Dorris, their collaborative process is as individualistic as it is cooperative, her description of this further emphasizes its simultaneous aggressions and permissions: "We're collaborators, but also individual writers. Michael and I plunge into each other's work with very little ceremony. We plot together, we dream up our characters together, we do everything together, except write the actual drafts, although even the writing is subject to one another's deepest desires. We go over every manuscript word by word. Then we argue over whatever we feel should be changed and we try to come to some sort of agreement on everything that goes out" (Bonetti 79). Writing allows a relationship between lovers, whose boundaries yield continually to the "plunge into each other's work." Even their individual drafts are mutually "subject" not to "domination" as that adjective might suggest, but to "one another's deepest desires."

These interviews are themselves acts of collaboration with their interviewers. Dorris and Erdrich prove proficient at public relations, and the intimacy reenacted for interviewers reinforces Erdrich's description of how their relationship worked:

> Wong: Louise, what are you working on right now?
> Erdrich: I'm starting on *Tracks* which is the next book that goes before *The Beet Queen*—just writing drafts of it.
> Dorris: But really the answer to your question is more complicated. I mean Louise is working on . . .

Erdrich: I was just thinking . . .

Dorris: . . . revisions for *Yellow Raft*.

Erdrich: . . . that I am working on Michael's. I'm really getting so up to working on *The Broken Cord*. I think it's a terribly important book. Right now I'm really in love with *A Yellow Raft on Blue Water* because as something is being finished, you feel this mixture of can't let it go and glory because it's beautiful. Right now my primary concern is go keep Michael . . .

Dorris: . . . from taking out that line.

Erdrich: . . . from taking out that line. [Laughter.] Exactly. That's what I'm working on. I'm very worried that he doesn't know how much this means. (216)

They are as emphatic about the fact that they "argue" with each other as that they "desire" each other's writing, and whenever the question of collaboration is raised by Wong or Bonetti, they reopen and reenact old arguments. Yet here again they clearly like exposing to interviewers the pleasure they get even from disagreement:

Dorris: And we trust each other's judgment.

Erdrich: Good, I'm glad you said that.

Dorris: Oh, see, she's lobbying for me to put back a line. [Laughter from both. To Louise:] I put it back, while you were gone, but I left the second line as was. (Wong 202)

Differences in style and tone emerge between Erdrich and Dorris in these interviews, but the differences are less salient than their presentation of themselves as straddling contradictions between individual and joint authorship, between personal argument and agreement. Their presentation of the logistics of their relationship is no less complex, no more prone to settle for a single label than is their self-presentation as Native American writers.

But their presentation of their marriage *is* more consistently celebratory. In their accounts of their coauthorship, its origin coincides with the origins of their relationship and marriage, so that their coauthorship and cohabitation become increasingly closely linked in these interviews. Early in the interview with Bonetti, Erdrich locates the beginning of their coauthorship in their romantic first meeting, when they "Met. Capital m": "I didn't really get anywhere [with writing] until I went to Dartmouth as a visiting writer. Then Michael and I fell in love, married, and started working together. It was like overdrive, or something. I finally began to really get things together" (81). Erdrich's ability to "get things together" as a writer begins with their collaboration and their relationship. (Given the importance of spiritualism to other collaborators, it is perhaps notable that the interviewer asks them at this point whether the rumor is true that they practice telepathy; Dorris says, "Oh, that was a joke," and Erdrich says, "It's true, though, we can read each other's minds" [81].) Contradictory as are Erdrich and Dorris's descriptions of their identities as authors, they inevitably recur to the image of the nuclear family: the happy married couple with their textual children.

Erdrich speaks of another occasion, perhaps less romantic, when in the first year of marriage they decided to enter a story in the Nelson Algren competition because "we were kind of looking for money" (Bonetti 85). Erdrich had a "very" rough draft for a story, but had never had "anywhere to put it" (84–85), and they thought it might be developed for the competition. Lacking "the guts to do anything with it," she waited until the last minute, when "Michael got ill—he was flat on his back—so it was in this very strange kind of frenzy that that story was written. A very uncomfortable kind of writing, in fact, because I would be writing on the kitchen table with people about to come in at any minute. Michael would read it, make adjustments, and, you know, it was very much the beginning of that kind of process" (85). This story, "The World's Greatest Fisherman," became the first chapter of *Love Medicine*. If their collaboration began as a romantic mystery of veiled coauthorship or as a real-life romance of working marriage, it also began as a mutually beneficial commercial partnership: Romance proved profitable.

––––––––––

How mutual, how equitable, how mutually beneficial was this coauthorship while it lasted? In an earlier era, Erdrich might well have become a Lady Gregory to some budding Yeats, a Viv for some Tom. Instead, the scale was tipped not in Dorris's direction, but in hers; she became a kind of Wordsworth to Dorris's Coleridge, or Eliot to Dorris's Pound. Whereas he is known best as an established scholar and nonfiction writer (the author in particular of *The Broken Cord*, the story of a boy he adopted with fetal alcohol syndrome) and he wrote two novels, *A Yellow Raft on Blue Water* and *Cloud Chamber*, after beginning to work with Erdrich, hers remains the greater literary reputation, based on her wholly impressive six novels and on her poetry, all of which appeared solely under her name. In the order of their publication, Erdrich's novels are *Love Medicine, The Beet Queen, Tracks, The Bingo Palace, Tales of Burning Love*, and *The Antelope Wife*.[26] Readers must now see not only that a woman might collaborate with a man without being overshadowed by him, but that she might overshadow him.

It may have been necessary, however—although Erdrich and Dorris did not plan this[27]—for the balance to tip in her direction if she was to achieve recognition as a woman *co*author. Thanks to the appearance of her numerous works only under her name, the increasingly widespread knowledge of their collaboration enhanced his reputation without damaging hers. Their one cosigned novel, despite mixed reviews, paradoxically boosted her individual reputation because critics were wary of its coauthorship and often compared it unfavorably with their noncoauthored works.[28] As all their interviews indicate, nonetheless, Dorris played a crucial role in the development of their "joint vision" (Bonetti 84). When they met, she was writing poems and stories; as she developed these stories through conversations with him that generated characters and plots, her writing grew into a novel, *Love Medicine,* which launched her very successful career.[29] As they neared the end of it, Dorris saw the possibility for "four books" (Bonetti 92), which eventually became her famous series of five novels.

In their interviews, Erdrich herself eagerly contributes these bits of information about the history of their coauthorship, acknowledging her indebtedness to Dorris,[30] whereas Dorris complicates her story, sometimes downplaying his role: "I think that probably there was a moment, you know—'Great Moments in Medicine'—in which I said it should be a quartet. . . . But they go through so many drafts that unless traced back from draft number one through draft number twelve it would be hard to figure out who had suggested what at any given moment" (Bonetti 89). Erdrich in turn redescribes the process as something that "as time went on . . . became shaped through conversations into a novel" (89). Much as Jael B. Juba became a fictional character larger than and distinct from either of her coauthors, Dorris and Erdrich experienced fiction writing as taking over from, superseding, and transforming their individual acts of authorship into an inseparably intertwined and merged coauthorship.

The interview process—when the interviewers are friendly, as they obviously are in this case—ultimately elicits healing effects rather than rifts, however, and this relationship ended disastrously. Meanwhile, most of Dorris and Erdrich's fiction dwells on contradiction rather than resolution. Their novels are filled with broken relationships: The stronger the bond, the fiercer the antagonism. Families are as torn as tribal communities and nations even while remaining bound together. Siblings, grandparents, parents, and children are set stubbornly against each other or blithely abandon each other and then less blithely return. Women are very powerful at times, and men often are weak, but male or female, people are adept at giving pain.[31] Women rarely form same-sex alliances for great-er strength, and neither do men. Desire itself is antagonistic: Sexual in-tercourse develops as a kind of violence, and sexual attraction thrusts men and women apart.

Despite these distancings, fragile affiliations are forged across the wide gaps between people. In the rest of this section, I touch on several such moments in the conclusions of Dorris and Erdrich's novels, in or-der to suggest how pivotal such moments are and how deeply contradic-tory their reconciliations remain.

So much comes apart, both comically and tragically in the course of a novel, that the affiliations never seem much more than fleeting mo-ments even when they occur during the novels' conclusions—when, for example, at the end of *Love Medicine*, Lipsha Morrissey (who has never known either of his parents) forms a momentary alliance with the man he has finally identified as his father, political fugitive Gerry Nanapush, and they drive off toward Canada in Lipsha's dead mother June's car. Generational differences prove especially difficult to bridge in these nov-els, as if every parent's primary bequest were the parent's rifts from his or her own parents, partners, and tribe.

In *Tracks*, Lulu Lamartine returns home to be received by Nanapush, who has deliberately become a Western-style "bureaucrat" (tribal chair-man) in order to "prove" that Lulu is his own daughter (she is, in fact, the daughter of Fleur and Eli). What draws Nanapush—the last survivor of his clan—to Lulu is a voluntary allegiance born from his prior rescue of a woman from another clan, the Pillager Fleur, which is narrated at the start of the novel. But as the schoolgirl Lulu (who, as we know from *Love Medicine*, eventually rips stormily through the lives of many men) runs to embrace Nanapush and his wife, the reunion is described as a *dis-*union of wind and trees: "We gave against your rush like creaking oaks, held on, braced ourselves together in the fierce dry wind."[32]

Wind turns out to be a recurrent trope in such scenes of provisional affinity. This sign of ceaseless change is made (transformatively) to stand for the bonds or affiliations between people. In *The Beet Queen*, after Dot Adare has been forced by the fragmented, short-lived coalition of adults who care about her to be crowned Queen (in a festival embarrassingly manufactured by a self-elected "Uncle"), she lies in bed wishing she could "lean into" her mother "the way wheat leans into wind." Instead of ac-tually approaching her mother, however, she goes to her room alone and waits for the real wind and rain to hit. The novel ends with imagined affiliation in this case, as she suddenly recognizes that her mother must be doing the same thing. Her mother "waits" like Dot for the wind, both of them "lying open" Danaë-like to the wind and rain: "I breathe it in, and I think of her lying in the next room, her covers thrown back too, eyes wide open, waiting."[33]

Crossing borders is an equally prevalent and equally contradictory trope in these novels, in that it is usually one person alone on whom the narrative focuses at such moments, so that—as in Erdrich and Dorris's contrary descriptions of their collaboration—the motifs of solitary journey and of relational bonding become oddly combined. Thus in *Love Medicine,* after his fugitive father has left Lipsha to flee into the heart of Canada, Lipsha recrosses the Canadian border in his mother's car. This moment may be seen (and has been by some readers) as a kind of reunion with both parents and between the child and his father's "native" country, but it is an intensely solitary reunion: "So there was nothing to do but cross the water, and bring her home"; "her" in this last sentence is June's car.[34] In the conclusion of *The Bingo Palace,* the uncanny ghost presence of Fleur crosses back and forth alone between "her island," where the spirits of her lost family reside (a world of ancient tradition), and "our brilliant houses," a material realm of card games, money collection, and "personal wars" (a world of contemporary Western pastimes).[35] Summing up these themes early in Dorris and Erdrich's last novel, *Cloud Chamber,* one of the protagonists, Martin McGarry, says—at the moment when he has permanently altered his beloved's life yet is alone and forgotten by her—"It's an odd thing how your life can change in the wisp of a breeze. A tinder may ignite or a fire blow out, but either way a boundary has been breached, a threshold irrevocably crossed, a key to the door."[36]

Adalaide Morris describes a comparably dual process in the ways racial, sexual, generational, and familial borders are crossed in *A Yellow Raft in Blue Water:*

> Part of the cultural work literature performs is to help us imagine ourselves across apparently intractable boundaries, the kind of boundaries Michael Dorris breaches in conceiving the lives of the three women who join as the plural protagonist of *A Yellow Raft in Blue Water.* . . . The palimpsestic plural of Dorris's novel suggests an ethics of coalition. . . . The bonding across race, gender, generation, and sexual preference in the family this novel constructs is rough-edged and adhesive, as dependent on difference as it is on relation. ("First Persons Plural" 22–24)

Weaving between "I and I," *A Yellow Raft in Blue Water* shows such alliances across multiple differences to be (in Morris's words) "temporary but tenacious" (24). This analysis could be applied to most of these novels, all of which possess multiple narrators who are as divided from each other by socially constructed differences as they are bonded by transitory, lived affiliations. Weaving in this fiction is an activity, not a result, and as such is as much a matter of "letting go" as of "blending, of catching."[37] Thus *Cloud Chamber* ends with a character from *A Yellow Raft in Blue Water*, Rayona, receiving in the penultimate paragraph the gift of a multifaceted vase. This vase, which once held a domineering ancestress' braid and later her ashes, now catches uncannily refracted lights, transparently symbolizing both Rayona's individual multiracial identity and the plural racial and sexual identities of her family heritage: "I turn the vase in my palms, letting each facet catch a distinct light, its own individual color of sky and earth. It's like looking at a thousand faces, each different from all the rest."[38]

In the conclusion of *Tales of Burning Love,* the "tenacious" yet impermanent act of affiliation becomes rhapsodic. Much as at the end of Toni Morrison's novel *Jazz*, Erdrich and Dorris choose in *Cloud Chamber* and in *Tales of Burning Love* (both published after *Crown of Columbus*, with its happy ending) almost unequivocally to celebrate the triumphs of "adhesion" over the "rough edges." All the characters are adults in the latter novel, their childhood, familial, and tribal backgrounds a thing of the past, and they inhabit a contemporary, divisively American world of hard work, careerism, and yuppie pleasures (luxury houses, secure marriages, money-making deals, readily available love affairs). We get to hear about this world from the perspectives of Jack and four of his former wives and to guess at the perspective of a fifth (actually his first) wife, the dead June of *Love Medicine.* The novel's emphasis is on the living women, however, and despite their anger at Jack's betrayals of them, all of them have forgiven Jack by the end and each has found a familial nest: Dot (of *The Beet Queen*) has returned to her own first husband, the political fugitive Gerry; Candice and Marlis (in Erdrich and Dorris's first story of lesbian cohabitation) have settled down together and are bringing up Marlis and Jack's child as theirs; and Eleanor and Jack have acknowledged that they are drawn more to each other than to anyone else, so that Jack too seems finally to have found a single helpmeet.

But even in this novel, although couples are destined to survive their painful pasts by finding love with each other, they are still alone in their thoughts at the end and are simply, as Eleanor says, seizing "a momentary chance to get the steps right, to move in harmony until the music stops." The language of affiliation remains severely oxymoronic: At the touch of Eleanor's hand, "Jack flinched closer." The conclusion of this novel is interesting in part because of its contrast to prior, less rhapsodic novels, a context deliberately invoked by a closing reference to June. Jack has just had sexual intercourse with Eleanor on the front steps of her house, on one step after another. They have both enjoyed it and at last are hurting no one else with it. Jack's final ecstasy is nonetheless torn by "the depth of what he felt about Eleanor [that] broke in upon" him and by the grief abruptly aroused in him for June: "He began to weep beside this woman, for the other woman. . . . It had not been easy for her, for June, when she froze to death, no. But it was also hard to bear the pain of coming back to life."[39]

The ending of Erdrich and Dorris's only cosigned novel is less ecstatic and more complex: *The Crown of Columbus* is interesting because of the way its primary plot wraps itself up yet leaves much of the novel still unwrapped. Of all of Dorris and Erdrich's novels, the ending of this happy Columbus-Day novel is actually among the least resolved. One of the two primary protagonists, the WASP Roger Williams, makes the great discovery of his paternity, of his daughter (Violet), yet also of the accompanying loss of "certainty." His transformation entails his rejection of identification with the European Columbus; he becomes part of a Navajo creation myth. The other major protagonist, Native American Vivian Twostar, meanwhile accepts in Roger "the European side of her own mixed heritage"—as Carla Freccero, Marianne Hirsch, Ivy Schweitzer, and Suzanne Zantop argue in an exceptionally intelligent coauthored review—while reconstituting Columbus in a spectacular scholarly discovery that enables her to argue "for the legal recognition of native sovereignty" (Freccero et al. 17). The unlikely affinity these two characters develop for each other is based from beginning to end on their finding in each other their opposite. As the reviewers mentioned earlier point out, however, this central plot is itself a version of American mythologizing, one in which romantic love conquers all, on one hand, and, on the other hand, civil protest works toward an enriched heritage for, and increased equality of, American peoples.

Meanwhile, one of the novel's subplots reopens the questions that are closed by this plot: A black Bahamian woman, Valerie Clock, finds the baby Violet, who has come ashore on a raft: "When Vivian reclaims her rescued child without a word of thanks, this lack of recognition raises the crucial question *The Crown of Columbus* leaves unanswered: Where, indeed, in this history, are the other inhabitants of the New World who arrived, not as conquerors, but as slaves?" (Freccero et al. 18). The African-

American Valerie is left alone at the end of this novel of strange encounters, and her lonely presence protests the other narratives of discovery and reconciliation. At the same time, the "dreamy" Valerie's brief encounter with and unlikely affinity for the baby Violet has awakened her from apathy to the possibility that anything might happen, even though Violet has just been wrenched away from her ("Her fingers were still clenched from letting go").[40] This conclusion thus hints not only at the possibility specifically of reencounter between America, Europe, and Africa, but also more vaguely at "other things." The ending forecasts something both sparer and less specific than nationalist/racial reconnoiter: "This meant that other things might happen to her, too, she was sure" (511). As I would further argue, the novel does this, as in Erdrich and Dorris's other conclusions, in acutely contradictory terms.

The "other things" that might happen to Valerie are already happening at the end: She is for the first time thinking about the sea as "alive, breathing, full of fish," where "people died" though also "sometimes a marvelous thing washed up" (510). By the end of the novel, she has started (in the novel's last words) "to think of the sea as a place to cross, but once she did, she couldn't stop" (511). It is "crossing" itself that matters for Valerie, the possibilities of something much less grand than "forg[ing] her own history" (or rewriting Columbian history [Freccero et al. 18]), namely, her small moment in time, and at the same time of something much greater, namely, that "everything" might "change" and be "different" (510). The vocabulary of this ending allows her both particularity and universality; she is both Eleutherian and Shakespearean, Central American and universal.

Freccero and her colleagues point out that the relationship between Vivian and Roger, between native and colonizer, between man and woman, and between preservationist and capitalist is one of "fierce, life-threatening competition," not easy cooperation. The novel thus "treats marriage and collaboration as central issues in American history," and Roger and Vivian's relationship is "like, one imagines, Erdrich and Dorris, work[ing] through competition to an (albeit imperfect) cooperation" (18). Such a relationship ultimately enables Dorris and Erdrich, these reviewers conclude, to resee American history: "Perhaps it is only in the struggles of a working partnership that the 'discovery' can be re-imagined as a true 'encounter'" (18). But this too remains a utopian fantasy of the novel, which its own ending undermines, not only because Vivian has failed even to acknowledge Valerie as the savior of her baby, but also because, as Roger stays at home with the new baby, Vivian takes her archaeological discovery of the Crown of Columbus and its alternative meanings and disappears with these into the public limelight in a simple reversal of traditional male/female roles.

This novel shows how violent competition can be (Dartmouth alumnus and capitalist Henry Cobb is nearly drowned in his attempt to kill Vivian for the results of her research), how easily cooperation can fail, and how little affinity people—all of whom are marked as different—generally discover between each other. What Erdrich and Dorris envision at the end in Valerie Clock is a single character who must make up her mind, utterly alone, to cross an occasionally merciful sea. As in their descriptions of their coauthorship, there are opposite truths here: the fact of Erdrich and Dorris's "joint vision" of cross-cultural conjunction and the fact of each writer's and character's disjunctive solitariness, the possibility of "miraculous" encounter and the prospect of a devouring abyss.

Between Sisters: Self-Reliance and Collaboration

"We were good citizens, good Americans!" A. Elizabeth Delany says of the large Delany family, "we loved our country, even though it didn't love us back."[41] And Amy Hill Hearth writes in her preface, "Their story, as the Delany sisters like to say, is not meant as 'black' history or 'women's' history, but American history" (xvi). Ossie Guffy claims for herself black and female American history: "I'm a woman, I'm black, I'm a little under forty, and I'm more of black America than Ralph Bunche or Rap Brown or Harry Belafonte because I'm one of the millions who ain't bright, militant, or talented."[42] In Caryl Ledner's preface, Guffy is "the real spirit of the black woman in America" (7). America in its turn paid attention to these women (for a short while at least)—in the case of the Delanys, paying homage as well—when their oral narratives hit the literary marketplace as mass-market paperbacks. For a mass audience—a middle-class, often white audience—the power and authenticity of these narratives was enhanced, not compromised, by their as-told-to collaborative production.

The preceding comments present the Delany sisters' story as the more universal of the two: Whereas Guffy's 1971 story is (as her subtitle announces) the "Autobiography of a Black Woman," Hearth asserts that the Delanys' 1993 autobiography is simply "American" history. But the Delanys' title, *Having Our Say*, rings of the rights movements to which both autobiographies pay tribute, and its cover displays an oval cutout through which the Delanys' faces smile, allowing instant identification of the sisters as black, female, and elderly. Both stories invoke the topicality of the moments in which they are narrated. Hearing about the Delanys, one would think one had discovered the poster seniors for 1990s political slogans about black middle-class self-reliance, whereas, narrated in the aftermath of one set of L.A. race riots and read in the aftermath of another a generation later, Guffy's story (already forgotten by most readers and dismissed or patronized by historians of black autobiography) speaks of America's unsolved social and racial problems, for the need for reform and intervention.

Read in juxtaposition with each other, the two texts thus retell American history from the marginalized points of view of African-American women, yet their stories differ radically from each other, each accenting what the other omits. Read closely, each may also be seen to differ within itself, contradicting itself or exceeding the formulas with which the narrators sum up their tales. The narrators often gesture toward alternative stories, toward their own rejected or unreachable options, so that, like each other's double—or indeed like sisters—they continually remind the reader of the other. At the same time, for these collaborators, as in the other collaborations explored in this study, it is not merely the claiming of differences, but the coalescence of similarities in the midst of difference that produces a rapturous sense of themselves as subjects, agents, and authors breaking boundaries imposed from without and within their particular social and familial circumstances. The differing literary success of these collaborations (the Delanys achieved fame almost overnight; Guffy's text disappeared from public consideration nearly as quickly) should not distract us from the strong affinities in the collaborative process. Without mention of name and number, one would not know whether Ledner or Hearth wrote the following account of her collaboration: "When we met, we liked each other immediately, and we . . . felt that we would like to spend a little time together getting to know each other and that, if at the end of that time we both wanted it, I would try to get _____'s story down on paper. We . . . wanted it, and this is the result" (Ledner 8). Whether short-lived or not, both sets of collaborations produced at least temporary bonds across race between black narrators and the white journalists who transcribed and edited their books.

The two sets of stories, as I emphasize, collaborate not only with white middle-class versions of American history, but also with each other in both negative and positive senses of that term. At times they deny and conspire against each other's cultural situations even as they proclaim solidarity; at other times, although they resist, they also support each other's differences. By reading them in conjunction with, rather than in ignorance of, each other, it becomes possible to expose and cultivate their differences with each other, within themselves, and with contemporary versions of the myth of American self-reliance.

The few scholars who have thus far paid attention to the collaborative relations behind these texts have been critical of their popularizing, journalistic transmission, faulting the white female transcribers for failing to disclose fully the gaps between their interviews and their narratives and for failing to confront the extent to which their own perspectives limit and govern the points of view of their interviewees. For Albert Stone, who is concerned with the history of black autobiographies and oral narratives, the problem with *Ossie* is inauthenticity, self-contradiction, and made-for-Madison Avenue sentiments.[43] For Mary Helen Washington, in a piece published in *The Women's Review of Books*, *Having Our Say* is similarly compromised by lack of disclosure of the interview process and by what she suspects is overemphasis by a white female interviewer of the racial difference in the Delanys' history.[44] In an article seeking possible feminist postmodern alternatives to "Stone's model of dual collaboration" in "Ossie Guffy, Nate Shaw, Malcolm X," Carole Boyce Davies does not discuss *Ossie,* preferring instead the "*collective life story,*" which she sees as challenging and "mov[ing] beyond the sense of a *dually authored* text [such as that of Guffy] to a *multiply articulated* text," thus opening up the linear, single-voiced autobiography to allow a wider range of voices by women of color.[45]

Although Stone, Washington, and Davies make salient arguments about these less than fully collaborative texts (Stone's argument to my mind less persuasively than Washington's), they neglect not only the political advantages of this kind of black/white collaboration, but also the ways in which a popular text of this sort—written to be widely accessible to readers—may not only reach and affect a larger audience than would be possible otherwise, but may also, in less obtrusive ways than those sought by the highly educated academic reader, confront a variety of socially constructed differences.

These texts do reflect their interviewers' circumscribed perspectives and streamlined narrative methods, but while conniving with readers' desires for plot and personal drama, they introduce historicized narratives and realms of experience quite unlike those of most white readers. In the case of *Having Our Say*, Hearth produces a plural testimonial, negotiating among four sets of narrative perspectives. Divided into parts and chapters, her narratives are organized sequentially and chronologically, so that it remains as easy for a reader to glide through this autobiography as through Ossie Guffy's. Yet each part is prefaced with a summary by Hearth herself, and the chapters are then told from points of view that alternate between Sadie, Bessie, and Sadie and Bessie.[46] Through this effort to re-enact the ways in which the collaboration between Sadie and Bessie Delany works, Hearth provides more direct exposure to differences of view than one would normally obtain in the single-authored autobiography. But, as I further argue, the so-called linear narrative does not intrinsically exclude variant perspectives: I go on to suggest that Ossie Guffy's text manifests differing points of view through ironic juxtaposition.

In what follows, I emphasize the divergent perspectives that are represented in these texts—primarily through inequalities between sisters, other family members, and other members of their race—more than the writers' aesthetic choices of single- or plural-voiced narratives in presenting this diversity. As in my discussion of Harriet Jacobs, I am interested in the ways a collaboratively produced book treats incidents of collaboration in the life story it narratives. *Having Our Say* stresses both the individual successes and successful collaborations of the Delany sisters, whereas *Ossie* focuses on personal failure and failed relationships, but when they are read together, it becomes obvious that in both narratives individual self-reliance and achievement are highly contingent on reliance on others, in assertions and narratives as contradictory as those of Erdrich and Dorris.

It was their old age and sisterhood that first won them attention: "The Delany Sisters' First 100 Years" is the cheerful subtitle of *Having Our Say*. They became wise women of the 1990s, dispensing advice for a happy long life. Before Bessie Delany's death in 1995 at the age of 104, the two sisters witnessed the stunning successes not only of their best-seller *Having Our Say* but of its sequel, *The Delany Sisters' Book of Everyday Wisdom* (which they wrote to answer the deluge of letters received after their first book), and of the Broadway production of *Having Our Say*, adapted and directed by Emily Mann.[47] (Meanwhile, Ossie, approximately forty years younger than the Delany sisters, probably turned 63 in 1995). But a reader of *Having Our Say* rapidly finds herself immersed in a flock of identity issues beyond those heralded by its cover. The kinds of identity differences simultaneously dividing and uniting these two sisters include not only those of race, gender, class, and age, but also of religious, sexual, and familial beliefs and attitudes. These various categories are closely entwined and often at odds with each other. Moreover, the Delany sisters want to see themselves as proud agents of their own fate and as models for others (it is not merely a publicity stunt that they called their second book *The Delany Sisters' Book of Everyday Wisdom*), yet they also see their lives as structured by innumerable conditions beyond their control, conditions ambiguously both constraining and enabling.

The conditions they recognize include a racist and sexist, though somewhat mobile American society; an ancestral history of free or manumitted literate black ancestors; a large, carefully supervised, publicly prominent immediate family; a strict religious upbringing by parents who combined Methodism with Episcopalianism (although the Delany parents were raised as Methodists, the Episcopal church gave the Delanys' father his chance to become a minister); and a set of powerful paternal admonitions. They were admonished by their father to pay their own way (including refusal of scholarships) and to better their race both through education (rather than through labor organization) and through service to others less privileged than they, sacrificing their own financial betterment and comfort to do so. Above all, that they were closely bonded oldest daughters from this tightly knit family intent on improving itself was foundational for nearly everything else they subsequently became, from their becoming successful, highly educated, professional women to their also becoming (in Sadie's phrase) "maiden ladies" who had "beaus" but never married (sex is hardly ever mentioned).

Yet there existed also in the Delany family a hierarchical structure wherein age alone gave Sadie (eventually the oldest child in the family) a higher position than her strong-willed "baby sister" Bessie. The additional criteria that Sadie was lighter in color and more charitable than her pugnacious sister—more "Christian," in the sisters' shared belief—gave her further advantages that, paradoxically, secured their relations to each other even while creating friction between them. The frequent separation of Sadie's and Bessie's narratives reinforces these personality differences, so that the reader is distanced from their intimacy and is invited to laugh at rather than with them (as too often is the case in representations of collaboration). The polyvocal arrangement of this text thus has some disadvantages that undermine its advantages.

What is ultimately more striking than their differences is their entrenched habit of agreeing to disagree. They are so accustomed to the friction between them as to have reached nearly complete consensus precisely about their differences. What emerges from their parallel and joint narratives is thus not rivalry, but an energetically playful sisterhood in which they finish each other's thoughts and confirm each other's stories. Their settled, idiosyncratic habits are an inexhaustible source of entertainment for them. The sisters attribute their longevity to a number of factors (above all to a healthy, active lifestyle), but the psychological factor that stands out for both is this devoted sisterhood, in which they can argue without constraint and do not have to be "worried" by men (24). They celebrate their successes in middle-class America, additionally, as triumphs for their race and their sex, even while acknowledging their own privileged upbringing.

Thus far, the portrait of the Delanys suppresses fewer complexities in the sisters' collaboration than one might have expected from a best-seller in the 1990s. But in portraying the Delany sisters as models of the proud, independent American middle class, this autobiography provides almost no picture of, and has little to say about, what it is like to be destitute or to be unable to rise out of the black lower classes. The possibility that they might be criticized for their privileges—or, more specifically, for presenting their unusual family as representative of their race—is briefly acknowledged by Hearth in her preface to Part I, where she outlines the Delany family as "one of the nation's preeminent black families" (3). This context and Hearth's rhetoric turn her acknowledgment into an uncomprehending dismissal of criticism, however. Detractors are "surprising": "The Delanys had to face some surprising detractors. Sadie and Bessie recall that lower-class blacks at times viewed achievers as being cliquish or arrogant, and that some cautioned that families such as the Delanys set impossibly high standards for other black Americans of that era. Their success, some felt, set up the larger black community for criticism by white America: If they can do it, why can't the rest of you?" (4–5). From this short paragraph, Hearth moves on to the "Delany creed," which "centered on self-improvement through education, civic-mindedness, and ethical living, along with a strong belief in God. The family motto was, 'Your job is to help somebody.' According to Bessie and Sadie Delany, this code applied to anyone who needed help, regardless of color. Their accomplishments could not shield them from discrimination and the pain of racism, but they held themselves to high standards of fair-minded idealism" (5). If the family motto is to "help somebody," then "self-improvement" is not alone thought to be sufficient for a good life for all. Yet Hearth's paragraph implicitly faults potential critics for not being like the Delanys—that is, for not sustaining a "creed centered on self-improvement" and upholding "high standards of fair-minded idealism," whereby people are altruistic (and not critical of each other), help others "regardless of color," and do not seek help themselves.

When Hearth recalls criticism that families like the Delanys set unattainable standards for most other African Americans "*of that era,*" she hints that this is no longer the case today. These paragraphs amount to a dismissal of any criticism of the Delanys' autobiography that might emerge from political activists or from the perspectives of people occupying more oppressed class positions. Hearth's preface differs notably from the way the sisters narrate their story, however, for the sisters make no reference at all in the autobiography to these detractors. In this one might find evidence of Washington's argument that the sisters probably focused, as storytellers, less on reporting divisions within their own race (as they might have done if their interviewer/coauthor/editor had been black) than on shaping their case as African Americans for a white middle-class journalist and, through her, for a white middle-class audience: "Things have kind of slid down as far as equality is concerned. The 1980s were the worst, yes, sir!" (283). Rarely is it other African Americans whose criticism the sisters rebut. On one or two occasions, they defend their belief that Booker T. Washington (with his Delany-like arguments for self-improvement and education) was as great a man as W. E. B. Du Bois, and they try to justify themselves when they choose self-betterment or charitable activity over political activism, but they also recall their participation—Bessie's in particular—in activist protest (115, 198–202). It is, rather, white groups or individuals whose lack of charity and altruism is deplored by the Delanys. Hearth's remark thus reveals a species of defensiveness or protectiveness, which is based on discussions with the Delanys but concerns Hearth more than it concerns the sisters in this autobiography.

The sisters' sections of the autobiography both contradict and contribute to a portrait of themselves as representative of their race. Clearly, the sisters want to be taken as representative of African-American capacities for Christian virtue, self-reliance, and intellectual and practical achievement, but they do not see themselves as typical of their race in their achievements and self-sufficiency, and they blame this fact not on other members of their race but on racism. The sisters continually remind their readers of the exceptional character of their achievements and the enormous odds against which any black person must struggle to attain a secure place in white society. Their autobiography reads like a series of exceptions and firsts. Their maternal grandmother, for example, was treated as a deeply beloved wife by her white companion at a time when black and white were not permitted to marry. Their father, a freed slave, became the first black Episcopalian bishop. Sadie was the first black teacher in the New York public high school system; Bessie was the second black woman dentist in American history. Based on their own experience, the Delany sisters argue persuasively that, for less able black people than themselves to reach the middle class, some special action must be taken. Thus they remark, "When Negroes are average, *they fail*, unless they are very, very lucky. Now, if you're average and *white*, honey, you can go far. Just look at Dan Quayle. If that boy was colored he'd be washing dishes somewhere" (162).

While reminding readers of the exceptional character of their achievements, the Delanys also attribute their most cherished habits to their family's tight network and to African-American communal customs, seeing them as characteristic of their race. In a review for *The Washington Post*, Sherley Anne Williams rephrases the Delany creed as part of a "tradition of personal advancement and racial uplift," which has unfortunately been "co-opted by self-styled conservatives, who read this bootstrap metaphor as every black (man) for himself." Williams argues that *Having Our Say* "deftly reinterprets that metaphor, setting it within a context of sharing and service to the race so persuasive that it may awaken, even in these philistines, some sense of the pride that was one of the values of that old black middle-class."[48]

Yet the sisters themselves occasionally fall into the rhetoric of self-reliance when, for example, they declare themselves against affirmative action. Bessie oscillates on this issue while narrating an event in which it was hinted that she might have a better chance at getting a job in a cinema if she presented herself as Hispanic rather than black. Bessie refused, asserting, "I am an *American Negro!*" and proudly left the theater. This incident suggests to her the usefulness of affirmative action for correcting job discrimination, yet she then goes on to pronounce her stand against it: "Today I know they have this thing called Affirmative Action. I can see why they need it. There are some places where colored folks would *never*, not in a thousand years, get a job. But you know what? I really am philosophically against it. I say: 'Let the best person get the job, period.' Everybody's better off in the long run" (156). How Bessie can take a stand against affirmative action on the basis of thinking that everyone is better off "in the long run" when she sees the "best person" as partly determined by racial criteria—when there are places where "colored folks would *never*" get a job—and partly influenced by the moral luck of upbringing, is a question she does not pause to consider and that Hearth apparently did not ask.

In general, though, *Having Our Say* does not purvey genial clichés about race. It offers, on one hand, a particularized narrative of racial oppression and discrimination and, on the other, the impressive resource of talent in African-American communities (unrealized by whites) that the Delany family exemplifies. As Hearth points out, "In the white world, with the possible exception of Hubert, the sisters' younger brother who was a New York political leader, the Delanys were almost unknown," whereas "in the black society of Raleigh, North Carolina, where they grew up, and later in Harlem, the Delanys were legendary" (4).

Some white middle-class readers of this autobiography might not identify the Delanys as middle class at every period in their story. For example, at a time when maids were common for middle-class American families, the Delanys did everything themselves, from hauling their water in pails from the river to clothing their children in second-hand clothes. In New York City, five of the ten adult Delany sisters and brothers lived together, "packed like sardines" in a three-room apartment (143). The borders between the black middle and lower classes, and between the black professional and working classes, sometimes seem open in this text, not only because the Delany family lives so economically, but because it feels deeply affiliated to more deprived members of its race. Moreover, the Delanys are acutely aware of the eagerness of many whites (particularly during Jim Crow) to deprive them even of the modest privileges they have. Relating an incident in which she was harassed by a drunken white man, Bessie muses, "It didn't matter to that white fella— and I doubt it would have mattered to the police—that I was a doctor of dentistry and a good citizen of Harlem. There was little respect from white people, no matter how accomplished you were. It was like you were invisible. It was so strange to be so respected among Negroes, but to white people you were just some little pickaninny" (196). The Delanys' story of black middle-class success thus alternately gestures toward, mirrors or merges into, rejects, and allies itself with black lower-class struggle. What their family's exceptionalism nonetheless masks becomes strikingly obvious when one turns to another collaboratively produced African-American woman's story, *Ossie.*

Women like Ossie[49] appear in the margins of the Delanys' autobiography, primarily as recipients of charity, and the sisters associate a lower-class lifestyle, from which their family saved them, with uncleanness, disease, and ignorance (it is no coincidence that Sadie becomes a teacher of domestic science). But Ossie's family values cleanliness, folk knowledge and wisdom, self-reliance, and self-improvement as much as the Delanys do, and Ossie is even more prone than the Delanys to attributing lapses in self-responsibility to failures of moral character, not only to racism. At the same time, as I noted at the outset, a constellation of differences of gender, race, religion, family, age, and sexuality distinguish these stories, and although I do not do equal justice here to all of these, it is important to suggest how these variables interweave. In all these categories, the Delany sisters have far more in common with each other than with Ossie.

The Delanys' doctrine of self-improvement through education has a corollary unmentioned in Hearth's preface, one that Ossie's mother firmly rejects. The Delanys' mother insisted that they never work as maids for white people, and the sisters are especially proud of their success in avoiding this. Not once did either of them work for white people "in their homes," and "that is one of the accomplishments in my life," Bessie exults, "of which I am most proud, yes sir!" (108). Summing up their achievements later on, Bessie writes an imaginary letter to David Duke: "Dear Mr. Duke: This is just to set the record straight. I am a Negro woman. I was brought up in a good family. My Papa was a devoted father. I went to college; I paid my own way. I am not stupid. I'm not on welfare. And I'm not scrubbing floors. Especially not yours" (231). This doctrine helps both to preserve the Delanys from an experience of direct servitude to whites and to propel them toward professional careers (when they had to earn money, they did so by teaching black children, by making candy to sell, or by working as ushers in movie theaters). But it also sharply divides them from one of the most common job experiences of black women of their generation.

Ossie's family had access to public education, and her older sister, Alice, took advantage of it in much the way the Delany sisters did, but Ossie's mother assumed, with good reason, that such access was limited. Unlike the Delanys' mother, she had not received an education herself and, as a widowed single mother, had to work her way through life as a housekeeper. In an argument with Alice, she says, "Reading and knowing how to write a good sentence are nice, but if a girl has to earn enough to buy food, she can't do it with them tools, leastwise not a black girl." Alice retorts (as the Delanys might have), "This isn't slavery; things have changed and they're gonna change still more. *I'm* not going to spend my life working in some white kitchen!" (64). To this, Ossie's mother responds, "How come you're doing it now? . . . When a black girl needs money she can always get it if she knows how to cook and clean and wash and iron. . . . When the day comes that all of you can be sure if you want to work at something highfalutin, you can get a highfalutin job, that's the day I'll say I'm wrong and you're right. Until that time, which ain't here yet, you all gonna know how to keep from starving, and that's that" (64–66). Both Alice and Ossie started to learn self-sufficiency by doing housework for white families when they were in their mid-teens. Thus Ossie began to work in high school. Ossie was not expected to go to college, however, as the strong-minded Alice planned to do, and Ossie subsequently dropped out of high school when she became pregnant. Still, her mother could assure Ossie that, in addition to being able to save some money for herself, "you'll be able to pay your own carfare and buy your own lunches, and that'll be a big help. Besides, you'll be building references, and that's important" (65).

Alice went on to advance herself until she could be "dressed real nice, like the girls who lived in Madisonville" (164), but this is Ossie's story, and Ossie confronts directly the seemingly impossible odds against which poor black families strove in midcentury to raise themselves in America. In fact, one of the odds Ossie must face is her elder sister's superior attitude. In sharp contrast to the Delany sisters, who grow up apparently joyously sharing everything, especially their spiritual beliefs and professional aspirations, Alice and Ossie are deeply divided: "It's funny the way there are always some close people in your life that you live with like you're sisters, but inside the two of you are as strange to each other as if you'd never even met," Ossie explains, and "that's the way it was with Alice and me then, and that's the way it's always stayed" (27). The older sister in this case treats the younger with derisive contempt, attacking Ossie's intelligence (as uncontrolled elder siblings are prone to do) while presenting herself as meant for better things. A kind of class division as well as familial rupture thus characterizes Ossie's most important sibling relation from an early age, as Ossie is "taught" by her older sister not to expect support or respect from those closest to her or from those placed above her.

Addressing a white middle-class readership, Ossie speaks of herself as one of millions who have not had a voice because they are not famous or not educated:

> We're the women you got used to seeing in your kitchens and the men you got used to seeing as Red Caps . . . the people who lived over on the other side of town. We lived there and we suffered there and we died there, and we did all three quietly. But now that time is past, and it ain't never going to come back. . . . Your TV screens are showing more black faces, and you're reading about us in your papers, but you ain't getting any picture of what we're really like, 'cause most of us ain't got any voices speaking for us. . . . I got a lot of kids growing up, and I guess you do, too, and I sure hope they have a chance to be the best they can be. So I'm going to try to tell it like it was, hoping it will throw a little light on the millions of us that ain't been rightly seen before. (9–10)

At the same time, Ossie qualifies her claims to representativeness as the autobiography develops by reminding readers of how happenstance aided or deserted her and how her life deviated from the lives of her mother and older sister—how a single family, not only a society or race, may divide among alternative life paths.

One reviewer of *Ossie* wrote, "This is a book filled with love and self-respect, with courage and accomplishment—at the bottom of the ladder."[50] As Ossie's story shows, however, there are many rungs even at "the bottom of the ladder" which can only be imagined through a variety of stories. Ossie's own story does not take place entirely at the bottom. As different as Ossie's story is from the Delanys', it recalls how close she once came, and could someday come again, to attaining the middle-class economic status that the Delanys enjoyed. In her preface, Ledner writes,

> This may seem like a strange book, like a voice out of the past. During this turbulent time of the emergence of the black American from the shadow world in which he has been pushed by white society, it isn't stylish to talk about black life as it has been lived by the majority of black people. Books are being written by the dozen on the sociological, psychological, and economic plight of blacks en masse, and more books are being written by black men, writing subjectively about the hell of the ghetto, drug addiction, crime, and degradation. This is a book unlike any of these. It is subjective, but its protagonist is neither male nor degraded. Rather, it is the personal history of one black woman, growing up in the less dramatic but more usual world of lower-middle-class America, in the period from 1931 to the present. (7)

Yet Ossie's story is also "dramatic" and, indeed, sensational in such journalistic terms, for her story of "lower-middle-class America" also happens to be—and here again it is sharply unlike that of the Delanys—a story of childhood neglect, adolescent pregnancy, single motherhood, welfare, and urban poverty. Ossie gives a personal body, mind, and name to all such social abstractions. In turning to that litany of familial and social struggles, one discovers further differences in the way the Delanys and Ossie introduce readers to their educations in race, gender, religion, sex, and familial collaboration.

Whereas the Delanys' story begins with the remarkable achievement of their sisterhood and old age—"Bessie and I have been together since time began, or so it seems. . . . She is 101 years old, and I am 103 . . . we are in some ways like one person" (7–8)—Ossie's story begins with a question that inscribes in the narrative the white/black collaboration that produces it. "A white lady who really wanted to know" asks Ossie, "How does it feel to be born black?" Ossie answers, "I guess you can't say what it's like to be *born* black, because when you're born—and for a long time after—you don't know you *are* black" (13). Sadie Delany too, by necessity, winds up answering that question in her first chapter and does so only slightly differently from Ossie: "As children, we were aware we were colored but we never gave it a second thought. Papa was dark and Mama was light and so what? It's just the way it was" (10). As a child, Sadie is aware of "being colored," whereas Ossie is not, but for neither of them does it signify. The problems, and thus significations, of blackness come later. Both Sadie and Ossie respond in much the way that Zora Neale Hurston does in her famous essay, "How It Feels to Be Colored Me": "I remember the very day that I became colored. . . . When I disembarked from the river-boat at Jacksonville . . . It seemed that I had suffered a sea change. I was not Zora of Orange County any more, I was now a little colored girl."[51] Blackness for all these autobiographers is a social construction, acquired retrospectively, not something they are born with.

But quite unlike both Hurston and the Delanys, Ossie does not adopt a tone of nonchalance toward what it is like to be black and continues with these words: "When you're little you haven't learned yet that the color of your skin is going to be the most important fact of your life, the prison that locks you out instead of in, the package around your soul that sets up an immediate reaction in the white world and makes you forever an inferior, unless proven otherwise. No, when you're very young, you're just Ossie, a little girl with one brother and three sisters, a mother who doesn't live with you but visits every Thursday and every other Sunday, and no father" (13). The Delany sisters' story focuses on how well they lived, how long they lived, and thus how little race ultimately made a difference to their lifestyles. By the end of Ossie's first chapter, she has narrated the death of her father from asthma, the newly straitened circumstances of her family as they move from their comfortable middle-class house to live with their maternal grandparents, and the burning of her oldest sister due to their drunken grandfather's neglect. The neglect is directly attributed to the psychological damage done by racism: "If you don't know by now," Ossie's grandmother tells her mother, "that a black woman can get a job when a black man can't, you got a lot to learn. And natchully, he turns to the drink when he can't get nothing to bring home to his family" (18–19).

Ossie's story is narrated in the shape of an ironic *Bildungsroman*, so that major (tragic) episodes of this sort bring with them a new hard "lesson," learned usually from a broken alliance with a family member, friend, or lover. Enriching the irony, each of these lessons is indefinite (so that the narrator and reader discover several sometimes contradictory lessons about cultural differences being learned in any given episode) or it is understated; the lesson in this case is not merely in being black but in being female. Ossie finds gender—again unlike the Delanys—to be as constitutive in her trials as racial difference:

> "There, there," my grandma soothed. "You got to be strong. The Lord gives us the strength to face what we gotta face."
> My mother stopped crying.
> "If that's true, Mama," she said accusingly, "how come he only gives it to women?"
> I became aware that I was cold and I was frightened, and I started to whimper, but nobody heard me. I didn't, I couldn't know it then, but I was starting my education as a black woman. (19)

In fact, the gender crisis, induced though it appears to be (to Ossie) by racial and economic difference, is a more pressing, immediate problem than either race or class in this story in almost every stage of Ossie's life. She suffers in severe ways from what is for her—as black feminist critics eventually articulated it—dual marginalization as both black and female.[52] If black men neglect, abandon, or abuse women, it is primarily because they have been abused, abandoned, and denigrated by whites, but the black woman is left to deal with abuse from both whites and black men. Ossie suffers men's failure to take responsibility for themselves, their families, and their race.

No particular religious denomination or church is ever mentioned in Ossie's story, but references to "the Lord" are threaded through Ossie's narrative, and belief in God and in the values of charity, honesty, and hard work is taken for granted. Ossie's paternal grandfather was a Southern minister, much respected in his community, who preached a similar creed to that of the Delanys' father. From him Ossie learns her second lesson that "we got to live in the world we got, and in this world it's enough to know you doing the best you can. A man can respect himself when he knows that. . . . What you think about *you*, that's what really matters" (41). However, Ossie concludes this episode by speculating that her grandfather's atypical "manhood," not his religion, must have enabled him to live by this creed: "Because Grandpa knew he was a man, he didn't have to prove it by throwing his weight around, so he faced the world and really looked at it and then picked his way through the best way for him and his. Funny, isn't it? I got lesson two in being a black woman from Grandpa, who was really a man" (42).

But this gently ironic conclusion occludes the complexity of what Ossie learns on her visit to her grandfather. She does not simply learn that anyone may live as a self-respecting person (whether white or black, male or female); she learns rather that she must expect herself precisely to endure circumstances in which she cannot anticipate respect from anyone else, much less "throw her weight around." For it is this Southern visit that instructs Ossie once and for all in both the significance of her skin and the vulnerability of her sex. When her sister is nearly raped by white boys, Ossie discovers racism and sexism at first hand. Thanks to her grandfather's successful interventions, Ossie receives a lesson in self-respect as well as in the racist/sexist social structure that denies respect to blacks and women. But these things rarely seem as reconcilable as they do at this moment, when her sister, brothers, and she have an influential grandfather to protect them, and shortly afterward her mother, in sharp dissension from her grandfather, provides a counterdoctrine of prudent deference: "It's like your Mr. Bob said that first night we come here— 'Nigra kids got to be taught to stay outa trouble.' . . . You want your black boy to stay out of trouble, you teach him his place when he's young" (50).

Ossie herself introduces the term *irony* much later in the autobiography, and in an ironic context, when a fellow worker, Callie, says, " 'Isn't it ironic the way the good ones [good black men] die and the bastards live on?'" Ossie's agreement is qualified: "I nodded, even though I wasn't too sure what ironic meant. The meaning of what she was saying was clear enough so's not knowing the word didn't confuse it none, but I went and looked it up anyhow, and after I got used to it, I found myself thinking that the real irony of Connie was that he was a good man and a bastard all at the same time. I was still pretty young when I was thinking that, 'cause now I know that combination of good and evil shows up in mostly everybody, one way or another. Like with Callie" (198). Irony in this text comes to seem an education in irony's endless self-replications, as it shifts here, for example, from Connie (who encouraged Ossie to read and to "look up" things but committed suicide when Ossie became pregnant with his child) to Callie (who got Ossie "a card so's I could borrow books" but then "lied" about waitressing tips and "pocketed some that was mine"). Yet at the same time, to be educated in irony, not only in "books," is to discover the saving grace of—in Erdrich and Dorris's phrase—"survival humor" (Bonetti 96). For Ossie, survival itself becomes possible when she finds a way to recognize, collaborate with, and reconcile herself to others' discrepancies and to her own.

Nothing is more striking, as one turns from the Delanys to Ossie, than the contrast between their sexual educations, and it is also here that Ossie's text becomes most ironic. The specifically female stories of sex and motherhood are almost entirely missing, barely mentioned, in the

Delanys' autobiography. The Delanys were told by their mother that they would have to make a choice between work and marriage (157), and their lives were so sheltered that they did not learn about sex until they were young adults. Bessie and Sadie describe themselves cheerfully as having had "lots of beaus" (121), and Bessie mentions a possible regret for Sadie over a beau her father and brother scared away long ago (119–20). But the sisters sound relieved never to have been "worr[ied] to death" by husbands (24) and to have escaped having children. (Bessie adds that she feels, with her eight younger siblings and the countless families she helped, as if she had "raised half the world," 158.) They are persuaded that their mother was right: For women of their generation to have professional lives, they had to stick together, choosing work and their own relationship over marriage.

It is on the subject of her sexual development that Ossie's story becomes most compelling. Her story also becomes contradictory on this issue. Irony points the way to constitutive contradictions in Ossie's life. If there are two Delanys, there are also two Ossies, a younger and an older one; predictably, they appear as the "innocent" Ossie-protagonist and "experienced" Ossie-narrator. These two sides seem always to have existed, the younger one acting in spontaneous, uninformed, often adventurous or reckless ways to seize life or simply survive, the older one commenting on, criticizing, and moralizing over the younger. When Ossie's father died, the household was broken up (older brothers and sisters going to other relatives, the younger ones cared for by maternal grandparents or aunts), and Ossie would never again experience the close, loving supervision of her mother or the tightly bound, united family she had heretofore known. As a result, her older sister, Alice, became a far greater influence in Ossie's life—a rivalrous, hostile one. Alice poured onto Ossie all the contempt Alice had for the situation she was trying to escape. Alice's different path in life is partly responsible not only for the self-critic in the experienced Ossie, but for the inexperienced Ossie's sexual mistakes and self-defeatism. Much as Alice and Ossie's distance from each other is never entirely bridged, the two Ossies' beliefs conflict with each other in ways that are not resolved.

Thanks to the teenage Alice's chiding Ossie for ignorance and naivety in contrast to Alice's greater knowledge and experience of men and of sex—about which she was also, however, mysterious—it did not occur to Ossie to say "no" when a boy led her into her first experience of sexual intercourse at age twelve. At age fourteen or fifteen, following some more advice from her sister, she attempted to exploit her attractiveness to a wayward male cousin, but without her sister's aggressive wiliness, this rapidly turned into more sex. When she became pregnant, Ossie and her cousin Charles were forced by their parents to marry (at age fifteen), and because her mother now felt that Ossie was independent, the family moved away. Soon after this, Charles disappeared when Ossie was pregnant with their second child; he deserted his army post and fled with the help of an aunt. Ossie's history is from then on a story of single motherhood and pregnancy, as she proceeded to have one child after another with a variety of unfaithful lovers. "Self-reliance" is thus forced on her, but she is in fact never able to rely on herself alone.

This is a history not just of single motherhood, but of very active heterosexuality (there is, unsurprisingly, no reference to lesbian sexuality in either book) and of serial dependencies. In commenting on her sexual activity, Ossie straddles several contradictory sets of beliefs. After her adventure as a twelve-year-old, she recalls being told sex was "evil" and she writes, "If Grandpa had done a sermon about me, he would have said that I had bitten the apple of knowledge and been expelled from the garden of innocence, and he would have been right, because from that time on I've wandered where the fruit was lush but poisoned, and I've eaten my fill, getting a little sicker with each bite, but unable to stop" (60). She condemns her act, but subsequently justifies herself in biblical terms; as a result of the guilt and loneliness she felt, she began to read the Bible for guidance and comfort and, soon after her first pregnancy, discovered there the sacred dictum that people should multiply. This became an absolute article of faith for Ossie—one that she shared with most of the other women (white and black) she would subsequently encounter in similar circumstances— and so she let lectures about birth control "slide over" her (192).

Ossie does not have sex only in order to reproduce, however; she takes pleasure in it with each lover in turn, and her children continually appear as accidents. Indeed, on this point the contradictions in her discourse multiply: She suggests that she fell into corruption (in accordance with her grandfather's moral views), that it was her intrinsic nature to want sex (a propensity to "lust," in contrast to her sister, as if this, as well as the stupidity her sister attributes to her, marked a genetic trait), that her sexual experiences resulted from being rushed into circumstances she was too young to manage (and so became explicable in the sociopsychological terms of the social workers she encounters), and that she chose sex freely, knowing the consequences, accepting them unashamed (in keeping perhaps with others in her community or with late 1960s attitudes toward sex). She continues to have lovers as she grows older and more knowing, and, as I have already suggested, she continues to enjoy the consequences—both the sex and the children. As Henrietta Buckmaster puts it in a *Christian Science Monitor* review (in a similarly contradictory manner), "A sort of promiscuity, yes—but her relations with the four men who fathered her children were loving, there was self-respect and integrity."[53] In the most tenacious contradiction of all, she remains throughout both proudly self-reliant and deeply dependent on these successive lovers and her cooperative arrangements with them, hoping each man will be the last, permanent partner.

As she concludes her narrative, she seems to have learned yet another lesson, and that is not to "multiply" so freely and to use birth control; she also at last has a loyal spouse and permanent home. Albert Stone sees Ossie as having an "abrupt switch in outlook" at this point and sees this "switch" as "insufficiently explored or justified" (240). Ossie writes,

> Judging by myself, I knew that the reason I kept having babies wasn't because I didn't know how to prevent them, it was because I didn't believe in not having them, and I'll bet a lot of those women sitting there felt pretty much like I did, and of course if you feel like that you just let the lecture slide over you, and it don't mean much of anything. Later, when I started working with kids and I saw how wrong I had always been about having babies, I had some groups of girls, and we got together and talked about having babies. (192)

But in fact Ossie has been anticipating this conclusion throughout her narrative, recounting the difficulty she has had in taking care of her children and her failure to stay home with them; moreover, this failure is the one she most decries in her own mother and most wishes to avoid. She eventually dedicates herself to community work with teenagers after her oldest boy attaches himself to a gang. She is forced to confront in her son the reasons why she should not have more children than she can care for closely.

Stone's critique casts doubt on the appropriateness of the Ledner/Guffy collaboration. He writes that the preceding passage "sounds suspiciously like a convenient conversion or accommodation negotiated by Ledner in recognition of middle-class white mores" (240). To argue in this way is not only to suggest that Ledner has seriously redirected Ossie's account of herself but also that "contradictions between [Ossie's] deepest convictions" or "compromise" (239–40) between opposed ideological stances are flaws of collaborative method rather than reenactments of contradictions inscribed in Ossie's situation, relationships, and thought.

Stone describes compromise explicitly as the result of the wrong sort of collaboration. He admires, by contrast, that between the "Harvard historian" (Theodore Rosengarten) and the "illiterate farmer" and "folk historian" (Nate Shaw). Rosengarten provides a long preface to make "explicit" his "careful" editorship and his "notions about history, autobiography, and personal identity," and Shaw's "understanding of historical autobiography is so intuitively accurate and complete that there is little likelihood of his being seriously controlled or molded by the educated questioner from Cambridge" (241–42, 244). Ledner, a "television writer living in Beverly Hills," is evidently less scrupulous, or at any rate less elaborate, in distinguishing her voice from her collaborator's, and Ossie's narrative is flawed for Stone by its "oscillation in mood, attitude, and idiom," which he finds "extreme." Ossie is "all too willing to skip over the contradictions between her deepest convictions, especially those represented by her nine children" (236, 239–40). Such preferences are conditioned by Stone's training as an academic, and he is concerned with establishing distinctions between the merely "popular" and the genuinely "artistic" and "historical" (229–30).

But one suspects that Stone's sense of artistry and authenticity is shaped also by cultural differences that cut closer to home. He does not pause to label or describe Ossie as he does Shaw, beyond calling her politics "middle-of-the-road" (240), but she is neither "illiterate" nor a "farmer," so her language reflects the rhetoric of the "compromising" urban middle class rather than the "vernacular poetry" (244) of the exotic rural man. Stone does not mention Ossie's detailing of her sexual history, so there may be an element of male discomfort in his distaste for the messy oscillations of her narrative. Meanwhile, when Stone remarks that "neither [Ledner nor Ossie] seems to know how difficult it is to establish an authentic self through the words and assumptions of another who, though a woman like herself, comes from a very different world" (240), he not only betrays a belief in particular kinds of discourse, rhetoric, and storytelling as more "authentic" than others, but shows his assumption that "authenticity" is achievable only by insisting on the difficulty of cross-racial collaboration.

Stone is wrong in assuming that every reader would find this narrative unauthentic or uncompelling. To the extent that Ossie's narrative is not "complete" (for example, she omits actual names for almost everyone in her family), it seems a more rather than less "authentic" act of storytelling, yet her "memory" for the events that had the greatest impact in her life is both detailed and credible. At least one reader found it as moving as I did when I first encountered it: As Buckmaster (herself a novelist) says, "This poignant, irresistible, tough-tender, shaking-up book gives us something to be greatly prized. Ossie's conclusions alone are worth the price of the book many times over."[54] Indeed, the book received favorable notice from nearly all its reviewers. At least two reviewers compared it—only partially to its disadvantage—to the poet Maya Angelou's far more literary, fictionalized autobiography *I Know Why the Caged Bird Sings.* Adjudicating its literary merit for libraries, one of these cautions that "since there are a number of contemporary autobiographies of this type available, librarians will have to weigh the needs of their collections" and then opines that "the book does not reflect the skill or style of Maya Angelou's *I Know Why the Caged Bird Sings.* . . . It is comparable rather to Piri Thomas' *Down These Mean Streets* and Claude Brown's *Manchild in the Promised Land.*"[55] This same reviewer describes the story, quite unlike Stone, as told "in [Ossie's] own colloquial language." The other reviewer writes that "Ossie's story while [by] no means as exceptional as Maya Angelou's . . . either in real life or on the page, has its own human interest" and finds in *Ossie* "an inalienable strength—hers."[56] More often, the reviewers simply note their opinions of the story, though less eloquently than Buckmaster, as "moving" and "pitilessly honest."[57]

Whether or not Ossie's narrative seems authentic to a reader less academically oriented and with closer affinities to Ossie, it remains valuable for quite another reason, and that is in providing what Stone pejoratively calls a "topical" historical document (230). Because all such texts reflect the collaboration through which they are produced, whether that of a scholar and a farmer or that of a television writer and a welfare mother–turned–community activist, they embed reminders of salient American differences, ironies, and contradictions. Placed next to artful autobiographical writing (like that of Angelou or Gertrude Stein), Ossie's journal might seem tame and formulaic. Placed next to a text that resembles it far more closely in its generic aspirations—such as *Having Our Say*—Ossie's narrative seems courageous and fresh. Moreover, it remains highly relevant at the turn of the twenty-first century for the picture it paints of America's vast underclasses and of a woman who learned lessons from having lovers and children rather than from having a formal education and a white-collar job. And although Ossie's narrative, like the Delanys', reflects its own moment at the height of the civil rights movement, if read now, it could not be co-opted by conservatives in the way that the Delany sisters' text could; it would have to be spurned. But in its day it was quickly overshadowed by other more sensational or more literary autobiographies, and if it is now ignored by academic literary historians and postmodernist feminists, any possibility of its confrontation with, and contradiction of, today's "topical" clichés will be lost.

But it would be a mistake, too, to dismiss *Having Our Say* in favor of *Ossie*—to choose the latter over the former. As I urge at the end of chapter 6, collaborative stories and writers should be read together for their differences as well as kinships to each other. Together, the texts discussed in this chapter dramatize the range and particularity of African-American women's histories in this century while witnessing also women's collaborations across differences of family position, gender, race, and class. Each tells a story that is only implied in the other. By noting the pleasures of lovers and children amid the struggles, Ossie indicates how much the Delanys had to sacrifice to obtain the security they enjoy in old age; by highlighting individual achievement and sisterhood, the Delanys alert us to the cost Ossie paid in her more typical life as an impoverished single mother. These autobiographies also show that although there may be different ways to tell a story, the variations themselves follow certain by-now well-trodden paths for storytelling, whether of the linear "realistic" narrative or of the polymorphic type, whether more self-conscious and "literary" or more streamlined and "popular." Moreover, both, in their collaborative production, testify to the considerable social cooperation necessary in moving stories from orality to textuality. If equally crafted, their formal options may mean less in themselves than a reader's willingness to cultivate the differences all these kinds of storytelling try to represent: the differences between sisters, races, genders, classes, religions, families, ages, and sexualities.

Ossie and Ledner end their text by shifting from *I* and *they* to *we* and *you*, eschewing discrimination (whether aesthetic or social) in their "concern" about the "trouble we don't need," even while recalling the many differences among American people:

> By people I mean everybody from the President of the United States down through the middle class, black and white, to the poor, the sick, the aged. Ain't nobody I mentioned who ain't got a stake of some kind in what's going to happen, so they should be concerned.
>
> Lord knows, I'm concerned. My neighbors are concerned. We tried to write down how we feel. Maybe you and your neighbors could do the same, and we could send all our thinking straight on to Washington. We think the government should enforce laws that outlaw segregation. . . . We think that all of us have to share in the responsibility of trying to turn out kids that respect the law because it's just, their parents because they're loving and fair, and themselves because they are willing to pay for what they get, so long as getting is possible. To do that, we can't start tomorrow. It will be too late. (224)

For the Delanys, as for Ledner and Ossie, social hope lies in the conflicts of collaboration.

At the end of Sadie's final narrative, Hearth and Sadie recall the triumphant moment when Sadie becomes, like and with Bessie, able to stand up to a gang of "young men": "Bessie was kind of surprised that I took those boys on like that. To tell you the truth, so was I" (294). "I'll tell you a little secret," Bessie herself says (and Hearth writes) at the end Bessie's final narrative in *Having Our Say*, which also ends the book: "I'm starting to get optimistic. I'm thinking: *Maybe I'll get into Heaven after all.* Why, I've helped a lot of folks—even some white folks! I surely do have some redeeming qualities that must count for something. So I just might do it: I just might get into Heaven. I may have to hang on to Sadie's heels, but I'll get there" (299). If bridged, different elevations—as one sister hangs onto her sibling's heels (and vice versa)—produce redoubled possibilities, the hard-won ironies of collaborative survival.

Where authenticity is seen as purity, collaborations will seem inauthentic as dilutions of pure authorship, and cross-racial collaborations will seem inauthentic as dilutions of a particular racial position or viewpoint. But authenticity, seen as acknowledgment and reflection of a thing's origin or making, is not purity. It is an effect or position occupied and argued for from within a context of interactive exchange. Race itself, as both an intellectual category and a social issue, can arise only in a context of cross-racial interactions, whether collaborative, conflictive, or a mixture of both. My study of collaborative authorship has led me to the perhaps paradoxical position that autobiographies that are acknowledged as collaborative carry a kind of legitimacy exceeding that of alleged solitarily authored autobiographies; among the texts under discussion in this book, cross-racial autobiographies yield especially complex, authentic representations of the complexities of race in America.

Conclusion

To the marriage of true minds there would be no impediment.

Nor was there. . . .

For a considerable time the sex of the authors was a matter of heated interest, speculation, and controversy. One
inquirer held that both writers were men: one of them an
old man and the other a young one. Another, on what
grounds it is difficult to determine, said that he knew one
author was a very old lady, and the other was her nephew,
a young soldier, but which was which he wasn't quite sure.

These cats are now out of the bag. Uncertainty is at an
end, and this brief introduction may close with the candid
admission of a fox-hunting gentleman. He said:

"The first time I read it, I read it at top speed. And the
second time I read it *very* slowly, chewing every word. And
then I read it a third time, going over the bits I liked best.
And then—and I thank God not till then!—I heard it was
written by two women!"[1]

MARRIAGE IS A RECURRENT trope in the testimonies of collaborative writers, but is it a true one? The coauthorships discussed in this
book range from the marriage of Louise Erdrich and Michael Dorris, which
collapsed so stunningly, through the mimicry of traditional roles in the
lesbian marriage between husband Gertrude Stein and wife Alice B. Toklas, to the lifelong hymeneal bond of the Fields, "closer married"[2] than
the Brownings. Or was the partnership of Edith Somerville and Martin
Ross—"Two of a Trade," who continued to collaborate (as on the preceding passage) through spirit communication long after Ross's death—a truer
partnership than that of the Fields? Then again, there are the numerous

approximate collaborations, such as that between John Stuart Mill and his platonic mistress and later wife, Harriet Taylor; or H.D.'s "writing on the wall" with Bryher, which turned out not to mean that they would live together until death and beyond. Such marriage indeed encounters impediments and alters when it alteration finds.

As Somerville and Ross claim, the truth and endurance of such marriagelike relations between coauthors are material to their joint writing. Despite all the possible impediments to their relationships, coauthors somehow manage to write together, at least for a time. In this respect, coauthors appear to be a distinctive literary and erotic phenomenon quite unlike the solitary author. But the relational circumstances of coauthors are also highly variable, and the degree of collaboration in particular is almost endlessly alterable. Likewise, the single author rarely truly writes alone.

What this passage, from Somerville's 1944 Preface to a reissue of *Some Experiences of an Irish R. M.* (1899) and *Further Experiences of an Irish R. M.* (1908), further demonstrates is the major impediment to coauthorship that comes from the *presumption* of single (male) authorship. Somerville and Ross's readers gossiped among themselves (based on the dual signature of "E. Œ. Somerville and Martin Ross") because they had to struggle to reimagine authorship as not single. In so doing they reimagined it first as male and cross-generational: Like teacher and student, the authors were surely "an old man" and a "young one." Then, admitting the possibility that these were cross-gendered pseudonyms—and admitting the weirdness of this possibility—a reader surmised that the authors were instead a "very old lady" and her "nephew." What readers could not guess, until told, was the text's actual authorship by two "cats": two not very old, highly vocal, slightly dangerous feminist women. Bending gender as well as authorship in their signatures, Somerville and Ross dented the norms of writing. As the passage's last reader notes, only by *not* knowing who and what the real authors were could he enjoy their book as thoroughly as he did. This story is a complex feminist joke on readers' assumptions about authorship, which works toward the modern moral that readers should trust the tale rather than worry about the teller. But if this is just another fiction constructed by Somerville and Ross, it is to my mind a more useful one than that of a text as possible, authentic, great only when authored by a single writer.

As Somerville and Ross's second commentator says, even if one "knows" that the authors of a coauthored text are an old lady and her nephew, it remains impossible to tell which is which. This study has asked why we want or need to tell them apart. Partly, I think, it is because coauthorship lacks shape for most readers, whereas authorship offers an intense focus of desire, ambition, and imagination. This study has attempted to suggest ways in which literary collaboration may be as or more, though differently, desirable than solitary authorship, focusing on the ways coauthors have figured collaborative relationships in their texts.

But although the solitary author may, as Stillinger claims, be a myth, he will remain a very successful one. It is difficult for most authors—and scholars—to imagine themselves writing in full collaboration. Most writers are accustomed to writing alone and to reaping individual benefits—if not recognition as a solitary genius, at least personal intellectual property in some piece of writing and being perceived by a peer, relative, student, or teacher as having originated something. Moreover, most writers are not used to writing together; those with college educations are accustomed to an ethical expectation that their most important pieces of writing will be entirely their own. Producing writing by means of a relationship with someone else can strike writers as simply undoable.

Yet if this study has shown anything, it has demonstrated that the relational possibilities are among the most fascinating, challenging, and attractive aspects of coauthorship. Literary collaborators blur the boundary not only between each other in writing, but between text and speech, between a text and its writerly contexts. To *con*-fabulate is not only to talk together, to *con*-verse,[3] but also to tell stories together. Confabulation assumes not the interaction of a single teller with a captive audience, but an assembly of speakers who are also listeners, a mutually enraptured set of tale-tellers. When thought of in this way, collaboration obviously is not an anomalous process, although it has come to seem so in the production of modern copyrighted literary texts. Nor is it at all a difficult thing to wish for oneself.

Readers of this study might, then, appropriately ask why I undertook this study alone. It could possibly be described as an approximate collaboration as I have defined that term, but I have received few editorial suggestions, and before submitting the book to the University of Illinois Press, I received these for only two sections. Although I have sometimes suggested a collaboration with another writer, none has ever materialized. This particular study began not in the recognition of collaboration between writers or the possibility of collaboration for myself but rather in reaction against an arbitrary criterion for hiring (discussed in chapter 1); only then did I become interested in this question in relation to particular texts. From that point of departure and for the next several years, this study evolved without my recognizing that I had begun to think through a book on collaboration. When I did finally recognize that a book was in the offing, I made a series of difficult decisions *not* to collaborate—the book had already moved too far along to allow a full collaboration.[4] The contexts in which my developing work was shared thus were almost exclusively presentational—at the lecture podium—rather than conversational. Meanwhile, this study had taken me into an area of research in which there is little prior scholarship with which to work.

Although I wish to argue for collaboration in this study, even while exploring its limitations, this book is not an argument against single authorship. I wish to leave the reader with two kinds of heightened awareness: first of the power, frequency, and interest of coauthorship and literary collaboration, and second of single authorship as itself not solitary, as participating rather in the wide range of kinds and degrees of multiple authorship. Authoring this study has been rich in collaborative difficulties and pleasures. These have taken place for me—as my chapter on Field is intended to clarify and problematize—in interaction primarily with the various literary collaborations exhumed here. In my representation of coauthorship, I am deeply swayed by what these coauthors have said about themselves, even as I have brought my own more skeptical, critical temper to bear on their self-representations. I am influenced obviously by feminist, gender, and multicultural criticism and theory, read and discussed with others over the years, some of which is documented here. As Deleuze and Guattari explain (their) authorship in the opening of their book *A Thousand Plateaus*, "The two of us wrote *Anti-Oedipus* together. Since each of us was several, that was already quite a crowd. Here we have made use of everything that came within range, what was closest as well as farthest away. . . . We have been aided, inspired, multiplied."[5] Each of us is already quite a crowd.

Notes

Introduction

1. Outside literary studies, the term *collaboration* occasionally produces confusion because it is broadly applicable to any form of joint labor. Yet in the literary field *collaboration* has become the term most commonly used to refer to coauthorship; for example, the Modern Language Association (MLA) bibliography records more than five hundred items under *collaboration* (nearly all of which pertain to coauthorship), whereas fewer than twenty references show up under *coauthorship* and its cognates.

2. Lisa Ede and Andrea Lunsford, "Why Write . . . Together?" *Rhetoric Review* 1.2 (1983), 150–57; "Why Write . . . Together: A Research Update," *Rhetoric Review* 5.1 (1986), 71–81; "Rhetoric in a New Key: Women and Collaboration," *Rhetoric Review* 8.2 (1990), 234–41; and *Singular Texts/Plural Authors: Perspectives on Collaborative Writing* (Carbondale: Southern Illinois University Press, 1990); Jack Stillinger, *Multiple Authorship and the Myth of Solitary Genius* (Oxford: Oxford University Press, 1991); and Wayne Koestenbaum, *Double Talk: The Erotics of Male Literary Collaboration* (New York: Routledge, 1989). Laura Ann Brady investigates economic pressures in conjunction with issues of authority in her dissertation on men's and women's collaborations (including Conrad and Ford's coauthorships, Maxwell Perkins's editorship, *Frankenstein*, *The Gilded Age*, *Love Medicine*, and *The Whole Family*); see "Collaborative Literary Writing: Issues of Authorship and Authority," Dissertation, University of Minnesota, 1988. For a study of feminist scholarly collaborations, which appeared too late for discussion here, see *Common Ground: Feminist Collaboration in the Academy*, ed. Elizabeth G. Peck and JoAnna Stephens Mink (Albany: SUNY Press, 1998). Subsequent citations of Stillinger and Koestenbaum appear parenthetically in the text.

3. For a discussion of the interactive possibilities computers offer writers of fiction, see Jay David Bolter, *Writing Space: The Computer, Hypertext, and the History of Writing* (Hillsdale, N.J.: Erlbaum, 1991).

4. A number of short studies have appeared on canonized male writers' collaborations, most notably by Wordsworth and Coleridge, Eliot and Pound. In addition to Stillinger's bibliographical references in *Multiple Authorship*, see Jewel Spears Brooker, "Common Ground and Collaboration in T. S. Eliot," *The Centennial Review* 25.3 (1981), 225–38; Stephen Parrish, "'Leaping and Lingering': Coleridge's Lyrical Ballads," in *Coleridge's Imagination: Essays in Memory of Pete Laver*, ed. Richard Gravil, Lucy Newlyn, and Nicholas Roe (Cambridge: Cambridge University Press, 1985), 102–16; Gordon K. Thomas, "The *Lyrical Ballads* Ode: 'Dialogized Heteroglossia,'" *The Wordsworth Circle* 20.1 (1981), 102–6; and Philip Sicker, "*Pale Fire* and *Lyrical Ballads:* The Dynamics of Collaboration," *Papers on Language and Literature* 28.3 (1992), 305–18.

5. Other important examples of famous male writers and female partners include Hardy's and Yeats's collaborations; for particularly useful discussions, see Pamela Dalziel, "Hardy as Collaborator: The Composition of 'The Spectre of the Real,'" *Papers of the Bibliographic Society of America* 83.4 (1989), 473–501; and James Pethica, "'Our Kathleen': Yeats's Collaboration with Lady Gregory in the Writing of *Cathleen ni Houlihan*," *Yeats Annual* 6 (1988), 3–31. See also Bradford Mudge, *Sara Coleridge, a Victorian Daughter, Her Life and Essays* (New Haven, Conn.: Yale University Press, 1989).

6. In chapter 3, on Michael Field, I explore some of the issues raised by feminist "restoration" and consider the problems as well as the benefits of archival reconstruction. However, I do not take up the broad phenomenon of ghostwriting or ghostwriters here. Ghostwriting usually presumes a lopsided distribution of tasks and recognition in writing, involving a nominal author, who is not a writer (or does not write well) but whose fame on other grounds makes him or her a marketable author, and a subordinately named or altogether suppressed "ghost" author, who does write well and is responsible for much or most of the given text but who is not famous. Several texts in this study could be redescribed as ghostwritten, including *The Autobiography of Alice B. Toklas*, the Delany sisters' and Ossie Guffy's transcribed autobiographies, and the texts coauthored by Erdrich and Dorris, Redgrove and Shuttle that were not cosigned. There is much ghostwriting in popular genres, such as science fiction, which merits study.

7. E. Œ. Somerville and Martin Ross, "Two of a Trade," *Irish Writing* 1 (1946), 79.

8. See Jonathan Culler, "Reading as a Woman," in *On Deconstruction: Theory and Criticism after Structuralism* (Ithaca, N.Y.: Cornell University Press, 1982), 43–64; Joan Kelly, "The Doubled Vision of Feminist Theory," in *Sex and Class in Women's History*, ed. Judith L. Newton, Mary P. Ryan, and Judith R. Walkowitz (London: Routledge & Kegan Paul, 1983), 259–70; Naomi Schor, "Reading Double: Sand's Difference," in *The Poetics of Gender*, ed. Nancy K. Miller (New York: Columbia University Press, 1986), 248–69; Paul Smith, *Discerning the Subject* (Minneapolis: University of Minnesota Press, 1988), 134–51; Kristina Straub, "Women, Gender, and Criticism," in *Literary Criticism and Theory: The Greeks to the Present*, ed. Robert Con Davis and Laurie Finke (New York: Longman, 1989), 859–66, 871–76; Bonnie Zimmerman, "What Has Never Been: An Overview of Lesbian Feminist Criticism," in *The New Feminist Criticism: Essays on Women, Literature, and Theory*, ed. Elaine Showalter (New York: Pantheon, 1985), 200–224; and my "*Aurora Leigh:* An Epical *Ars Poetica*," in *Writ-*

ing the Woman Artist: Essays on Poetics, Politics, and Portraiture, ed. Suzanne W. Jones (Philadelphia: University of Pennsylvania Press, 1991), 359–63.

9. The Women's Caucus for the 1991 Convention of the MLA (San Francisco) sponsored a pathbreaking session, "Feminist Collaboration"; as panelists Carey Kaplan and Ellen Cronan Rose explain, this session represented the many women who have joined in "formal and informal collective and collaborative work" of many types, "from coedited and cowritten books to graduate study groups formed for mutual support and sustenance," in "Strange Bedfellows: Feminist Collaboration," *Signs* 18.3 (1993), 557n.8. Kaplan and Rose's important essay in the spring 1993 issue of *Signs* derived from this session. Subsequently, a panel sponsored in April 1992 by the Narrative Conference (at Vanderbilt University) and a Dec. 1992 MLA panel (in New York) sponsored by *Tulsa Studies in Women's Literature* spawned a two-part forum of papers by feminist collaborators, published in the fall 1994 and spring 1995 issues of *Tulsa Studies.* The collaborative scholars included in the *Tulsa Studies* published forum were Susan Leonardi and Rebecca Pope, Darlene Dralus and Jen Shelton, Stacey Schlau and Electa Arenal, Janice Doane and Devon Hodges, and Linda Hutcheon and Michael Hutcheon. Coauthors Joyce Elbrecht and Lydia Fakundiny (Jael B. Juba) also took part in this forum.

10. Ede and Lunsford generally are credited with first theorizing the idea of conversation in collaborative writing, but this concept appears in all feminist scholarly and literary collaborators' self-descriptions that I have encountered, whether or not they are aware of Ede and Lunsford's work. Though less prevalent than "conversation," the figure of the dance also occurs at some point in almost all collaborators' discussions of their writing practices. The term *mosaic,* often cited by scholars, was first adopted by Michael Field; see Mary Sturgeon, *Michael Field* (London: George G. Harrap, 1922), 47. *Jazz* is favored by Rose in Kaplan and Rose's essay, "Strange Bedfellows" (553). The metaphors of the quilt and of cooking ("Screaming Diva Stew" and "mixed green metaphors") are explored by Susan Leonardi and Rebecca Pope, "Screaming Divas: Collaboration as Feminist Practice," *Tulsa Studies in Women's Literature* 13.2 (1994), 262–64, 269–70. See also Stacey Schlau and Electa Arenal, who make the term *co-labor* central to discussion of their scholarly collaboration in "*Escribiendo yo, escribiendo ella, escribiendo nosotras:* On Co-Laboring," *Tulsa Studies in Women's Literature* 14.1 (1995), 39–49.

11. Jane Gallop, *The Daughter's Seduction: Feminism and Psychoanalysis* (Ithaca, N.Y.: Cornell University Press, 1982), 29–32.

12. This study mostly omits plays and cinematic writing to focus on collaborative novels, poems, and autobiographies. The one exception occurs in chapter 3, on Michael Field, which culminates with a brief discussion of their closet verse drama, *Canute the Great.* More could be written on collaboration in drama and film, but these are traditionally collaborative media and would enlarge this already large project by necessitating attention to a vast body of literature and adding genre to the questions posed. Yet there is nothing particularly mysterious about what would make collaborative writing more likely in group projects such as plays and films than in other forms of literature, and generic distinctions barely begin to account for the sparsity of acknowledged and deliberate authorship in novels and poetry. The collaborative writing that most intrigues me is (thus far) a rare event.

13. Janice Doane and Devon Hodges, "Writing from the Trenches: Women's Work and Collaborative Writing," *Tulsa Studies in Women's Literature* 14.1 (1995), 56.

14. Joyce Elbrecht and Lydia Fakundiny, "Scenes from a Collaboration: Or Becoming Jael B. Juba," *Tulsa Studies in Women's Literature* 13.2 (1994), 241–57. Subsequent citations of this essay appear parenthetically in the text. Among other notable contemporary collaborations, see the verse sequence by the U.S. poets Olga Broumas and Jane Miller, *Black Holes, Black Stockings* (Middletown, Conn.: Wesleyan University Press, 1985); the epistolary novel by the British writers Sara Maitland and Michelene Wandor, *Arky Types* (London: Methuen, 1987); and the verse sequence by Suniti Namjoshi (of Indian birth) and Gillian Hanscombe (of Australian birth), *Flesh and Paper* (Seaton, Devon, U.K.: Jezebel Tapes and Books, 1986).

15. The work of "Pansy" and her friends advocates domesticity in devoutly Christian terms. The Gerard sisters were Scottish writers who set their work in various European, Eastern European, and Mexican contexts, exploring situations with mildly political and occasionally complex gender implications. Marjorie Barnard and Flora Eldershaw were two single career women (one working in a library, the other in education) involved in various leftist organizations; their 1947 censored novel *Tomorrow and Tomorrow and Tomorrow* was reproduced in an uncensored version by Virago in 1983. For discussion of M. Barnard Eldershaw's collaboration and its treatment by critics, see Maryanne Dever, "'No Mine and Thine but Ours': Finding 'M. Barnard Eldershaw,'" *Tulsa Studies in Women's Literature* 14.1 (1995), 65–75. British authors Mary Howitt and her husband and the Taylor sisters (popular authors of children's and domestic literature) wrote during a moment in the nineteenth century earlier than that encompassed by the present study.

16. For a study of a case in which twelve coauthors were involved in writing a novel, see Dale M. Bauer, "The Politics of Collaboration in *The Whole Family*," in *Old Maids to Radical Spinsters: Unmarried Women in the Twentieth-Century Novel*, ed. Laura L. Doan (Urbana: University of Illinois Press, 1991), 107–22.

17. Among the few studies that include attention to collaborative group dynamics are Bauer's "The Politics of Collaboration"; Carole Boyce Davies, "Collaboration and the Ordering Imperative in Life Story Production," in *De/Colonizing the Subject: The Politics of Gender in Women's Autobiography*, ed. Julia Watson (Minneapolis: University of Minnesota Press, 1992), 3–19; Ede and Lunsford, *Singular Texts/Plural Authors*; Anne Ruggles Gere, *Writing Groups: History, Theory, and Implications* (Carbondale: Southern Illinois University Press, 1987); Valerie Miner, "Writing Feminist Fiction: Solitary Genesis or Collective Criticism?" *Frontiers* 6.1 (1981), 26–29; *New Visions of Collaborative Writing*, ed. Janis Forman (Portsmouth, N.H.: Boynton/Cook, 1992); and *Writing With: New Directions in Collaborative Teaching, Learning, and Research*, ed. Sally Barr Reagan, Thomas Fox, and David Bleich (Albany: SUNY Press, 1994).

18. Marjorie Garber, *Vice Versa: Bisexuality and the Eroticism of Everyday Life* (New York: Simon & Schuster, 1995).

19. See Pansy and Her Friends, *A Sevenfold Trouble* (Boston: D. Lathrop, 1889); Zoë Fairbairns, Sara Maitland, Valerie Miner, Michele Roberts, and Michelene Wandor, *Tales I Tell My Mother: A Collection of Feminist Short Stories* (Boston:

South End Press, 1978); and Victoria Byerly, *Hard Times Cotton Mill Girls: Personal Histories of Womanhood and Poverty in the South* (Ithaca, N.Y.: Cornell University, 1986).

20. Kaplan and Rose focus on their own scholarly collaboration in "Strange Bedfellows."

21. Jacques Lacan, *Feminine Sexuality: Jacques Lacan and the école freudienne,* ed. Juliet Mitchell and Jacqueline Rose, trans. Jacqueline Rose (New York: Norton, 1985), 147.

22. Michael Field, *Works and Days: From the Journal of Michael Field,* ed. T. and D. C. Sturge Moore (London: John Murray, 1933), 6.

23. Leonardi and Pope, "Screaming Divas," 260.

24. Barbara Johnson, "Lesbian Spectacles: Reading *Sula, Passing, Thelma and Louise,* and *The Accused,*" in *Media Spectacles,* ed. Marjorie Garber, Jann Matlock, and Rebecca L. Walkowitz (New York: Routledge, 1993), 160; rpt. in Barbara Johnson, *The Feminist Difference: Literature, Psychoanalysis, Race, and Gender* (Cambridge, Mass.: Harvard University Press, 1998), 157–65. Subsequent citations refer to *Media Spectacles* and appear parenthetically in the text.

25. Field creates pronominal problems; I refer primarily to the collaborative team that called itself Michael Field (rather than to the individuals Bradley or Cooper), but I also wish to acknowledge—indeed to emphasize—the unconventional plurality of this author, so Field is referred to as "they" in this study.

26. Bonnie Zimmerman, "Lesbians Like This and That: Some Notes on Lesbian Criticism for the Nineties," in *New Lesbian Criticism: Literary and Cultural Readings,* ed. Sally Munt (New York: Columbia University Press, 1992), 4; Kaplan and Rose, "Strange Bedfellows," 552. Although the use of the lesbian as metaphor has attracted criticism, the practice is so widespread now as to be common among lesbian/feminist critics. See also Marilyn Farwell, "Toward a Definition of the Lesbian Literary Imagination," *Signs* 14.1 (1988), 110–12.

27. Barbara Smith, "Toward a Black Feminist Criticism," in *All the Women Are White, All the Blacks Are Men, But Some of Us Are Brave,* ed. Gloria T. Hull, Patricia Bell Scott, and Barbara Smith (Old Westbury, N.Y.: Feminist Press, 1982), 157–75; Deborah E. McDowell, Introduction, *Quicksand and Passing,* by Nella Larsen (New Brunswick, N.J.: Rutgers University Press, 1986), ix–xxxviii.

28. Adrienne Rich, "Compulsory Heterosexuality and Lesbian Existence" (1980), in *Blood, Bread, and Poetry: Selected Prose, 1979–1985* (New York: Norton, 1986), 23–75.

29. Teresa de Lauretis, "Sexual Indifference and Lesbian Representation," in *The Lesbian and Gay Studies Reader,* ed. Henry Abelove, Michèle Aina Barale, and David M. Halperin (New York: Routledge, 1993), 144. Subsequent citations appear parenthetically in the text.

30. Eve Kosofsky Sedgwick, *Tendencies* (Durham, N.C.: Duke University Press, 1993), 81. Before this passage, Sedgwick makes the perhaps more familiar point that psychoanalytic feminists tend to grant "special status" to "the identities 'male' and 'female'" and to treat "all other complex intersections of behavior, subjectivity, self-perceived identity and other-ascribed identity" as "completely transparent and historyless"; she goes on to cite the unhistoricized use of the terms *sodomy* and *pederasty* by Kaja Silverman as examples (80). Because most of the collaborative texts treated in my study reflect the dominant binarisms in mod-

ern culture in foregrounding male/female and heterosexual/homosexual differences, my argument is concerned more explicitly with those categories than with more diverse "tendencies."

31. Toni Morrison, *Sula* (1973; rpt. New York: Plume, 1982), 51.

32. Mary Ann Doane, *The Desire to Desire: The Woman's Film of the 1940s* (Bloomington: Indiana University Press, 1987), 11–12.

33. Doane criticizes the concept of contiguity as theorized by French theorists such as Irigaray, Cixous, Montrelay, and Kofman, arguing that "these theorists activate the tropes of proximity, overpresence or excessive closeness to the body, and contiguity in the construction of a kind of 'ghetto politics' which maintains and applauds woman's exclusion from language and the symbolic order" (*The Desire to Desire* 12). I believe these theories to be somewhat more complex than Doane suggests, and contiguity is viewed in my argument not as opposite to or an absolute alternative to lack but as a condition or trope that is always already embedded in lack.

34. For a related use of *oscillation* in a different context, see Laura Mulvey, *Visual and Other Pleasures* (Bloomington: Indiana University Press, 1989), 35.

35. Sturgeon, *Michael Field*; Emma Donoghue, *We Are Michael Field* (Bath, U.K.: Absolute Press, 1998), 9. Subsequent citations of Donoghue appear parenthetically in the text.

36. Janet Todd, ed., *British Women Writers: A Critical Reference Guide* (New York: Continuum, 1989), 244–45.

37. Donoghue, *We Are Michael Field*, 15; Sturgeon, *Michael Field*, 17; Angela Leighton, *Victorian Women Poets: Writing against the Heart* (Charlottesville: University Press of Virginia, 1992), 204. Subsequent citations of Leighton appear parenthetically in the text.

38. Some intriguing correspondences and contrasts might be pursued between the pseudonym of Jael B. Juba and the four protagonists of Joanna Russ's *The Female Man* (1975; rpt. Boston: Beacon, 1986)—the four J's (who include a Jael). Elbrecht and Fakundiny report in e-mail correspondence that this is unintentional.

39. Joyce Elbrecht and Lydia Fakundiny, *The Restorationist: Text One—A Collaborative Fiction by Jael B. Juba* (Albany: SUNY Press, 1993). Subsequent citations appear parenthetically in the text.

40. Sturgeon, *Michael Field*, 47.

41. See Christine (Chris) White's much-cited article, "'Poets and Lovers Evermore': Interpreting Female Love in the Poetry and Journals of Michael Field," *Textual Practice* 4.2 (1990), 197–212. A subsequent article by White qualifies her description of Field's lesbianism but still takes issue with Lillian Faderman's model of "romantic friendship"; see White, "The Tiresian Poet: Michael Field," in *Victorian Women Poets: A Critical Reader*, ed. Angela Leighton (Cambridge, Mass.: Blackwell, 1996), 148–61.

42. Field, *Works and Days*, 16.

43. Ellen Moers, *Literary Women: The Great Writers* (1976; rpt. Oxford: Oxford University Press, 1985), 41.

44. Michael Field, *Underneath the Bough* (London: George Bell, 1893), 68–69. A facsimile of this volume may be found in *"Sight and Song" (1892) with "Underneath the Bough" (1893)* (New York: Woodstock Books, 1993).

45. Although Sturgeon and Leighton (and also Donoghue) do not explain their reasons for this attribution, probably the poem appears early in Bradley and Cooper's diaries and in Bradley's handwriting. Bradley and Cooper describe themselves in their private diaries and confidential letters as writing separately as well as together (writing separately especially in their poems), but handwriting itself is not an adequate index of authorship because, as I note at other points in this study, coauthors often first conceive their poems or fiction together in conversation with each other and may continue to converse as one of them wields the pen. Lost drafts indicating the authors' interwoven revisions may intervene between a work's first conception and its final form. In the case of Michael Field, the emphasis of critics on attributions of individual authorship unfortunately reinforces an old archaeology of the Bradley/Cooper relationship (and thence of their poetry) that frames Katherine as dominant initiator and Edith as submissive receiver; this model relies too simply on patriarchal views of how relationships work. Bradley and Cooper themselves vigorously resisted their friends' and acquaintances' tendency to refer to them other than as one Michael Field. Donoghue's new biography goes far to correct this archaeology of their relationship. My primary concern here is not with how the poem was originally composed, moreover, but with how, once published under the name Michael Field, it is read.

46. A volume of poems, *The New Minnesinger*, by Bradley (London: Longmans, Green), appeared in 1875 under the name Arran Leigh; Bradley and Cooper's first coauthored work, the play *Bellerophôn* (London: Kegan Paul), appeared in 1881 under the names Arran and Isla Leigh; their second work, the plays *Callirhoë and Fair Rosamund*, appeared under the name Michael Field, and from then on, all their work appeared either under the name Field or anonymously.

47. Michael Field, *Sight and Song* (London: Elkin Matthews and John Lane, 1892), 99. Subsequent citations appear parenthetically in the text. See also Leighton's account of this passage (*Writing against the Heart* 215).

48. Judith Butler, *Gender Trouble: Feminism and the Subversion of Identity* (New York: Routledge, 1990), 147.

49. Judith Butler, *Bodies That Matter: On the Discursive Limits of "Sex"* (New York: Routledge, 1993), xi.

50. For an analogous process of which Juba may be aware, see the end of Julia Kristeva's "Women's Time," in *The Kristeva Reader*, ed. Toril Moi (New York: Columbia University Press, 1986), 210.

51. Michel Foucault, *The History of Sexuality: An Introduction*, vol. 1, trans. Robert Hurley (New York: Random House–Vintage Books, 1978, 1980), 157.

52. Butler, *Gender Trouble*, 93–106.

53. Gilles Deleuze and Felix Guattari, *A Thousand Plateaus: Capitalism and Schizophrenia*, trans. Brian Massumi (Minneapolis: University of Minnesota Press, 1987), 149–66 and passim.

54. See also de Lauretis on the ways "lesbian writers and artists have sought variously to escape gender [as an essentialized set of differences], to deny it, transcend it, or perform it to excess, and to inscribe the erotic in cryptic, allegorical, realistic, camp, or other modes of representation" ("Sexual Indifference" 144). Although in the following chapters I focus on the contradictions, complicities, problematic engagements, and challenges of women's coauthorships, I also discern a comparable variety of evasive strategies.

Chapter 1: Originality and Collaboration

1. Harold Bloom, *The Anxiety of Influence: A Theory of Poetry* (Oxford: Oxford University Press, 1973), 5–6.

2. Sandra M. Gilbert and Susan Gubar, *The Madwoman in the Attic: The Woman Writer and the Nineteenth-Century Literary Imagination* (New Haven, Conn.: Yale University Press, 1979), 49–50. Subsequent citations appear parenthetically in the text.

3. Bloom, *The Anxiety of Influence*, 9, 14, and passim.

4. Koestenbaum, *Double Talk*, 6; Gallop, *The Daughter's Seduction*, 29–31.

5. For accounts that highlight the relationship between the *Autobiography* and *On Liberty* and downplay collaboration, see the arguments of Jerome Buckley, "John Stuart Mill's 'True' Autobiography," *Studies in the Literary Imagination* 23.2 (1990), 230; Avrom Fleishman, "Personal Myth: Three Victorian Autobiographers," in *Approaches to Victorian Autobiography*, ed. George P. Landow (Athens: Ohio University Press, 1979), 223; and James Olney, *Metaphors of Self: The Meaning of Autobiography* (Princeton, N.J.: Princeton University Press, 1972), 257–58. For accounts that stress an association between Mill's collaboration with his wife and their views about liberty, see Gertrude Himmelfarb, *On Liberty and Liberalism: The Case of John Stuart Mill* (New York: Knopf, 1974); Alice S. Rossi, ed., *Essays on Sex Equality*, by John Stuart Mill and Harriet Taylor Mill (Chicago: University of Chicago Press, 1970); Gail Tulloch, *Mill and Sexual Equality* (Hertfordshire, U.K.: Harvester Wheatsheaf, 1989); and Jo Ellen Jacobs, "'The Lot of Gifted Ladies Is Hard': A Study of Harriet Taylor Mill Criticism," *Hypatia* 9.3 (1994), 132–62. For a highly critical account of Mill's views of gender and liberty and of the linkage between them, see Christine Di Stefano, "Rereading J. S. Mill: Interpolations from the (M)Otherworld," in *Discontented Discourses: Feminism/Textual Intervention/Psychoanalysis*, ed. Marleen S. Barr and Richard Feldstein (Urbana: University of Illinois Press, 1989), 160–72. Subsequent citations of Di Stefano appear parenthetically in the text.

6. Jonathan Loesberg, *Fictions of Consciousness: Mill, Newman, and the Reading of Victorian Prose* (New Brunswick, N.J.: Rutgers, 1986), 25. Subsequent citations appear parenthetically in the text.

7. Loesberg makes no reference to Jack Stillinger's attention to this problem in "Who Wrote Mill's *Autobiography*?" (cited in note 12) but in an endnote explains that "no arguments in favor of anything more than influence have, in my opinion, ever met [the] objections" of Robson and Pappe (*Fictions of Consciousness* 253). See H. O. Pappe, *John Stuart Mill and the Harriet Taylor Myth* (Melbourne, Australia: Melbourne University Press, 1960); and John M. Robson, *The Improvement of Mankind: The Social and Political Thought of John Stuart Mill* (London: University of Toronto Press and Routledge & Kegan Paul, 1968). However, see Phyllis Rose's assertion that among recent critics, "every serious scholar of Mill's life and work has believed what Mill says about Harriet's share in his intellectual life," in *Parallel Lives: Five Victorian Marriages* (New York: Vintage, 1984), 128–29. In support of this statement, Rose cites Michael St. John Packe, *The Life of John Stuart Mill* (London: Secker & Warburg, 1954); Ruth Borchard, *John Stuart Mill: The Man* (London: Watts, 1957); F. A. Hayek, *John Stuart Mill and Harriet Taylor: Their Correspondence and Subsequent Marriage* (Chicago: University of

Chicago Press, 1951); and Himmelfarb, *On Liberty and Liberalism.* But see Jacobs's discussion of the ways Packe, Borchard, and Himmelfarb criticize Taylor ("'The Lot of Gifted Ladies'" 141–43).

8. See Janice Carlisle, *John Stuart Mill and the Writing of Character* (Athens: University of Georgia Press, 1991): "The most evenhanded account is still Jack Stillinger's" (310n.19). Subsequent citations appear parenthetically in the text.

9. Jack Stillinger, Introduction, *Autobiography,* by John Stuart Mill (Boston: Houghton Mifflin, 1969), xvii. Subsequent citations of this Introduction appear parenthetically in the text.

10. Olney also expresses "squirming discomfort" with Mill's tributes (*Metaphors of Self* 250).

11. Jack Stillinger, ed., *The Early Draft of John Stuart Mill's "Autobiography"* (Urbana: University of Illinois Press, 1961).

12. Jack Stillinger, "Who Wrote J. S. Mill's *Autobiography?" Victorian Studies* 27 (1983), 21. Subsequent citations appear parenthetically in the text.

13. See Diana Trilling: The correspondence shows "Mrs. Taylor to have been one of the meanest and dullest ladies in literary history, a monument of nasty self-regard. . . . This was no woman, no real woman," in "Mill's Intellectual Beacon," *Partisan Review* 19.1 (1952), 116, 119.

14. Hayek, *John Stuart Mill,* 194.

15. For example, see Himmelfarb, *On Liberty and Liberalism,* 252–53, 256–57; Rose, *Parallel Lives,* 114–22, 127; Trilling, "Mill's Intellectual Beacon"; Packe, "The Life of John Stuart Mill"; and Bruce Mazlish, *James and John Stuart Mill: Father and Son in the Nineteenth Century* (New York: Basic, 1975).

16. Jacobs, "'The Lot of Gifted Ladies,'" 134, 148–51. See Tulloch, *Mill and Sexual Equality,* chapters 5, 6, and passim; and Leah D. Hackleman, "Suppressed Speech: The Language of Emotion in Harriet Taylor's *The Enfranchisement of Women," Women's Studies* 20 (1992), 273–86. Arguments in favor of Taylor's intelligence focus on what Mill called her "boldness in speculation" and on what Di Stefano describes as a "feminism more sophisticated and developed" than Mill's ("Rereading J. S. Mill" 164); also see Rossi, *Essays on Sex Equality,* and Tulloch, *Mill and Sexual Equality.* Mill himself attributed many ideas in most of his major works after *A System of Logic* to Taylor but insisted that he had believed in the equality of men and women long before he met her.

17. See Rossi, *Essays on Sex Equality,* 57.

18. John Stuart Mill, *Autobiography and Literary Essays, Collected Works of John Stuart Mill,* vol. 1, ed. John M. Robson and Jack Stillinger (Toronto: University of Toronto Press; London: Routledge & Kegan Paul, 1981), 194, 195. Subsequent citations of the autobiography refer to this edition and appear parenthetically in the text.

19. See Buckley, "'True' Autobiography," 229; and Susan Groag Bell, "The Feminization of John Stuart Mill," in *Revealing Lives: Autobiography, Biography, and Gender,* ed. Bell and Marilyn Yalom (Albany: SUNY Press, 1990), 86–89.

20. See also Bell, who restores Mill's thought to its historical contexts in nineteenth-century debates about gender ("Feminization" 85, 90). Linda M.-G. Zerilli focuses on this tropology but, influenced in part by Bloom, sees Taylor as absorbed by Mill: "Constructing 'Harriet Taylor': Another Look at J. S. Mill's *Autobiography,"* in *Constructions of the Self,* ed. George Levine (New Brunswick, N.J.: Rut-

gers University Press, 1992), 197. I argue for the relative value of Mill's celebration of Taylor in a genre normally focused exclusively on celebrating the "I" of the autobiography.

21. Buckley, "'True' Autobiography," 229.

22. Moreover, as Hayek and Zerilli indicate, Mill believed that "a proper memoir of his wife could [not] be written" (Hayek, *John Stuart Mill* 15; Zerilli, "Constructing" 194).

23. Rose sees Mill's "subjection" ironically (*Parallel Lives* 135–40), whereas Bell sees courage in Mill's deliberate self-feminization ("Feminization" 91).

24. I use the term *overdetermined* here in a loose psycholiterary sense; for a comprehensive psychoanalytic portrait of Taylor as an "overdetermined" choice for Mill, see Mazlish, *James and John Stuart Mill*, 283 and passim.

25. The "early draft" of the *Autobiography* was written in late 1853 and early 1854 and covered Mill's life until his marriage in 1851; Mill added three more pages in 1861 and then another forty-eight in winter 1869–70. See *Autobiography and Literary Essays*, xix–xx.

26. Luce Irigaray, *This Sex Which Is Not One*, trans. Catherine Porter and Carolyn Burke (1977; Ithaca, N.Y.: Cornell University Press, 1985).

27. Zerilli, "Constructing," 192–93, 202–6. Himmelfarb associates the works to which Di Stefano refers with Mill's intellectual debt to Taylor and attributes the essay on nature in particular to Taylor's influence; in this, as in other instances, Taylor and Mill (at the very least) collaborated in allowing some women more equality than others.

28. For Mill's collaboration with his stepdaughter after his wife's death, see Ann P. Robson, "Mill's Second Prize in the Lottery of Life," in *A Cultivated Mind: Essays on J. S. Mill Presented to John M. Robson*, ed. Michael Laine (Toronto: University of Toronto Press, 1991), 215–41.

Chapter 2: Black/White, Author/Editor Friction

1. Jacobs writes ironically of the "beautiful 'patriarchal institution'" of slavery in *Incidents in the Life of a Slave Girl*, ed. L. Maria Child, introd. Valerie Smith (1861; Oxford: Oxford University Press, 1988), 114. Subsequent citations appear parenthetically in the text.

2. Lydia Maria Child to Harriet Jacobs, 27 Sept. 1860, in *Incidents in the Life of a Slave Girl: Written by Herself*, ed. Jean Fagan Yellin (Cambridge, Mass.: Harvard University Press, 1987), 246.

3. Mary Childers and bell hooks, "A Conversation about Race and Class," in *Conflicts in Feminism*, ed. Marianne Hirsch and Evelyn Fox Keller (New York: Routledge, 1990), 60–81. For an influential discussion of the desirability of such conversation, see also Elizabeth Abel, "Black Writing, White Reading: Race and the Politics of Feminist Interpretation," *Critical Inquiry* 19.3 (1993), 470–98.

4. For a related discussion of another coproduced autobiography less completely authored by its primary subject, see Jean M. Humez, "Reading *The Narrative of Sojourner Truth* as a Collaborative Text," *Frontiers* 16.1 (1996), 29–52.

5. Patricia G. Holland and Milton Meltzer, *The Collected Correspondence of Lydia Maria Child, 1817–1880* (New York: Kraus Microform, 1979), nos. 1243, 1255, and 1282; Jean Fagan Yellin, "*Written by Herself:* Harriet Jacobs' Slave

Narrative," *American Literature* 53.3 (1981), 479–86; Holland and Meltzer, eds., *Lydia Maria Child: Selected Letters, 1817–1880* (Amherst: University of Massachusetts Press, 1982), 357–59, 364, 374–75, 378–79, 420; Dorothy Sterling, ed., *We Are Your Sisters: Black Women in the Nineteenth Century* (New York: Norton, 1984); Yellin, "Text and Contexts of Harriet Jacobs' *Incidents in the Life of a Slave Girl, Written by Herself,*" in *The Slave's Narrative,* ed. Charles Davis and Henry L. Gates Jr. (Oxford: Oxford University Press, 1985), 262–82; Alice Deck, "Whose Book Is This?: Authorial versus Editorial Control of Harriet Brent Jacobs' *Incidents in the Life of a Slave Girl: Written by Herself,*" *Women's Studies International Forum* 10.1 (1987), 33–40; and Yellin, Introduction, Correspondence, Chronology, and Notes to *Incidents in the Life of a Slave Girl: Written by Herself* (1987). Subsequent citations of these references appear parenthetically in the text.

6. Margaret Homans, *Bearing the Word: Language and Female Experience in Nineteenth-Century Women's Writing* (Chicago: University of Chicago Press, 1986), 13–16 and passim.

7. Yellin sought to correct views established of this text by critics such as John W. Blassingame, who categorized Jacobs's autobiography with other "fictional accounts" in which "the major character may have been a real fugitive, but the narrative of his life is probably false" and found it "not credible"; see Blassingame's *The Slave Community: Plantation Life in the Antebellum South* (Oxford: Oxford University Press, 1972), 233–34. Since Yellin's pioneering work in the 1980s, culminating in her 1987 edition, a small flood of criticism on Jacobs's text has appeared. But the arguments about authenticity rage on. See especially Elizabeth Fox-Genovese's doubts about the claim in Jacobs's text that her slave master did not rape her and that she spent seven years in a tiny attic to escape him. Fox-Genovese acknowledges Jacobs as this text's author but sees her autobiography as fictionalized; see Fox-Genovese's *Within the Plantation Household: Black and White Women of the Old South* (Chapel Hill: University of North Carolina Press, 1988), 374–75, 381, 392, 462n.5. Also see Carolyn Sorisio's negotiation of this "debate" in "'There Is Might in Each': Conceptions of Self in Harriet Jacobs's *Incidents in the Life of a Slave Girl, Written by Herself,*" *Legacy* 13.1 (1996), 1–2. Yellin has carefully modified earlier biographical arguments—involving Jacobs's choice of Jacobs rather than Knox as her surname and her omission of her father's second marriage and family in telling his story—and now acknowledges the "constructed" character of this text, but Yellin still insists on Jacobs's control over it; see "Harriet Jacobs's Family History," *American Literature* 66.4 (1994), 765–67.

8. Yellin argues that the "contrasting voices" of this text—for example, its straightforward moments and its melodrama—are all Jacobs's own (Introduction xix, xxxiv), whereas I see Jacobs's writing as collaborative with previous slave narratives, sentimental novels, news accounts, and so forth (which Jacobs had read) as well as with her editor. Most critics devote either part or all of their accounts to the problem of "true womanhood" and the concomitant clash of genres in this autobiography.

9. For commentary on Child's editing of the John Brown episode, see Bruce Mills, "Lydia Maria Child and the Endings to Harriet Jacobs's *Incidents in the Life of a Slave Girl,*" *American Literature* 64.2 (1992), 265; and Michelle Burnham, "Loopholes of Resistance: Harriet Jacobs' Slave Narrative and the Critique of Agency in Foucault," *Arizona Quarterly* 49.2 (1993), 69.

10. Deck reads this "reference to her own small ideas" as sarcastic ("Whose Book" 40).

11. For a useful discussion of the relations between orality and literacy in African-American women's texts and particularly in Jacobs, see Harryette Mullen, "Runaway Tongue: Resistant Orality in *Uncle Tom's Cabin, Our Nig, Incidents in the Life of a Slave Girl,* and *Beloved,*" in *The Culture of Sentiment: Race, Gender, and Sentimentality in Nineteenth-Century America,* ed. Shirley Samuels (Oxford: Oxford University Press, 1992), 251–52.

12. See especially Yellin's account of Jacobs's activism after publication of her book (Introduction xxiv–xxv).

13. See also William L. Andrews's account of Jacobs's importance to Child and to Amy Post in *To Tell a Free Story: The First Century of Afro-American Autobiography, 1760–1865* (Urbana: University of Illinois Press, 1986), 247.

14. In seeing Brent as facing a series of nonchoices, my account differs from others that emphasize her self-determination or acquisition of an autonomous self; see Nellie Y. McKay, "The Girls Who Became the Women: Childhood Memories in the Autobiographies of Harriet Jacobs, Mary Church Terrell, and Anne Moody," in *Tradition and the Talents of Women,* ed. Florence Howe (Urbana: University of Illinois Press, 1991), 110–13; and Mary Helen Washington, *Invented Lives: Narratives of Black Women 1860–1960* (New York: Doubleday, 1987), 3–15. For articles that offer reconsideration of agency in this text, see Burnham, "Loopholes of Resistance," 53–73; Franny Nudelman, "Harriet Jacobs and the Sentimental Politics of Female Suffering," *English Literary History* 59 (1992), 939–64; Sidonie Smith, "Elizabeth Cady Stanton, Harriet Jacobs, and Resistances to 'True Womanhood,'" in *Subjectivity, Identity, and the Body: Women's Autobiographical Practices in the Twentieth Century* (Bloomington: Indiana University Press, 1993), 45; and Carla Kaplan, "Narrative Contracts and Emancipatory Readers: *Incidents in the Life of a Slave Girl,*" *The Yale Journal of Criticism* 6.1 (1993), 93–119, and (a shortened version of this essay) "Recuperating Agents: Narrative Contracts, Emancipatory Readers, and *Incidents in the Life of a Slave Girl,*" in *Provoking Agents: Gender and Agency in Theory and Practice,* ed. Judith Kegan Gardiner (Urbana: University of Illinois Press, 1995), 280–301. In contrast to Kaplan, however, I see the impulse among contemporary feminist critics to "recuperate" Jacobs's text as participating in a process of "approximate" collaboration in which Jacobs herself engaged. For another response to Kaplan's argument, see Deborah M. Garfield, "Speech, Listening, and Female Sexuality in *Incidents in the Life of a Slave Girl,*" *Arizona Quarterly* 50.2 (1994), 46–47n.29.

15. The two intermediate chapters—one on New Year's Day, when slaves are sold, the other on her uncle's escape—introduce the hideousness of slave conditions, with which readers of slave narratives would already have been familiar. Their effect is thus to suggest what is different in Brent's situation: Brent's is the story of a relatively privileged slave girl who is able to remain in close proximity to her natal family, yet this "privileged" slave must lead a life that would horrify a Northern white woman.

16. In this two-chapter gap, she describes the catch-22 in which slaves generally are caught by explaining the misinformation they are given about the North and the ugly lives led by slaves in neighboring households, where men and women submit to both psychological and physical brutalities.

17. As Robert B. Stepto notes, this "snug cottage in the clearing" is a familiar trope in antislavery literature, and it is a "lure forsaken by Linda Brent"—a false hearth, as I would call it; see *From Behind the Veil: A Study of Afro-American Narrative*, 2d ed. (Urbana: University of Illinois Press, 1991), 103.

18. Valerie Smith adopts this figure to describe the dilemma posed by Mr. Sands; see "'Loopholes of Retreat': Architecture and Ideology in Harriet Jacobs's *Incidents in the Life of a Slave Girl*," in *Reading Black, Reading Feminist: A Critical Anthology*, ed. Henry Louis Gates Jr. (New York: Penguin, 1990), 215–16. Subsequent citations appear parenthetically in the text.

19. For discussion of the problematics of this sexual story, see Karen Sánchez-Eppler, "Righting Slavery and Writing Sex: The Erotics of Narration in Harriet Jacobs's *Incidents*," in *Touching Liberty: Abolition, Feminism, and the Politics of the Body* (Berkeley: University of California Press, 1993), 83–104; Garfield, "Speech," 19–49; and Mauri Skinfill, "Nation and Miscegenation: *Incidents in the Life of a Slave Girl*," *Arizona Quarterly* 52.2 (1995), 63–79.

20. For a description of silence as "an instrument for the assertion of her personal and sexual autonomy," see Joanne M. Braxton and Sharon Zuber, "Silences in Harriet 'Linda Brent' Jacobs's *Incidents in the Life of a Slave Girl*," in *Listening to Silences: New Essays in Feminist Criticism*, ed. Elaine Hedges and Shelley Fisher Fishkin (Oxford: Oxford University Press, 1994), 147. Compare Garfield's extensive discussion of "speech" and "listening."

21. On the "loophole," see especially Valerie Smith on its paradoxicality in this text, in "'Loopholes of Retreat'"; Burnham on its associations of surveillance, warfare, and legal escape and its allusions to William Cowper and to Child's novel *Hobomok* ("Loopholes of Resistance" 54, 56–60); and Deck, "Whose Book," 39.

22. It is a telling symbol of how ill that decision bodes for Brent that the first chapter in which she describes "The Flight" (chapter 17) begins with her being bitten by a snake in the backyard of the friend's house where she first hides. Before her escape, she had rescued her baby daughter asleep beside a snake under the Flint plantation house. Mirroring her daughter's plight in this way, her escape is no such thing.

23. Claudia Tate, "Allegories of Black Female Desire; or, Rereading Nineteenth-Century Sentimental Narratives of Black Female Authority," in *Changing Our Own Words: Essays on Criticism, Theory, and Writing by Black Women*, ed. Cheryl A. Wall (1989; New Brunswick, N.J.: Rutgers University Press, 1991), 109, 111.

24. See also my discussion of choice in relation to its "constitutive constraints" (in Judith Butler's terminology) in the Introduction.

25. Hortense Spillers argues that if Brent has an alter ego in this account, it is Mrs. Flint. "But," Spillers continues, "just as we duly regard similarities between life conditions of American women—captive and free—we must observe those undeniable contrasts and differences so decisive that the African-American female's historic claim to the territory of womanhood and 'femininity' still tends to rest too solidly on the subtle and shifting calibrations of a liberal ideology," in "Mama's Baby, Papa's Maybe: An American Grammar Book," *Diacritics* 17 (Summer 1987), 77.

26. See Mary Helen Washington's account of this scene as "the pivotal moment in the Brent text," when Brent "affirm[s] a self in a world equally determined to annihilate that self" (*Invented Lives* 10–11). For an analysis of the "commercial

set of negotiations represented" in this text, see Houston A. Baker Jr., *Blues, Ideology, and Afro-American Literature: A Vernacular Theory* (Chicago: Chicago University Press, 1984), 50–56.

27. See also Elizabeth C. Becker's argument for Carby against Andrews's emphasis on "women's community" in "Harriet Jacobs's Search for Home," *College Language Association Journal* 35.4 (1992), 419–21; Andrews, *To Tell a Free Story*, 253–54, 257, 260.

28. Hazel Carby, *Reconstructing Womanhood: The Emergence of the Afro-American Woman Novelist* (Oxford: Oxford University Press, 1987), 6, 51.

Chapter 3: Contradictory Legacies

1. As of MLA's fall 1999 listings, seven pre-1990 citations appear in the MLA bibliography, five of them in French; four more articles (all in English) have been indexed in the 1990s.

2. Sturgeon makes the same point amid her more widely cited remarks about what critics "reviled" in Field: "But in the meantime the critics learned that Michael Field was not a man, and work much finer than *Callirrhoë* passed unnoticed or was reviled; while on the other hand *Borgia*, published *anonymously*, was noticed and appreciated. One might guess at reasons for this, if it were worth while. Perhaps the poets neglected to attach themselves to a useful little log-rolling coterie, and to pay the proper attentions to the Press. Or it may be that something in the fact of a collaboration was obscurely repellent; or even that their true sex was not revealed with tact to sensitive sensibilities" (*Michael Field* 29). Subsequent citations appear parenthetically in the text.

3. The "female aesthete" was in itself a contradiction in terms and a role difficult to succeed in, as Linda K. Hughes shows in her discussion of Graham R. Tomson, in "A Fin-de-Siècle Beauty and the Beast: Configuring the Body in Works by 'Graham R. Tomson' (Rosamund Marriott Watson)," *Tulsa Studies in Women's Literature* 14.1 (1995), 95–121.

4. An excerpted version of Leighton's chapter has been reprinted in an anthology of *Victorian Women Poets*, ed. Tess Cosslett (New York: Longman, 1996), 237–57. See also Chris White's article "'Poets and Lovers Evermore,'" cited in the Introduction (note 41) and reprinted in *Sexual Sameness: Textual Differences in Lesbian and Gay Writing*, ed. Joseph Bristow (New York: Routledge, 1992), 26–43. White's more recent article, "The Tiresian Poet" (1996), works along some similar lines to my 1995 essay "Contradictory Legacies: Michael Field and Feminist Restoration," *Victorian Poetry* 33.1 (1995), 111–28. However, White's 1996 article focuses on contradictions of gender and sexuality, and it seeks to reconcile these contradictions where I do not. For Prins's articles, see "A Metaphorical Field: Katherine Bradley and Edith Cooper," *Victorian Poetry* 33.1 (1995), 129–48; and "Sappho Doubled: Michael Field," *The Yale Journal of Criticism* 8.1 (1995), 165–86. See also Donoghue's 1998 biography, *We Are Michael Field*, for critical and biographical sources (149–52). Subsequent citations of Leighton's unexcerpted chapter, White, and Prins appear parenthetically in the text.

5. As in the Introduction, I refer here primarily to the collaborative team that called itself the singular Michael Field (rather than to Bradley or Cooper as individuals), while also stressing Field's plurality, so I generally refer to Field as "they."

Donoghue's biography (which appeared several years after the earlier version of this chapter was published and after this larger study of collaboration was substantially completed) also notes Field's contradictoriness (9) but does so in passing and without examining its ramifications for readers.

6. For a summary of some defenses undertaken in the 1920s, see Leighton (*Writing against the Heart* 204).

7. Elaine Showalter, *A Literature of Their Own: British Women Novelists from Brontë to Lessing* (Princeton, N.J.: Princeton University Press, 1977), 19.

8. Field, *Works and Days*, xvi. Subsequent citations appear parenthetically in the text.

9. While reminding readers of Michael Field's precedent, Leonardi and Pope also write, "[They] called themselves 'Michael Field.' I'd prefer something more explicitly allied with women and women's work" ("Screaming Divas" 262).

10. In *Works and Days*, they refer to each other as a bird and a cat, with Bradley "Sig" (the bird) and Cooper "Puss."

11. For discussion of sexually allusive play in women's poetry, see Amelia Williams, "Venus' Hand: Laughter and the Language of Children's Culture in the Poetry of Christina Rossetti, Edith Sitwell, Edna St. Vincent Millay and Stevie Smith," Dissertation, University of Virginia, 1993.

12. Field entrusted their journals and letters to T. S. Moore to publish selectively fifteen years after their death; the original manuscripts are now available in the Bodleian and British Libraries.

13. Field, *Underneath the Bough*, 79. Subsequent citations appear parenthetically in the text.

14. Lillian Faderman, *Surpassing the Love of Men: Romantic Friendship and Love between Women from the Renaissance to the Present* (New York: William Morrow, 1981), 210.

15. Faderman, *Surpassing the Love of Men*, 211.

16. Donoghue negotiates this terrain more effectively (*We Are Michael Field* 27–32).

17. For White's more detailed 1996 argument, which includes attention also to the heterosexual and passionate Sapphic moments in *Long Ago*, see "The Tiresian Poet," 150–52, 155, 161.

18. Biographical information in the available printed sources is incomplete, not mentioning a date for Amy's birth. For example, *British Authors of the Nineteenth Century*, ed. Stanley J. Kunitz and Howard Haycraft (New York: H. W. Wilson, 1936), 222, notes that Edith was three at the time of the illness, but they also date Katherine's birth as 1848 rather than 1846, as it is recorded almost everywhere else. Though far more detailed than previous reference sources, Donoghue's short biography also omits the exact date of Amy's birth (*We Are Michael Field* 15).

19. Henri Locard found in the diaries evidence of "quite distinct personalities" and "unequal intellectual and literary gifts" that undercut their descriptions of themselves; he fastened on Cooper as the more brilliant of the two, with an "uncanny spiritual nature and poetic gifts," and he characterized their relationship harshly as "narcissistic mutual adulation" in "Works and Days: The Journals of 'Michael Field,'" *Journal of the Eighteen Nineties Society* 10 (1979), 1, 7. He thus joined a long tradition of critics who have sought not only to separate but to judge between partners in collaborations. Yet he notes accurately sources of tension and

difficulty between the two women that they were slow to admit themselves. See Donoghue, *We Are Michael Field,* for her important correction of this history for the Fields and for the most balanced characterizations of Cooper and Bradley to date.

20. See Prins's intriguing discussions of these intertextual exchanges in "A Metaphorical Field" and "Sappho Doubled."

21. Eve Kosofsky Sedgwick, *Epistemology of the Closet* (Berkeley: University of California Press, 1990), 10.

22. David J. Moriarty, "'Michael Field' (Edith Cooper and Katherine Bradley) and Their Male Critics," in *Nineteenth-Century Women Writers of the English-Speaking World,* ed. Rhoda B. Nathan (New York: Greenwood, 1986), 124. See also Donoghue's biography for her review of Field's entire career as playwrights.

23. Michael Field, *Canute the Great* and *The Cup of Water* (Westport, Conn.: George Bell & Sons, 1887), 97–98. Subsequent citations appear parenthetically in the text.

24. Diana Fuss, "Inside/Out," in *Inside/Out: Lesbian Theories, Gay Theories,* ed. Fuss (New York: Routledge, 1991), 7.

Chapter 4: Uncanny Couplings

1. Edith Somerville adopted the pseudonym Geilles Herring, the name of an ancestress, when her mother would not allow her to use her own name; this pseudonym was misread as "grilled herring" and used only for the first edition of *An Irish Cousin.* In the second edition, Somerville appeared under the name Viva Graham. She persuaded her mother to allow her own name for their second novel, *Naboth's Vineyard,* and all subsequent work (including the third, revised Longmans edition of *An Irish Cousin*) appeared under E. Œ. Somerville and Martin Ross. Violet Martin had begun using her pseudonym earlier, in articles published in *The World;* her name was taken from the family patriarch, dating back to 1590, Martin of Ross. See E. Œ. Somerville and Martin Ross, *Irish Memories* (1917; rpt. New York: Longman, 1918), 137; for Viva Graham, see Geraldine Cummins, *Dr. E. Œ. Somerville: A Biography* (London: Andrew Dakers Ltd., 1952), 16; for Martin of Ross, see Maurice Collis, *Somerville and Ross: A Biography* (London: Faber & Faber, 1968), 18. Subsequent citations of *Irish Memories* appear parenthetically in the text. I follow general convention in this chapter in referring to these authors as Somerville and Ross.

2. J.G. Paul Delaney describes "their fellowship [as] a match for [Ricketts's] with Shannon," in *Letters from Charles Ricketts to "Michael Field" (1903–1913),* ed. J. G. Paul Delaney (Edinburgh: Tragara Press, 1981), 7.

3. For a description of their formal and "elaborate" "manners," their working habits, and the dogs that gave their otherwise impeccably arranged household a "touch of the Zoo," see Editor's Preface, *Works and Days,* xix, xviii.

4. Gifford Lewis disputes previous biographers' representation of this first meeting as equally galvanic for Somerville and Ross (a representation that originated with Somerville in *Irish Memories*), saying that "On meeting Edith Somerville, Martin, for the first time, experienced a strong voluntary attachment to another person: as her letters will show, Martin had the greatest difficulty in getting Edith's attention," in *Somerville and Ross: The World of the Irish R. M.* (Harmondsworth, U.K.: Penguin, 1985), 47. But Lewis's arguments are defensively constructed to

combat Maurice Collis's influential psychological portrait of Somerville as homosexual (Collis was the first biographer authorized by Edith Somerville's nephews, Sir Nevill Coghill and Sir Patrick Coghill, to write a biography based on their aunt's papers).

5. Violet Powell, *The Irish Cousins: The Books and Background of Somerville and Ross* (London: Heinemann, 1970), 191; Cummins, *Dr. E. Œ. Somerville,* 104.

6. Hilary Robinson, *Somerville & Ross: A Critical Appreciation* (New York: St. Martin's, 1980), 19. Subsequent citations appear parenthetically in the text. Somerville visited Oscar Wilde in 1888 to interest him in drawings and articles "on studio life in Paris" (Somerville had gone to Paris to study art in 1884 and again in 1887). He was not helpful and created a bad impression on her, though also a comic one (Collis, *Somerville and Ross* 48–49). But these women were not unaware of their peers in London.

7. For a transcription of Ethel Smyth's letters to Somerville after the latter's apparent refusal of Smyth, see Collis, *Somerville and Ross,* 195–96. In one letter, Smyth writes, "Never would I have called you a prude or—good heavens—wished to pull you round to my point of view. It all came about because you were so often—or anyway sometimes—a little shocked at me" (196). For another transcription of these letters and Sir Nevill Coghill's account, see Lewis, *Somerville and Ross,* 205–7. Coghill writes, "My Aunt was a little shocked by Ethel, especially in the matter of her terrific romantic passions in the past" (206). Elizabeth Wood explains that the source of Coghill's account (which Lewis does not document) is a letter to Christopher St. John, Ethel Smyth's biographer; see *Ethel Smyth: A Biography* (London: Longmans, Green, 1959), 203, cited in Wood, "Ghost Shockers: A Parable of Lesbian Life," *Australian Feminist Studies* 20 (Summer 1994), 15–16.

8. The first biography of Edith Somerville, produced in 1952 by Geraldine Cummins, a companion of Edith's last twenty-two years (beginning in 1927), recalls Somerville's remarks against "sexual immorality" and uncovers no "romance in Edith's life" (although "I have searched diligently"; *Dr. E. Œ. Somerville* 104, 234). The next by Maurice Collis in 1968, focused on both Somerville and Ross, applies a dated sexological analysis to Somerville's homosexual "obsession" (*Somerville and Ross* 33) and Ross's need to "find an outlet for her genius" (37). Powell's literary biography, *The Irish Cousins,* describes Somerville and Ross's response to visiting the site of the Ladies of Llangollen as suggesting the Irish collaborators' unconsciousness of lesbianism, and her disapproving reference to the search for "evidence of perverse affections" presumably refers to the scrutiny initiated by Collis (46). For Lillian Faderman, who published *Surpassing the Love of Men* in the year (1981) after Robinson's critical appreciation and insistence on platonic "friendship," the concept of "romantic friendship" *allows* inclusion of Somerville and Ross as her first and foremost example of "Love and 'Women Who Live by Their Brains'" (the title of her chapter 5, which borrows a phrase directly from Somerville's *Irish Memories*). In 1985, however, Gifford Lewis published an elaborately illustrated trade press biography, many passages and an entire appendix of which are devoted to defending Somerville and Ross (especially Somerville) against the insinuations of homosexuality inaugurated by Collis: "That Edith was a lesbian has gained general acceptance through an unlovely combination of affected liberalism, ignorant salaciousness and the sad assumption that huge vital-

ity and strength in a woman implies masculinity" (*Somerville and Ross* 203). Lewis nonetheless presents extensive evidence of romantic friendship coupled with considerable physical intimacy: "Martin loved bed—she wrote there, thought there, and when at Ross, up in her attic bedroom, liked nothing better than to have the visiting Edith all to herself, in bed. . . . Both Hildegarde [Edith's sister] and Martin were cold in bed, and Edith was in some demand as a hot-water bottle" (201–2). Two recent articles analyze homophobia in biographies of Somerville and Ross: Shawn R. Mooney, "'Colliding Stars': Heterosexism in Biographical Representations of Somerville and Ross," *The Canadian Journal of Irish Studies* 18.1 (1992), 157–75; and Wood, "Ghost Shockers," 10.

9. On this see Seán McMahon, "John Bull's Other Ireland: A Consideration of *The Real Charlotte* by Somerville & Ross," *Eire-Ireland* 3 (Winter 1968), 119.

10. John Cronin notes this "nostalgia" in *Somerville and Ross* (Lewisburg, Pa.: Bucknell University Press, 1972), 45; and Wayne Hall notes the "regret for [a] lost way of life" in *Shadowy Heroes: Irish Literature of the 1890s* (Syracuse, N.Y.: Syracuse University Press, 1980), 64.

11. The *Irish R. M.* stories were so successful that for decades Somerville and Ross were known primarily as Irish humorists; they built upon this reputation by publishing sequels to these stories. But they are increasingly remembered as much for their novels as for their stories. Most critics cite Stephen Gwynn's opinion of *The Real Charlotte* as "the best novel ever written in Ireland," in preface to an evaluation of it as among the best, in Gwynn, "Lever's Successors," *Edinburgh Review* 478 (Oct. 1921), 351.

12. Powell is alone among Somerville and Ross's literary biographers in noticing even a slight connection: "Possibly in the fascination of their new-made relationship the title represented a reflection of themselves to the authors" (*The Irish Cousins* 22).

13. Somerville recalls the early influence of her aunt Louisa and Louisa's cousin, Willy Wills, who "had collaborated, in what, in the then current slang, was called 'a Shilling Shocker.'" However, she goes on to attribute the origin of their collaboration to Somerville and Ross's mothers, "who incited [them] to the first writing that [they] did together" (that is, a *Dictionary of the Family Language*), because "in those days Mothers had to be obeyed," in E. Œ. Somerville and Martin Ross, "Two of a Trade," *Irish Writing* 1 (1946), 81. John Cronin sees Theo as "a combination of Violet's and Edith's images of themselves—pretty, determined, a great rider to hounds, excited by the rigors of the chase" (*Somerville and Ross* 27).

14. There has been practically no extended discussion of this novel among Somerville and Ross's few critics. Powell records Somerville's understanding of the significance of *An Irish Cousin* when first published in this way: "Looking back, Edith Somerville considered that the success of *An Irish Cousin* was partly due to the lack of competitors in its particular field. . . . Since the appearance of *Castle Rackrent* eighty-eight years earlier there had been few, if any, novels about the Irish countryside and its people, written from the point of view of someone who, like Maria Edgeworth, had this as the background of their everyday life" (*The Irish Cousins* 28–29).

15. Concurring with Robinson, I disagree with John Cronin when he says, "All the horror and mystification are finally explained away rather easily" (*Somerville and Ross* 27).

16. E. Œ. Somerville and Martin Ross, *An Irish Cousin* (1889, 1903; New York: Longman, 1922), 29. Subsequent citations appear parenthetically in the text.

17. Early in the novel, Willy remarks, "Is it old Moll Hourihane? She's as old as two men—or looks it, anyhow" (28).

18. Powell writes, "Uncle Dominick seems to have had an affair with Moll Hourihane, so might he have been the father of Anstey who marries Willie? His drinking concealed, perhaps, a horror of incest as well as remorse for a possible murder" (*The Irish Cousins* 24). In the novel itself, a neighboring country woman hints heavily at Moll's involvement with Dominick, yet says that Anstey "favours" the Brians, "nice quiet people" (*An Irish Cousin* 213).

19. As discussed later, Somerville and Ross originally conceived of *An Irish Cousin* as a "shocker" (*Irish Memories* 128).

20. Powell, *The Irish Cousins*, 23.

21. For objections among the Anglo-Irish gentry to matches between cousins, see Lewis, *Somerville and Ross*, 36.

22. Her offer follows a moment when Theo "kissed his cheek" and thinks, "He was my only cousin, and I was never going to see him again—and then I tried to draw myself away from the grasp that was tightening round me, but it was too late" (288).

23. Biographers disagree about why love scenes or romances often lack credibility or are missing altogether from Somerville and Ross's novels, and their disagreement echoes their arguments about whether Somerville and Ross's relationship was homosexual and whether they see Somerville or Ross as the more important partner in the collaboration. Cummins attributes the lack of credible love scenes in Somerville's work to her Irish "reticence" about "sexual love": "When writing alone Edith was typical of her own little Irish world in skirting the love-affair as if it were a dangerous bog hole. But Martin was not shy of it and to some degree supplied this lack in her partner" (*Dr. E. Œ. Somerville* 234). This self-contradictory apologetic—after all, Martin is no less Irish than Edith and was reportedly far more reticent than Edith when it came to writing about love in *An Irish Cousin*—is typical of biographers' approach to these issues. Against Collis's subsequent, more extended argument for Ross's greater abilities as a writer and greater heterosexual tendencies, Lewis defends Somerville: "In writing *An Irish Cousin* [Martin] showed a positive dislike of passionate romantic passages that dwelt on physical love. It was Edith who, backed up by her mother's protestations, overrode Martin and put in 'most fiery love' (first edition, chapter 9), and it was Edith who wrote the intense proposal scene where Willy and Theo so distress each other, for it was she who had had experience of, and had the capacity for, passion" (*Somerville and Ross* 200).

24. For Dominick's articulation of a landlord's dominion over tenants as "the natural arrangement of things," against the progressive ideas of Nugent's sister Henrietta, see especially 102–3.

25. Virginia Beards, Introduction, *The Real Charlotte*, by E. Œ. Somerville and Martin Ross (New Brunswick, N.J.: Rutgers University Press, 1986), xiii–xiv. Subsequent citations of this Introduction and of the novel appear parenthetically in the text.

26. Somerville and Ross were referred to by their family and, more playfully,

referred to themselves as "Shockers" in "Two of a Trade" (80, 84) and *Irish Memories* (128).

27. Somerville and Ross thought of *An Irish Cousin* also as "The Shaughraun" (*Irish Memories* 128), which Powell notes is "synonymous with sentimental language and artificial situations" (*The Irish Cousins* 19).

28. John Cronin, *The Anglo-Irish Novel: Vol. 1: The Nineteenth Century* (Totowa, N.J.: Barnes & Noble, 1980), 139. Although most critics speak of this as an experience undergone together by Somerville and Ross, as Somerville herself writes about it here, Lewis and John Cronin cite a letter of 21 Aug. 1889 (soon after the book's publication) in which Ross says, "I seem to remember very much the first beginnings of the Shocker just now—when . . . you told me of the old maniacs face at the window over the Whitehall door," in Lewis, *Somerville and Ross,* 73, and John Cronin, "'An Ideal of Art': The Assertion of Realities in the Fiction of Somerville and Ross," *The Canadian Journal of Irish Studies* 11.1 (1985), 5. But Powell writes that "Martin, in an interview they both gave in 1896, had referred to this slightly blood-chilling episode as marking a change in their point of view when they were in the early stages of their novel" (*The Irish Cousins* 19). (Powell does not indicate her source for this interview.) Meanwhile, John Cronin notes that even if Ross did not share the experience Somerville describes, she had a similar one that directly informed *The Big House at Inver* ("'An Ideal of Art'" 5–6).

Cronin is the only critic I have discovered who has analyzed this passage from *Irish Memories* as a "carefully structured set-piece . . . a piece of fiction, or, at any rate, not entirely fact" (5). His article, which appeared in the year before Beards's edition of *The Real Charlotte,* analogizes an earlier moment in Somerville's narrative of this experience to Joyce's writing: Somerville's ability to capture a manner of speech is "as sharply attuned to linguistic nuance as James Joyce himself (one thinks of Stephen Dedalus's sensitivities in the celebrated passage concerning the funnel and the tundish in *A Portrait of the Artist as a Young Man*)" ("'An Ideal of Art'" 5). Critics often emphasize the parallels between Joyce's methods and vision and those of Somerville and Ross.

29. These now-classic analyses of *Jane Eyre* appear in Gilbert and Gubar's *The Madwoman in the Attic* (336–71) and Showalter's *A Literature of Their Own* (114–25).

30. Moll recovers her voice after Dominick's death, when she keens for him (303–4).

31. E. Œ. Somerville and Martin Ross, *Naboth's Vineyard* (London: Spencer Blackett, 1891).

32. For a different account of the strong women in Somerville and Ross's novels, see Anthony Cronin, "Edith Somerville and Martin Ross: Women Fighting Back," *Heritage Now: Irish Literature in the English Language* (Kerry, Ireland: Brandon, 1982), 75–86.

33. Few readers note the operation of chance and coincidence in this "causative" plot, but see Anthony Cronin, "Edith Somerville," 84.

34. Meanwhile, Francie offends her lover, Roderick Lambert, by reminding him of the gap of sixteen years between them, but although "Roddy" and Charlotte are contemporaries, he holds the conventional view that it is far more normal for a young woman to love an older man than for a man to love an older or a plain

woman. He has married an older woman for her money and seeks the sympathy of both Charlotte and Francie for having had to "throw[] himself . . . away" (29).

35. Ross's experiences in Dublin provided much of the background for Francie, and Somerville knew the woman (Emily Herbert) on whom Charlotte was based. I do not count myself among the many readers (especially early readers) who find Francie more sympathetic, if less intelligent, than her older cousin. See V. S. Pritchett, *The Living Novel* (London: Chatto & Windus, 1966), 151. At the same time, despite the centrality of their cousinship in this novel, I do not focus equally in this account on Charlotte and Francie because my concern is with the relations between this type of oppositional doubling (Charlotte and Francie constitute only one of several character doublings in this novel) and the problems of Charlotte's commanding agency and titular "reality" in this novel.

36. In her Introduction, Beards writes, somewhat contradictorily, that "in a society that places such high value on women's looks, it is no wonder that Francie and Charlotte suffer as they do. Their complementary careers bear out the accuracy of the proposition 'anatomy is destiny'" (xvi); Beards sees the novel as "consistently validat[ing] Freud's judgment" (xi).

37. See Anthony Cronin for an argument (against Conor Cruise O'Brien's view of Charlotte as "evil") that Somerville and Ross's "rational view of the world" led them to develop in Charlotte a worldly woman who, though not attractive, is "superior" to others in her "energy." Cronin further argues against O'Brien (and here I agree with Cronin) that "to believe that [the Dysarts] are superior to her in any mode of conduct or activity except those dependent on prior possession, is to convict oneself of snobbery" ("Edith Somerville" 79–80). See O'Brien, *Writers and Politics* (New York: Pantheon, 1955), 106–15. John Cronin argues that "The book develops into an effective exposé of the essential irrelevance of evil. Charlotte is a figure of Faustian stature who can do everything except what she most desires" (*Somerville and Ross* 41). "Evil" is not entirely irrelevant in this novel, I argue, but it is also not sheerly definitive of Charlotte or clearly deterministic of the plot.

38. McMahon is the only critic I have discovered who has noticed "the vein of gothic atmosphere" in *The Real Charlotte* and this novel's parallels with *An Irish Cousin*, particularly in the "gloom and decay of Gurthnamuckla" and Julia Duffy's "dispossession" ("John Bull's Other Ireland," 133–34).

39. Tally Ho is the name of a house owned by the Townshends where Martin and her mother moved in Jan. 1886, the year she first met Somerville. As John Cronin notes, it is also the house where Somerville died in 1949 (*The Anglo-Irish Novel* 138).

40. John Cronin also notes the way the novelists have "prepared" for Francie's fall (*The Anglo-Irish Novel* 151).

41. Sigmund Freud, "The 'Uncanny,'" *Collected Papers: Volume IV: Papers on Metapsychology; Papers on Applied Psychoanalysis*, trans. Joan Riviere (New York: Basic Books, 1959), 371–77. Subsequent citations appear parenthetically in the text.

42. Powell, *The Irish Cousins*, 64.

43. Two notable exceptions include Lewis, who devotes chapter 10 of *Somerville and Ross* to a respectful description of Somerville and Ross's interest in and experiences with the "super-normal," and Wood, who concludes her article on

biographical censorship of Somerville and Ross's letters with an anecdote about an uncanny moment in Wood's personal tour of Drishane ("Ghost Shockers" 22).

44. For detailed descriptions of this postmortem collaboration, see Collis, *Somerville and Ross*, 177–84; Lewis, *Somerville and Ross*, 192–93.

45. For accounts of the ways Somerville and Ross collaborated with each other, see "Two of a Trade," 79–85; *Irish Memories*, 124–34. As with Field, biographers and critics have made efforts to separate their hands, based in part on Somerville's account of their complementary aptitudes ("Two of a Trade" 85). Yet readers generally acknowledge most of their work as an inseparable "mystery"; see Collis, *Somerville and Ross*, 64–65; John Cronin, *Somerville and Ross*, 21–23; Robinson, *Somerville & Ross*, 38–48; and Lewis, *Somerville and Ross*, 73–74, 108.

46. Cummins, *Dr. E. Œ. Somerville*, 104. As Wood notes, Cummins does not mention the fact that Cummins's own "psychic powers and pursuits" inaugurated her friendship with Somerville ("Ghost Shockers" 17).

Chapter 5: Rewriting the Uncanny

1. On Symonds, Ellis, and sexology, see Koestenbaum, *Double Talk*, 43–44. Koestenbaum's interest in the roots of psychoanalysis, and thus also in Symonds, is in its gay acculturation, whereas mine is in the ways psychoanalysis has been challenged by feminist interrogation of its roots and models. Koestenbaum nonetheless contributes important insights into a feminist critique of Freudian psychoanalysis.

2. Koestenbaum, *Double Talk*, 17–18, 21–22, 25–32, 34–35.

3. For recent critical appropriations of the uncanny, see Terry Castle, *The Female Thermometer: Eighteenth-Century Culture and the Invention of the Uncanny* (Oxford: Oxford University Press, 1995); Sarah Webster Goodwin, "Domesticity and Uncanny Kitsch in 'The Rime of the Ancient Mariner' and *Frankenstein*," *Tulsa Studies in Women's Literature* 10.1 (1991), 93–108; Mieke Bal, "Murder and Difference: Uncanny Sites in an Uncanny World," *Journal of Literature and Theology* 5.1 (1991), 11–19; Marjorie Garber, *Shakespeare's Ghost Writers: Literature as Uncanny Causality* (London: Methuen, 1987); and Lars Engle, "The Political Uncanny: The Novels of Nadine Gordimer," *The Yale Journal of Criticism* 2.2 (1989), 101–27.

4. Since 1974 *Tribute to Freud* has consisted of not one text but two: "Writing on the Wall" and "Advent." "Advent" (w. 1948) was published by Norman Holmes Pearson in conjunction with "Writing on the Wall," after H.D.'s 1961 death, so that they now appear together as separate titles with their original titles under the joint title *Tribute to Freud*. My discussion focuses on the memoir "Writing on the Wall" (w. 1944), published by H.D. in serial form in 1945–46, then republished in book form as *Tribute to Freud* (1956). H.D. described "Advent" as a postwar "continuation . . . or . . . prelude" to "Writing on the Wall" that she "assembled" in 1948 from the original notebooks in which she recorded her first impressions of analysis with Freud. (Some critics mistakenly refer to "Advent" as the original journal in which she took notes on her sessions.) See H.D., *Tribute to Freud* (1974; rpt. New York: New Directions, 1984), xiv. Subsequent citations of *Tribute to Freud* refer to this edition and appear parenthetically in the

text. H.D. had two sets of sessions with Freud, which took place from 1 March to 12 June 1933 and from 31 Oct. to 2 Dec. 1934.

5. Susan Stanford Friedman, "Against Discipleship: Collaboration and Intimacy in the Relationship of H.D. and Freud," *Literature and Psychology* 33.3–4 (1987), 91, 98, 103. Friedman first suggested this idea when she described H.D.'s therapy with Freud as a "collaboration" in *Psyche Reborn: The Emergence of H.D.* (1981; Bloomington: Indiana University Press, 1987), 12.

6. Norman N. Holland, "H.D. and the 'Blameless Physician,'" *Contemporary Literature* 10.4 (1969), 474–506; Holland's article was subsequently revised and expanded to form the first chapter of *Poems in Persons: An Introduction to the Psychoanalysis of Literature* (New York: Norton, 1973), 5–59; Joseph N. Riddel, "H.D. and the Poetics of 'Spiritual Realism,'" *Contemporary Literature* 10.4 (1969), 447–73; Susan Stanford Friedman, "Who Buried H.D.? A Poet, Her Critics, and Her Place in 'The Literary Tradition,'" *College English* 36.7 (1975), 804–7. Riddel comments briefly on this exchange in "H.D.'s Scene of Writing—Poetry as (and) Analysis" (1979), in *American Critics at Work: Examinations of Contemporary Literary Theories*, ed. Victor A. Kramer (Troy, N.Y.: Whitson, 1984), 151.

7. Claire Buck, *H.D. and Freud: Bisexuality and a Feminine Discourse* (New York: St. Martin's, 1991), 98. In addition to Buck, Holland, and Riddel, critics who place Freud and psychoanalysis at the center of their discussions of H.D. include Susan Stanford Friedman, *Psyche Reborn*; Janice S. Robinson, *H.D.: The Life and Work of an American Poet* (Boston: Houghton Mifflin, 1982); Marilyn B. Arthur, "Psychomythology: The Case of H.D.," *Bucknell Review* 28.2 (1983), 65–79; Peggy A. Knapp, "Women's Freud(e): H.D.'s *Tribute to Freud* and Gladys Schmitt's *Sonnets for an Analyst*," *Massachusetts Review* 24.2 (1983), 338–52; Elizabeth A. Hirsh, "Imaginary Images: 'H.D.,' Modernism, and the Psychoanalysis of Seeing" (1989), in *Signets: Reading H.D.*, ed. Friedman and Rachel Blau DuPlessis (Madison: University of Wisconsin Press, 1990), 430–51; Deborah Kelly Kloepfer, *The Unspeakable Mother: Forbidden Discourse in Jean Rhys and H.D.* (Ithaca, N.Y.: Cornell University Press, 1989); Dianne Chisholm, *H.D.'s Freudian Poetics: Psychoanalysis in Translation* (Ithaca, N.Y.: Cornell University Press, 1992); and Katherine Arens, "H.D.'s Post-Freudian Cultural Analysis: Nike versus Oedipus," *American Imago* 52.4 (1995), 359–404.

8. Rachel Blau DuPlessis coauthored with Friedman a groundbreaking article whose thesis is the modification of Freud's views of women by H.D., in "'Woman Is Perfect': H.D.'s Debate with Freud," *Feminist Studies* 7.3 (1981), 417–29. Following their lead are Nora Crow Jaffe, "'She Herself Is the Writing': Language and Sexual Identity in H.D.," in *Literature and Medicine* 4 (1985), 99–106; Knapp, "Women's Freud(e)," 340–49; and Robinson, *H.D.: The Life and Work*, 296–97 and passim. Friedman also develops these arguments in *Psyche Reborn*, passim, as does DuPlessis in *H.D.: The Career of That Struggle* (Bloomington: Indiana University Press, 1986), 74–75 and passim.

9. Other critics who have adopted this term include Chisholm, who describes Freud and H.D. as "collaborative readers" (*H.D.'s Freudian Poetics* 10 and passim); Knapp, "Women's Freud(e)," 338; and Jaffe, who sees this as an "unconscious collaboration" ("'She Herself'" 107).

10. Riddel, "H.D.'s Scene of Writing," 147.

11. In a famous passage of *Tribute to Freud*, H.D. records Freud as beating his

fist on the headpiece of her sofa and exclaiming, "The trouble is—I am an old man—*you do not think it worth your while to love me*" (15–16).

12. Friedman, *Psyche Reborn*, 12–13, 70–74, 157–60, 175, 193–95, and passim; Adalaide Morris, "The Concept of Projection: H.D.'s Visionary Powers" (1984), in *Signets*, 273–96.

13. Chisholm and Riddel are the only critics to have applied the "uncanny" to *Tribute to Freud*, although Riddel treats the uncanny briefly and exclusively in keeping with Freud's use of the term ("H.D.'s Scene of Writing" 148–49). For a revisionary theory (very different from mine) of a "feminist uncanny" that occurs through "masochistic jouissance," see Chisholm, *H.D.'s Freudian Poetics*, 109–10, 145–59.

14. This observation about the affiliation between H.D.'s thought and Jung's is common in criticism of H.D. See Barbara Guest, *Herself Defined: The Poet H.D. and Her World* (New York: Doubleday, 1984), 328; Friedman, *Psyche Reborn*, 191–92; Norman Holmes Pearson, Foreword, *Hermetic Definition* by H.D. (1958; rpt. New York: New Directions, 1972), vi.

15. Robinson sees H.D. as especially anxious about "crossing the line" with father figures (*H.D.: The Life and Work* 292, 296); following DuPlessis (*H.D.: The Career* 114), Kloepfer focuses on H.D.'s anxiety about incestuous relations with the maternal (*The Unspeakable Mother* 19).

16. From the earliest reviewers, numerous critics have seen the relationship between Freud and H.D. as a relation of opposites. Where I differ from such accounts is in seeing H.D. as interesting herself as much in identities as in differences, affirming both sides even of antinomial constructs. Thus, she slides directly from affirming the fact that "there were two's and two's and two's in my life . . . two actual brothers . . . two half-brothers . . . two tiny graves of the two sisters" (a passage occasionally misremembered by critics as expressing dualism when it refers to twinnings or identities) to affirming the fact that there were also dualities, "then in later life, there were two countries . . . separated by a wide gap in consciousness . . . two distinct racial or biological or psychological entities." "Two" thus becomes a conceptual pun. These "distinct . . . entities," in their turn, slide together to become almost, but never quite, one and the same: "two distinct racial or biological or psychological entities [that] tend to grow nearer or to blend, even, as time heals old breaks in consciousness" (31–32).

17. It is not clear from the text what terms H.D. believes Freud actually used. The only words she sets in quotations are "dangerous," "symptom," and "symptom of importance" (41, 173). Moreover, she uses the word "dangerous" several times, so that in the single instance where she drops it into quotations, it could be herself whom she cites or a quotation for emphasis.

18. Critics often treat this incident as if it had not occurred (even while reporting it in their description of the vision), so that the writing on the wall is analyzed as if entirely "seen" by H.D. Even Morris says little about Bryher's participation.

19. H.D. perceived the writing on the wall as shadows of light: "shadow- or . . . light-pictures" (41), "dim light on shadow, not shadow on light," "'a shadow thrown' . . . this shadow was, 'light'" (45). The phenomenon was inexplicable because it occurred too late in the day for shadows to be thrown by the sun outside.

20. H.D. alludes at several points in "Writing on the Wall" and "Advent" to the "severe shocks" (40) she experienced particularly in the period from 1914 to 1920; these experiences have been much discussed and documented by H.D.'s biographers and critics. Most critics see her analysis with Freud as a crucial threshold for her writing, breaking her writer's block; see Friedman, *Psyche Reborn*, 9; Guest, *Herself Defined*, 218; DuPlessis and Friedman, "'Woman Is Perfect,'" 425; DuPlessis, *H.D.: The Career*, 71–73. In addition, several critics see her analysis as enabling her to sort through and accept her sexual identity; see especially Jaffe, "'She Herself.'"

21. However, Friedman reports that Freud offered to give one of his chow's pups to H.D.'s daughter Perdita (Pup was also Perdita's nickname), and amid H.D.'s anxiety about some of the "dying pups" and Bryher's refusal to accept a dog, H.D.'s "dreams and distress began to link the pups with her own childbirths, associations she brought to Freud. 'Evidently I was afraid of becoming pregnant by papa Freud; funny?????'" ("Against Discipleship" 102). See "Against Discipleship" for discussion of Freud's attitude toward "leaks" in analysis (97).

22. In 1927 Bryher married H.D.'s lover Kenneth Macpherson, by whom in 1928 H.D. conceived and aborted a child; Macpherson had been and became again more interested in men. In 1928 the Macphersons adopted Perdita, and Perdita and the three adults all lived together as a family. For Freud's interest in gossiping with H.D., see Guest, *Herself Defined*, 213; Friedman, "Against Discipleship," 99–100.

23. Friedman, "Against Discipleship," 102–3; Robinson, *H.D.: The Life and Work*, 403.

24. See especially DuPlessis and Friedman, "'Woman Is Perfect'"; DuPlessis, *H.D.: The Career*, passim; Arens, "H.D.'s Post-Freudian Cultural Analysis"; Jaffe, "'She Herself'"; Knapp, "Women's Freud(e)"; and Robinson, *H.D.: The Life and Work*, passim.

25. H.D., *Collected Poems 1912–1944*, ed. Louis L. Martz (New York: New Directions, 1983), 455, 456.

26. Although critics tend to stress the divergence of Freud and H.D.'s views on gender, theirs is also an argument about sexuality (see H.D.'s note in "Advent" about his disagreement with her over the happiness she might have had with her first woman lover, Frances Josepha, in *Tribute to Freud*, 152); as Jaffe shows, H.D. experienced this argument ultimately as collaborative.

27. These occult experiences include hallucinations of a Mr. Van Eck on a ship to Greece and the sensation of being in a "bell-jar" as well as the writing on the wall, but—although she does not understand why—the only experience Freud saw as "dangerous" was that of the writing on the wall, and she too focuses on this in *Tribute to Freud* (39–41).

28. H.D., *Collected Poems*, 460.

29. See also Jaffe's discussion of H.D.'s discovery, through her argument with Freud, of her "perfect" bisexuality ("'She Herself'" 99–100).

30. L. S. Dembo, "Norman Holmes Pearson on H.D.: An Interview," *Contemporary Literature* 10.4 (1969), 443; Friedman, *Psyche Reborn*, 154; Jaffe, "'She Herself,'" 96.

31. But, as DuPlessis and Friedman (among others) point out, "H.D.'s personal defiance of Nazi anti-Semitism is vividly evident in *Tribute to Freud* (p. 61) in her description of her visit to Freud's house . . . when, among other things, Nazis

had chalked swastikas on the walk leading to Freud's door" ("'Woman Is Perfect'" 429n.17).

32. For a brief discussion of the shaman as the kind of artist H.D. wanted to be, see Susan Gubar, "The Echoing Spell of H.D.'s *Trilogy*" (1978), *Signets*, 317n.23.

33. Holland first diagnosed her vision as a form of "megalomania" ("H.D. and the 'Blameless Physician'" 503), but the text itself suggests that H.D., not Freud, considered this possibility without embracing it: "Megalomania they call it—a hidden desire to 'found a new religion' which the Professor ferreted out in the later Moses picture" (51). Unfortunately, others occasionally have followed Holland's observation in attributing this directly to Freud. Kloepfer and Chisholm offer interesting psychological explanations of this experience as, respectively, "bicameral" (*The Unspeakable Mother* 113) and "the optical illusion of 'eidetic vision'" (*H.D.'s Freudian Poetics* 32). Critics who see the visions primarily as poetry also often attribute this explanation, at least in part, to Freud, although again H.D. never quotes him directly describing the writing on the wall as a form of poetry. The phrase "metaphors for poetry" is used by Denis Donoghue in his review of *H.D.: The Life and Work of an American Poet* by Janice S. Robinson, *New York Times Book Review*, 14 Feb. 1982, 3. DuPlessis and Friedman see H.D. as benefiting from Freud's observation in "The Master" that "you are a poet," and they see the writing on the wall as "inspiration" (*Tribute to Freud* 47) for poetry ("'Woman Is Perfect'" 426–27); the "word 'prophesy' appears repeatedly throughout ["The Master"] as a synonym for 'writing'" ("'Woman Is Perfect'" 425). Kloepfer describes H.D.'s vision on Corfu as a "murex," such that "vision, verses, identity merge into one so that 'she herself is the writing'" (*The Unspeakable Mother* 116).

34. Morris, "The Concept of Projection," 274.

35. Friedman, *Psyche Reborn*, 203, 204–5, 275.

36. See Friedman, "Against Discipleship," 101; DuPlessis, *H.D.: The Career*, 84–85; Buck, *H.D. and Freud*, 114, 121, 127.

37. These terms appear, respectively, in a review of *Tribute to Freud* by "C. G."; in "Brief Mention," *American Literature* 29 (March 1959), 112; and in Riddel, "H.D.'s Scene of Writing," 152.

38. H.D., *Collected Poems*, 456, 460.

39. H.D.'s writing is densely "palimpsestic" (Kloepfer, *The Unspeakable Mother*, passim) not only in its "intertextuality" (Chisholm, *H.D.'s Freudian Poetics*, passim) but in its layering of relationships on which H.D. relied for survival, so that while Bryher and Freud double as spiritual midwives for H.D.'s vision and the Princess doubles for Bryher as financial midwife for the survival of Freud's science, Freud in his turn doubles for Eric Heydt (and vice versa), with whom H.D. was again in analysis. H.D. wrote *Tribute to Freud* (and a second analysis-oriented memoir as well, *end to torment*) under Heydt's care and stimulus.

40. Guest, *Herself Defined*, 215.

41. Guest, *Herself Defined*, 212; Arens, "H.D.'s Post-Freudian Cultural Analysis," 360. But see Morris's discussion of H.D.'s "gift economy" in "A Relay of Power and of Peace: H.D. and the Spirit of the Gift" (1986), in *Signets*, 52 and passim.

42. Arens, "H.D.'s Post-Freudian Cultural Analysis," 359.

43. H.D., Letter to Bryher, 22 Nov. 1934, qtd. in Friedman, "Against Discipleship," 101.

44. Arens, "H.D.'s Post-Freudian Cultural Analysis," 359–60.

45. These authors' names appear in their texts sometimes as Penelope Shuttle and Peter Redgrove, at other times as Peter Redgrove and Penelope Shuttle, so I follow their practice.

46. Penelope Shuttle and Peter Redgrove, *The Wise Wound: Menstruation and Everywoman* (London: Gollancz, 1978), 254. Subsequent citations appear parenthetically in the text. With slightly variant titles (including *The Wise Wound: Eve's Curse and Everywoman* and *The Wise Wound: Myths, Realities, and Meanings of Menstruation*), the book has been reprinted at least four times since 1978, most recently as *The Wise Wound: Menstruation and Everywoman* (London: Marion Boyars, 1999).

47. For two 1990s discussions of menstruation that parallel Redgrove and Shuttle's arguments, see Judy Grahn, *Blood, Bread, and Roses: How Menstruation Created the World* (Boston: Beacon, 1993); and Ana Castillo, "La Macha: Toward a Beautiful Whole Self," in *Chicana Lesbians: The Girls Our Mothers Warned Us About*, ed. Carla Trujillo (Berkeley, Calif.: Third Woman Press, 1991), 26–35.

48. For Redgrove's equivocal relation to postmodernism, see Neil Roberts, *The Lover, the Dreamer, and the World: The Poetry of Peter Redgrove* (Sheffield, U.K.: Sheffield Academic Press, 1994), 16. See also Roberts, "Peter Redgrove: The Science of the Subjective," *Poetry Review* 77.3 (1987), 4.

49. Penelope Shuttle and Peter Redgrove, "The Dialogue of Gender," in *On Gender and Writing*, ed. Michelene Wandor (London: Pandora, 1983), 145. Subsequent citations appear parenthetically in the text. *The Hermaphrodite Album* (London: Fuller d'Arch Smith, 1973) is a cosigned book of poems by Redgrove and Shuttle.

50. Shuttle and Redgrove recently published a sequel to *The Wise Wound, Alchemy for Women: Personal Transformation through Dreams and the Female Cycle* (London: Rider, 1995), a practical guide to menstrual dreaming and other techniques to reconnect with one's inner cycles. For a review that struggles to find the right patronizing categorization, settling uneasily on "New Age," see Roy Porter, "Bleeding Liberty," *TLS*, 30 June 1995, 9.

51. Peter Redgrove and Penelope Shuttle, *The Terrors of Dr Treviles* (London: Routledge & Kegan Paul, 1974), 24. Subsequent citations appear parenthetically in the text.

52. For a contemporary discussion of various literary erotic threesomes, which has increased visibility (and perhaps acceptability) of the *ménage à trois*, see Garber, *Vice Versa*, especially 423–524.

53. It should be noted here that Redgrove and Shuttle nonetheless observe a line between sanity and insanity: "We hasten to say that there are conditions that are considered unprofitable mere madness, even in cultures that recognise shamanism" (*The Wise Wound* 247).

54. Especially useful discussions of African-American cultures in relation to postmodernism may be found in Cornel West's "Black Culture and Postmodernism," in *Remaking History*, ed. Barbara Kruger and Phil Mariani (Seattle: Bay Press, 1989), 87–96; and in bell hooks's *Yearning: Race, Gender, and Cultural Politics* (Boston: South End Press, 1990), 23–31.

55. Erika Duncan, "Peter Redgrove and Penelope Shuttle: The Joys and Perils

of Collaboration," *Book Forum* 7.4 (1986), 22. Subsequent citations appear parenthetically in the text.

56. Peter Redgrove, "Peter Redgrove," in *We Two: Couples Talk about Living, Loving and Working Partnerships for the '90s,* ed. Roger Housden and Chloe Goodchild (New York: HarperCollins, 1992), 135. Subsequent citations appear parenthetically in the text.

57. Duncan erroneously speaks of the age difference between Redgrove and Shuttle as 25 years (18).

58. In his 1992 essay, Redgrove returns to this vocabulary of stealing when he says, "It is best to say that we live a 'poetic' life together and as we are freelance writers this also means hard graft, as the first thing that suffers in a recession is trifles like authorship. I say this in response to your [the editor's] query about whether the individual sense of purpose or destiny conflicts with our relationship. All our writing is so closely shared and formed between us that there is not (so far in 20 years and some 30 books written together) this conflict" (*We Two* 139). It is like Redgrove (and Shuttle), however, to face directly an assumption embedded in single authorship and in copyright law: that to "borrow" someone else's words is to "steal." By borrowing the terminology that would indict them, Redgrove redefines and revalues it in the context of their very different authorial practices.

59. Shuttle sees Redgrove's subsequent work *The Black Goddess* as "a man's menstrual vision" (*We Two* 125).

60. Theirs was not the first study to appear, although they see *The Wise Wound* as the first to focus on "the inward experience and significance" of menstruation (note on p. 15). For prior studies, see Katharina Dalton, *The Menstrual Cycle* (Harmondsworth, U.K.: Penguin, 1969); Paula Weideger, *Menstruation and Menopause: The Physiology and Psychology, the Myth and the Reality* (New York: Knopf, 1975); Janice Delaney, Mary Jane Lupton, and Emily Toth, *The Curse* (1976; Urbana: University of Illinois Press, 1988).

61. Homans, *Bearing the Word,* 1–29.

62. Whereas the interview with Duncan is presented as a first-person observer's account, interspersed with quotations of Redgrove and Shuttle, Wandor (herself a successful British writer and feminist) sent her contributors to *On Gender and Writing* a set of questions and left it to the authors to respond in whatever form they wished. Redgrove and Shuttle replied in the form of an interview, with "Michelene" posing the questions, and "Penelope and Peter" answering them with "one" voice, never separating themselves in the course of the interview. Though conversational and animated in tone, their responses are carefully composed. This piece thus seems closer to the views propounded in *The Wise Wound* than does Duncan's and, though less problematic in the views it expresses, is both more complex and more compelling to a feminist audience.

63. Their roles split when their child, Zoe, was born and, primarily for economic reasons, Redgrove had to take up the role of the breadwinner while the parenting fell more entirely to Shuttle. Yet as a result of the disappointments of his first marriage, Redgrove worked harder and more successfully to resist the effects of this distribution of tasks and, when Zoe was old enough to require less time, Shuttle and Redgrove were able to return to the more fluid relations they had enjoyed previously (which they enjoy much more). See Wandor, "The Dialogue of Gender," 145.

64. See *The Wise Wound*, chapter 2.

65. Redgrove and Shuttle appear far less interested in the literal experiences of penile erection and ejaculation than in female sexual process, in part because Redgrove feels that he has experienced greater intensities and breadths of sexual experience through stretching and bending himself to stay with Shuttle's rhythms, in part because they both feel penile experience has been overstressed, inscribed in our language and literature, and so determines much of what is said and written whether an author wishes it or not. Redgrove and Shuttle do address the issue Freud raised of women's "lack," responding to this as various other feminists have done by valuing everything women do have; if anyone "lacks" something, in their argument, it is men rather than women because men lack the complex sexual capacities of women. In addition, they see women as included in, rather than utterly excluded from, men's penile experience in much the same way that they see men as able to participate in women's experiences; for example, in intercourse "sex-difference [is] important, clearly, as Peter has the penis and Penelope the vagina. However, as all lovers who become practised know, it is sometimes difficult to remember who has the penis and who is being penetrated during the excitements of the act" (Wandor 143). See *The Wise Wound*, 68–70, 92, and passim, for Redgrove and Shuttle's critique and revisions of Freud.

66. For a discussion of the ways Freud and Wilhelm Fliess's collaboration dovetailed with their mutual interest in male menstruation, nasal surgery, and anal bleeding, see Koestenbaum, *Double Talk*, 35–41. See also *The Wise Wound*: "'Vicarious menstruation' by bleeding from the nose or elsewhere is not all that uncommon in men" (76).

67. Marriage itself, as they both hasten to explain in their separate 1992 essays, was dictated by economic factors. Three years after their daughter was born, they realized that none of them—not Redgrove, Shuttle, or Zoe—would be permitted any rights to each other's literary (as Shuttle points out) and material (as Redgrove explains) estate if one of the parents died, so they felt compelled to become part of the socioeconomic system of marriage, which is also in this case a literary and sexual property system.

68. Later, Brid Hare asks an old cobbler (a nationalist who has studied Cornish) what *Treviles* means, and he says "it means 'the house on the old cliff'" (137).

69. Brid Hare's surname is especially resonant in relation to Redgrove and Shuttle's sources and arguments. It echoes Layard's *The Lady of the Hare*, which, as they explain in *The Wise Wound*, "turns upon recognition of a dream-hare as 'willing sacrifice,' and a young girl apparently recovers from mental retardation"; a "young woman becomes a 'superwoman' compared to her former self, through dream analysis of her *mother*. The crux is an acceptance of the 'willing sacrifice' of the moon-animal by the mother" (112, 270; italics theirs). In addition, one of the "moon creatures" or "moon-familiars" is the hare (140): It is "a frequent witch-animal in folklore," it is another word "for the period," and it is associated both with erotic ecstasy and fertility (226). Brid Hare further reverses and transforms age-old stories of the "old witch of whom the young one is jealous, until she has acquired the magic power, the sexuality, to overcome her. The jealousy is harmlessly earthed, the contest is accomplished in the story, everyone laughs, and a relationship with one's real mother is preserved" (237). See John Layard, *The Lady*

of the Hare: Being a Study in the Healing Power of Dreams (London: Faber & Faber, 1944).

70. For extensive discussion of the concept and phenomenon of the "other husband," see *The Wise Wound*, 64, 101–3, 127, 129, 146–47, 226–27, 270.

71. Redgrove and Shuttle also note the importance of "psychodramas" and "active imagination" for the enaction and articulation of menstrual experiences for both men and women, in *The Wise Wound*, 63, 173.

72. Note, in particular, the crossing of womb imagery with male figuration: "If you look at well-drawn anatomical pictures of the womb, you will be able to see in it the appearance of a wise goat-head bent forward, with magnificent sweeping horns, which are the Fallopian tubes" (*The Wise Wound* 225).

73. Similarly, the imagery of both Satan's and the stag's "branching" horns, which appear at many points in this narrative, is glossed in *The Wise Wound* as displaced, masculinized figures (bullish, double phalloi) for what in earlier cultures was a divine imagery of fallopian tubes; in this novel, the imagery becomes cross-gendered (126, 214, 223, 225).

74. Bodkin's name is a standing joke in the novel.

75. See *The Wise Wound* for description of the important experience of the "afterglow" as "holy" for both men and women (234).

76. Thus they write, "It is only in exceptional circumstances that a man has to go so far as to *become* a woman" in order to develop female capacities of thought and feeling; "We are certainly not recommending 'the operation'!" (134). The lack of close attention to transsexualism is notable in a project that presents itself as a comprehensive paradigm shift in sexual relations. For a challenging argument for attention to transsexualism and transgenderedness, see Susan Stryker, "My Words to Victor Frankenstein above the Village of Chamounix: Performing Transgender Rage," *GLQ* 1.3 (1994), 237–54.

Chapter 6: Rewriting Writing

1. Bella Brodzki, Celeste Schenck, and (following these critics) Leigh Gilmore point out that, given Stein's "anticipation of and affiliation with poststructuralism," it is surprising to see her so rarely discussed in "contemporary studies of autobiography written by men"; they "question how male critics, lured by the postmodernist possibilities of autobiography, could have missed a star source such as Stein," in Gilmore, "A Signature of Lesbian Autobiography: 'Gertrice/Altrude,'" in *Autobiography and Questions of Gender*, ed. Shirley Neuman (London: Frank Cass, 1991), 61; she paraphrases Brodzki and Schenck's Introduction, *Life/Lines: Theorizing Women's Autobiography*, ed. Brodzki and Schenck (Ithaca, N.Y.: Cornell University Press, 1988), 10–11. Marianne DeKoven argues that Stein went even further than modernist, postmodern, and avant-garde writers have done in "violat[ing] and reshap[ing] not just the conventions of literature . . . but, in addition, the conventions of language itself," although she sees this latter "experimental" writing as postdating *The Autobiography of Alice B. Toklas*, in *A Different Language: Gertrude Stein's Experimental Writing* (Madison: University of Wisconsin Press, 1983), xiii. Lisa Ruddick also does not analyze *The Autobiography of Alice B. Toklas*, but she takes a "poststructuralist" view of Stein's work gen-

erally as "polysemous," in *Reading Gertrude Stein: Body, Gnosis, Text* (Ithaca, N.Y.: Cornell University Press, 1990), 7–8, 11.

2. Gillian Hanscombe and Virginia L. Smyers, *Writing for Their Lives: The Modernist Women 1910–1940* (London: Women's Press, 1987), xiv, xvii. Hanscombe also coauthored a book of poems with Namjoshi, *Flesh and Paper.*

3. Hélène Cixous and Catherine Clément, *The Newly Born Woman,* trans. Betsy Wing (Minneapolis: University of Minnesota Press, 1986); Monique Wittig and Sande Zeig, *Lesbian Peoples: Materials for a Dictionary* (London: Virago, 1980); Maitland and Wandor, *Arky Types.*

4. There is still interest in the 1990s in exploring what is odd in this coupling, as evidenced by Diane Elam's *Feminism and Deconstruction: Ms. en Abyme* (New York: Routledge, 1994).

5. See D. A. Miller's "Secret Subjects, Open Secrets," chapter 6 of *The Novel and the Police* (Berkeley: University of California Press, 1988), 192–220. Coincidentally, Timothy Dow Adams uses the phrase "the open secret" in reference to Stein and Toklas in *Telling Lies in Modern American Autobiography* (Chapel Hill: University of North Carolina Press, 1990), 25.

6. James Joyce, *Ulysses* (New York: Vintage, 1961), 256.

7. *The Autobiography of Alice B. Toklas* (New York: Harcourt, Brace, 1933); Gertrude Stein, *The Autobiography of Alice B. Toklas* (1961; rpt. New York: Random House–Vintage Books, 1990). Subsequent citations of this text refer to the Random House Vintage Books edition and appear parenthetically in the text. As Gilmore points out, the name Gertrude Stein dwarfs the title of the book in the 1961 Vintage edition both on its cover and on its title page, thus obliterating the effect of the first edition ("A Signature of Lesbian Autobiography" 66). See also James E. Breslin, "Gertrude Stein and the Problems of Autobiography," in *Women's Autobiography: Essays in Criticism,* ed. Estelle C. Jelinek (Bloomington: Indiana University Press, 1980), 152.

8. Adams, *Telling Lies,* 31–32, and Sidonie Smith emphasize that the text offers "hints" of Stein's authorship throughout; see Smith's *Subjectivity, Identity, and the Body,* 66.

9. This is the title of a brief memoir by George Wickes in which he reports Toklas's claim that she authored the autobiography, in *Lost Generation Journal* 2.1 (1974), 38, 37 (this article is continued on 37 from the back cover, 38).

10. For the argument for Toklas's authorship, see Bridgman, *Gertrude Stein in Pieces* (Oxford: Oxford University Press, 1970), 209–38. Although others who knew Toklas have joined him in this (cited in note 42), he is nearly alone among scholars in seriously considering this possibility. In a note to one of her essays on Stein, Catharine Stimpson writes, "I believe that Toklas's typing, appraising, and editing often became a mild rewriting, but to call Toklas the writer, rather than the frame that kept the writer within bounds, would be excessive," in "Gertrice/Altrude: Stein, Toklas, and the Paradox of the Happy Marriage," in *Mothering the Mind: Twelve Studies of Writers and Their Silent Partners,* ed. Ruth Perry and Martine Watson Brownley (New York: Holmes & Meier, 1984), 137n.25. In *Exact Resemblance to Exact Resemblance: The Literary Portraiture of Gertrude Stein* (New Haven, Conn.: Yale University Press, 1978), Wendy Steiner observes that "the same doubling" found in "The doodle, 'Gertrice/Altrude,'" in the manuscript of 'Lend a Hand' . . . can be seen in the manuscript of *Toklas* it-

self, where large stretches appear in Toklas's handwriting. [But] I do not believe as some critics . . . have suggested, that she in fact composed large parts of the work, Stein hiding this fact in her joy at producing a comprehensible, saleable piece of writing. Toklas was probably transcribing Stein's dictation, thus creating in real life the same confusion of identity upon which the artful *Toklas* is based. Indeed, the realms of reality and fiction were not discrete" (187). Such contradictory comments suggest widespread lack of awareness of the processes of coauthorship.

11. On this type of intertextual reference, see Georgia Johnston, "Narratologies of Pleasure: Gertrude Stein's *The Autobiography of Alice B. Toklas*," *MFS: Modern Fiction Studies* 42.3 (1996), 590–606.

12. For a view of the text as both open and secretive about issues other than lesbianism, see Marjorie Perloff, "(Im)Personating Gertrude Stein," in *Gertrude Stein and the Making of Literature*, ed. Shirley Neuman and Ira B. Nadel (Boston: Northeastern University Press, 1988), 61–63. Ulla E. Dydo places this text in the context of Toklas's jealousy at discovering an earlier love affair of Stein's in "*Stanzas in Meditation:* The Other Autobiography," *Chicago Review* 35.2 (1985), 4–20. Sidonie Smith connects the complexity that results from the creation of a "fictive autobiographer, 'Alice B. Toklas,'" to the aim of semicovertly "represent[ing] the lesbian couple" (*Subjectivity, Identity, and the Body* 67). See also Johnston, "Narratologies of Pleasure"; Catharine Stimpson, "Gertrude Stein and the Lesbian Lie," in *American Women's Autobiography: Fea(s)ts of Memory*, ed. Margo Culley (Madison: University of Wisconsin Press, 1992), 152–66; Shari Benstock, "Expatriate Sapphic Modernism: Entering Literary History," in *Lesbian Texts and Contexts: Radical Revisions*, ed. Karla Jay and Joanne Glasgow (New York: New York University Press, 1990), 195; Adams, *Telling Lies*, 17–38; Estelle Jelinek, chapter 10 of *The Tradition of Women's Autobiography: From Antiquity to the Present* (Boston: Twayne, 1986), 135–45; Stimpson, "Gertrice/Altrude," 126, 130, 135; Elizabeth Fifer, "Is Flesh Advisable? The Interior Theater of Gertrude Stein," *Signs* 4.3 (1979), 472; and Stimpson, "The Mind, the Body, and Gertrude Stein," *Critical Inquiry* 3.3 (1977), 499. Gilmore warns against seeing the autobiography (and other writings by Stein) as a "code" to be cracked and argues, in lines parallel to mine, that Stein develops a "deconstructive" writing that "trace[s] the oscillation between the visible and the invisible in Stein's lesbian representation," in "A Signature of Lesbian Autobiography" (59) and in her revised version of this essay, chapter 6 of *Autobiographics: A Feminist Theory of Women's Self-Representation* (Ithaca, N.Y.: Cornell University Press, 1994), 203.

13. The frontispiece to the original edition depicts Stein writing at a table in the foreground and Toklas entering a door in the background, thus reminding the reader of Stein's status as writer and Toklas's as writer's companion. See Paul K. Alkon, "Visual Rhetoric in *The Autobiography of Alice B. Toklas*," *Critical Inquiry* 1 (1975), 849–81; Bridgman, *Gertrude Stein in Pieces*, 219; Breslin, "Gertrude Stein," 152; Neil Schmitz, *Of Huck and Alice: Humorous Writing in American Literature* (Minneapolis: University of Minnesota Press, 1983), 204–6; Harriet Scott Chessman, *The Public Is Invited to Dance: Representation, the Body, and Dialogue in Gertrude Stein* (Stanford, Calif.: Stanford University Press, 1989), 61–62; Smith, *Subjectivity, Identity, and the Body*, 66; and Gilmore, "A Signature of Lesbian Autobiography," 66, and chapter 6, 214–15.

14. In general I refer to this autobiography as Stein and Toklas's text rather than

as Stein's, not because I believe that the external proof definitively shows that it is fully coauthored but because the text presents itself as having in some sense dual authors. Other texts and ideas associated thus far exclusively with Stein I refer to as Stein's. I refer to Toklas as narrator or subject of the autobiography.

15. Similarly, Stein gave up a career in pathological psychology, toward which William James had steered her, out of boredom, saying "she dislikes the abnormal, it is so obvious. She says the normal is so much more simply complicated and interesting" (*Autobiography of Alice B. Toklas* 83).

16. Miller, "Secret Subjects, Open Secrets," 200.

17. See Stimpson's list of repetitions in *Three Lives* in her 1977 article, "The Mind, the Body, and Gertrude Stein," 50on.25.

18. On its status as memoir, see also Adams, *Telling Lies*, 30.

19. See Chessman's discussion of the "uncanny" doubling of Stein and Toklas in the frontispiece (*The Public Is Invited* 61–62). Chessman interestingly argues that although Man Ray's photograph portrays Toklas as "a secondary, shadowy doppelgänger," it also "evokes a second and contrasting possibility. . . . The two women may hover on the brink of a dialogue" (62). See also Lynn Z. Bloom, "Gertrude Is Alice Is Everybody: Innovation and Point of View in Gertrude Stein's Autobiographies," *Twentieth Century Literature* 24.1 (1978), 82–83. Schmitz describes Alice's function as humorous double (*Of Huck and Alice* 202).

20. See Schmitz, *Of Huck and Alice*, 204–11, and Smith, *Subjectivity, Identity, and the Body*, 69–70, on Stein's place at the storm center of modernism in this text.

21. For a brief, contradictory pair of allusions to automatic writing, see *The Autobiography of Alice B. Toklas*, 77, 79. For an illuminating discussion, see Steven Meyer, "Writing Psychology Over: Gertrude Stein and William James," *The Yale Journal of Criticism* 8.1 (1995), 133–63.

22. *Value* is the term preferred, for example, in "A Transatlantic Interview 1946," ed. Marianne DeKoven, in *The Gender of Modernism: A Critical Anthology*, ed. Bonnie Kime Scott (Bloomington: Indiana University Press, 1990), 502; rpt. from *A Primer for the Gradual Understanding of Gertrude Stein*, ed. Robert Bartlett Haas (Los Angeles: Black Sparrow Press, 1971), 15–35.

23. See "How Writing Is Written," in *The Gender of Modernism*, 494; rpt. from *How Writing Is Written: Volume II of the Previously Uncollected Works of Gertrude Stein*, ed. Robert Bartlett Haas (Los Angeles: Black Sparrow Press, 1974), 151–60.

24. Jacques Derrida, *Of Grammatology*, trans. Gayatri Chakravorty Spivak (Baltimore: Johns Hopkins University Press, 1974), 25.

25. See Jacques Derrida, "Différance," *Margins of Philosophy*, trans. Alan Bass (Chicago: University of Chicago Press, 1982), 1–27.

26. Umberto Eco, Postscript to *The Name of the Rose*, trans. William Weaver (New York: Harcourt Brace Jovanovich, 1984), 66–67. This passage by Eco has received special attention as a statement of "postmodern" aims in a paperback guide to twentieth-century art movements; see Matei Calinescu, *Five Faces of Modernity: Modernism, Avant-Garde, Decadence, Kitsch, Postmodernism* (Durham, N.C.: Duke University Press, 1987), 276–77.

27. However, Stein and Toklas cannily note further that camouflage cannot in itself prevent nationalist differentiation: "Another thing that interested us enor-

mously was how different the camouflage of the french looked from the camouflage of the germans, and then once we came across some very very neat camouflage and it was american" (187).

28. See also Hanscombe and Smyers's description of Stein and Toklas's early work together (*Writing for Their Lives* 80).

29. The "male"- and "female"-marked roles, to which Stein and Toklas partly adhere, have been the occasion of much criticism and some dispute among critics. For a critique, see Catharine Stimpson, "Gertrude Stein and the Lesbian Lie," 152–66; for redescription in terms of butch-femme relations, see Gilmore, "A Signature of Lesbian Autobiography," 63–65, and chapter 6, 208–11; for similar redescription, drawing on Judith Butler, see Smith, *Subjectivity, Identity, and the Body;* also see Gabriele Griffin, "What Is [Not] Remembered: The Autobiography of Alice B. Toklas," in *Women's Lives/Women's Times: New Essays on Auto/Biography,* ed. Trev Lynn Broughton and Linda Anderson (Albany: State University of New York Press, 1997), 143–56.

30. DuPlessis, *H.D.: The Career,* 76.

31. Of special interest in this context is the "Love poem in two voices, written alternately by Gertrude Stein and Alice Toklas" in both their handwritings, reproduced in *Gertrude Stein In Words and Pictures,* ed. Renate Stendhal (Chapel Hill, N.C.: Algonquin Books, 1994), 64. (I wish to thank Adale Sholock for drawing my attention to this source.) In arguing for Toklas's possible authorship of the autobiography, Richard Bridgman considers the manuscript evidence for related texts, especially "Ada," Stein's first portrait of Toklas, which alternates between their hands; manuscript evidence of Toklas's interpolations and cancellations in the autobiography; the marked stylistic shift between the notebook for the autobiography and the final full-length manuscript of the autobiography (in Stein's hand, possibly a fair copy); internal evidence derived from a rereading of "Stanzas in Meditation," written concurrently with the autobiography; the biographical evidence of Stein's writer's block following the success of the autobiography; and (according to her own report) her return to her earlier style (*Gertrude Stein in Pieces* 209–17, 234–38).

32. See Bridgman, *Gertrude Stein in Pieces,* 210–13, as opposed to Steiner, *Exact Resemblance,* 187.

33. "Ada," in *Geography and Plays* (New York: Something Else Press, 1968), 16.

34. Thus Sidonie Smith asks rhetorically, "When precisely did she do the reading? When precisely did they eat their supper?" (*Subjectivity, Identity, and the Body* 71). See also the connections observed by Chessman between cooking, reading, and writing in this scene (*The Public Is Invited* 63–64).

35. On the multiple significances of the "ring-shaped insignia embossed on the cover," see Smith, *Subjectivity, Identity, and the Body,* 65–66.

36. See *Multiple Authorship and the Myth of the Solitary Genius,* as discussed in chapter 1 of this study.

37. Alice B. Toklas, *What Is Remembered* (New York: Sphere, 1963).

38. Bridgman observes that "Gertrude Stein originally ended the manuscript as Mark Twain had the *Adventures of Huckleberry Finn*—'Sincerely yours, Alice B. Toklas,'—then cancelled it" (*Gertrude Stein in Pieces* 219, note).

39. In an essay by Emile Benveniste, "Subjectivity in Language," to which I return in discussion of Marlatt and Warland, Benveniste proposes his now-famous

argument that the "I" "cannot be identified except in what we have called else-
where an instance of discourse and that has only a momentary reference," in
Problems in General Linguistics, trans. Mary Elizabeth Meek (Coral Gables, Fla.:
University of Miami Press, 1971), 226. This is an activity of language that Stein
and Toklas use to mock and unsettle conventional autobiographical referentiali-
ty. Parallel discussions of this dual, decentered "I" may be found in Gilmore, "A
Signature of Lesbian Autobiography"; Breslin, "Gertrude Stein"; Chessman, *The
Public Is Invited*; Smith *Subjectivity, Identity, and the Body*; Johnston, "Narra-
tologies of Pleasure"; and Griffin, "What Is [Not] Remembered."

40. Toklas's earlier citation of Henry McBride of the *New York Sun* suggests how
to take a joke in the autobiography: "Laugh with and not at her, in that way you
will enjoy it all much better" (121). In *What Is Remembered*, Toklas recalls McBride
as saying, "Laugh if you like, . . . but laugh with her and not at her" (69).

41. Bridgman, *Gertrude Stein in Pieces*, 219.

42. When George Wickes suggested that Toklas and he might tape-record "interviews that would present the autobiography of Gertrude Stein by Alice B. Toklas," she responded, "'Oh, but I couldn't do that. . . . You see,' she said, 'I wrote
the Autobiography in the first place.'" Toklas offers a long explanation of this
process, which sounds (once again) like coauthorship:

> She went on to explain that Gertrude Stein had been after her to write a book
> of memoirs to be called "My 25 Years with Gertrude Stein." . . . Gertrude
> helped her as much as she could, at first revising what Alice had written, at
> last taking down Alice's words and revising them as she went along. For that
> reason Alice said the book should be called *The Autobiography of Alice B.
> Toklas* by Gertrude Stein.
>   At first this was just a little joke between them. . . . But when Harcourt
> Brace accepted the book and the *Atlantic Monthly* decided to publish an
> excerpt, this was too much for Gertrude Stein to resist. It had been her life-
> long ambition to be published in the *Atlantic*. Alice said she didn't mind.
> . . . As far as she was concerned, it had been Gertrude's book all along.

When Toklas finally wrote her own autobiography (that is, with herself as primary
subject), she told Wickes, "'The difficulty this time . . . was not the writing. It was
the remembering.' And from those ancient depths came something like a chuck-
le. 'That's the point of the title,'" *What Is Remembered* (Wickes, "Who Really
Wrote *The Autobiography*" 38, 37). See also Bridgman's account, *Gertrude Stein
in Pieces*, 209.

Most readers and critics appear to be unaware of this article by Wickes, but some
readers (not critics) nonetheless believe Toklas wrote *The Autobiography of Alice B. Toklas*. See especially Maurice Grosser, who writes that the autobiography
"is made up word for word of the stories I have heard Alice tell. In fact, the autobiography presents an exact rendition of Alice's conversation, of the rhythm of
her speech and of the prose style of her acknowledged works. . . . I remain con-
vinced that the book is entirely Alice's work," in *The New York Review of Books*
33.17 (1986), 36.

43. In an interview with Robert Bartlett Haas, Stein says, "As a joke I began to
write the *Autobiography of Alice B. Toklas* and at that moment I had made a rather
interesting discovery . . . that other people's words are quite different from one's

own and that they cannot be the result of your internal troubles as a writer. They have a totally different sense than when they are your own words. . . . So I did a tour de force with the *Autobiography of Alice B. Toklas* and when I sent the first half to the agent they sent back a telegram to see which one of us had written it," in Afterword, *What Are Masterpieces?* by Gertrude Stein (New York: Pitman, 1970), 102. Alice B. Toklas herself writes, in *What Is Remembered*, "It was Bertie, Sir Robert Abdy, who had said to Gertrude, You should write the history of your friends and time. Which she did, *The Autobiography of Alice B. Toklas*" (172). Such declarations are not particularly trustworthy, however, especially when articulated by an experimental writer and her chief cohort struggling to build and maintain a reputation. I find notably ambiguous the passages in *Everybody's Autobiography* (1937; rpt. London: Virago, 1985) where Stein presumably takes credit for *The Autobiography of Alice B. Toklas:* "Alice B. Toklas did hers and now everybody will do theirs. . . . In the first place she did not want it to be Alice B. Toklas" (xxi), and "if one has succeeded in doing anything one is certain that anybody who really has it in them to really do anything will really do that thing. Anyway I have done something and anyway I did write *The Autobiography of Alice B. Toklas* and since then a great many things happened" (1).

44. This association of the text with gossip (as well as of gossip with Toklas) has been used to devalue it, as S. C. Neuman explains in *Gertrude Stein: Autobiography and the Problem of Narration* (Victoria, B.C.: University of Victoria English Literary Studies, 1979), 23. See also Bridgman, *Gertrude Stein in Pieces,* 218; and Smith, *Subjectivity, Identity, and the Body,* 80.

45. For a still more positive description than mine of this issue of equality in Stein's texts, including the autobiography, see Marianne DeKoven, "'Excellent Not a Hull House': Gertrude Stein, Jane Addams, and Feminist-Modernist Political Culture," in *Rereading Modernism: New Directions in Feminist Criticism,* ed. Lisa Rado (New York: Garland, 1994), 321–50.

46. Miller, "Secret Subjects, Open Secrets," 195.

47. Although these writers consistently sign themselves in alphabetical order, as Daphne Marlatt and Betsy Warland, I occasionally reverse their names in this chapter.

48. Daphne Marlatt and Betsy Warland, "Reading and Writing between the Lines," *Tessera* 5 (1988), 84. Subsequent citations refer to this publication and appear parenthetically in the text.

49. H.D. and Stein are both major influences (among other modernist woman writers) on the new lesbian feminist poetics emerging in the last twenty years in Canada. In her introduction to the anthology *In the Feminine,* for example, Marlatt heralds Woolf and Stein: "As the Québec writers reach back to Virginia Woolf and Gertrude Stein in English literature, we [English-Canadian writers] can reach forward to their new writing in French with its well-developed analysis, its radical deconstruction of male-biased language, its creative invention of new words and new ways of speaking, so that, with a new horizon, we can return to and build on our own roots to develop our culture in the feminine," in *In the Feminine: Women and Words/Les femmes et les mots (Conference Proceedings 1983),* ed. Ann Dybikowski, Victoria Freeman, Daphne Marlatt, Barbara Pulling, and Betsy Warland (Edmonton: Longspoon, 1985), 13.

50. The coin itself becomes a pivotal trope in their work; see the opening pages

of "Subject to Change" in Marlatt and Warland, *Two Women in a Birth* (New York: Guernica, 1994), 149–50.

51. Betsy Warland, "Introduction: Inventing *InVersions*," in *InVersions: Writing by Dykes, Queers and Lesbians,* ed. Betsy Warland (Vancouver: Press Gang, 1991), xi.

52. *Double Negative* (Charlottetown, P.E.I.: gynergy, 1988), 20.

53. In the first monograph devoted to either of these writers, Douglas Barbour traces the development in Marlatt's poetics from the 1960s, when she was influenced by Robert Creeley, Charles Olson, Robert Duncan, Warren Tallman, and Earle Birney, to her focus on feminist theory and women's writing in the early 1980s, in *Daphne Marlatt and Her Works* (Toronto: ECW, 1992), 4–7. See also Marlatt's account in "Between Continuity and Difference: An Interview with Daphne Marlatt," by Brenda Carr, in *Beyond TISH,* ed. Douglas Barbour (Vancouver: NeWest, 1991), 99–102.

54. For similar play on *invert, verse,* and *version,* see "Vers-ions Con-verse: A Sequence of Translations," Barbara Godard, Susan Knutson, Daphne Marlatt, Kathy Mezei, Gail Scott, and Lola Lemire Tostevin, in *Collaboration in the Feminine: Writings on Women and Culture from "Tessera,"* ed. Barbara Godard (Toronto: Second Story, 1994), 158–59. The polyvalent term *re-verse* appears in Marlatt and Warland's *Double Negative,* 25.

55. Barbour notes in 1992 that Marlatt and Warland have lived together in Vancouver since 1983 (*Daphne Marlatt* 3). But in combination with Marlatt's new collaborations with Nicole Brossard (see note 56), see hints of the end of this relationship in Jodey Castricano and Jacqueline Larson, "Blue Period—That's a Story: A Conversation with Nicole Brossard and Daphne Marlatt," *West Coast Line* 28.3 (1994–95), 47, 49.

56. Marlatt has collaborated on texts with Nicole Brossard, although these appear as separately authored pieces, subsequently conjoined in a single volume or article; see *Character* (Marlatt)/*Jeu de lettres* (Brossard) (Montréal: Editions nbj, 1986) and "Only a Body to Measure Reality By: Writing the In-Between," Text of the Arthur Ravenscroft Memorial Lecture, jointly delivered at the University of Leeds, 29 February 1996, *Journal of Commonwealth Literature* 31.2 (1996), 5–17.

57. *Sp/Elles: Poetry by Canadian Women/Poésie de femmes canadiennes,* ed. Judith Fitzgerald (Windsor, Ont.: Black Moss, 1986).

58. As Brenda Carr points out, Marlatt and Warland's ecofeminism is accompanied by "gesture[s] of decolonization," in "Collaboration in the Feminine: Daphne Marlatt/Betsy Warland's 'Re-versed Writing' in *Double Negative,*" *Tessera* 9 (Fall 1990), 116–18.

59. "Moving Parts," in *InVersions,* 181.

60. As Marlatt explains, in elaborating points made by Kristeva, the language sought by many feminist writers in Quebec "returns us to the body, a woman's body and the largely unverbalized, presyntactic, postlexical field it knows. postlexical in that, as Mary Daly shows, with intelligence (that gathering hand) certain words (dandelion sparks) seed themselves back to original and originally-related meaning. this is a field where words mutually attract each other, fused by connection, enthused (inspired) into variation (puns, word play, rime at all levels) fertile in proliferation." In "Musing with Mothertongue," *Touch to My Tongue,* in *Two Women in a Birth,* 29.

61. Barbour notes that "on a reading tour to promote" their books *Touch to My Tongue* and *open is broken*, "the poets set up a dialogue between the books, alternating poems" (*Daphne Marlatt* 63n.27).

62. For use of the term *postmodern* in relation to Marlatt's work, see Frank Davey, "Daphne Marlatt," in *From There to Here: A Guide to English-Canadian Literature Since 1960* (Erin, Ont.: Porcépic, 1974), 195; Barbour, *Daphne Marlatt*, 18. Pamela Banting prefers the term *postcolonial* to *postmodern* for Marlatt's writing, but her definition of the postcolonial closely resembles political postmodernism; see "The Phantom Limb Syndrome: Writing the Postcolonial Body in Daphne Marlatt's 'Touch to My Tongue,'" *Ariel* 23.3 (1993), 7–8. Marlatt uses the term herself when she speaks approvingly of the way "Québec women writers have taken what was useful to their own thought from European (post)modernist thought, but instead of trying to insert themselves into the tradition they have initiated a feminine culture based on difference that looks forward, is almost utopian in its vision and devastating in its criticism of what it leaves behind" (*In the Feminine* 13). In "Between Continuity and Difference," Marlatt distances herself from the term *postcolonial:* "Our world certainly isn't post-colonial or post-feminist" (105).

63. On Marlatt's use of a psychoanalytic poststructuralist vocabulary and her refusal of "any one psychoanalytic metanarrative," see Keith Green and Jill Le-Bihan, "The Speaking Object: Daphne Marlatt's Pronouns and Lesbian Poetics," *Style* 28.3 (1994), 436. See also their related discussion of the Lacanian "Symbolic" and the male "gaze" in Marlatt's novel (438).

64. I assume an allusion here to Julia Kristeva's *Polylogue* (Paris: Seuil, 1977).

65. Benveniste's determinate distinction between the supposedly fixed concept of *tree* as signified and the unfixed signified concept of *I* ("Subjectivity in Language," 226) would be observed by a poststructuralist thinker as less than absolute. The *tree* does not gesture in speech toward precisely the same concept; its signified shifts along with *I* from subject to subject and from situation to situation.

66. Benveniste completes this sentence by (somewhat contradictorily) adding, "They are complementary, although according to an 'interior/exterior' opposition, and, at the same time, they are reversible" ("Subjectivity in Language," 224–25).

67. Monique Wittig, *The Lesbian Body* (1973), trans. David Le Vay (Boston: Beacon, 1986), 10–11. See also Wittig's "The Mark of Gender," in *The Poetics of Gender,* ed. Nancy K. Miller (New York: Columbia University Press, 1986), 71–72. Interestingly, Gilmore applies Wittig's "j/e" to Stein, though noting their historically differentiated situations, in "A Signature of Lesbian Autobiography," 60.

68. As I note in the preface to "On Collaborations: Part II," "when people write and talk together, they become acutely aware of how they perform together," and collaborative scholars and writers thus often create texts that double as performable scripts; see Preface, *Tulsa Studies in Women's Literature,* 14.1 (1995), 16.

69. Gallop, *The Daughter's Seduction,* 29–32.

70. See Derrida, "Différance," 3–5.

71. Grahn, *Blood, Bread, and Roses;* Elaine Showalter, "Feminist Criticism in the Wilderness," in *The New Feminist Criticism: Essays on Women, Literature, and Theory* (New York: Pantheon, 1985), 259–67.

72. Eve Kosofsky Sedgwick, *Between Men: English Literature and Male Ho-*

mosocial Desire (New York: Columbia University Press, 1985). See also Koesten-baum, *Double Talk*, passim.

73. Of Lacan's "*Lalangue,*" Rose writes, "Lacan's term displaces [Saussure's] opposition [between *langue* and *parole*] in so far as, for him, the organisation of language can only be understood in terms of the subject's relationship to it. *La-langue* indicates that part of language which reflects the laws of unconscious processes, but whose effects go beyond the reflection, and escape the grasp of the subject," in Lacan's *Feminine Sexuality*, 46n.11.

74. For a striking account of the growth of trust through collaborative writing, see Darlene Dralus and Jen Shelton, "What Is the Subject? Speaking, Silencing, (Self) Censorship," *Tulsa Studies in Women's Literature* 14.1 (1995), 19–37.

75. "Subject to Change," in *Two Women in a Birth*, 159. Subsequent references appear parenthetically in the text.

76. See Green and LeBihan, "The Speaking Object," 436–38, for a discussion of this criticism of Marlatt.

77. Marlatt eloquently counters this charge of essentialism—which she sees as itself grounded in a "patriarchal" definition—in "Between Continuity and Dif-ference," 105–7.

78. Marlatt and Warland both discuss what is a decidedly complex understand-ing of the term *utopia* in "Speaking In and Of Each Other," an interview by Jan-ice Williamson, *Fuse* 8.5 (1985), 27–28. (This interview focuses on *Touch to my Tongue* and *open is broken* and precedes the writing of their coauthored texts.)

79. Warland, "Moving Parts," in *InVersions*, 181–82.

80. Warland, in *Sp/Elles*, 112. In "Between Continuity and Difference," Mar-latt speaks against the "universal" in poetry and says, "my work . . . is marked by my gender as well as my history, class, national identity, race, all those things," and goes on briefly to discuss her personal sense of "emigrant" alienation (103). For Marlatt's immigrant experience, see Banting, "The Phantom Limb Syndrome," 10–11; Barbour, *Daphne Marlatt*, 1.

81. Sue Schenk, "Woman—Identified," rev. of *Tide Lines*, ed. Lee Felming, and of *InVersions*, ed. Betsy Warland, in *Canadian Literature* 138–39 (Fall 1993), 158.

Chapter 7: Rewriting America

1. Michael Dorris, *Paper Trail: Essays* (New York: HarperCollins, 1994), 160–61, 147. "Rewriting History" is the title of an essay reprinted in this collection (133–44).

2. Erdrich received an undergraduate degree from Dartmouth and a master's in creative writing from Johns Hopkins and sees herself exclusively as a writer ("I can't seem to get a feel for critical theory," she says, in "An Interview with Louise Er-drich"): *Conversations with Louise Erdrich and Michael Dorris*, ed. Allan Chavkin and Nancy Feyl Chavkin (Jackson: University Press of Mississippi, 1994), 234.

3. Although a film based on *The Broken Cord* won a number of media awards, and other novels by Erdrich and Dorris have formed the basis for screenplays, neither of them has been interested in becoming more involved in filmmaking. In Dorris's words, "I found [working in Hollywood and writing screenplays for *The Broken Cord*] a very frustrating experience because there are so many layers a work

has to go through in which people with their own agendas make decisions about it and changes in it and so forth and so on. . . . It's much more of a collaborative process, and the only person I really want to collaborate with is Louise," *Conversations with Louise Erdrich and Michael Dorris*, 215–16.

4. Kay Bonetti, "An Interview with Louise Erdrich and Michael Dorris," *The Missouri Review* 11.2 (1988), 96. Subsequent citations appear parenthetically in the text. See also *Conversations with Louise Erdrich and Michael Dorris*, 144.

5. When they cosign their texts, their names appear sometimes as Louise Erdrich and Michael Dorris and sometimes as Michael Dorris and Louise Erdrich, and I have varied the order in this chapter.

6. A vivid example of the differences within feminism emerges when one considers Michael Dorris's self-described feminism in relation to Katha Pollitt's critique of *The Broken Cord*, in "A New Assault on Feminism," in *The Nation*, 26 March 1990, 416–17, and Dorris's understandably heated but (to this reader) not entirely persuasive response to Pollitt's analysis of the "fetal rights" debate, in *Conversations with Louise Erdrich and Michael Dorris*, 205–6.

7. Except for tense changes and brief mentions of Dorris's suicide, this section on Erdrich and Dorris has not been revised in response to, or as a result of, his death. This collaboration always troubled me (for reasons suggested within) yet nonetheless deserves admiration for its manifold achievements.

8. The nonfictional narrative they cosigned is a tale of travel: *Route 2* (Northridge, Calif.: Lord John Press, 1991). They also cosigned occasional pieces, including the introduction to *Wigwam Evenings: Sioux Folk Tales Retold* (Lincoln: University of Nebraska Press, 1990), a group of stories coauthored by a turn-of-the-century interracial couple, Charles A. Eastman (Ohiyesa) and Elaine Goodale Eastman (ix–xii); "Who Owns the Land?" *The New York Times Magazine*, 4 Sept. 1988, 32, 34–35, 51–52, 57, and 65; and "Bangs and Whimpers: Novelists at Armageddon," *The New York Times Book Review*, 13 March 1988, 1, 24–25.

9. But Erdrich complicates this assertion, as she does on a number of other points that I discuss here: "We're not saying there is no individual creativity. . . . But it is really mixed in with collaboration," in "An Interview with Louise Erdrich and Michael Dorris," by Hertha D. Wong, *North Dakota Quarterly* 55.1 (1987), 202. Subsequent citations of the Wong interview appear parenthetically in the text.

10. Yet in speaking of their collaboration on *The Crown of Columbus*, Erdrich sees their minds and writing as having "meshed": "Mind-meld! That's what it was! It was the Vulcan mind-meld," in *Conversations with Louise Erdrich and Michael Dorris*, 170.

11. Kaplan and Rose, "Strange Bedfellows," 559.

12. The transcript of the PBS conversation, published in *Conversations with Louise Erdrich and Michael Dorris*, does not in my view support Kaplan and Rose's perception of Erdrich as "nearly silent" or as a parrot. Kaplan and Rose were by no means alone, however, in perceiving Erdrich and Dorris's relationship in this way. Primarily because Erdrich had already established a reputation, reporters at first saw Dorris as a "Svengali"; see *Conversations with Louise Erdrich and Michael Dorris*, 57.

13. The court records on the custody case involving the charges of sexual abuse against Dorris are now closed.

14. See the newspaper obituaries and stories that appeared in *The New York*

Times, 15 April 1997, C24 (note that this obituary inaccurately reports Dorris's survivors as including an adopted daughter "Sava"; Jeffrey Sava was their second adopted *son;* this article also neglects to mention the accidental death of his oldest adopted son, Abel); *The Washington Post,* 15 April 1997, D1–2; *The New York Times,* 16 April 1997, A12; *The Washington Post,* 16 April 1997, D1, D6; *Boston Sunday Globe,* 20 April 1997, A1, A26; *Publishers Weekly,* 21 April 1997, 14; *Newsweek,* 28 April 1997, 82–83. The circumstances surrounding Dorris's death may eventually inspire cultural analysis by critics, but an extensive biographical postmortem of this sort exceeds the bounds of the present study.

15. The cost of their fame becomes noticeable in their 1991 interview with Vince Passaro, yet after ten years of marriage, they still "look[ed] like newlyweds" even to this skeptical interviewer (*Conversations with Louise Erdrich and Michael Dorris* 157, 159, 160).

16. See William H. Pritchard, rev. of *The Crown of Columbus,* in *The Hudson Review* 44 (1991), 504–5; Kirkpatrick Sale, "Roll On, Columbus, Roll On," *The Nation,* 21 Oct. 1991, 488; and Robert Allen Warrior, "Columbus Fiction: The Real Treasure," rev. of *The Crown of Columbus,* in *Christianity and Crisis,* 16 Dec. 1991, 393–94. See its announcement by Paul Nathan, "Two on the Block," *Publisher's Weekly,* 5 Aug. 1988, 27. What troubled reviewers as much as the advance publicity, however—and what they mention more often than the money Dorris and Erdrich received—is their collaboration. Erdrich and Dorris did not originally plan the novel to coincide with the quincentenary, they researched and wrote the novel over the course of ten years before its publication, and for them it was as serious a novel as their others; see *Conversations with Louise Erdrich and Michael Dorris,* 164. See also Helmbrecht Breinig's discussion of the issue of this novel's popularity in "(Hi)storytelling as Deconstruction and Seduction: The Columbus Novels of Stephen Marlowe and Michael Dorris/Louise Erdrich," in *Historiographic Metafiction in Modern American and Canadian Literature,* ed. Bernd Engler and Kurt Müller (Paderborn, Germany: Ferdinand Schöningh, 1994), 337–46.

17. Passaro saw in Erdrich and Dorris two writers who "manage[d] their careers avidly, shrewdly and almost entirely by themselves" (*Conversations with Louise Erdrich and Michael Dorris* 159). Dorris presented himself as a writers' agent in order to get the attention of major publishers for Erdrich's *Love Medicine,* and his ploy worked (Bonetti, "An Interview" 93). Dorris notes that "eschewing the byline has its advantages" when it comes to acting as one's own agent, in *Conversations with Louise Erdrich and Michael Dorris,* 18. Similarly, Erdrich and he "made the decision" deliberately to seek "a trade publisher" for *The Broken Cord,* thus ensuring a "popular audience" rather than a "specialist" one for Dorris's book on fetal alcohol syndrome (Wong, "An Interview" 216). Nonetheless, Erdrich and Dorris consider their efforts almost always those of "serious" writers; see Erdrich on *The Beet Queen* and Dorris on *The Broken Cord,* in *Conversations with Louise Erdrich and Michael Dorris,* 76, 130: "The greater danger to artists in this country" than that of being political, Erdrich says, "is commercialism" (241).

18. On their success in achieving this, see Hans Bak, "Toward a Native American 'Realism': The Amphibious Fiction of Louise Erdrich," in *Neo-Realism in Contemporary American Fiction,* ed. Kristiaan Versluys (Amsterdam: Rodopi,

1992), 145. Dorris and Erdrich have also done much to support other Native American writers (even while questioning "Native American literature" as a viable category for writing): In a story published shortly after Dorris's death, for example, he is credited with being "a tireless promoter of a range of young American Indian talent, both as a reviewer and behind the scenes," Dinitia Smith, "The Indian in Literature Is Catching Up," *New York Times*, 21 April 1997, B1.

19. See Carla Freccero, Marianne Hirsch, Ivy Schweitzer, and Susanne Zantop, "Columbus Circles," rev. of *The Crown of Columbus*, in *The Women's Review of Books*, 9, 17 Oct. 1991, 17–18; and Diane D. Quantic, rev. of *The Crown of Columbus*, in *Western American Literature* 26 (1992), 369–71. For a favorable scholarly article that links postmodernism primarily to the mix of genres in *The Crown of Columbus*, see Teresa Cid, "Wanting America Back: *The Crown of Columbus* as Tentative Epic in an Age of Multiculturalism," in *The Insular Dream: Obsession and Resistance*, ed. Kristiaan Versluys (Amsterdam: VU University Press, 1995), 347. Subsequent citations of Freccero, Hirsch, Schweitzer, and Zantop appear parenthetically in the text.

20. See especially Nancy J. Peterson, "History, Postmodernism, and Louise Erdrich's *Tracks*," *PMLA* 109.5 (1994), 982–94; Gerald Vizenor, Preface, *Narrative Chance: Postmodern Discourse on Native American Indian Literatures* (Albuquerque: University of New Mexico Press, 1989), xii; and Breinig, "(Hi)storytelling," 325–46. See also Leslie Marmon Silko's critique of the postmodernism of *The Beet Queen* in "Here's an Odd Artifact for the Fairy-Tale Shelf," rev. of *The Beet Queen*, *Impact/Albuquerque Journal Magazine*, 7 Oct. 1986, 10–11. For responses to this critique, see Susan Pérez Castillo, "Postmodernism, Native American Literature and the Real: The Silko-Erdrich Controversy," *The Massachusetts Review* 32.2 (1991), 285–94; and Erdrich, *Conversations with Louise Erdrich and Michael Dorris*, 237–38. See also Catherine Rainwater, "Reading between Worlds: Narrativity in the Fiction of Louise Erdrich," *American Literature* 62.3 (1990), 414–15; Bak, "Toward a Native American 'Realism,'" 149–50; and Paula Gunn Allen, *The Sacred Hoop: Recovering the Feminine in American Indian Traditions* (Boston: Beacon, 1986), 79–81. For accounts in interviews with Erdrich and Dorris of, respectively, the influence of postmodernism on Erdrich's writing and the political in their novels, see *Conversations with Louise Erdrich and Michael Dorris*, 68, 174, 237–38.

21. See also Erdrich's comments on her early story of Mustache Maude in *Conversations with Louise Erdrich and Michael Dorris*, 250–51.

22. Most criticism focuses on Erdrich's novels (with little or no reference to Dorris's coauthorship). A few articles focus on Dorris's novels (with little or no reference to Erdrich's coauthorship). Fewer still focus on Erdrich and Dorris's writing together, and these articles all analyze *The Crown of Columbus*; these include Breinig, Cid, and Thomas Matchie, "Exploring the Meaning of Discovery in *The Crown of Columbus*," *The North Dakota Quarterly* 59.4 (1991), 243–50; and Ann Rayson, "Shifting Identity in the Work of Louise Erdrich and Michael Dorris," *Studies in American Indian Literature* 3.4 (1991), 27–36. Useful articles on identity issues in Erdrich's novels include Susan Stanford Friedman's "Identity Politics, Syncretism, Catholicism, and Anishinabe Religion in Louise Erdrich's *Tracks*," *Religion and Literature* 26.1 (1994), 107–33; Susan Meisenhelder's "Race and Gender in Louise Erdrich's *The Beet Queen*," *Ariel* 25.1 (1994), 45–57; and Louise Flavin's "Gender Construction amid Family Dissolution in Louise Erdrich's

The Beet Queen," Studies in American Indian Literatures 7.2 (1995), 17–24. See also Rayson, "Shifting Identity."

23. Donna Haraway, "A Manifesto for Cyborgs: Science, Technology, and Socialist Feminism in the 1980s," in *Feminism/Postmodernism,* ed. Linda J. Nicholson (New York: Routledge, 1990), 196; Adalaide Morris, "First Persons Plural in Contemporary Feminist Fiction," *Tulsa Studies in Women's Literature* 11.1 (1992), 11–29. Haraway defines affinity as relation "not by blood but by choice, the appeal of one chemical nuclear group for another, avidity." Subsequent citations of Morris appear parenthetically in the text.

24. My discussion of their interviews focuses on those by Hertha Wong and Kay Bonetti because these are two of the most extensive interviews (appearing, not surprisingly, in learned journals), because they are formatted *as* interviews rather than as narratives interspersed with quotations, and because the interviews include both Dorris and Erdrich. One might compare these interviews with other dual interviews, especially those by Laura Coltelli, Sharon White and Glenda Burnside, Bill Moyers, and Michael Schumacher, and with interviews of Erdrich or Dorris alone, by Joseph Bruchac (with Erdrich), and by Allan Chavkin and Nancy Feyl Chavkin (with Dorris, and then with Erdrich)—all in *Conversations with Louise Erdrich and Michael Dorris.*

25. In another interview, Dorris says, "The common denominator of being Americans crosses all ethnic lines," in *Conversations with Louise Erdrich and Michael Dorris,* 88.

26. The following analyses stop short of *The Antelope Wife;* though begun before Dorris's death, it is the first of Erdrich's novels not to be dedicated to Dorris and to contain no acknowledgment of his influence.

27. Dorris and Erdrich, on the contrary, see Dorris as only gradually discovering his talent and drive to be a writer in years of collaboration with and support from Erdrich; see *Conversations with Louise Erdrich and Michael Dorris,* 121, 167.

28. See Robert Houston, "Take It Back for the Indians," rev. of *The Crown of Columbus, New York Times Book Review,* 29 April 1991, 10; John Elson, "1 + 1 = 2," rev. of *The Crown of Columbus,* in *Time,* 29 April 1991, 76; Joanne Kaufman, rev. of *The Crown of Columbus,* in *People Weekly* 35 (10 June 1991), 26, 28; Warrior, "Columbus Fiction"; and Pritchard's review. Reviewers in academic publications were notably more sympathetic; see especially Freccero, Hirsch, Schweitzer, and Zantop, "Columbus Circles"; Quantic's review; and Gerda Oldham, rev. of *The Crown of Columbus,* in *Antioch Review* 49.2 (Spring 1991), 303. For favorable reviews, see also Erica Abeel, who calls it "partly a feminist fable," rev. of *The Crown of Columbus,* in *New Woman* 21 (May 1991), 28; David Finkle, who calls it "brilliant hokum," rev. of *The Crown of Columbus,* in *Village Voice Literary Supplement,* 7 May 1991, 7; Don G. Campbell, rev. of *The Crown of Columbus,* in *Los Angeles Times Book Review,* 12 May 1991, 3, 13; and Michael Kerrigan (although he hedges his bets about the results of their "seamless" coauthorship), in "Seeking an America of the Heart," *TLS,* 19 July 1991, 21. Another mixed review appeared from Guy Mannes-Abbott, "Native Speech," rev. of *White People: Stories* and *The Crown of Columbus,* in *New Statesman and Society,* 26 July 1991, 35. An unusually sympathetic and corrective news article, carefully reporting on the collaboration behind and previous reviews of *The Crown*

of Columbus, was produced by Josh Getlin, "Novel Route to Discovery of America," *Los Angeles Times,* 3 May 1991, E1, E11.

29. For the importance of conversation in all their collaborations, see *Conversations with Louise Erdrich and Michael Dorris,* 65, 176.

30. See also Erdrich's comments in *Conversations with Louise Erdrich and Michael Dorris,* 88, 121, 167, and in interviews conducted between Sept. 1992 and April 1993, 232, 243, 245.

31. On the strong women in their fiction, Dorris notes, "It is sometimes said that the women characters are stronger in Louise's and my fiction than the men— well, I think that the women are simply *equally* as strong as the men. . . . I think they simply appear strong because we are so used to seeing women portrayed as not strong"; for his fuller account, see *Conversations with Louise Erdrich and Michael Dorris,* 217.

32. Louise Erdrich, *Tracks* (New York: Harper & Row, 1988), 226.

33. Louise Erdrich, *The Beet Queen* (1986; rpt. New York: Bantam, 1989), 338.

34. Louise Erdrich, *Love Medicine* (1984; rpt. New York: HarperCollins, 1993), 367.

35. Louise Erdrich, *The Bingo Palace* (New York: HarperCollins, 1994), 273–74.

36. Michael Dorris, *Cloud Chamber* (New York: Scribner, 1997), 31.

37. Michael Dorris, *A Yellow Raft in Blue Water* (1987; rpt. New York: Warner, 1988), 372.

38. *Cloud Chamber,* 316. For an insightful discussion of the "catch" in relation to *The Crown of Columbus,* see Rayson, "Shifting Identity," 28.

39. Louise Erdrich, *Tales of Burning Love* (New York: HarperCollins, 1996), 452.

40. Louise Erdrich and Michael Dorris, *The Crown of Columbus* (1991; rpt. New York: HarperCollins, 1992), 504–5, 511. Subsequent citations appear parenthetically in the text.

41. Sarah L. Delany and A. Elizabeth Delany with Amy Hill Hearth, *Having Our Say: The Delany Sisters' First 100 Years* (New York: Dell, 1993), 87. Subsequent citations appear parenthetically in the text.

42. Ossie Guffy, as told to Caryl Ledner, *Ossie: The Autobiography of a Black Woman* (New York: Norton, 1971), 9. Subsequent citations appear parenthetically in the text.

43. Albert E. Stone, "Two Recreate One: The Act of Collaboration in Recent Black Autobiography," *Real* 1 (1982), 236–40. See also chapter 7 in Stone's *Autobiographical Occasions and Original Acts: Versions of American Identity from Henry Adams to Nate Shaw* (Philadelphia: University of Pennsylvania Press, 1982), 231–64. Subsequent citations refer to the article in *Real* and appear parenthetically in the text.

44. Mary Helen Washington, "Reading between the Lines," rev. of *Having Our Say,* in *The Women's Review of Books* 11.4 (1994), 10.

45. Davies, *De/Colonizing the Subject,* 4.

46. I refer to the sisters not only as the Delanys or the Delany sisters but by the names given them in this narrative: their nicknames Bessie and Sadie.

47. Their saga began with an article by Hearth, "Two 'Maiden Ladies' with Century-Old Stories to Tell," that appeared in *The New York Times,* 22 Sept. 1991, section WC, 1, 12–14; it proceeded through eighteen months of interviews to publication in *Having Our Say;* continued through live television interviews, for

example, on CBS's *Sunday Morning,* the *Oprah Winfrey Show,* Black Entertainment Television, and CNN; issued in a second book, *The Delany Sisters' Book of Everyday Wisdom* by Sarah and A. Elizabeth Delany with Amy Hill Hearth, (New York: Kodansha International, 1994); and climaxed in the highly successful Broadway show based on *Having Our Say.* After her sister's death, Sarah L. Delany and Amy Hill Hearth published yet another book, *On My Own at 107: Reflections on Life without Bessie* (New York: HarperCollins, 1997). Sarah Delany died at age 109 in 1999.

48. Sherley Anne Williams, "Witnesses to a Century," rev. of *Having Our Say,* in *The Washington Post,* 23, 12 Sept. 1993, 1.

49. I refer to Ossie Guffy also by her first name, the name most often used in this narrative.

50. Henrietta Buckmaster, "So Farewell Welfare," rev. of *Ossie: The Autobiography of a Black Woman, Christian Science Monitor,* 24 June 1971, 9.

51. Zora Neale Hurston, "How It Feels to Be Colored Me," in *I Love Myself When I Am Laughing . . . And Then Again When I Am Looking Mean and Impressive: A Zora Neale Hurston Reader,* ed. Alice Walker (New York: Feminist Press, 1979), 152–53.

52. The dual marginalization of black women is broached in such early writings as Barbara Smith's "Toward a Black Feminist Criticism" (1977), in *The New Feminist Criticism,* ed. Showalter, 168–85; *All the Women Are White,* ed. Hull, Scott, and Smith; and bell hooks, *Feminist Theory: From Margin to Center* (Boston: South End Press, 1984).

53. Buckmaster, "So Farewell Welfare," 9. If one includes her husband at the time of *Ossie's* narration, there were five men who fathered her children, and thus at least seven lovers in her life before she had reached the age of forty.

54. Buckmaster, "So Farewell Welfare," 9.

55. Elizabeth M. Guiney, rev. of *Ossie,* in *Library Journal* 96 (15 May 1971), 1703.

56. Rev. of *Ossie,* "Non-Fiction," *Kirkus Reviews* 39 (15 March 1971), 333.

57. Rev. of *Ossie* in "Young Adult Best Books," *Top of the News* 28 (April 1972), 312; rev. of *Ossie* in *The Booklist* 68 (1 April 1972), 664; rev. of *Ossie* in *Publisher's Weekly* 199 (22 March 1971), 51.

Conclusion

1. E. Œ. Somerville, Preface, *Some Experiences and Further Experiences of an Irish R. M.,* by Edith Somerville and Martin Ross (1899, 1944; London: Dent, 1991), xviii, xx.

2. Field, *Works and Days,* 16.

3. The hyphenated term *con-verse* has been used interestingly in relation to a "chain" of commentaries on verse translations; see Godard et al., "Vers-ions Converse: A Sequence of Translations," in *Collaboration in the Feminine,* 153–61.

4. After giving one public lecture and writing two chapters of this study, I taught a graduate course on collaboration, in which it occurred to me to attempt a multiply authored study with my students. I realized, however, that this would involve me in a hierarchical collaboration because the ideas and impetus for this project were already in place and the students were following my lead rather than

taking independent initiative. Then again, after writing a complete draft of the study, I thought of someone with whom I would have liked to collaborate, and I considered this seriously until the humor of it hit me: I had practically finished this book. The only text I have successfully coauthored thus far is an essay written when I was a senior in college, a parody of literary critical analysis, lost or destroyed long ago.

5. Deleuze and Guattari, *A Thousand Plateaus*, 3.

Index

latt and Warland, 204, 207; and
Mill, 48; between Stein and Toklas, 189, 194–97; in *The Terrors of
Dr Treviles,* 166; therapeutic, 133–
36, 153–54, 155, 160

Lacan, Jacques, 155, 184, 203, 220,
273n.21, 306n.63; on desire, 6, 14,
18, 218; and "ex-istence," 13; and
Gallop, 5, 208; and *Lalangue,* 213,
307n.73. *See also* Freud, Sigmund

Langue, 208, 212–13, 307n.73

Larsen, Nella, 273n.27; *Passing,* 15–
18, 27, 35

Larson, Jacqueline: and Jodey Castricano, 305n.55

Lawrence, D. H., 151, 176

Layard, Dr. John, 148, 154, 297–
98n.69

LeBihan, Jill: and Keith Green, 220,
306n.63, 307n.76

Ledner, Caryl, 2, 222, 224, 242–63.
See also Guffy, Ossie

Leigh, Arran, 84, 275n.46; *Belle-
rophôn* (with Isla Leigh), 84; *The
New Minnesinger,* 84. *See also*
Bradley, Katherine; Field, Michael

Leigh, Isla, 84, 275n.46; *Bellerophôn*
(with Arran Leigh), 84. *See also*
Cooper, Edith; Field, Michael

Leighton, Angela, 24, 81–83, 85–86,
88, 274n.37, 275nn.45 and 47,
282n.4, 283n.6

Leonardi, Susan: and Rebecca Pope,
13–14, 84, 271nn.9 and 10,
273n.23, 283n.9

Lesbianism, 11, 14–19, 81, 88–89;
and Erdrich, 310n.21; and Field, 14,
21, 24–25, 27, 82, 83, 88–89, 91,
94; and H.D., 134, 137, 150,
293n.26; and Marlatt and Warland,
199–201, 208, 215, 219, 220, 221;
as metaphor, 14, 226, 273n.26; and
Redgrove and Shuttle, 150, 178;
and Somerville and Ross, 99–100,
285–86n.8, 287n.23; and Stein and
Toklas, 186, 300n.12; and *Tales of
Burning Love,* 239. *See also* Desire;
Sexuality; *coauthors' names*

Lewis, Gifford, 284n.4, 285nn.7 and
8, 286n.8, 287nn.21 and 23,
288n.28, 289n.43, 290nn.44 and 45

Livingston, C. M.: writing with Pansy, 272nn.15 and 19

Locard, Henri, 283n.19

Loesburg, Jonathan, 43–44, 276nn.6
and 7

Lunsford, Andrea: and Lisa Ede, 2,
12, 269n.2, 271n.10, 272n.17

Lupton, Mary Jane, 296n.60

Macpherson, Kenneth, 147, 293n.22

Maitland, Sara: and Michelene Wandor, 183, 272nn.14 and 19, 299n.3

Mann, Emily, 245

Mannes-Abbott, Guy, 311n.28

Marlatt, Daphne, 307n.77; *Character,*
305n.56; critical attention to,
306nn.62 and 63, 307n.76; development of, 305n.53; as immigrant,
307n.80; "Only a Body to Measure
Reality By" (with Nicole Brossard),
305n.56; and Nicole Brossard,
305nn.55 and 56; *Touch to My
Tongue,* 202, 305n.60, 306n.61,
307n.78; "Vers-ions Con-verse,"
305n.54, 313n.3

—and Betsy Warland, 1, 3, 8, 182–84,
195, 199–221, 224, 227, 304nn.47
and 49, 305n.55, 306n.61, 307n.78;
on colonialism, 201, 305n.58,
306n.62; critical attention to, 201–
2, 220–21, 305n.58; and distinguishing between collaborators,
216–19, 220–21; *Double Negative,*
199–202, 305nn.52, 54, and 58; and
feminism, 200–202, 304n.49,
305n.58; *In the Feminine,* 201,
304n.49; relationship between,
305n.55; representation of collaboration between, 202–15, 215–19,
220; and sexual relations, 199–200,
210, 215; social differences between, 220–21, 307n.80; "Subject
to Change," 202, 215–19, 304–
5n.50, 307n.75; *Two Women in a
Birth,* 202, 305nn.50 and 60,
307n.75

—"Reading and Writing between the
Lines" (with Betsy Warland), 202–
15, 219–20, 304n.48; collaborationism in, 203–4; collaborative cohabitation in, 214–15; "collectivity"

HOLLY A. LAIRD is editor of *Tulsa Studies in Women's Literature* and a professor of English at the University of Tulsa, where she teaches modern and Victorian literature, theory, and women's studies. A past president of the Council of Editors of Learned Journals, she is also the author of *Self and Sequence: The Poetry of D. H. Lawrence,* which was selected as an Outstanding Academic Book by *Choice.*

Typeset in 9.5/12.5 Trump Mediaeval
with Trump display
Composed by Celia Shapland
for the University of Illinois Press
Manufactured by Thomson-Shore, Inc.

University of Illinois Press
1325 South Oak Street
Champaign, IL 61820-6903
www.press.uillinois.edu

WITHDRAWN